LEGAL ASPECTS OF
RECEIVABLES FINANCING

AUSTRALIA
The Law Book Company Ltd.
Sydney : Melbourne : Brisbane : Perth

CANADA
The Carswell Company Ltd.
Toronto : Calgary : Vancouver : Ottawa

INDIA
N. M. Tripathi Private Ltd.
Bombay
and
Eastern Law House Private Ltd.
Calcutta *and* Delhi

M.P.P. House
Bangalore

Universal Book Traders
Delhi

ISRAEL
Steimatzky's Agency Ltd.
Jerusalem : Tel Aviv : Haifa

PAKISTAN
Pakistan Law House
Karachi

LEGAL ASPECTS OF RECEIVABLES FINANCING

BY

FIDELIS ODITAH, LL.B., B.C.L., M.A., D.Phil.,
*Fellow of Merton College, Travers Smith Braithwaite Lecturer in
Corporate Finance Law, University of Oxford*

LONDON
SWEET & MAXWELL
1991

Published in 1991 by
Sweet & Maxwell Limited of
South Quay Plaza, 183 Marsh Wall
London E14 9FT
Phototypeset by
LBJ Enterprises Limited
Chilcompton, Somerset
Printed by
Butler and Tanner
of Frome, Somerset

British Library Cataloguing in Publication Data
Oditah, Fidelis
  Legal aspects of receivables financing.
  1. Great Britain. Loans. Securities. Law
  I. Title
  344.10674

ISBN 0–421–43860–6

For
my parents

PREFACE

The management of corporate finance is of critical importance to any firm regardless of its size. The tools of management are many and varied. This book examines the legal aspects of one such tool, namely, receivables financing.

Receivables are simple contract debts. In developed economies the bulk of corporate wealth is locked up in debts. The recycling of these valuable assets as well as their utilisation in the provision of working capital is the focus of this book. Given some of the unique problems of corporate finance, it has been considered proper to organise the book around the legal status of the "borrower". As a result, only corporate "borrowers" are examined.

This book is an attempt to provide an integrated analysis of receivables financing. It explores some of the fundamental legal propositions around which receivables financing is usually organised. It examines the legal nature of receivables; the anatomy of security interests; the theory of secured financing the patterns of receivables financing and the considerations relevant to the choice of any one technique of receivables financing; priority problems; enforcement of the financing agreement; equities affecting assigned receivables; and the impact of insolvency on receivables financing. Assignment law provides the basic framework for receivables financing. The triangular relationship between financier/assignor/ debtor raises a number of policy questions not encountered in other types of asset based financing. In no area of the law are the rules of preference among adverse claimants more confused than in relation to dealings in debts. The book shows that a number of propositions on which financing practices are predicated are conceptually unsound. The result of these problems is that receivables financing is less secure than is often assumed.

The book is written on the assumption that Part IV of the Companies Act 1989 is in force. This book, the result of a dissertation submitted for the degree of doctor of philosophy at Oxford University, has benefited from the generosity of a number of individuals. My primary debt is to my supervisor, Mr. D. D. Prentice who, through numerous discussions, has helped to sharpen my views on a number of issues. I am also grateful to Professor B. R. Rudden for supervision in the early stages of the dissertation and for his continual support and advice. Professor Roy Goode and Mr. Philip Wood were my examiners. I am indebted to them for their comments. Bill Anton, Lorraine Desai and Toby Landau checked some of the citations. Their help is gratefully acknowledged. I must record my thanks to Jane Higgins for her invaluable secretarial assistance and to the editorial staff of Sweet & Maxwell, for the speed and efficiency which they brought to bear on the publication of this book.

Money for this project was provided primarily by the Commonwealth Scholarship Commission. Support was also received from the Alexander Maxwell Law Scholarship Trust.

The law is stated on the basis of material available to me as of September 20, 1990.

Fidelis Oditah
Merton College
Oxford
September 20, 1990

TABLE OF CONTENTS

TABLE OF CASES

TABLE OF STATUTES

TABLE OF STATUTORY INSTRUMENTS

CHAPTER ONE

CONCEPTS AND DEFINITIONS

Introduction

In a barter economy there may be no need for credit since goods, **1.1**
services, and facilities will be exchanged immediately for the bargained
consideration. Such an economy necessarily assumes that performance
and counter-performance of contractual obligations will be simultaneous.
Debts would be unknown as there would be no moment of time during
which one party gives credit to the other. This, however, is unrealistic
because in practice it is difficult to conceive a situation where a debt or
other obligation does not arise prior to its discharge. Even where money
is paid over the counter at the time of sale, there must be a moment of
time during which the purchaser is indebted to the vendor.[1] In most, if
not all transactions, there is always a *scintilla temporis* during which one
party is a creditor of the other. This primary obligation to pay money is
probably the most common of all types of obligation.

The provision of credit for trade and industry stimulates production
and encourages enterprise. Credit also tides individuals and companies
over difficult times. When credit is provided, the creditor will in most
cases find the debtor's promise to discharge his obligations sufficient. But
when default is something which can occur, it becomes important for the
creditor to receive full or partial satisfaction of his claim. In the sphere of
private finance, considerations of default alone may not necessarily lead
the creditor into asking for security. For example, the debtor's assets may
be sufficient to meet the claims of all creditors in full. Experience shows,
however, that this is often not the case. A creditor, even though
cautiously optimistic about the debtor's ability and willingness to perform
his obligations, will often, as a matter of prudence, seek additional
protection over and above the bare promise of the debtor to perform.
This, not uncommonly, may take the form of warranties particularly in
unsecured financing. Warranties, however, may or may not offer the
desired level of protection, not least because a breach of warranty will
sound only (if at all) in damages, the sufficiency of which depends on the
solvency of the debtor. For practical purposes security will offer more
protection. From the debtor's point of view, security may lower the cost

---

[1] *Timmins* v. *Gibbins* (1852) 18 Q.B. 722 at 726, 118 E.R. 273, 274; *Littlechild* v. *Banks*
(1845) 7 Q.B. 739. *Cf. Bussey* v. *Barnett* (1842) 9 M. & W. 312; Farnsworth, *Contracts*
(1982), p. 4.

1

of credit. In the case of money obligations, the reduction will normally be reflected in the rate of interest. The result is that credit and security are, in the average case, aspects of the same phenomenon.

Receivables financing is a part of this phenomenon. The expression "receivables financing" is ambiguous.[2] In this book, however, the expression is used to denote any arrangement by which money is raised on the strength of contractual receivables. Receivables form an integral part of the assets of every trading company. Mortgage and charge debts, car loans, insurance premiums, credit card debts, secured consumer loans, equipment loans, freights (including sub-freights), rentals from real and personal property, debts for goods sold or services rendered, are all receivables. So important is this category of liquid assets that Macleod was compelled to write over a hundred years ago:

> " . . . if we were asked—who made the discovery which has most deeply affected the fortunes of the human race? We think, after full consideration we might safely answer—the man who first discovered that a debt is a saleable commodity.[3] When Daniel Webster said that credit has done more a thousand times to enrich nations than all the mines of the world, he meant discovery that a debt is a saleable chattel."[4]

A hundred years on, nothing has diminished the importance of receivables as a basis for raising money. If anything, the indications are to the contrary. In developed economies the bulk of corporate wealth is locked up in debts. The recycling of these valuable assets as well as their utilisation in the provision of working capital is the primary focus of this book. As would be expected both the recycling and utilisation take a variety of forms. Receivables could be, and frequently are, discounted either privately or in the money markets. Also they may be, and often are, assigned or charged as security for a loan, or an overdraft or other revolving credit facility. Between discounting and security lies a third possibility—outright assignment in discharge or reduction of a pre-existing debt, very little known and almost completely ignored in discussions of forms and patterns of receivables financing. There could also be more complex combinations of these. Normative arguments as to which form is better are not useful because there is no absolute, universal objective criterion by reference to which their relative merits may be ascertained. A number of considerations are relevant to the choice of any one form. The technique chosen will normally reflect the desire to give the company a financing package tailored to meet its own particular circumstances and needs.

---

[2] In one sense receivables financing means financing the creation of contractual receivables. This is usually the sense in which the related expression "stock-in-trade financing" is used. Since every going concern necessarily generates receivables, the financing of receivables would in this sense be the financing of an enterprise. The expression, however, has a narrower meaning, namely, the raising of money on the strength of receivables.

[3] Macleod, *Principles of Economical Philosophy* (2nd ed., 1872), p. 481, cited in 1 Gilmore, *Security Interests in Personal Property* (1965), p. 213, n. 7.

[4] Macleod, *Elements of Economics* (1881), p. 327, cited in 1 Gilmore, *op. cit.*, p. 213, n. 7.

Given the incidence of the debt obligation, its rigour (it is not ordinarily affected by impossibility of performance[5] nor modifiable except in response to some defect in its formation or a variation in counter-performance) and the fact that it has very few, if any, latent defects (money does not, unlike other forms of property, go wrong[6]), it is not surprising that receivables are generally considered an ideal basis for short-term finance. Receivables are localised and less abstract than tangible personalty. They are almost entirely dependent for their value on the ability and willingness of the debtor to pay. A breach may not change the nature of the debt obligation but will almost certainly affect its value. As a result, receivables financing meets with additional problems not ordinarily encountered in other forms of financing. For example, where long-term contracts are involved, or where substantial after-sales services are called for, the resulting receivables are precarious and liable to be affected by the account debtor's rights of set-off unless excluded. Also the very feature of receivables—liquidity, which is the main attraction, may in time become problematic both because receivables are highly fungible, so that the law soon abandons all attempt to trace the proceeds, and because enforcement against a recalcitrant debtor may not be easy.

From this, it is obvious that the subject of receivables financing is a broad one and the legal issues involved are both intricate and diverse. Issues such as assignability, registration and remedies of secured creditors are covered. The subject is also affected to a large extent by the complexity of set-off laws. In no area of the law are the rules of preference among adverse claimants more confused than in relation to dealings in debts. The rule in *Dearle* v. *Hall*[7] was developed in the context of priority conflicts between assignees of a trust fund which was insufficient to pay them. It was, therefore, not wholly unreasonable to regulate their priorities by the order in which notice of their assignments was given to the trustees. In those circumstances notice "perfected" the assignment as it was the nearest step to taking possession. Over 160 years have elapsed since the rule was crystallised but nothing has been done to adapt it to the realities of modern times. It is a poor reflection on our law that in this day and age an account debtor should be treated as a kind of public register of notices of assignment. The results of this have been profound. The heartland of receivables financing is occupied by charges and mortgages. These security interests raise many interesting legal questions. The securities will be enforced if the secured obligation is not performed. Where there are two or more chargeholders secured, among others, by a floating charge, which of them may appoint an administrative receiver? Can there be more than one administrative receiver at the same time? What are the powers and duties of a receiver? What are the effects of automatic and partial crystallization clauses on priorities? Does the

---

[5] This is one explanation of *Paradine* v. *Jane* (1647) Aleyn 26. The court looked on the lease as a fully executed contract so that the tenant bore the risk of eviction, just like the buyer of goods bears the risk of their loss or destruction after risk or property or both have passed to him. See 6 Corbin, *Contracts* (1962), para. 1322.

[6] This assumes the absence of inflation.

[7] (1828) 3 Russ 1.

3

petition for, or the order of, an administration automatically crystallise a floating charge? How far does the insolvency legislation erode the remedies for the enforcement of security interests over receivables? How does one reconcile the dispositive and other dealing powers of an administrator with the rights of a chargeholder whose security over receivables is fixed? What is the meaning of "proceeding" in the context of administration? Can an administrator disclaim onerous contracts? To what extent, if any, can the company's debtors exercise rights of set-off in relation to pre-administration cross-claims? What is the impact of the avoidance provisions on receivables financing? Who is entitled to property recovered in exercise of avoidance powers? These and many other questions are examined in this book. Now we shall examine some more general recurring themes in receivables financing. The remainder of this chapter is devoted to the examination of the anatomy of real security, the need for security and the theory of secured financing.

The uncertain anatomy of security interests

1.2   A financier insisting on security is not content with the normal remedy for breach of the debtor's obligation to pay. Real security entitles him to take the security for the discharge of his own debt in priority to other creditors of the same debtor. Moreover, save in cases of secured non-recourse lending, the personal obligation of the debtor to repay entitles the secured creditor to prove for any unpaid balance if the security does not exhaust his claim.[8] Even where absolute title is transferred, provided it is by way of security, equity recognises the transfer as being for the purpose of *security* even though the security is *title*. Although the ability to take security is, in most cases, a matter of contract, the law plays some role in determining enforceability as well as timing and manner of enforcement of security interests. For example, a charge in order to be enforceable against certain persons must be registered.[9] A charge for this purpose is any form of security interest over property, other than an interest arising by operation of law.[10] Also after the presentation of a petition for, or the making of an order of, an administration, no steps may be taken to enforce a security interest over the company's property.[11] Security in this context means any mortgage, charge, lien or other security.[12] Despite these restrictions on the rights of a security holder and the statutory attempt at definition, the anatomy of security interests remains obscure. The extent of these statutory erosion of freedom of contract cannot be fully appreciated unless we know what is a security interest. Does a debtor who exercises his right of set-off during an

---

[8] *Re Barned's Banking Co., Kellock's case* (1868) L.R. 3 Ch.App. 769 at 776; *White* v. *Simmons* (1871) L.R. 6 Ch.App. 555; *Quatermaine's case, Re London, Windsor & Greenwich Hotels Ltd.* [1892] 1 Ch. 639.
[9] Companies Act 1985, s.399(1).
[10] *Ibid.*, s.395(2).
[11] Insolvency Act 1986, ss.10(1)(b) and 11(3)(c).
[12] *Ibid.*, s.248(b).

administration enforce a security over property? Is a right of set-off "other security"? What about a retention of title agreement in a sale or supply contract? Is it a registrable charge? The answers to these questions are anything but obvious. Some of the analytical problems in this area arise from the fact that many discussions of the nature of security interests seek a level of common generality between them and assume the existence of identifying features present in all security interests.[13] Hence a security interest has been defined as "a right given to one party in the asset of another party" to secure the performance of an obligation.[14] Inherent in this definition are two subsidiary propositions: first, that a security interest is a right *in rem*; secondly, that such a right is the result of a grant to the creditor rather than a reservation by him. For the sake of completeness a third proposition may be added: English law recognises only four types of consensual security.[15] The first two propositions are undoubtedly good law in so far as they indicate what is *sufficient* to constitute a right over property a security interest. However, in so far as they also stipulate what is *necessary* to the constitution of a security interest, they are, in my view, difficult to accept. In particular, proposition three is very doubtful, and unless the premiss of the second proposition can be sustained, the third must necessarily fall.

For purposes of argument the first proposition may be accepted as law, although it must be said that the distinction between rights *in rem* and rights *in personam* is neither a reliable nor a satisfactory criterion for identifying security interests because there are proprietary rights frequently used as security which are not rights *in rem*.[16] The second proposition is questionable. It is not at all obvious that security in the legal sense must always derive from a grant by the debtor, rather than a reservation by the creditor. Goode[17] argues that the effect of a reservation is not to create a security, but to ensure the continuance of the owner's absolute interest in the asset. No doubt, the distinction between security and absolute interests is important to an understanding of the nature of security interests. It does not, however, follow from this that security in the legal sense must always lie in *grant*. The only reason given by Goode is that it is a corollary of his fourfold classification of consensual security interests.[18] The premise of the "grant" theory is unsustainable unless indeed English law recognises a closed list of security interests. This is doubtful. Before we examine the evidence in support of the closed list, it would be helpful to consider whether as a matter of principle a security interest must always lie in grant. It is submitted that the criterion of grant is neither necessary nor sufficient to distinguish a security from other interests: unnecessary, because any contract under which a defeasible title to goods sold is retained by the seller as security for the payment of the price creates a security interest in law; insufficient, because a grant is not,

---

[13] See, *e.g.* R. M. Goode, *Legal Problems of Credit and Security* (2nd ed., 1988), p. 1; Sykes, *Law of Securities* (4th ed., 1986), pp. 12–13.

[14] Goode, *op. cit.*, p. 1.

[15] Goode, *op. cit.*, pp. 10 *et seq*.

[16] For a discussion of the proprietorial nature of debts, see para. 2.7, *infra*.

[17] Goode, *op. cit.*, p. 5. See also, Goode (1990) Monash L.R.

[18] The categories are mortgage, charge, pledge, and contractual lien.

5

for instance, inconsistent with a gift or other transaction. Hence it is necessary to distinguish those grants which create a security interest from other kinds of grant.

The test of a security interest is whether the debtor has an equity of redemption in the property, the subject-matter of the alleged security.[19] If this be so, the question is really whether in a transaction under which an owner of property reserves title until he is paid, the buyer has an equity of redemption. It is submitted that the buyer does indeed have an equity of redemption. Where he has paid part of the purchase price before the goods are repossessed, there are in reality two proprietary interests: the seller's interest and the buyer's.[20] If the seller resells, he must account to the buyer for this interest. It follows that whatever the seller is liable to account to the buyer upon a resale on account of sums already paid by the buyer under the contract, constitutes the buyer's equity of redemption. It matters little whether, as a matter of legal analysis, the seller's liability is described as arising from a contractual obligation to account in cases where the contract of sale is still afoot,[21] or from the buyer's restitutionary right to recover as on a failure of consideration, in those cases where the sale contract has already determined.[22]

The fact that the motive of a retention of title seller is to give himself a security does not, of course, make his retention a security interest. But where title is retained *until* payment for the goods, the retention contains a built-in temporal and quantitative limitation on the seller's title[23]: it is limited to the amount due but unpaid; it does not survive payment of that amount. This defeasible interest is a security interest. Prior to 1989 it was not sufficient to make a retention of title agreement registrable as a charge to show that it is a security interest; it was necessary to show that the security, if any, was conferred rather than retained.[24] This provided very little immunity from registration on retention agreements.[25] Today, however, there is no requirement that a registrable security be one which is conferred rather than retained; all that is necessary is that the security interest be not conferred by operation of law.[26] A retention of title agreement, without doubt, is not an interest arising by operation of law.[27] It seems, therefore, that once it is accepted that a retention agreement is a security interest, it is registrable as a charge unless it is a charge under which the seller is entitled to possession of the goods.[28] A retention of title seller is only contingently entitled to possession. This contingent entitlement would not seem sufficient to bring him within the exception.

---

[19] *Re George Inglefield Ltd.* [1933] Ch. 1.
[20] *Wickham Holdings Ltd.* v. *Brooke House Motors Ltd.* [1967] 1 W.L.R. 295 at 300.
[21] *Clough Mill Ltd.* v. *Martin* [1985] 1 W.L.R. 111 at 117–118, 124, 125.
[22] *Ibid.*
[23] *Ibid.* at 126.
[24] *Clough Mill Ltd.* v. *Martin, supra*; *John Snow & Co. Ltd.* v. *D.B.G. Woodcroft Ltd.* [1985] B.C.L.C. 54 at 63.
[25] *Re Bond Worth Ltd.* [1980] Ch. 228; *Pfeiffer GmbH & Co.* v. *Arbuthnot Factors Ltd.* [1988] 1 W.L.R. 150; *Tatung (UK) Ltd.* v. *Galex Telesure Ltd.* (1989) 5 B.C.C. 325.
[26] Companies Act 1985, s.395(2).
[27] *Tatung (UK) Ltd.* v. *Galex Telesure Ltd., supra.*
[28] Companies Act 1985, s.396(1)(b).

Besides, a chargee is not exempted from registration if he is only entitled to take possession in the event of default or on the occurrence of some other event.[29]

The nature of real security has never been authoritatively or exhaustively discussed in English law. This is due partly to the fact that there has never been a comprehenisve regulation of security interests along the lines of Article 9 of the United States Uniform Commercial Code.[30] Because the efforts at regulation have been piecemeal and directed at particular forms of security, the need to examine the juridical nature of real security has never arisen. Now that a charge is defined as any consensual interest over property, it is hoped that the anatomy of a security interest will one day be examined. What can, however, be said is that it is impossible to draw up a comprehensive list of security interests, let alone on any basis which excludes retention of title agreements and limits the categories of consensual security interests to mortgage, charge, pledge, and contractual lien. On the contrary, funded building contract retentions could properly be regarded as security interests. Where the retention has not been segregated from the employer's other assets, so that it remains a debt owed to the builder, the perceived conceptual difficulty in having a charge over one's obligation to another[31] may, if the perception is well founded, argue against the possibility of a charge in such circumstances. But once the retention is deposited in a bank account, the conceptual difficulty disappears and the retention could then be appropriately described as a registrable charge. That the security is retained rather than conferred no longer gives immunity from registration. Also the right to forfeit a lease for non-payment of rent is regarded by equity simply as a security for the payment of the rent.[32] It is therefore important that this new shift in emphasis by the charges provisions is kept in mind. More importantly, since consensual security is a matter of contract, it will always remain possible to obtain real security in personal property in different ways with different legal consequences. The principal authority relied upon[33] for the "grant" and "closed list" theory is *McEntire* v. *Crossley Brothers*.[34] In that case a lessor hired out goods on terms that he was to remain the absolute owner thereof until full payment of the agreed rentals by the lessee. The House of Lords held that the agreement was not void as an unregistered bill of sale. Whether it created any other form of security interest did not arise and so was not decided. The case can only be regarded as authority for the theory that security

---

[29] *Ibid.*, s.396(2)(c).
[30] Art. 9–102 of the U.S. Uniform Commercial Code provides that Art. 9 applies "(a) to any transaction (regardless of its form) which is intended to create a security interest in personal property." What transactions are so intended is left to the courts to decide. In the U.K. there is no statutory or case law equivalent to Art. 9–102 UCC.
[31] *Re Charge Card Services Ltd.* [1987] 1 Ch. 150. In *Welsh Development Agency* v. *Export Finance Co. Ltd.* (1990) B.C.C. Brown-Wilkinson V.-C. doubted whether he would have reached the same conclusion, as did Millett J. in *Charge Card*. However, in the interest of preserving consistency in matters which had an important general commercial impact, he followed that decision.
[32] *Ladup Ltd.* v. *Williams & Glyn's Bank plc* [1985] 1 W.L.R. 851.
[33] Goode, *op. cit.*, p. 6.
[34] [1895] A.C. 459.

must always lie in a grant if bills of sale are exhaustive of security interests capable of subsisting in personal property. This is, of course, not the case. Also since a bill of sale is always the result of a grant, it is not surprising that their Lordships declined the invitation to treat a security obtained by retention as if it were by grant. On any view, therefore, the case is a rather weak authority for the "grant" theory.

So far, we have been concerned with definitions of security interests proposed by others. We shall now attempt a description of what are the essentials of a security interest. As uncertainties must always remain in the penumbra of every definition, what is proposed here is the core of real security. Having said that, a security interest may be described as a creditor's interest in property in which the debtor or an associated third party has some interest, whether arising consensually or by operation of law, which renders the performance of the debtor's obligation more assured.[35] This description is admittedly imprecise. When, for example, does an interest in property render performance of an obligation more assured? What is a right of property? These are some of the questions which the above description does not answer. The first question is, however, not difficult to answer: an interest in property renders the enjoyment of a right more assured when the interest-holder can resort to his interest for the satisfaction of his claim, in priority to other claimants of the same property, in the event of default in the performance of the obligation secured. This emphasises the right of priority incident to real security. But two problems remain. First, the criterion of priority, on its own, is insufficient to determine the existence of a security interest because there are other arrangements such as a contractual set-off, deposit, factoring with recourse, negative pledge in unsecured financing agreement, flawed asset,[36] and a host of other self-help remedies, which, by achieving limited priority for the party entitled to enforce the remedy, produce at least one of the results of real security. Secondly, the ability of the security holder to resort to his security in priority to other creditors is a consequence, rather than an element, of real security and so throws little (if any) light on its juridical nature. There is also the associated

---

[35] In *Re Paramount Airways Ltd.* (1990) B.C.C. 130 at 149, Browne-Wilkinson V.-C. accepted the following definition of security proposed by counsel:

"security is created where a person (the creditor) . . . obtains rights exercisable against some property in which the debtor has an interest in order to enforce the discharge of the debtor's obligation to the creditor."

Although the definition does not pretend to be comprehensive, it is certainly no wider than the ordinary meaning of security.

[36] Flawed asset is an arrangement under which a creditor (usually a bank) restricts the right of the debtor to deal with his asset in the custody of the creditor until certain conditions are fulfilled. Typically, the "asset" is a cash deposit with the bank and the restriction on the freedom to deal with it is the "flaw." It is in effect a condition of repayment of the deposit and since it is usually a "security" for some contingent obligation the agreement will provide that the bank is under no liability to pay until the contingency ceases to be capable of occurring. If the money is on time deposit the agreement may provide for automatic renewal upon maturity. In some cases the agreement may not forbid withdrawals altogether but merely provide a limit beyond which the deposit must not be reduced. Whatever form the flawed asset arrangement takes, no security interest is thereby created because the bank has no property interest in the deposit even though its ability to exercise a right of set-off will entitle it to priority if there is the requisite degree of mutuality.

difficulty that, very often, the issue for determination is the extent of a right and this can only be deduced from the nature of the right itself. In such cases it would be circular to use the effect of an agreement to determine its legal nature.

The first problem is very easily met. Although arrangements such as contractual set-off, flawed asset, deposit, and other self-help remedies may, in appropriate cases, achieve limited priority for the party entitled to enforce the right, the difference between them and real security is that the priority which they may achieve is not a consequence of an underlying property right. Self-help remedies are not necessarily proprietary. A person who sets off a debt due from him against another debt owed to him is exercising a purely personal right. He does not do so by virtue of any property interest. The same is true of a person who exercises a right to forfeit a deposit. For example, under a flawed asset arrangement, the creditor's right to withdraw his deposit is postponed or restricted until a designated contigency happens. But this restriction does not, on its own, confer any property interest on the depositee over the deposit. The restriction, no doubt, affords the depositee some protection by way of set-off. What, however, distinguishes these contractual self-help remedies from a real security is that a security holder asserts his right of priority by virtue of the property interest which his security gives him. In addition, his security gives him far wider enforcement rights than is exercisable by virtue of contractual self-help remedies; for example, he may have the right to appoint a receiver, not by way of equitable execution, but in exercise of a contractual right. In contrast, none of the self-help remedies creates a property right in the party entitled to enforce the remedy, nor a right to appoint a receiver.

The second problem is, however, more difficult for there is no easy way out. The problem raises the fundamental question whether in the treatment of securities one has to adopt an empirical approach of looking at the devices of mortgage, charge, pledge, lien, reservation of title agreements, funded retentions, etc., with a view to finding what is common to them, or a functional approach of looking at the end contemplated by a particular transaction. To a large extent, the latter is the more reliable approach, albeit circular. The difficulty with the former is that it assumes a closed list of security interests; nothing is common to the enumerated categories apart from the fact that they all involve a property interest in the creditor by virtue of which he can assert a right of priority. In determining whether or not a security interest exists, it is better to proceed in two stages: the first is to decide whether the creditor has a right of priority—a right to resort to the interest, the subject-matter of the security, and secondly, whether that right is asserted by virtue of an underlying property interest in property in which the debtor or an associated third party has some interest, whether arising from a grant, a reservation or howsoever, provided, of course, that the debtor or third party has an equity of redemption in the property. The proviso is necessary in order not to confuse a security interest with absolute beneficial ownership. However, since equity will imply a right of redemption and other constituents of the equity of redemption, once the character of the transaction as a security is established,[37] the question

---

[37] *Durham Bros.* v. *Robertson* [1898] 1 Q.B. 765 at 772.

whether a transaction creates a security interest is logically precedent to the ascertainment of what residual rights make up the debtor's equity of redemption.

As we have seen, property and priority are the essence of real security. It is therefore necessary to ascertain exactly what is meant by a property interest. For the present purpose, a property interest may be described as a bundle of rights exercisable against a *res* by virtue of the interest. It is normally defined by reference to the existence and location of a *res*, the subject-matter of the property interest. The interest will in its nature be capable of assumption by third parties and have some degree of stability.[38] The ability of the secured creditor to recover the property, the subject-matter of his security interest, is a property right; this may be compared with the recovery of monetary compensation (the main remedy for the vindication of a personal right). It does not matter that in some cases the property (*i.e.* the *res*) itself is a mere right as with non-negotiable debts and other choses in action. Thus a security interest is a bundle of proprietary rights exercisable over a given *res* and designed to render performance of the secured obligation more certain. When the interest is a product of contract, the content of the security interest will be determined by the terms of the contract. The extent to which the interest can be asserted against third parties is a matter, not of private contractual negotiation, but of *priority*; this will depend largely on its legal incidents.

One consequence of the description of a security interest as a property interest is that it cannot survive the extinction of the *res* over which it exists.[39] Extinction does not, however, mean strict and literal disappearance of the original *res*, for legal analysis recognises that the original *res* may have become substituted for something new or different.[40] When substitutions occur the task of the court is to identify the new thing into which the original security survives. This will normally be the product or proceed of the original *res* which, in turn, becomes derivative security unless the contract expressly provides that such new product or proceed will be part of the original security. The exercise of identifying the surviving security is called tracing. However, the process of identification is complex and artificial.[41] The ability to trace the original security interest distinguishes a secured creditor from his unsecured counterpart who

---

[38] *National Provincial Bank Ltd.* v. *Ainsworth* [1965] A.C. 1175 at 1247.
[39] See, *e.g. Borden (UK) Ltd.* v. *Scottish Timber Products Ltd.* [1981] Ch. 25.
[40] In *Taylor* v. *Plumer* (1815) 3 M. & S. 562 at 575, Lord Ellenborough C.J. put the attitude of common law to substitutions very pointedly when he said:
   " . . . it matters not what other form, different from the original, the change may have been made, whether into promissory notes as in *Scott* v. *Surman* (1742) Wiles 400, or merchandise as in *Whitecomb* v. *Jacob* (1710) 2 Salk 160, for the product of, or substitute for the original thing follows the nature of the thing itself"
so long as it can be identified as such. Equity adopts a similar approach, although the equitable rules for identifying the original thing are more elaborate, sophisticated and artificial: see *Re Diplock* [1948] 1 Ch. 465 at 531 *et seq.*
[41] Birks, *Introduction to the Law of Restitution* (1985), pp. 358 *et seq.* where the rules of tracing are discussed.

cannot trace for want of the requisite proprietary base.[42] However, the extent to which a property interest may be displaced in favour of competing dealings by the same grantor or others with that interest is a question of priorities, and, by itself, an unreliable indicator of the existence of a security interest.[43]

Quasi security interests

The flexibility of contract law has led to a proliferation of self-help **1.3** rights in the nature of security. For the sake of clarity we may refer to these rights as quasi security interests because some of them *behave* like security interests. Examples include the recourse provision in a factoring agreement, the right to forfeit a deposit, set-off agreement, the negative pledge in an unsecured financing agreement, and the flawed asset arrangement. These contractual devices afford the creditor or the party entitled to invoke them some measure of protection. The fact that they are capable of achieving limited priority, at times, makes the task of classifying security interests (properly so called) difficult, especially if emphasis is placed on priority as an incident of real security. Even when real security is defined as something designed to render the performance of an obligation more assured, one is still faced with the problem of distinguishing arrangements which assure performance as an incident of an underlying right of property from others which, though behaving like real security (in the sense of guaranteeing priority), are not security interests at all because the limited priority which they guarantee is not consequent on any underlying right of property. The latter arrangements are purely personal rights exercisable by virtue of contract.

The need for security

Many debtors discharge their financial obligations without being com- **1.4** pelled to do so. This may satisfy most creditors who will therefore content themselves with the debtor's promise to pay especially in short-term debt obligations. But when a debtor undertakes medium and long-term obligations, unforeseeable future changes in its fortunes may affect its ability to pay. Such changes may lead to default in performance and even liquidation. If its likely liquidation value is sufficient to meet the claims of its creditors, none would in theory seek additional protection by way of

---

[42] The idea of "proprietary base" is Birks's: see *op. cit.*, p. 379. In the present context it means that a creditor asserting a right to any property as derivative or substitutionary security must show that at the beginning of the story he had a proprietary interest in that property and that nothing happened to deprive him of that interest. It is for this reason that a creditor entitled to a set-off cannot pursue the proceeds or product of the debt once paid. All he ever had was a personal right.

[43] This question of equitable priorities was the very issue raised in *Re Connolly Bros. Ltd. (No. 2)* [1912] 2 Ch. 25, and *Security Trust Co. v. Royal Bank of Canada* [1976] A.C. 503. See also, *Capital Finance Co. Ltd. v. Stokes* [1969] 1 Ch. 261 at 277; *Re Bond Worth Ltd.* [1980] Ch. 228 at 253.

real security. For many reasons, however, this is often not the case. When insolvent liquidation supervenes, the promise to pay is no more valuable than the piece of paper on which the promise to pay is written. Creditors know this and will in practice not rest content on the debtor's personal credit, but will seek additional protection by taking real security. In this sense, the need for security is a derived need for the insulation from the consequences of corporate insolvency which real security affords.

The primary purpose of real security is to render the performance of the secured obligation more certain though once taken, the security may perform other subsidiary functions. Real security achieves this certainty by giving the secured party a right of property (including a right of pursuit) and a right of preference or priority. The extensive right of enforcement (principally through the appointment of a receiver) which some securities give, is a sub-category of the right of property. The right of property and pursuit is the right to take specific property, the subject of the security interest, without needing to go to court and to follow that property into whatever new thing it survives. This also includes the right to follow it into the hands of any person who receives it, though in some cases this possibility may be limited by special common law or equitable rules designed for the protection of recipients of property, for example, the plea of holder in due course of a bill of exchange or acquisition by a bona fide purchaser of the legal title to that property without notice of the security interest.[44] Notwithstanding these constraints on the right of pursuit, the right is nonetheless a valuable one. It enables the secured creditor to bypass the slowness with which the mills of justice grind. This right to proceed against the security after the debtor's default is at the heart of real security, and distinguishes the secured creditor from his unsecured brother. Occasionally, this distinction is said to be between ownership and obligation.[45] Even where the secured creditor cannot proceed against his security peaceably and requires the intervention of the court, the procedure is cheaper and less time-consuming. In contrast, an unsecured creditor has no property right in the assets of his debtor either before, during, or after liquidation.[46] To enforce his claim, he must

---

[44] The plea of bona fide purchaser for value without notice is said to be an absolute, unqualified and unanswerable plea to the jurisdiction of a court of equity: *Pilcher* v. *Rawlins* (1872) L.R. 7 Ch.App. 259 at 269, 271; *Heath* v. *Crealock* (1874) L.R. 10 Ch.App. 22 at 23; *Taylor* v. *London & County Banking Co.* [1901] 2 Ch. 231 at 256.

[45] R. M. Goode (1987) 103 L.Q.R. 433 at 434–438. He argues that the impact of this distinction has been reduced significantly by the development of equitable rights; the principle of subrogation; and the availability of procedural securities for the protection of a party to proceedings.

[46] Commencement of winding-up terminates the company's power to manage its property which thus becomes available for the discharge of its liabilities. But this does not give the unsecured creditors a proprietary interest in any specific property of the company. Jointly they own the fund of assets represented by the corporate debtor's unincumbered property, but are more like residuary legatees of an estate in the course of administration: see *Knowles* v. *Scott* [1891] 1 Ch. 717 at 722–723; *Re Paul & Gray Ltd.* (1932) 32 S.R. (NSW) 386 at 393; *Re a Caveat, ex p. Canowie Pastoral Co. Ltd.* [1931] S.A.S.R. 502 at 504; *United Fuel Investments Ltd.* v. *Union Gas Co. of Canada Ltd.* (1966) 53 D.L.R. (2d) 12; *Calgary & Edmonton Land Co. Ltd.* v. *Dobinson* [1974] Ch. 102 at 108; *Re Calgary & Edmonton Land Co. Ltd.* [1975] 1 W.L.R. 355 at 359; *Ayerst* v. *C. & K. (Constructions) Ltd.* [1976] A.C. 167 at 178–180; *cf. Re Ashpurton Estates Ltd.* [1983] 1 Ch. 110 at 123.

sue and obtain judgment for a debt before proceeding to levy execution. The law suit to obtain judgment and the enforcement procedures are tedious and costly both in time and money.

The secured creditor's right to appropriate some specific property in satisfaction of his claim in the face of competing claims of third parties is known as the right of preference or priority. This right is available whether or not the debtor is in liquidation. In insolvent liquidation, it is one of the main departures from the rhetoric that assets of the insolvent must be distributed *pari passu* among creditors.[47] Another way of expressing this conclusion is to say that assets available for distribution do not include those subject to trust or valid security interests.[48] This enables the secured creditor to resort to his security and stay outside the debtor's liquidation to the extent of his security. So much does the law cherish the interests of secured creditors that it recognises their unlimited right to enforce their security even after a liquidator has been appointed.[49] Also, in the enforcement of security the law does not generally impose any duty of care on the secured creditor as to the timing of enforcement even where it is calculated to spite the debtor, provided that in exercising any power of sale he does so with reasonable care.[50] Enforcement powers are, however, not entirely free from restraints. In particular, where an administrator is appointed[51] the secured creditor may lose control over both the timing and conduct of the enforcement of his security.[52]

Unsecured creditors, on the other hand, have no proprietary interest in any specific property of the debtor even after liquidation, and since they rank behind preferential creditors in the "pecking order," the value of their right to dividend is usually negligible. They thus bear the burden of insolvent liquidation.[53] However, security is not academic outside the context of insolvency. On the contrary, questions of priority may, and

---

[47] Insolvency Act 1986, s.107. See also, *British Eagle International Airlines Ltd.* v. *Compagnie Nationale Air France* [1975] 1 W.L.R. 758.

[48] Insolvency Act 1986, s.283(3) provides that the property of the bankrupt which vests in his trustee in bankruptcy does not include those held on trust for third parties by the bankrupt. Although there is no statutory equivalent for insolvent companies, there can be little doubt that the same principle applies to corporate liquidation. This conclusion derives inferential support from *Re Margart Property Ltd., Hamilton* v. *Westpac Banking Corp.* [1985] B.C.L.C. 314.

[49] *Re Henry Pound, Son & Hutchins* (1889) 42 Ch.D. 402; *Re Potters Oils Ltd.* [1986] 1 W.L.R. 201. *Cf. Re Landmark Corp. Ltd.* (1968) 88 W.N. (Pt. 1) (NSW) 195 at 196. For a discussion of challenge to enforcement of security, see Chap. 7, *infra*.

[50] See para. 7.3, *infra*.

[51] Under Pt. II of the Insolvency Act 1986.

[52] See para. 7.4, *infra*.

[53] *Salomon* v. *A. Salomon & Co. Ltd.* [1897] A.C. 22 at 53 (everybody knows that when there is a winding-up debenture holders step in and sweep off everything; and a great scandal it is); *Re London Pressed Hinge Co. Ltd.* [1905] 1 Ch. 576 at 581 (the facts are that the undertaking is substantially carried on only for the benefit of the debenture holders who have a floating security over it); *Business Computers Ltd.* v. *Anglo-African Leasing Ltd.* [1977] 1 W.L.R. 578 at 580 (the background facts are simple and depressingly typical . . . the question whether in this day and age it is necessary to permit the Crown and the holders of floating charges the totality of the priorities which can be exercised under the existing law is not the subject of debate in this court, though it is at least debatable elsewhere); *Borden (UK) Ltd.* v. *Scottish Timber Products Ltd.* [1981] Ch. 25 at 42 (unsecured creditors receive a raw deal in insolvency).

often do, arise outside insolvency.[54] Moreover, save in secured non-recourse lending,[55] the personal obligation of the debtor to repay the loan means that if the security does not exhaust the secured creditor's claim, he may prove for the unpaid balance in the debtor's liquidation. He must elect whether to prove for his entire claim and surrender his security or realise it (including placing a value on it) and prove for any balance.[56]

An interesting question is whether an unsecured creditor can steal a march on other creditors by writing into his loan documentation, a provision entitling him to priority over other creditors without taking real security. In jurisdictions like Spain this is possible. But can it be done in English law? The question has nothing to do with self-help remedies like set-off agreement or the right to forfeit a deposit. A debtor can agree to prefer one of his creditors provided the preference is not given during the prohibited statutory period before the onset of insolvency,[57] and that the asset given was not subject to a specific security. Such an agreement is valid between debtor and creditor, but unenforceable against other creditors in any subsequent liquidation of the corporate debtor for at least two reasons: first, there is no appropriation of any property in favour of the creditor. Secondly, the provision may be contrary to public policy on the ground that it is an attempt to contract out of the *pari passu* rule.[58]

A general theory of secured financing?

1.5   A general theory of secured financing may seek to explain either the incidence of secured financing or the reasons why the law allows secured creditors to enjoy the totality of priorities exercisable under existing law. An explanation which focuses on the incidence of the secured debt will show why creditors insist on security. This has already been examined in the previous section and need not be repeated. What we shall consider in this section are the reasons the law allows secured creditors to enjoy preferential treatment. It may be argued that this question does not arise because the ability to take security and enjoy the rights attached to it is

---

[54] See, *e.g. Cave* v. *Cave* (1880) 15 Ch.D. 639; *Re Morgan* (1881) 18 Ch.D. 93, where questions of relative priority arose outside the insolvency context.

[55] The concept of secured non-recourse lending could be misleading for at least two reasons: first, the right of the lender to be repaid is, as a matter of principle, unlimited. This means that there will always be recourse against the borrower even where the right of repayment depends on a contingency, as in *Waite Hill Holdings Ltd.* v. *Marshall* (1983) 133 N.L.J. 745. Secondly, it is inconceivable that a financing agreement will not contain covenants and warranties by the party being financed. If it does, their presence imports limited recourse, in so far as a breach will give the financier a right of redress against the debtor. Therefore, if the concept of secured non-recourse lending has any meaning at all, it can only mean that the source of repayment is limited to designated assets of the debtor.

[56] Insolvency Rules (S.I. 1986 No. 1925), r. 4.88. See also, *Moor* v. *Anglo-Italian Bank* (1879) 10 Ch.D. 681 at 689; *Re Hopkins* (1881) 18 Ch.D. 371 at 373, 374.

[57] The prohibited period is six months before the onset of insolvency or two years in the case of connected persons, provided that the company was, during that period, unable to pay its debts within s.123 of the Insolvency Act 1986, or became unable to do so in consequence of the preference: Insolvency Act 1986, s.240(1) and (2).

[58] *British Eagle International Airlines Ltd.* v. *Compagnie Nationale Air France* [1975] 1 W.L.R. 758; *Carreras Rothman Ltd.* v. *Freeman Matthews Treasure Ltd.* [1985] Ch. 207.

the result of freedom of contract. This, however, is only partly sound. For one thing, it does not explain why freedom of contract is ignored when reopening a number of pre-insolvency transactions if the debtor becomes insolvent, or why registration is imposed on the security, as these prevent freedom of contract from applying freely according to its tenor. For another, it is not easy to reconcile the priority of unsecured preferential claims over a floating charge[59] with the theory that secured creditors prevail because they have bargained for their priority. Indeed it may be asked why parties should have the freedom to enter into such a bargain at all. Does freedom of contract, for example, enable an unsecured creditor to bargain for preferential treatment with the debtor without taking a security? Considerations of this nature suggest that the explanation must be sought elsewhere.

There are three topical theses: informational explanations; monitoring explanations; the conventional explanation. Informational and monitoring explanations seek to solve the puzzle of the secured debt through the parameters of economic efficiency. The law accords priority to secured creditors because security is efficient—the welfare gains arising from security exceed the losses, given certain assumptions such as a perfect market and the absence of transaction costs. Informational theorists focus on the pre-contractual role of security. They argue that because of differences in risk aversion among creditors, market imperfections and information asymmetries, it is difficult for creditors to classify debtors into risk-groups before extending credit. Gathering the required information is costly. This cost is borne by debtors in the form of higher credit cost. Debtors therefore give security in order to minimise the cost of obtaining credit. Security is able to have this effect because of its inherent quality as a signalling device. Not only does it reduce the cost of obtaining information as to debtors' creditworthiness, but also the ability to provide security is, by itself, evidence of creditworthiness.[60]

There are variations on the theme of information but we need not go into these.[61] These explanations shed considerable light on the benefit of security. However, like all explanations based on economic efficiency, they are predicated on somewhat unrealistic assumptions. Besides, a security interest may be an insufficiently precise or clear signal as to a debtor's creditworthiness. This may arise, for example, if there is a pre-existing security over the property tendered as security but which does not require registration. In such situations, the debtor's apparent ability to create another security over the property is a misleading indication of his creditworthiness. Also, unless it can be shown that security is cheaper than other devices available for ascertaining a debtor's creditworthiness, it is unclear why a creditor should prefer the information which he can gather from a security interest to that obtainable from other sources.

In contrast to informational theories which focus on the pre-contract role of security, monitoring explanations look at post-contract position

[59] Insolvency Act 1986, ss.40, 175, 386 and Sched. 6.
[60] Schwartz (1981) 10 *Journal of Legal Studies* 1 at 14 *et seq.*
[61] For a good general survey, see Schwartz, *op. cit.*; (1984) 37 Vand. L.R. 1051; White (1984) 37 Vand. L.R. 473; Buckley (1986) 72 Vand.L.R. 1393.

and evaluate the role of security in the context of an existing contractual relationship. The premiss of monitoring explanations is that debtor/ creditor relationships generate conflicts (or agency costs) which increase the cost of credit. These conflicts arise from debtor misbehaviour and have the effect of altering retrospectively the terms on which credit was given. For example, lenders adjust their interest rates, among other things, to reflect the risk class of borrowers. A borrower who converts business assets to private use or switches into a riskier venture after a loan has been made, unilaterally reduces the rate of interest because the lender would have charged a higher rate of interest for this. Lenders are alive to these forms of debtor misbehaviour and would monitor the borrower to prevent this. Some creditors are better at monitoring the debtor than others. Better monitors are typically unsecured while ineffi- cient monitors take security. This exploitation of creditors' comparative monitoring advantages reduces the cost of credit to the debtor. The cost reduction is a benefit to the borrower; the result is efficient and justifies the priority accorded to secured creditors.[62] A variation on this theme is that creditors take security in order to avoid freerider problems.[63] Less efficient creditors tend to freeride on the policing efforts of more efficient creditors. The latter take security in order to focus their policing efforts on their security and avoid freerider problems. A further refinement on the theme of monitoring regards security as a form of relational contract in which lending is a joint venture.[64] The function of security in such a relationship is to give the creditor a leverage over the debtor's business. The relational contract theory does not claim to provide the whole explanation for the incidence of secured credit; it is only a complemen- tary vision to the existing monitoring cost explanations.[65]

Monitoring theses provide a significant insight into the role of security. Protective and restrictive clauses found in the documentation of finance agreements show that creditors are alive to the need to keep a close watch on the debtor's business activities. Examples include the provision of financial information and compliance certificates as well as the negative pledge.[66] However, it is far from obvious that similar provisions cannot be found in unsecured debt instruments. On the contrary, they are more common in such instruments. If this be so, monitoring explanations are unpersuasive to the extent that they fail to explain why monitoring is better accomplished by taking security. In this country the floating charge is one of the commonest forms of security. Where, as will very often be the case, the charge covers the entire undertaking of the debtor, the task of monitoring is burdensome, not least because of the breadth of the security. If policing is carried out through the security the creditor in effect monitors the whole business. Charged assets can no longer be regarded as focal points of monitoring. Hence freerider problems will

---

[62] Jackson & Kronman (1979) 88 Yale L.J. 1143. See also, Baird & Jackson, *Cases, Problems and Materials on Security Interests in Personal Property* (1984), pp. 361–367.
[63] Levmore (1982) 92 Yale L.J. 49.
[64] Scott (1986) 86 Col.L.R. 901 at 925 *et seq.*
[65] *Ibid.* at 970.
[66] See, *e.g. Encyclopaedia of Forms and Precedents* (4th ed.), Vol. 6, Form 18: 48, cl. 27.

remain. Moreover, excessive monitoring may expose the creditor to a possible liability for wrongful trading[67] on the basis of shadow directorship.[68]

The relational model, by moving away from the focal point analysis, avoids some of the pitfalls inherent in other monitoring explanations. Limited to project finance on which it is modelled, it may be considered persuasive, at least to the extent that it gives due weight to the interests at play in the somewhat peculiar situation of project finance. But even so limited, it ignores the important fact that in many project financings the financier is often a co-venturer with a stake in the equity. This feature distinguishes project finance from the conventional debt financing. Also, the relational theory, like other monitoring explanations, does not explore fully the potential leverage over a debtor's business which can be obtained by a power to declare an event a default entitling the creditor to call in the debt and invoke whatever remedies are available for the enforcement of payment.

Monitoring explanations exaggerate the role of debtor misbehaviour as a cause of corporate insolvency. That misbehaviour accounts for some insolvencies is beyond argument. But it does not necessarily follow that all insolvencies result from mismanagement. Unforeseeable changes in the debtor's fortunes may lead to insolvency: the market for its products may be misjudged or decline; it may be affected by a general depression; its business may depend heavily on that of a third party in which case it is unlikely to survive the collapse of that third party. Therefore, creditors do not take security simply and solely because of fear of debtor misbehaviour, but principally to insulate themselves from contingencies such as corporate insolvency howsoever arising.

Since neither the need to reduce the cost of obtaining information nor the monitoring potential of security satisfactorily explains the priority accorded security interests, we may now turn to the third topical thesis. This is the "conventional explanation." The premiss of this explanation is that security makes the credit market accessible to many debtors who, in the absence of security, may be unable to obtain unsecured finance. Some debtors have good credit rating and are able to raise unsecured finance at prime rates.[69] On the other hand, many debtors have such unimpressive credit rating that they can only obtain small, unsecured loans at high rates of interest. Their loans represent a high degree of risk and can be administered and policed only at a clerical cost relatively high in relation to any sum with which they could possibly be trusted.[70] Between these extremes lie most debtors. Many of them cannot obtain unsecured financing on terms which do not encroach significantly upon their profit margins, but they have assets which, if the law allows them to be taken as security, would enable them to obtain credit on competitive terms. This promotes prosperity and gives debtors in this category access to funds

---

[67] Insolvency Act 1986, s.214.
[68] *Ibid.*, ss.214(7) and 251; *Ex p. Copp* [1989] B.C.L.C. 13.
[69] Van Horne, *Financial Management and Policy* (3rd ed., 1974), pp. 458 *et seq.*; Kripke (1985) 133 U.Pa.L.R. 929 at 946–961.
[70] J. Maclachlan (1960) 60 Col.L.R. 593 at 607.

which, without the priority accorded to security interests, would be inaccessible. This explanation, it is submitted, convincingly accounts for the priority accorded to security interests.[71] The conventional explanation does not deny that security performs other functions: it may provide information; it may be useful for policing the debtor; it may be a defensive mechanism to prevent other creditors from acquiring superior rights in the debtor's assets.[72] However, the law recognises and gives effect to the priority of secured creditors because security makes available funds which may otherwise be employed elsewhere, or made available only on terms which the average debtor can ill afford. This may or may not be perceived as detrimental to unsecured creditors of a common debtor, but it can scarcely be shown to be at their expense.[73] Indeed a secured creditor has already paid for his priority through receipt of a lower return on his investment. On the other hand, unsecured creditors have already been paid for allowing this priority and they receive a higher rate of return because of their lower priority position. Since most creditors are free to select the terms on which they would lend, there is no compelling argument based on considerations of fairness for adopting one legal rule rather than the other.[74] Insolvency law derogates from the rights of secured creditors only where there is a perceived overriding insolvency goal which recognition of security in some circumstances would compromise.[75] The question whether security is good, neutral or bad is not, however, an insolvency question. It is because this fact is not often kept in mind that certain insolvency rules pursue a redistributional goal and one sometimes hears arguments for the enhancement of insolvency rights of unsecured creditors. Ideally insolvent liquidation should be a forum for the translation of assets and liabilities of the debtor according to pre-insolvency entitlement of creditors under substantive law, and not an occasion for the dislocation of pre-insolvency entitlements unless this is dictated by a clear insolvency goal.[76]

[71] *Cf.* Schwartz (1981) 10 *Journal of Legal Studies* 1 at 27 (security is a zero sum game because the reduction in the interest rate consequent on security is offset by the correspondingly high rate charged by unsecured creditors of the same debtor).

[72] Most commentators agree that the role of security in project financing is defensive: see Wood, *Law and Practice of International Finance* (1980), p. 323; Davies, *IBA Energy Law Seminar* (1979), Vol. 2, N. 3 at p. 9; McCormick (1983) 1 J.E.R.L. 21 at 37; [1986] I.F.L. Rev., Jan., 11 at 16.

[73] See Goode (1983) 8 Can.Bus.L.J. 53 (the priority of secured creditors is justified by the concepts of bargain, value and notice). Some forms of value recognised by law may appear to be rather shadowy, *e.g.* where the first in, first out rule applies. But this is not in fact so as a banker who honours cheques drawn on an overdrawn account gives value.

[74] Jackson (1982) 91 Yale L.J. 857 at 871.

[75] Jackson (1984) 36 Stan. L.R. 725 at 731 (at bottom, bankruptcy overrides non-bankruptcy rights because those rights interfere with the group advantages associated with creditors acting in concert).

[76] Jackson (1985) 14 *Journal of Legal Studies* 73.

CHAPTER TWO

MAIN FINANCING TECHNIQUES OVER RECEIVABLES

Introduction

In this chapter, we shall examine the legal meaning of receivables, **2.1** whether the debt created by a bank deposit is a receivable, the distinction between existing, future and contingent receivables, the legal treatment of proceeds of receivables, whether receivables are proprietary rights, the main forms of receivables financing and the considerations which may influence the choice of any one or more financing technique(s) over receivables.

Meaning of receivables

"Receivables" is nowhere defined in English law being more in use in **2.2** North America and Europe than in the United Kingdom. There is, however, nothing mysterious about the term receivables. As used in North America, the term is a generic description for rights to payment for goods sold or leased, facilities made available and services rendered.[1] This description equates receivables with simple trade debts. The term "receivables" is wider than "book debts" which is used in identifying charges requiring registration,[2] although both terms are often used interchangeably.[3] Receivables include, but are not limited to, book debts and would cover assets as diverse as rents issuing from land or personal

---

[1] Art. 9–106 UCC defines an account receivable as "any right to payment for goods sold or leased or for services rendered which is not evidenced by an instrument or chattel paper, whether or not it has been earned by performance." Contract rights have now been included in this definition since it was dropped in the 1972 Official Text as an unnecessary separate category of intangibles. Bills of sale and hire-purchase agreements are chattel papers which the UCC definition excludes but which no doubt embody receivables. See also, Ontario Personal Property Security Act, RSO 1980, Chap. 375, s.2(b).
[2] Companies Act 1985, s.396(1)(c).
[3] See *Bank of Nova Scotia* v. *Royal Bank of Canada* (1975) 59 D.L.R. (3d) 107 at 119 where the Alberta Supreme Court accepted evidence that "book debt" is a banking terminology while "receivable" is used by accountants.

property,[4] freights,[5] premiums payable to an insurer,[6] bank loans[7] and a simple debt for goods sold.[8] Most of these debts would also count as book debts. However, the courts take a narrow view of book debts. For example, book debts have been defined as debts arising in the ordinary course of business of a trader as would normally be entered in properly kept books of a company engaged in a business of that kind whether or not in fact entered.[9] On this basis rentals due under a hire-purchase agreement are book debts and hence receivables of the dealer whether or not the hire-purchase agreement contains a minimum payment clause and whether or not the hirer has an option to determine the agreement before it runs its full course.[10] In Australia some cases have taken a particularly narrow view of book debts. Thus, it has been held that nothing qualifies for inclusion in the category of book debts which is not *actually entered* in the books of the trader.[11] Similarly, it has been said that an entry in a company's book account is a book debt irrespective of any question of accountancy practice in regard to such debts and notwithstanding that as a practical matter, such debts would not normally be entered in properly

---

[4] *Re Ind, Coope & Co. Ltd.* [1911] 2 Ch. 223; *Rhodes* v. *Allied Dunbar Pension Services Ltd., Re Offshore Ventilation Ltd.* [1987] 1 W.L.R. 1703 at 1705, rvsd. [1989] 1 All E.R. 1161 (C.A.) (not on this point).

[5] *Re Welsh Irish Ferries Ltd., The Ugland Trailer* [1986] Ch. 471; *The Annangel Glory* [1988] 1 Lloyd's Rep. 45.

[6] *Re Law, Car & General Insurance Corpn.* [1911] W.N. 91.

[7] *Re Moulton Finance Ltd.* [1968] Ch. 325 at 332 (deposit of a charge certificate by way of an equitable sub-mortgage void as an unregistered charge on book debts).

[8] *Siebe Gorman & Co. Ltd.* v. *Barclays Bank Ltd.* [1979] 2 Lloyd's Rep. 142.

[9] *Shipley* v. *Marshall* (1863) 14 C.B.(N.S.) 566; *Tailby* v. *Official Receiver* (1887) 18 Q.B.D. 25 at 29 (C.A.); *Re Lawson Constructions Pty. Ltd.* [1942] S.A.S.R. 201; *Independent Automatic Sales Ltd.* v. *Knowles & Foster* [1962] 1 W.L.R. 974. The authorities are exhaustively reviewed in *Contemporary Cottages (NZ) Ltd.* v. *Margin Traders Ltd.* [1981] 2 N.Z.L.R. 114.

[10] *Independent Automatic Sales Ltd.* v. *Knowles* [1962] 1 W.L.R. 974. See also, *Blakey* v. *Trustee of Property of Pendlebury* [1931] 2 Ch 255 where the question was whether monthly payments under a hire-purchase agreement were "debts due or growing due" within the reputed ownership provision in s.38(c) of the Bankruptcy Act 1914. In *Australian Guarantee Corpn.* v. *Balding* (1930) 43 C.L.R. 140, future instalments under a hire-purchase agreement which gave the hirer an option to determine the agreement were held to be book debts within the definition in s.80 of the Instruments Act 1928 (Victoria). In *Re W. F. Le Cornu Ltd.* [1931] S.A.S.R. 425, there was no option to determine the hire-purchase agreements and the instalments due were *a fortiori* book debts within the meaning of s.5(1)(d) of the Companies (mortgages, charges and debentures) Act 1924 (South Australia). However, in *H.J. Wigmore & Co. Ltd.* v. *Rundle* (1930) 44 C.L.R. 222 the High Court of Australia held that there was no future promise by the hirer to pay rentals under a hire-purchase agreement because the agreement was determinable at his option. Even more difficult to reconcile are the decisions of Long Innes J. in *Motor Credits Ltd.* v. *W.F. Wollaston Ltd.* [1929] S.R.(NSW) 227 and *Blackwood's Ltd.* v. *Chartres* [1931] S.R.(NSW) 619.

[11] *Robertson* v. *Grigg* (1932) 47 C.L.R. 257 at 266. The explanation of Evatt J. at 272 is more satisfactory though it too is a narrow view of book debts. Evatt J. thought that sums due to a storekeeper under some road construction contracts carried out by him were not book debts because the contractor's *main* business was store-keeping and the construction contract lasted only for a short time. See also, *Lesser* v. *Shire of Wannon* (1897) 23 V.L.R. 446 where Madden C.J. held that sums payable under a construction contract were not book debts because there was no evidence that the contractor was engaged in the *business* of road construction.

kept books of companies engaged in the same business.[12] These revealed differences in the judicial approach to the meaning of book debts are a consequence of the circumstance accepted in all the cases that whether a given debt is a book debt is a mixed question of law and fact: law, to the extent that the debt must arise from the ordinary business of the company; fact, because accountancy evidence as to book-keeping practices in different industries is always admissible. Variations in recording practices lead to different conclusions as to the meaning of book debts.

It has indeed been suggested that the distinction to be drawn is probably between debts accruing due to the company in the course of carrying on the business for which it is formed, and debts which are merely incidental to the carrying on of that business, or which, although *intra vires*, are not directly connected with it.[13] The former are book debts; the latter are not. This solution is consistent with the result in some of the Australian cases,[14] but our courts have not generally adopted this narrow approach. There are practical problems with an approach based on *vires*. First, it is doubtful whether debts which are incidental to the carrying on of a business are to be excluded from the category of book debts merely because they are not directly connected with the main business of the company. Secondly, there are problems in defining with sufficient precision exactly how direct need the business be before debts arising from it can properly be described as book debts. It should also be noted that most of the cases which have considered the meaning of book debts were decided in the context of bankruptcy litigation and in some, the inarticulate judicial policy of fairness to the unsecured creditors may have influenced the outcome.[15] In other cases, the desire to protect the secured creditor has noticeably influenced the adoption of a narrower meaning of book debts.[16] These inarticulate and vague notions of fairness have obscured the meaning of book debts. They are not, however,

---

[12] J. G. Starke, *Assignment of Choses in Action in Australia* (1972), p. 79. In *Waters* v. *Widdows* [1984] V.R. 503 Nicholson J. held that an inter-company loan was a book debt partly because it had in fact been entered in the books of the lender as a debt due from the borrower. However, in *Stanley Stamp Co.* v. *Brodie* (1914) 34 N.Z.L.R. 129, Stout C.J. refused to treat as book debts entries in the company accounts because the entries were not in respect of any debts; they were in respect of stamps sent out to agents and clients for approval. More recently, Anderson J. held in *Hart* v. *Barnes* [1983] 2 V.R. 517 that the amount realised by the receiver on the sale of stock-in-trade and plant comprised in the charge under which he was appointed were not book debts. They were not proceeds of sale arising in the ordinary course of the company's business.

[13] R. R. Pennington, *Company Law* (5th ed., 1985), p. 525.

[14] See n. 10, *supra*.

[15] This is true of most of the cases which considered whether particular debts were caught by the reputed ownership provision in s.38(c) of the Bankruptcy Act 1914. See, *e.g. Blakey* v. *Trustees of Property of Pendlebury* [1931] 2 Ch. 255; *Shipley* v. *Marshall* (1863) 14 C.B.(N.S.) 566 (considered the older provision in s.137 of the Bankruptcy Act 1861). See also, *Waters* v. *Widdows* [1984] V.R. 503.

[16] *Lesser* v. *Shire of Wannon* (1897) 23 V.L.R. 446; *Robertson* v. *Grigg* (1932) 47 C.L.R. 257; *Hart* v. *Barnes* [1983] 2 V.R. 517. The policy of protecting secured creditors is most obvious from *Shackell* v. *Howe, Thornton & Palmer* (1909) 8 C.L.R. 170. There the High Court of Australia held that moneys which were payable by an agent to his principal for the sale of the latter's wool consigned to the agent for sale were not debts arising in connection with the business of the principal. This is very surprising because the way the pastoralist's business was conducted was to sell his wool through agents.

applicable to receivables and it would seem that all trading debts, whether arising from the company's main business or from a one-off business, are receivables, whether qualifying as book debts or not. It would not matter if such debts are not, as a matter of book-keeping practice, normally entered in any books. Further, the distinction between *ultra vires* and *intra vires* business activities has nothing to do with the quality of a right to payment as a receivable. From this, it is clear that though receivables comprehend book debts, they are not confined to what are commonly perceived as book debts, although book debts constitute the bulk of the receivables of every trader. Today the revolution in information technology makes it easy to store business records in computers so that book entry is on the way out. This makes it singularly odd to continue to use the expression "book debt." It may be that as the computer has marginalised ledger books the term "receivable" will gradually replace "book debt."

It must be emphasised that advance payment for goods or services does not prevent the supplier's right to payment from being described as a receivable of his trade or business.[17] Notwithstanding the prepayment, the receivables arise *eo instanti* when enjoyment of the contractual consideration commences.

It may be asked whether this examination of the meaning of receivables and book debts is at all necessary. In my view the discussion has both theoretical and practical significance. Theoretically, the discussion delineates the boundaries of the subject of receivables financing. It explains why topics as diverse as security over receivables and securitisation of receivables find a place in a discussion of legal aspects of receivables financing. But the examination has a practical dimension. First, it is not uncommon for businesses to be sold with the benefit of "book debts and other debts." The purchaser in such a case will be concerned to know what exactly are comprehended in the phrase "book debts" and "other debts." Secondly, a first charge may be executed over the entire undertaking of a company excluding its "book debts and other debts" whilst a second charge is taken over "book debts and other debts." To determine the relative priority of both charges over a given right to payment belonging to their common debtor, one must decide whether that right of payment is a book debt or other debt. A creditor may also secure his advance by a floating charge over book debts and a fixed charge over other debts. The preferential creditors will want to know whether a particular debt is a book debt because they are entitled to priority over the floating chargee.[18] An administrator appointed by a court would also want to know whether it is a book debt since he can deal with book debts the subject of a floating charge without leave of the court.[19] A charge may also be taken over a given contract right whether the right be

---

[17] *Australian Guarantee Corpn. Ltd.* v. *Balding* (1930) 40 C.L.R. 140 at 160–161. Contrast *Re Keenan Brothers* [1985] I.L.R.M. 641 at 643 where Walsh J. observed that book and other debts cease to be such once paid. This is broadly correct provided it is borne in mind that the payment is a proceed of the debts and would be caught by a security over such debts: *infra*, para. 2.4.

[18] See *Waters* v. *Widdows* [1984] V.R. 503.

[19] Insolvency Act 1986, s.15(1) and (3).

present or contingent, *e.g.* an Export Credit Guarantee (ECG) policy and the liquidator will want to characterise the right as a book debt so as to avoid it if the charge is not registered.[20] The list of situations in which the question whether a supplier's right to payment is a book debt can be multiplied almost infinitely.

Yet the question what is a book debt has regrettably remained one of those mysteries of company law.

Cash at bank

The question whether a cash balance at the bank is a book debt has **2.3** puzzled company lawyers for many generations. The banker/customer relationship is one of debtor/creditor.[21] If a cash balance is a debt due to the customer does that debt rank as a book debt of the customer? The answer to this question depends on the nature of business carried on by the depositor. If the depositor is an institutional investor specialising in the placement of funds at its bankers for relending to borrowers in the money market, the resulting debt created by the deposit is properly described as a book debt of that investor. This is because the debt is one which arises in its normal course of business and would normally be entered in properly kept books of traders engaged in that kind of business. On the other hand, where the depositor's business does not involve placement of funds at the disposal of banks for the purpose of relending (so that the deposit is no more than a surplus stacked away for convenience), the debt created by the deposit is not a book debt.[22] The question whether cash at bank is a book debt is relevant to the inquiry whether a fixed charge on such deposit is registrable as a charge on book debt or whether the deposit is covered by a charge on "book debts and other debts." No reported authority has considered the question whether cash balances *could* be book debts. When that question arises for decision the proper approach would be to consider the nature of the business carried on by the depositor. All the cases which have so far considered the nature of a bank deposit in this context have turned on their particular circumstances.[23] In *Re Brightlife Ltd.*,[24] for example, the question was whether a specific charge on all "book debts and other debts" of the corporate borrower caught cash at its bankers. Hoffmann J. held that the cash balance was not within the expression "book debts and other debts." That the cash balance was held not to be a book debt is hardly surprising, for the borrower was not engaged in the business of placing money with other bankers for relending. In this respect, the decision is consistent with a host of other cases dating back over a hundred years.[25] But why was the cash balance not comprehended in the

---

[20] *Paul & Frank Ltd.* v. *Discount Bank (Overseas) Ltd.* [1967] Ch. 348.

[21] *Foley* v. *Hill* (1848) 2 H.L. Cas. 28.

[22] *Re Stevens* [1888] W.N. 110, 116; *Re Haigh (deceased)* (1907) 51 S.J. 343; *Stanley Stamp Co.* v. *Brodie* (1914) 34 N.Z.L.R. 129 at 149; *Watson* v. *Parapara Coal Co.* (1915) 17 G.L.R. 791; *Re Brightlife Ltd.* [1987] Ch. 200; *Re Permanent Houses (Holdings) Ltd.* [1988] B.C.L.C. 563.

[23] This is true of all the cases cited in n. 22, *supra*.

[24] [1987] Ch. 200.

[25] See n. 22, *supra*.

expression "other debts"?[26] Hoffmann J. gave three reasons. First, a businessman or an accountant would not regard the cash balance as "other debts." He would regard it as cash at bank. This is not very convincing because a businessman's conception of cash at bank cannot dispose of the question whether such assets are debts. Secondly, clause 5(ii) of the deed of charge permitted the company to deal with the debts charged by "getting in" or "realising": a bank balance cannot "sensibly be got in or realised." Again this is a weak explanation. The fact that not all assets comprehended in the expression "other debts" are susceptible of dealing by "realising or getting in" does not diminish the quality of such assets as debts. Thirdly, the provision for written consent to dealing means that the chargor would have to obtain the consent of the chargee before withdrawing any money from its account or obtain such consent each time it issued a cheque. This negatived any inference that the cash balances were included in the phrase "other debts." Such an arrangement is an extreme commercial improbability.

But there is nothing extreme or commercially improbable in such an arrangement. It must be borne in mind that the charge was conceived as a specific charge on "book debts and other debts" of Brightlife Ltd. and the restraint on its freedom to deal with its bank account is one of the monitoring devices necessary for the constitution of a specific charge on book debts and other debts.[27] Besides, even if the cash balance was not covered by the charge on "book debts and other debts," it consisted entirely of the proceeds of the book debts and would have become derivative or substitutionary security.[28] This is by the mechanism of tracing. However, this argument was not advanced. In the light of these, it is difficult to accept this aspect of the decision in *Re Brightlife Ltd.*, although it was only a point of construction. The same question resurfaced in *Re Permanent Houses (Holdings) Ltd.*[29]—another decision of Hoffmann J. Here again, it was held, on what appears to be stronger facts, that a cash balance was, as a matter of construction, neither a book debt nor "other debts." The decision is important because it stresses that the issue is at bottom one of construction, and that *Re Brightlife Ltd.* is no authority for the view that cash at bank is never a book debt, or for that matter, a book debt within section 396(1)(c) of the Companies Act 1985. For the sake of completeness it may be added that a cash balance which is a book debt will count as a receivable, but a conclusion that cash at bank is not a book debt does not dispose of the question whether it is a receivable because receivables include, but are not limited to, book debts.

---

[26] *Cf. Watson* v. *Parapara Coal Co., supra,* where Chapman J. of the New Zealand Supreme Court held that although a bank balance was not a book debt, it was nevertheless a debt because the reference to "book debts" in the debenture could not restrict the meaning of the phrase "other debts," which phrase was intended to describe something not covered by book debts.

[27] *Siebe Gorman & Co. Ltd.* v. *Barclays Bank Ltd.* [1979] 2 Lloyd's Rep. 142; *Re Keenan Bros.* [1985] I.L.R.M. 641. *Cf. Re Armagh Shoes Ltd.* [1982] N.I. 59. For a detailed discussion, see paras. 5.7 and 5.8, *infra*.

[28] In *Re Permanent Houses (Holdings) Ltd.* [1988] B.C.L.C. 563, payment in respect of an indemnity agreement was rightly held to be a proceed of debts.

[29] See n. 28, *supra.*

Proceeds of receivables

Both at law and in equity, it is recognised that the product or proceeds **2.4** of, and substitutes for, the original thing follow the nature of the thing itself so long as they can be identified as such. The process of ascertaining into what thing the original survives is called tracing and both common law and equity have devised their own rules of ascertainment. Accordingly, a security over receivables could be asserted against its proceeds and for this purpose, proceeds of receivables are whatever is received upon a sale, exchange, collection or other disposition of receivables, and would frequently include cash whether or not at bank, cheques and other bills of exchange, and promissory notes. The purchaser or chargee of receivables is able to assert title to the proceeds because they are the fruits of the original asset. The importance of proceeds of receivables in the present context is twofold. First, the knowledge that receivables encompass their proceeds would dispel the misconception that once the obligor pays the debt, the money ceases to be caught by an assignment of receivables.[30] Secondly, it will narrow the compass within which the inquiry whether cash at bank is a receivable assumes significance. This is not to say that in practice it will always be easy to prove that a particular asset is a proceed or product of some underlying receivables. Apart from difficulties of proof, claimants of proceeds of receivables face two additional problems. The first is that title to receivables does not always endure until the *res* disappears because the right to trace into proceeds may be defeated by special rules designed to protect recipients, *e.g.* the equitable doctrine of bona fide purchaser for value.[31] Secondly, because receivables are in their nature fungible, both common law and equity are quick to abandon all effort at identification of the proceeds into which the original receivables survive.

Documentary receivables

The distinction between pure and documentary receivables has some **2.5** significance. Pure receivables are rights to payment for goods, services or facilities which are not *embodied* in any document. A simple contract debt is a pure receivable irrespective of the nature of the underlying transaction from which the debt arose. It is not uncommon for an obligor to give his creditor a bill of exchange or promissory note either as a

---

[30] *Cf. Re Keenan Bros.* [1985] I.L.R.M. 641 at 643.
[31] *Taylor* v. *Blakelock* (1886) 32 Ch.D. 560; *Thompson* v. *Clydesdale Bank Ltd.* [1893] A.C. 282; *Coleman* v. *Bucks & Oxon Union Bank* [1897] 2 Ch. 242. This is in some respects similar to the defence of holder in due course where the debts are paid by a note or bill of exchange.

security for performance, or as a discharge[32] of the obligation in respect of which it is given. Such a bill or note will frequently be negotiable. The quality of negotiability is important. First, the instrument is transmissible by delivery or by delivery and indorsement. Secondly, a holder in due course of the negotiable instrument takes the instrument free of equities.[33] Even a person who becomes a holder after the instrument has become overdue takes free of equities arising from the underlying contract in respect of which the instrument is issued.[34] This is because the instrument is regarded as autonomous of the underlying contract. Where negotiable instruments are tendered *in payment* of trade debts, they are documentary receivables.

It is in this sense that the courts have in the past held that bills receivable of a company are book debts whether or not they have been entered as bills receivable in the books of the company.[35] But even here, some qualifications are necessary. First, it is not every bill of exchange which counts as a documentary receivable. Only bills and notes *representing* the price of goods sold or leased, services rendered or facilities made available, qualify for inclusion in the list of documentary receivables. Accommodation[36] and other bills which do not represent an underlying trade debt are not receivables, though the cases are not always clear on this. Moreover, ordinary bills and notes given not as payment, but as *security* for payment or the discharge of some other obligation, are not receivables. This follows logically from the fact that documentary receivables, although autonomous of the underlying contract, are not independent rights in themselves, but are merely substitutionary rights

---

[32] A plea of discharge or payment by a bill of exchange means in law that the bill has been taken in satisfaction. In many cases this is unlikely. However, in a loose mode of speech, payment by a bill means that a bill has been given on account of the debt: *Currie* v. *Misa* (1875) L.R. 10 Ex. 153 at 163. It is in this second sense that the concept of discharge by tender of a bill is used in the text. Ordinarily, the bill tendered in payment is presumed to be a conditional payment only thus preserving the original debt but suspending the remedy for its enforcement until maturity of the bill: *Currie* v. *Misa, supra*; *Allen* v. *Royal Bank of Canada* (1926) 134 L.T. 194 at 196; *Re Charge Card Services Ltd.* [1987] Ch. 150 at 166. Unlike debt securities, the right to payment embodied in a documentary receivable does not merge with the instrument: *cf. Price* v. *Moulton* (1851) 10 C.B. 561; *Comr. of Stamps* v. *Hope* [1891] A.C. 476. A debt security merges with the remedy on the secured debt because the security being a higher remedy makes recourse to the action for money had and received on the debt unnecessary. Only the remedy (not the debt) is merged.

[33] Bills of Exchange Act 1882, ss.29(2) and 38(1).

[34] *Burrough* v. *Moss* (1830) 10 B. & C. 558; *Oulds* v. *Harrison* (1854) 10 Ex. 572.

[35] *Dawson* v. *Isle* [1906] 1 Ch. 633; *Siebe Gorman & Co. Ltd.* v. *Barclays Bank Ltd.* [1979] 2 Lloyd's Rep. 142. It is somewhat paradoxical that *Re Stevens* [1888] W.N. 110, 116, which was relied on in both cases does not quite decide that bills receivable were book debts. Although the report is extremely scanty, on p. 116 the reporter mentions that North J. decided that the debts *represented* by the bills were book debts. This is a more accurate statement of the law than the broad generalisation that bills receivable are book debts.

[36] Bills of exchange used to raise money for the drawer's own business and drawn pursuant to an acceptance credit are usually referred to as "accommodation bills." Although s.28 of the Bills of Exchange Act 1882 defines an accommodation party to a bill, the Act draws no distinction between ordinary bills and those drawn under acceptance credits.

representing some underlying pure receivables.[37] Thus, a security over receivables would carry through to bills given by the obligor.[38] A certificate of deposit[39] would count as a documentary receivable only where the depositor is engaged in the investment business and the deposits represented by the certificate are part of the trading debts due to him. Between pure and documentary receivables lies an intermediate stretch of what may loosely be referred to as hybrids. These are basically claims evidenced by some kind of writing, but the document is not the essence of the obligation to pay even where production of the document is a condition precedent to the obligor's performance. The document evidences, but does not embody, the debt. Examples include IOUs, conditional sale and hire-purchase agreements, and policies of insurance.

Future, potential and contingent receivables

The question whether receivables are present, potential, future, or **2.6** contingent is important for various reasons. First, whereas an assignment of present receivables need not be supported by consideration to be effective, an assignment of future receivables can only take effect in equity, and must be supported by consideration whether or not by deed.[40] Secondly, security assignments of book debts are registrable whether the book debts be present or future.[41] But fixed charges over contingent obligations are not registrable.[42] So, it is of importance that future receivables are distinguished from contingent obligations. In the distinction lies the question of registrability of present charges over future rights. Thirdly, an assignment of future and contingent rights can take effect, if at all, only in equity.[43] Such an assignment must necessarily be

---

[37] *Re Stevens* [1888] W.N. 110, 116; *Dawson* v. *Isle* [1906] 1 Ch. 633 at 637. The distinction between a bill given in payment of a debt and one given as security for a debt is important when characterising a bill as a documentary receivable. Unfortunately, unhelpful generalisations that bills are book debts tend to obscure this vital distinction. For example, while bills given as *security* are exempt from registration when sub-pledged (see Companies Act 1985, s.396(2)(f)), there is no similar exemption for a charge on bills tendered in *payment*.

[38] *Siebe Gorman & Co. Ltd.* v. *Barclays Bank Ltd., supra.*

[39] A certificate of deposit is defined in s.55(3) of the Finance Act 1968 as

" . . . a document relating to money, in any currency, which has been deposited with the issuer or some other person, being a document which recognises an obligation to pay a stated amount to bearer or to order, and being a document by delivery of which, with or without endorsement, the right to receive that stated amount, with or without interest, is transferable."

[40] *Tailby* v. *Official Receiver* (1888) 13 App.Cas. 523; *Re Ellenborough* [1903] 1 Ch. 697; *Norman* v. *Fed. Comr. of Taxation* (1962) 109 C.L.R. 9 at 21.

[41] *Re W. F. LeCornu Ltd.* [1931] S.A.S.R. 425; *Re George Inglefield Ltd.* [1933] Ch. 1 (Eve J.); *Independent Automatic Sales Ltd.* v. *Knowles & Foster* [1962] 1 W.L.R. 974; *Paul & Frank Ltd.* v. *Discount Bank (Overseas) Ltd.* [1967] Ch. 348; *Contemporary Cottages (NZ) Ltd.* v. *Marqin Traders Ltd.* [1981] 2 N.Z.L.R. 114. *Cf. Blackwood's Ltd.* v. *Chartres* [1931] S.R.(NSW) 619.

[42] Under s.396(1)(c) of the Companies Act 1985, only charges on book debts are registrable. Charges on contingent liabilities are registrable only if they are *floating*: s.396(1)(e). The result is that fixed charges on contingent obligations and debts other than book debts escape registration.

[43] In general future property is not assignable at law: *Lunn* v. *Thornton* (1845) 1 C.B. 379.

equitable. It is argued later[44] that the characterisation of an assignment as equitable or legal affects priorities in two ways: the first is that the rule in *Dearle* v. *Hall*[45] has no application to legal assignments because the rule is confined to equitable assignments. This conclusion is not affected by the provision which subjects legal assignments to existing equities.[46] Moreover, even as regards equitable assignments, it is settled law that the *Dearle* v. *Hall* notice has no application to future interests which are mere expectancies and possibilities, until they have a present existence.[47] This is because the equitable principle which underlies the rule treats notice as equivalent to possession. But alike in equity as at law, possession cannot be taken of things which have no existence, and in respect of which there can be no debtor or other obligor from whom performance is due. This makes it particularly important to distinguish clearly between existing and potential receivables to which the rule can apply if the assignment is equitable, and future receivables and other contingent obligations to which the rule is inapplicable until the subject-matter has a present existence. The distinction is also important in relation to the rule that an assignee takes subject to equities. The general rule is that an assignee takes subject only to equities in existence at the date of notice.[48] However, it is said that equities for this purpose do not include cross-claims which are wholly contingent at the date of notice.[49] If this is well founded the distinction between existing and contingent debts is important. Also, the general rule does not (it is thought) prevent an anticipatory debtor from setting off post-notice cross-claims against an assignee of expectant receivables.

English law draws an arbitrary distinction between existing and future receivables on the one hand, and future receivables and other contingent liabilities, on the other. All contractual rights are vested from the moment when the contract is made, even though they may not be presently enforceable, whether because the promisee must first perform his own part of the bargain, or because some condition independent of the will of either party (such as the elapsing of time) has to be satisfied.[50] The result is that English law treats as existing debts not only those which have been *earned* by the promisee, whether or not presently payable,[51] but also those which are *unearned*. The basis for the inclusion of unearned rights to payment in the category of *existing* receivables even where the contract is wholly executory is that they *grow out of a present obligation*. So it is that for a long time the courts have treated as existing

[44] See para. 6.14., *infra*.
[45] (1828) 3 Russ. 1.
[46] Law of Property Act 1925, s.136(1).
[47] See para. 6.4., *infra*.
[48] *Roxburghe* v. *Cox* (1878) 17 Ch.D. 520.
[49] *Jeffryes* v. *Agra & Masterman's Bank* (1866) L.R. 2 Eq. 674.
[50] *Colonial Bank Ltd.* v. *European Grain & Shipping Ltd., The Dominique* [1988] 3 W.L.R. 60 at 67, rvsd. [1989] 2 W.L.R. 440 (H.L.) (not on this ground).
[51] Under a building contract the promisor usually maintains a retention fund as security against bad workmanship. The fund represents sums earned though not payable: *Brice* v. *Bannister* (1878) 3 Q.B.D. 569; *Buck* v. *Robson* (1878) 3 Q.B.D. 686; *Ex p. Moss* (1884) 14 Q.B.D. 310; *Drew* v. *Josolyne* (1887) 18 Q.B.D. 590; *G. & T. Earle* v. *Hemsworth RDC* [1928] 44 T.L.R. 605, (1929) 140 L.T. 69 (C.A.); *Re Tout & Finch* [1954] 1 W.L.R. 178.

or present receivables a legal right to be paid only at a future date if it depends upon an existing contract on the repudiation of which an action could be brought for an anticipatory breach.[52] The contract is the *tree*, the future debts which *may* arise, the fruits. The unearned debts are *potential* and hence existing. But in so lumping earned (even though not presently payable) debts and unearned, albeit potential, debts, as existing debts, the common law has, in a somewhat extravagant fashion, destroyed the vital distinction between *rights in esse* and *rights in potentia*. Thus, a right to interest under a fixed-term loan,[53] future rent from existing leases,[54] sums payable under an existing construction contract,[55] royalties payable under an existing copyright,[56] freight payable under a signed bill of lading, and sums payable for goods or services not yet delivered or rendered, are all present receivables. Uncertainty as to the amount payable is immaterial. Similarly the fact that under some of these contracts nothing may be earned because the right is conditional on counter-performance is not considered important.

There are other problems with the assimilation of earned and unearned receivables in the category of present debts. First, what happens where the contract gives the party from whom payment is expected the right to terminate the contract at any stage before performance? Will the existence of the right prevent the prospective payments from being treated as existing receivables? Doubts on this score arise from the fact that it has been held that where a hire-purchase agreement is determinable at the option of the hirer, the future rentals payable if the option is not exercised are not debts at all until the hirer enjoys the consideration for the period covered by the future rental.[57] Further, in lump-sum contracts, entire performance is a condition precedent to the promisee's right to payment.[58] Does the fact that nothing is *due* until performance has been completed exclude such contract rights from the category of existing receivables? Problems may also arise where a contract provides that the supplier shall supply goods *if and when* requested by the buyer.[59] Will

---

[52] *Norman* v. *FCT* (1962) 109 C.L.R. 9 at 26; *Booth* v. *FCT* (1988) 76 A.L.R. 375.

[53] Cf. *Norman* v. *FCT* (1962) 109 C.L.R. 9.

[54] *Australian Guarantee Corpn.* v. *Balding* (1930) 43 C.L.R. 140; *Re W.F. LeCornu Ltd.* [1931] S.A.S.R. 425; *Independent Automatic Sales Ltd.* v. *Knowles & Foster* [1962] 1 W.L.R. 974; (future rentals under existing hire-purchase agreements). cf. *H.J. Wigmore & Co. Ltd.* v. *Rundle* (1930) 44 C.L.R. 222 and *Blackwood's Ltd.* v. *Chartres* [1931] S.R. (NSW) 619 where it was held that such rentals were not debts "due or growing due" under existing contracts because the hire-purchase agreements gave the hirer the option to determine the agreement.

[55] *Hughes* v. *Pump House Hotel Co. Ltd.* [1902] 2 K.B. 190. See also, *Edmunds* v. *Edmunds* [1904] P. 362.

[56] *Re Trytel* [1952] 2 T.L.R. 32. This should be contrasted with *Bergmann* v. *Macmillan* (1881) 17 Ch.D. 423 where the profits by way of royalty for the future working of some patents were treated as future property.

[57] *H.J. Wigmore & Co. Ltd.* v. *Rundle* (1930) 44 C.L.R. 222; *Blackwood's Ltd.* v. *Chartres* [1931] S.R.(NSW) 619.

[58] *Cutter* v. *Powell* (1795) 9 Term Rep. 320; *Sumpter* v. *Hedges* [1898] 1 Q.B. 673; *Bolton* v. *Mahadeva* [1972] 1 W.L.R. 1009. Contrast *Hoenig* v. *Isaacs* [1952] 2 All E.R. 176 where the defects in performance fell far short of what was required to deprive the contractor of the contract price.

[59] Cf. *Burton* v. *Great Northern Ry.* (1854) 9 Exch. 507; *Great Northern Ry.* v. *Witham* (1873) 29 L.T. 471.

such contracts be productive of *existing* receivables before goods are actually requested under the contract? These examples show the difficulty of treating all existing contracts as creative of existing debts. *Walker* v. *Bradford Old Bank Ltd.*[60] shows just how far the common law has strayed. A bank customer assigned all moneys then or thereafter to be standing to his credit at his bank. At the date of the assignment only a little over £48 was there. At his death the balance had increased to about £217. The Divisional Court held that the eventual balance of £217 was a sum growing out of an existing contract and hence a present debt at the date of the assignment. That the deposits created a debt in the customer's favour is undoubted. But the analogy with sums arising out of an existing construction contract, upon which the court relied, was inexact, if not strained. The customer was under no obligation to increase the amount on deposit at the date of the assignment. And surely, the additional deposits did not *grow out* of the contract as sums grow out of an existing contract to supply goods or render services. The customer could have refrained from increasing his bank deposit without committing a breach of contract.

Even more controversial is the distinction between future debts and contingent debts. The significance of the distinction for the present purpose is that a fixed charge over future book debts is registrable whereas one over contingent debts is not.[61] By definition future book debts are debts expected under contracts which have no present existence whatever, but which every going concern expects to result from future contracts into which it might enter. Such debts are neither earned nor payable. They are, however, frequently used in receivables financing to support advances of money. As valuable rights, they are the expected fruits of the business as a going concern; and are no more vague than a song as yet only in contemplation,[62] and less uncertain of coming into existence than a story reposing solely in the mind of the author.[63] Yet in the extravagant rhetoric of common law jurisprudence this category of future rights is distinguished from contingent debts. A contingent debt by definition is an obligation or promise which may in a certain future event become a debt.[64] In reality such a debt is no debt at all for the event on which the debt depends may never happen. There is a further distinction between contingent liabilities which may never become debts, and debts payable on a contingency. If the event is one which must happen at some time, for example, upon the delivery of goods contracted to be purchased, it is not the debt but the *time of payment* which is contingent.[65] It is on this basis that sums payable under a present contract are treated as existing debts even though payment is contingent on performance of the stipulated consideration. But where the contingency may never happen,

---

[60] (1884) 12 Q.B.D. 511.
[61] *Paul & Frank Ltd.* v. *Discount Bank (Overseas) Ltd.* [1967] Ch. 348. *Cf. Re Brush Aggregates Ltd.* [1983] B.C.L.C. 320.
[62] As in *Performing Right Society Ltd.* v. *London Theatre of Varieties Ltd.* [1924] A.C. 1.
[63] *Ward, Lock & Co. Ltd.* v. *Long* [1906] 2 Ch. 550.
[64] *Mortimer* v. *IRC* (1864) 2 H. & C. 838; *Marren* v. *Ingles* [1980] S.T.C. 500 at 503, 506; *Re Gasbourne Pty. Ltd.* (1984) 8 A.C.L.R. 618.
[65] *Mortimer* v. *IRC* (1864) 2 H. & C. 838 at 851.

the so-called debt is contingent in the fullest sense: both the existence of the obligation to pay and the amount payable are contingent.[66] Examples include contracts of guarantee, indemnity and insurance. It is arguable that future contracts produce contingent debts and that no realistic distinction can be drawn between future debts and contingent debts. In future contracts, both the existence of the obligation, and the amount payable, are contingent. A company is never bound to enter into future contracts and since entering into such contracts is an event which may or may not happen, the debts expected are contingent in the fullest sense.

However, in *Paul & Frank Ltd.* v. *Discount Bank (Overseas) Ltd.*,[67] Pennycuick J. held that a charge over contingent debt was not registrable as a charge on book debts whereas a charge on future book debts was registrable because

" . . . where the item of property is the benefit of a contract and at the date of the charge the benefit of the contract does not comprehend any book debt, . . . that contract [cannot] be brought within the section as being a book debt merely by reason that the contract may ultimately result in a book debt.[68]"

It is difficult to distinguish, as did Pennycuick J., between book debts which arise from existing contracts and book debts which arise from non-existent contracts on any basis which makes charges over the latter registrable but charges over the former non-registrable. Besides, there would seem to be a basic conflict between the proposition that registration may be required in respect of a charge over future book debts, and the concept that the test is the character of what is charged at the date of the charge. It has accordingly been suggested that registrable charges on book debts include both future book debts and contingent debts.[69] This is doubtful. True it is that Pennycuick J. thought that, though at the date of the charge the Export Credit Guarantee (ECG) policy did not comprehend any book debts, yet that book debts could arise from it in the future. But it does not follow that truly contingent debts are registrable. The truth is that at no point in time would such an existing contract produce book debts even after the contingency has occurred. If by contingent contracts one refers to contracts of insurance, guarantee and indemnity, the better view is that even where such contracts are in existence, the claims which may arise under them are not book debts at all. Moreover, although a charge over book debts may carry through to such contracts as "proceeds" of book debts, yet a charge on such contracts is not registrable as a charge on book debts.

It should also be emphasised that the Latin tag *debitum in praesenti solvendum in futuro*, useful as it may seem in expressing the idea that present debts are existing obligations even though not presently payable, does not illuminate the distinction between present and future receiv-

---

[66] *Ibid.*
[67] [1967] Ch. 348.
[68] *Ibid.* at 362.
[69] Penn, Shea & Arora, *Law Relating to Domestic Banking* (1987), Vol. 1, pp. 350–351.

31

ables. It does not help to identify those money obligations which are to be treated as earned even though payable only in future.

Receivables as property rights

2.7   The question whether receivables are property rights has no practical utility. Conceptually, though, the question bears on the propriety of including security interests over receivables in the category of consensual security interests. It is perhaps convenient to start the discussion by saying that a receivable, being a mere right of payment, is not an interest in any specific assets belonging to the debtor, save where the right to payment is secured.[70] Rather the creditor is entitled to look to the fund of assets, indeterminate though this may be, belonging to the debtor for payment. A receivable is not a sum of money belonging to the creditor but in the possession of the debtor. Yet the liability of the debtor to fulfil his obligation is a *thing*, a valuable one at that, capable of being dealt with like any other intangible property. The problem for the legal analyst lies chiefly in the fact that orthodox analysis describes proprietary rights as those exigible against a thing, the *res*. Proprietary rights are defined by reference to the existence and location of a *res*, for the existence of proprietary rights correlates with the liability of a *res*, the subject-matter of the rights. But a mere unsecured debt is a purely personal right defined by reference to the existence and location of a particular debtor. How, then, does one include a receivable in the category of proprietary rights? One solution is to distinguish between real and personal rights. Real rights are those exercisable against a *res* and this is not less so because the *res* itself is a mere right. This, however, is not very helpful. What real rights does a creditor of an unsecured debt have? He cannot point to any real assets over which his rights exist. The difficulty is partly the result of the duality in the conception of *res*. Not only are tangible objects included, but also rights as such are treated as *res* even where the rights are good only against *this debtor*. Property could mean either the *res*, the subject of ownership, or the rights exercisable over that *res*. In either sense receivables could be the subject of property rights save that this is only possible in the relationship between assignees and the debtor. As between the creditor and debtor, a debt, even where secured, is but a personal obligation. And even in such a case, the creditor's property right is not in the debt, but in his security.

Techniques of financing against receivables

2.8   Broadly speaking, there are only three ways of financing against contractual receivables. These are by:

> (1) an outright assignment in discharge or reduction of an existing indebtedness;

---

[70] *Arab Bank Ltd.* v. *Barclays Bank* [1954] A.C. 495 at 531. But even in the case of secured debts, the creditor's property right is limited to the subject-matter of his security; it is not in the general assets of the debtor.

(2) discounting the receivables; and

(3) an assignment of, or charge on, the receivables as security.

Although securitisation is sometimes, if inaccurately, referred to as a fourth method, in truth securitisation is something of a hybrid between sale and sub-charge of receivables. Also outright assignment is a species of sale.

Outright assignment

Receivables may be assigned outright in discharge or reduction of a **2.9** pre-existing indebtedness. A creditor who presses his debtor for payment may accept an assignment of a debt due to his debtor from a third party, in satisfaction of his claim.[71] The same is true in principle of any other creditor. In economic terms the result is as if money has been exchanged for money. Many would, however, treat this technique as a mercantile rather than a financing transaction. The creditor's debt is discharged by acceptance of an assignment of a debt due to his original debtor from a third party. This method of financing against receivables is usually an alternative of last resort and is only acceptable on the theory that the substituted debtor is more creditworthy. No problem of registration of the assignment arises where it is intended as an outright non-security assignment. Further, the law as to avoidance of charges and other security interests has no application. Where the assigned debt is equal to or less than the creditor's claim no question of disguised mortgage can arise. But difficulties abound, as we shall see, where the face value of the assigned debt is more than the creditor's claim against the assignor. The "extra" may suggest an equity of redemption, with the result that the assignment which appears outright on its face, falls to be treated as a mortgage. This form of receivables financing is considered in more detail in Chapter 4.

Discounting receivables

Receivables, whether in a pure or negotiable form, may be discounted for immediate cash. Discounting of bills of exchange is an important source of corporate refinancing particularly where, as is common, the bills are discounted before maturity. In this way, the drawer in effect provides finance for the drawee's trading. Apart from bills, pure receivables are regularly discounted for many small and medium size proprietary companies. This method of raising money on the strength of receivables is known by different names in different industries. In the instalment credit industry, for example, sale of receivables is known as block discounting, though a refinement of it is rather confusingly called agency block

---

[71] This was the factual situation in *Brice* v. *Bannister* (1878) 3 Q.B.D. 569; *Buck* v. *Robson* (1878) 3 Q.B.D. 686; *Ex p. Moss* (1884) 14 Q.B.D. 310; *G. & T. Earle* v. *Hemsworth RDC* (1929) 140 L.T. 69 (C.A.); *Ashby, Warner & Co. Ltd.* v. *Simmons* [1936] 2 All E.R. 697; *Re Lawson Constructions Pty Ltd.* [1942] S.A.S.R. 201; *Sandford* v. *D.V. Building & Constructions Co. Ltd.* [1963] V.R. 137; *Siebe Gorman & Co. Ltd.* v. *Barclays Bank Ltd.* [1979] 2 Lloyd's Rep. 142; *Re Brush Aggregates* [1983] B.C.L.C. 320.

discounting. In other cases the arrangement is referred to as factoring and where the facility does not include credit control, ledger administration and debt collection, practitioners call it invoice discounting. In essence, discounting of receivables involves the purchase of invoiced receivables at less than their face value. The assignor whose receivables are so discounted receives immediate cash to the extent of the purchase price. The financier deducts an administration charge in addition to the "discount" which, by being calculated on a daily yield basis, produces a sum equivalent to interest on the amount advanced to the assignor. In most cases the discounting agreement will contain a recourse provision entitling the financier to reassign some of the discounted receivables to the assignor in certain circumstances. This recourse provision is normally accompanied by a right to retain some of the collected receivables as security for the performance of the assignor's recourse obligation. This technique of financing receivables is considered in detail in Chapter 3.

Security interests over receivables

2.10   Receivables are frequently assigned or charged as security for an advance of money. The security may be fixed or floating and may extend to present and future receivables alike. Being liquid assets, receivables are suitable for revolving credit. In economic terms this process involves an exchange of money for money. Raising money on the security of receivables is considered in more detail in Chapter 5.

Securitisation of receivables

2.11   Securitisation is not a distinct method of financing against receivables since it involves a sale of a stream of receivables or a sale coupled with a sub-charge by the purchaser. It is, however, treated separately because it is an innovative trading of receivables as securities in the capital markets. In international banking sale of loan assets is partly the result of the boom and subsequent bust in sovereign borrowing. This has to some extent been shaped by the pressures of regulation. In the domestic arena, securitisation of credit card receivables, secured consumer and equipment loans, and home mortgages, has become an important source of funds for institutional financiers. Here, pools of receivables are packaged and transferred to a special purpose company (SPC). The purchase price is raised by the SPC through loan notes issued in the securities market. This arrangement enables the transferor to achieve two main results: it moves the assets (receivables) off its balance sheet. This improves its gearing ratio because the SPC is structured so as not to amount to a subsidiary for purposes of group accounting. Secondly, the transferor retains a profit margin represented by the difference between the interest rate paid to the noteholders and that paid on the original loan by the borrower.

On the international scene, sale of participations in syndicated loans is a well-established banking practice. Sales, in general, take one of three forms: sub-participation,[72] assignment and novation. Because obligations

---

[72] Sub-participation may be funded or involve only the assumption of risk of default by the borrower. Broking and direct placements are also used particularly in the trading of commercial bills.

cannot be transferred in English law,[73] only novation achieves a "clean" transfer of rights and obligations. In recent years banks have sought to make their participations more liquid by annexing Transferable Loan Instruments (TLI) and Transferable Loan Certificates (TLC) to the syndicated facility. Participations can then be sold more easily by the sale of TLIs, TLCs, and other more complex instruments. Sub-participations utilise the secondary market which exists for the sale and purchase of participations. Securitisation of sovereign debts, it has been said,[74] is the result of the high interest rates up to the early 1980s. Securitisation raises complex and interesting conceptual, tax, and regulatory issues. However, these issues will not further be considered.

Distinction between sale and security assignments of receivables

As we have seen, financing against receivables could take a variety of **2.12** forms. Therefore, when the issue for determination is the legal nature of a transaction, it is not to the point to say that it is a financing rather than a mercantile agreement. Such a statement does not illuminate the question whether the financing was effected by a loan secured by a mortgage of receivables, a sale, or an outright assignment. The distinction between the three methods is important. First, implicit in a mortgage of receivables is the assignor's equity of redemption which remains his until foreclosure.[75] By contrast a vendor of receivables has no contractual obligation to reacquire them unless the sale is with recourse.[76] Secondly, a mortgagee of receivables who realises his security for a sum less than the secured amount is entitled, save in non-recourse lending, to look to the general resources of the assignor for recoupment. This is in theory different from the position of a purchaser of receivables who bears the ordinary risks incident to his ownership of the assigned receivables. Thirdly, a mortgage of receivables may infringe existing restrictions on the assignor's ability to borrow, whether these be contained in its Articles or in prior debt instruments. Sale of receivables has no such effect because it does not involve a borrowing of money. However, sophisticated prohibitions on the creation of additional debt or security are almost certain to restrict all forms of dealing. More importantly, whereas a mortgage of receivables must, to be effective, be registered, there is, as yet, no provision for the registration of sales and outright non-security assignments of receivables. Also, the characterisation of a transaction as a sale or mortgage could have important accounting effects. In the United Kingdom accounting treatment of a transaction follows its legal rather than economic effect. The result is that for a company which is already highly geared, a mortgage could weaken its balance sheet whereas a sale could improve it since it involves no direct repayment obligation.

[73] *Tolhurst* v. *Associated Portland Cement Manufacturers (1900) Ltd.* [1902] 2 K.B. 660 at 668.
[74] T. Congdon, *The Debt Threat* (1988), p. 202.
[75] *Re George Inglefield Ltd.* [1933] Ch. 1 at 27.
[76] *Ibid.*

The distinction may also be of importance to the investor. The characterisation of a transaction as a sale or mortgage affects an investor's evaluation of the riskiness of a proposed investment because implicit in any risk analysis is the perceived ease with which the relevant asset can be liquidated. This makes it necessary for the investor to know whether, and if so, how much, the returns on his investment are likely to be interrupted by any subsequent receivership, administration, or liquidation of the corporate assignor. A purchase of receivables is less likely to be affected by these events than a mortgage. Other differences relate to the liability for stamp duty and value added tax (VAT). A sale of receivables is, in principle, liable to *ad valorem* tax on the instruments by which it is effected.[77] A loan secured by a mortgage of receivables is not liable to stamp duty.[78] Further, mortgages are exempt supplies for purposes of VAT.[79] The same cannot be said of sales.[80] Whereas the "discount," as the consideration for the financial services rendered by the purchaser, is VAT-free, the "administration charge" is certainly liable to VAT.[81]

In deciding on which side of the divide an assignment of receivables falls the duty of the court is to ascertain the real intention of the parties. Whether what appears on its face as an outright non-security assignment is to be treated as a sale or security depends on whether there can be discovered from the documents and the surrounding circumstances an equity of redemption either in express words or by necessary implication. For this purpose, the court must have regard to the substance of the transaction as disclosed by the documents, the course of dealings between the parties and every other relevant circumstance.[82] If, upon examination, the court finds that the form of the transaction masks the real bargain, the mask is disregarded as an unavailing sham.[83] It is this approach which has led the courts to disregard what on its face appears to be an outright non-

---

[77] Stamp Act 1891, ss.54, 59(1) and Sched. 1. See also, *West London Syndicate* v. *IRC* [1898] 1 Q.B. 226 rvsd. as to goodwill in [1898] 2 Q.B. 507 (C.A.); *Measures Bros Ltd.* v. *IRC* (1900) 82 L.T. 689; *Lloyd's & Scottish Finance Co. Ltd.* v. *Prentice* (1977) 121 S.J. 847 (C.A.).

[78] The duty chargeable on mortgages was removed by the repeal of the relevant parts of Sched. 1, Stamp Act 1891: see Finance Act 1971, s.64, Sched. 14, Pt. VI.

[79] Value Added Tax Act 1983, s.17(1), Sched. 6, Group 5; *Dyrham Park Country Club Ltd.* v. *The Comrs.* [1978] V.A.T.T.R. 244.

[80] Arguably, only block discounting of hire-purchase and conditional sale agreements are exempt supplies under item 3, Sched. 6, Group 5, VAT Act 1983. But the Commissioners of Customs & Excise take the view that discounting of other receivables (as well as those arising under instalment credit agreements) are exempt supplies. However, the "charge" or "fee" for debt collection, credit control and sales ledger administration are subject to VAT because these are non-financial services which do not come within Group 5 of Sched. 6: see HM Customs & Excise Leaflets Nos. 700/5/85, para. 6 and 701/29/85, para. 2, reproduced in 3 De Voil, *Value Added Tax*, pp. J 36, J 1143. This has now been confirmed by *Comrs. of C. & E.* v.*Diners Club Ltd.* [1988] 2 All E.R. 1016, aff'd. [1989] 2 All E.R. 385 (C.A.).

[81] HM Customs & Excise Leaflet No. 701/29/85, para. 7.

[82] *Re Kent & Sussex Sawmills Ltd.* [1947] Ch. 177; *Re Row Dal Constrtuctions Pty. Ltd.* [1966] V.R. 249; *Automobile Association (Canterbury) Inc.* v. *Australasian Secured Deposits Ltd.* [1973] 1 N.Z.L.R. 417 at 420 *et seq.*

[83] By definition a "sham" is a transaction designed to give the appearance of creating legal rights and obligations different from the *actual* legal rights and obligations which the parties intended to create: *Snook* v. *London & West Riding Investments Ltd.* [1967] 2 Q.B. 786 at 802; *Ramsay* v. *IRC* [1982] A.C. 300 at 323.

security assignment on the grounds that it is a thinly disguised mortgage.[84] Even if the documents are not a sham, they may yet show, upon analysis, that the transaction was intended to be one of loan, and that the adoption of a sale and resale structure is merely machinery.[85] In this exercise parol evidence of the factual matrix known to the parties as well as of the genesis of the transaction is admissible.[86] Thus, when a transaction is described as a sale, but the "vendor" is liable to pay interest *eo nomine* and is under a contractual obligation to repurchase the debts sold, the court will refuse to be misled by the form of the transaction.[87] For the same reason, the annexation of interest coupons to the document evidencing the purported sale is likely to be fatal.[88] Where the document recites that an outright sale is intended, but the operative part shows that the outright assignment is only for indemnity, the transaction is a secured loan whatever the parties choose to call it.[89] Sometimes the commercial improbability of the consequences of an outright assignment dictates that rather than strain credulity by enforcing the transaction as an out-and-out assignment, the court may treat it as a loan secured by a mortgage of receivables.[90] Further, if the "vendor" is under a contractual obligation to apply the proceeds of sale in a particular way, it is likely that the court will refuse to be a party to this sham and would appropriately treat the purported sale as a security. This is because it is beyond the powers of a purchaser to dictate how the purchase money is applied by the vendor. Such a power is the exclusive preserve of a lender.

It is, however, beyond the interpretational powers of a court, at any rate where the documents and circumstances do not disclose a different contract, to attribute falsity to the parties merely because the choice of the financing technique was motivated by a desire to stay outside the regulatory environment. It is for this reason that the courts have emphasised time and time again, that the motive of the parties is irrelevant because it throws no light on the legal nature of the transaction.[91] Also, the fact that in the implementation of their agreement the

---

[84] *Bower* v. *Foreign & Colonial Gas Co.* [1877] W.N. 222; *Saunderson & Co.* v. *Clark* (1913) 29 T.L.R. 579; *Re Kent & Sussex Sawmills Ltd., supra; Re Row Dal Constructions Pty. Ltd., supra; Automobile Association (Canterbury) Inc.* v. *Australasian Secured Deposits Ltd., supra; Re Universal Management Ltd.* [1983] N.Z.L.R. 462; *Bambury* v. *Hayes Securities Ltd.* [1986] B.C.L. 1591.
[85] *Curtain Dream plc* v. *Churchill Merchanting Ltd.* (1990) B.C.C. 341 at 349. See also, *Welsh Development Agency* v. *Export Finance Co. Ltd.* (1990) B.C.C.; *cf. Palette Shoes Pty. Ltd.* v. *Krohn* (1937) 58 C.L.R. 1.
[86] *Prenn* v. *Simmonds* [1971] 1 W.L.R. 1381 at 1385; *Reardon Smith Line Ltd.* v. *Yngvar Hansen-Tangen* [1976] 1 W.L.R. 989 at 997.
[87] *Automobile Association (Canterbury) Inc.* v. *Australasian Secured Deposits Ltd., supra.*
[88] *Bower* v. *Foreign & Colonial Gas Co.* [1877] W.N. 222.
[89] *Saunderson & Co.* v. *Clark* (1913) 29 T.L.R. 579.
[90] Similar considerations dictated the characterisation of the transactions in *Re Kent & Sussex Sawmills Ltd., supra; Re Row Dal Constructions Pty. Ltd.; Re Universal Management Ltd., supra; Bambury* v. *Hayes Securities Ltd., supra.*
[91] *Re George Inglefield Ltd.* [1933] Ch. 1; *Olds Discount Co. Ltd.* v. *John Playfair Ltd.* [1938] 3 All E.R. 275; *Olds Discount Co. Ltd.* v. *Cohen* [1938] 3 All E.R. 281n; *IRC* v. *Rowntree & Co. Ltd.* [1948] 1 All E.R. 482; *Chow Yoong Hong* v. *Choong Fah Rubber Manufactory* [1962] A.C. 209; *Hamilton Finance Co. Ltd.* v. *Coverley Westray* [1969] 1 Lloyd's Rep. 53 at 71; *United Dominions Trust Ltd.* v. *Beech* [1972] 1 Lloyd's Rep. 546; *Lloyds & Scottish Finance Ltd.* v. *Cyril Lord Carpet Sales Ltd.* (1979) 129 N.L.J. 366; *Clough Mill Ltd.* v. *Martin* [1985] 1 W.L.R. 111 at 125.

parties have not followed the exact details agreed upon does not alter the character of the transaction. Departures may be dictated by considerations of convenience; and not to enforce a legal right is one thing, foregoing the right by rescission, waiver, variation or estoppel, is another.[92] Besides, evidence of departures from the letter of the financing agreement is likely to be post-contractual; such evidence is generally inadmissible as an aid to the interpretation of the contract.[93] Moreover, terminological inexactitude, does not, on its own, alter the legal character of the bargain entered into by the parties. This explains why expressions such as "advance," "repayable," "loan," "credit line," "security," etc., in the documentation of the transaction, do not turn a true sale into a loan secured by a mortgage of receivables.[94] Exceptionally, the courts have treated a transaction described as an "assignment by way of security" as an outright non-security assignment in reduction of an existing indebtedness.[95] In such cases, however, the fact that the consideration for the assignment was a loan was regarded as a circumstance of importance.

The courts have been ambivalent in the treatment of repurchase provisions in so-called sale transactions involving receivables. In principle it is clear that an absolute transfer containing nothing to show that a relationship of debtor and creditor is to exist between the parties does not cease to be so and become a mortgage merely because the vendor stipulates that he is to have a *right* of repurchase.[96] There is, it is said, all the difference in the world, at any rate as regards the legal incidents, between a mortgage and a right of repurchase.[97] Of course, if the respective transactions are completed by redemption or repurchase, as the case may be, there is no difference in the result. But does the same principle hold good for a contractual *obligation* to repurchase? No general answer meets all the issues which such an obligation raises. It may be that the distinction to be drawn is between an obligation to repurchase on the happening of an uncertain future event, such as a failure of a condition subsequent, on the one hand, and an absolute future obligation to repurchase on the other. In the former, the presence of a contingent obligation to repurchase (which may never materialise) would not, it is thought, turn the sale transaction into a mortgage. It is on this basis that factoring and other discounting agreements containing recourse obliga-

---

[92] *Lloyds & Scottish Finance Ltd.* v. *Cyril Lord Carpet Sales Ltd.* (1979) 129 N.L.J. 366 at 372.

[93] *Whitworth Street Estates Ltd.* v. *Miller* [1970] A.C. 583; *Re Armagh Shoes Ltd.* [1982] N.I. 59.

[94] *Olds Discount Co. Ltd.* v. *John Playfair Ltd., supra; Olds Discount Co. Ltd.* v. *Cohen, supra; United Dominions Trust Ltd.* v. *Beech, supra; Lloyds & Scottish Finance Ltd.* v. *Cyril Lord Carpet Sales Ltd., supra. Cf. Kelter* v. *American Bankers' Finance Co.* 302 Pa 483 (1932).

[95] *Lyon* v. *TY-Wood Corp.* 239 A 2d 819 (1968); *Siebe Gorman & Co. Ltd.* v. *Barclays Bank Ltd.* [1979] 2 Lloyd's Rep. 142 at 162–163. In both cases the court found that the use of the word "security" was in the general sense of indicating that the assignee viewed the assignment as *assuring* him of the moneys owed him by the assignor.

[96] *Alderson* v. *White* (1858) 2 De G. & J. 97 at 105.

[97] *North Central Waggon Co.* v. *Manchester, Sheffield & Lincolnshire Ry. Co.* (1888) 13 App.Cas. 554 at 567. *Cf. Re George Inglefield Ltd.* [1933] Ch. 1 at 27.

tions have not been treated as mortgages. In the latter, the presence of an absolute obligation to repurchase ought to lead to the conclusion that the purported sale is only a sham masking a mortgage which is in reality the substance of the transaction.[98] However, the courts have not adopted any clear cut approach. Two cases illustrate the judicial ambivalence in this area. In *Automobile Association (Canterbury) Inc.* v. *Australasian Secured Deposits Ltd.*[99] it was held that the fact that the vendor bound itself to repurchase the stocks at a stated price and the purchaser bound itself to resell the same stocks, and the fact that the right of, and obligation to, repurchase may be exercised at any time after a specified date, meant that the purchaser was precluded indefinitely from dealing with the stocks as a beneficial owner and justified characterising the transaction as a mortgage. But in *Chase Manhattan (Asia) Ltd.* v. *First Bangkok City Finance Ltd.*,[1] the Hong Kong Court of Appeal came to a different conclusion. There, a lender sold one half of its interest in a real estate loan to Chase Manhattan (Asia) (CMA) on terms that it was to repurchase the half share in approximately three months from the date of sale and was to receive the interest paid on the loan in the meantime. The transaction was held to be a true sale and not a charge. This was so notwithstanding that the court also held that CMA's interest in the promissory note securing the original loan determined at the date when the lender was contractually bound to repurchase.

Most of the cases establishing the above principles arose in the context of deciding whether the transactions in question constituted registrable security bills of sale or were void under the moneylenders legislation. That probably accounts for what was an extremely lenient approach. Whether such cases should continue to be regarded as authoritative, is at the very least, problematic. It is, however, fair to say that as regards registration, the law has chosen to draw a difficult, and in some sense, arbitrary distinction between a mortgage of receivables which is registrable,[2] and a sale or discounting of receivables which is exempt. Nor is it altogether clear that some of the purported sales are true sales at all. The courts have been all too anxious without further analysis or investigation, to uphold discounting of receivables as true sales.[3] Such a "sale" might on

---

[98] *Curtain Dream plc* v. *Churchill Merchanting Ltd.* (1990) B.C.C. 341.
[99] [1973] 1 N.Z.L.R. 417. It seems the mood is to follow this approach which, it is submitted, is more realistic: see *Curtain Dream plc* v. *Churchill Merchanting Ltd.*, *supra*.
[1] [1988] 2 F.T.L.R. 450. On appeal [1990] 1 W.L.R. 1181, the Judicial Committee of the Privy Council reversed the Hong Kong Court of Appeal, holding that the arrangement created a registrable charge which, not being registered was void against the liquidator.
[2] Companies Act 1985, s.396(1)(c) & (e).
[3] See, *e.g. Lloyds & Scottish Finance Ltd.* v. *Cyril Lord Carpet Sales Ltd.* (1979) 129 N.L.J. 366 where the House of Lords ignored the overwhelming evidence that a loan was intended and placed too much reliance on the importance attached to the "master agreement" by the parties. *Cf. Wide Bay & Burnett Finance Co. Ltd.* v. *Andersens Ltd.* [1932] St. R. Qsd. 119 where a discounting agreement was held to be a money lending transaction partly because "discounts" fell within the definition of "loan" in the Money Lenders Act 1916 (Queensland), s.3, but also because in substance and effect, the transaction was a loan of money. American courts place emphasis on the incidence of transaction risks: see *Kelter* v. *American Bankers' Finance Co.* 306 Pa 483 (1932); *Major's Furniture Mart* v. *Castle Credit Corp.*, 602 F 2d 538 (1979); *In the Matter of Armando Gerstel Inc.*, 65 B.R. 602.

further analysis have been found to be a loan secured by a mortgage of receivables. No weight is attached to the incidence of transaction risks in the purported sale. While it is undesirable to reallocate contractual risks by declaring a discounting agreement a secured loan, a better approach is one which treats the incidence of risks in the transaction as a circumstance of significance. If the "vendor" assumes none of the risks of ownership, there is a case for treating the transaction as a secured loan regardless of the label the parties choose to attach to it. In some cases it is difficult to distinguish between a full recourse discounting of receivables and a non-recourse loan secured on receivables. The picture becomes even more blurred when the loan is repayable only on a contingency.[4] It is similar difficulties that persuaded the authors of Article 9 of the United States Uniform Commercial Code to bring both discounting of receivables and security assignments within the scope of the Article,[5] though the assimilation did not dispense entirely with the necessity for distinguishing a true sale from a secured loan.[6]

Considerations affecting the choice of financing technique

2.13 In choosing an appropriate financing technique over receivables, apart from the particular needs of the corporate client being financed, there are a host of other considerations which both the financier and the corporate client cannot safely ignore. One such consideration is the ability of the client to create additional debt or to sell its assets. Generally speaking, every trading company has an implied power to borrow money for its business activities and to secure such debt by a charge on its property, unless there is a prohibition in its Articles or Memorandum of Association.[7] So, the financier would be concerned to see whether there is any

---

[4] As in *Waite Hill Holdings Ltd.* v. *Marshall* (1983) 133 N.L.J. 745.
[5] UCC (1972 Official Text), Art. 9–102 provides that the Article applies to all transactions regardless of form, which are intended to create a security interest, and to any sale of accounts or chattel paper.
[6] Both Art. 9–502 (on collections) and Art. 9–504 (on dispositions) provide that if the security agreement secures an indebtedness, the secured party must account to the debtor for any surplus, and unless otherwise agreed, the debtor is liable for any deficiency. Therefore although both sale and security assignments of receivables are subject to the filling requirements of the UCC (subject to specified exceptions in Art. 9–104(f)), the ultimate destination of the surplus after the assignee has been recouped, necessitates a distinction between a sale and a security.
[7] *Re Patent File Co.* (1870) 6 Ch. App. 83 at 88; *Re General Provident Assurance Co.* (1872) L.R. 14 Eq. 507; *Re Hamilton Windsor's Ironworks* (1879) 12 Ch.D. 707; *General Auction Estates Co.* v. *Smith* [1891] 3 Ch. 432. The impact of corporate incapacity has been minimised, if not eliminated, by the new provisions inserted by the Companies Act 1989, s.108 into Chap. III, Pt. I of the Companies Act 1985. New s.35(1) provides that the validity of an act done by a company shall not be called into question on the ground of lack of capacity by reason of anything in the company's memorandum. However, this is without prejudice to the right of a member of the company to bring proceedings to restrain the doing of an act which, but for s.35(1), would have been beyond the company's capacity, except where the act sought to be restrained is in fulfilment of a legal obligation of the company: *ibid.*, s.35(2). Also, in favour of a person dealing with a company in good faith, the power of the board of directors to bind the company, or authorise others to do so, shall be deemed to be free of any limitation under the company's constitution: *ibid.*, s.35A(1).

prohibition on the client's ability to borrow; whether there is a limit on the amount which may be borrowed, and if so, whether the limit has been exceeded. It would be important to know whether any consents, apart from those of the directors, are required to borrow and give security. But a financier dealing with the company in good faith need not worry about these restrictions.[8] If there are existing debt instruments it is likely that there would be restrictions on the company's ability to create additional debt and to give a senior charge on its assets.[9] Similarly, a company can dispose of its assets just as freely,[10] subject, of course, to the usual formalities; but prior creditors may have imposed fetters on this power. The choice may occasionally depend on considerations affecting the lender alone. It may be unable to do business other than lending. In that event it cannot purchase receivables. Regulatory constraints affecting the lender may rule out additional lending so that quite apart from any question of corporate incapacity, it cannot make additional loans without moving them off its balance sheet. Where cross-border financing is carried out, there might be restrictions on the ability of foreign financial institutions to do particular businesses. In addition, domestic regulations in foreign jurisdictions particularly with respect to secured consumer loans, may make particular financing alternatives unattractive because of the difficulty of enforcing security against the receivables represented by the loans. This problem is likely to become more acute with the recent attempts at globalisation of securitisation of receivables and when the single European market becomes a reality.

Another relevant consideration is whether there is a contractual prohibition against assignment of receivables. Most properly drafted reservation of title clauses in sale of goods transactions are likely to contain such a prohibition. They are also common in construction contracts and may be found in the standard form contracts of some trade organisations. The prohibition may be absolute or partial. In the latter case consent may be required to any form of dealing with the receivables. At the moment, the effect of such a prohibition in English law is obscure.[11] Some factoring agreements contain a warranty that the receivables are not subject to any property reservation clause or any prohibition

---

[8] Companies Act 1985, ss.35–35B.

[9] Actual notice of a debt instrument is not constructive notice of any restrictions contained therein: *English & Scottish Mercantile Investment Trust Ltd.* v. *Brunton* [1892] 2 Q.B. 1 affd. *ibid.,* 700; *Re Castell & Brown Ltd.* [1898] 1 Ch. 315; *Re Valletort Sanitary Steam Laundry Co. Ltd.* [1903] 2 Ch. 654; *Re Standard Rotary Machine Co.* (1906) 95 L.T. 829; *Wilson* v. *Kelland* [1910] 2 Ch. 306; *G. & T. Earle* v. *Hemsworth RDC* (1928) 44 T.L.R. 605; *Siebe Gorman & Co. Ltd.* v. *Barclays Bank Ltd.* [1979] 2 Lloyd's Rep. 142. This reasoning is technical and unsatisfactory, and is not justified by judicial reluctance to extend constructive notice into commercial transactions. Under the new s.415(2) of the Companies Act 1985, registrable prescribed particulars of a charge may include whether the company has undertaken not to create any other charges ranking in priority to or *pari passu* with the charge. New s.416(1) provides that a person taking a charge over a company's property shall be taken to have notice of any matter requiring registration and disclosed on the register at the time the charge was created. This notice does not extend to purchasers of the company's property: s.416(2).

[10] See n. 7, *supra*.

[11] For a full discussion see para. 8.7, *infra*.

against dealing. In an appropriate case, the warranty may negative any suggestion that the factor had constructive notice of the prohibition. The efficacy of such a warranty in relative priority problems has not been fully tested,[12] but it is unlikely to avail a factor who wilfully shuts his eyes to the prohibition. This is one consideration which financiers will do well to keep in mind.

Some financing agreements contain a cross-default clause. The effect is to accelerate repayment of the loan where there is a default in another debt instrument. Most financiers avoid searching other debt instruments because of fear of discovering negative pledge clauses and similar prohibitions. However, since a cross-default clause in an earlier debt instrument could have grave implications for junior creditors, the existence of such a clause cannot safely be ignored in any evaluation of the riskiness of a proposed advance.

The choice of a particular technique or combination of techniques, may be affected by non-legal factors. Prominent among these is accounting considerations. Where the prevailing accountancy practice treats a transaction not according to its economic effect, but follows its legal characterisation as in the United Kingdom, the desire to achieve off-balance sheet results remains attractive.[13] A sale or discounting transaction improves the balance sheets of the corporate client because the sum advanced is credited whereas a loan is always entered as a liability even where it involves limited or no recourse. A corporate client who is highly geared will find a sale of receivables more attractive since, as regards economic effect, a sale is barely distinguishable from a non-recourse funding against receivables.

Tax considerations will always remain relevant. A loan secured by a mortgage of receivables is not liable to VAT or stamp duty. A sale of receivables is liable to *ad valorem* duty on the instruments by which the sale is effected. In some jurisdictions the amount could be substantial. Also, it may be liable to VAT if administration charge is imposed for debt collection, ledger administration and credit control.

From the financier's point of view the security of his investment is always a factor of some significance. The extent to which his returns could be interrupted by any subsequent receivership, administration or liquidation of the corporate client must be taken into account in selecting an appropriate financing technique. Legislation has made significant inroads into formal security interests. For instance, a loan secured by a mortgage of receivables must be registered to be effective against any subsequent secured creditor,[14] administrator or liquidator of the corporate client. Also, the Insolvency Act 1986 avoids, and in some circumstances, modifies, the rights of the secured creditor. Preferences given, and floating charges created, during the relevant time are vulnerable.[15]

---

[12] In *Pfeiffer GmbH* v. *Arbuthnot Factors Ltd.* [1988] 1 W.L.R. 150, it was conceded that such a warranty prevented the factor from being affected by constructive notice of the prohibition in the seller's agreement with the buyer.
[13] But see Pt. I of the Companies Act 1989.
[14] Companies Act 1985, ss.396(1) & 399(1).
[15] Insolvency Act 1986, ss.239 & 245.

Extortionate credit bargains,[16] transactions at an undervalue[17] and those defrauding creditors[18] are all liable to be reopened. The petition for, and the appointment of, an administrator, may impede expeditious enforcement of the rights of secured creditors.[19] The form of the security, whether fixed or floating, may determine whether the financier can block a proposed administration. Outright sale or discounting of receivables is unlikely to be avoided on any of the above grounds although they may be reopened if they are extortionate. The definition of "credit" is wide enough to cover discounting of receivables,[20] but how much "discount" and other charges will amount to an extortion, is a question of fact depending on all the circumstances. The fact that credit could have been obtained at a much lower cost by the client is a circumstance of some significance. All these should be borne in mind both in selecting the appropriate financing technique and its structure.

---

[16] Insolvency Act 1986, s.244.
[17] *Ibid.*, s.238.
[18] *Ibid.*, ss.423–425.
[19] *Ibid.*, ss.8, 10(1), 11(3) & 15.
[20] By s.9(1) of the Consumer Credit Act 1974, "credit" is defined as including a cash loan, and any form of financial accommodation. Discounting of receivables will no doubt count as a form of "financial accommodation."

CHAPTER THREE

DISCOUNTING OF RECEIVABLES

Introductory

3.1　The management of corporate finance is of critical importance to any business regardless of size, particularly in formative years. In this chapter we shall examine one tool of financial management. This is discounting of receivables. Reduced to its barest essentials, discounting of receivables means selling receivables at a discount, that is to say, at a price less than their face value. A single receivable may be discounted for immediate cash, although this would, for obvious reasons, be rare, except, perhaps, where a large amount is involved. More commonly, a stream of receivables is discounted, the aim being to provide working capital geared to the particular requirements of the company. As a financial service, it may be contrasted with long-term finance by way of a loan secured on receivables. Discounting is primarily to meet the need for short-term finance. It is therefore not a substitute for long-term capital even though a regular arrangement for discounting may be long-term in its aim and outcome. Short-term suppliers of capital, while not disinterested in the profitability of the company being financed, are of necessity primarily concerned with liquidity. Long-term financiers on the other hand, look primarily to profitability of the enterprise being financed.

Discounting of receivables is as old as historical records of business practices go, but institutional discounting has a more recent origin.[1] The patterns of discounting vary enormously from industry to industry. For example, film production is not uncommonly financed by discounting the distributor's covenant to pay under a "negative pick-up" agreement.[2] Bills of exchange used in inland and foreign trade are everyday discounted before maturity and in this way provide refinancing. More importantly, the extension of trade credit is made substantially easier by the institution of factoring. When goods, services or facilities are pro-

---

[1] Steffan and Danziger (1936) 36 Col. L.R. 745, chronicle the history of factoring and its association with the mercantile factor.

[2] Michael Henry, *The Film Business: a legal and commercial analysis* (1986), pp. 29 *et seq.* Even county councils now try to discount their anticipated future receipts from council house sales, the aim in some cases being to evade the statutory limits on their spending powers. Such arrangements raise interesting questions of public law, in particular, whether county councils have capacity to conclude such sales. In *R.* v. *Wirral Metropolitan BC, ex p. Milstead, The Independent*, March 28, 1989, the Divisional Court held that a council had no power to enter into a discounting agreement.

vided on short-term credit to the buyer, the unpaid account is a static, immobilised asset frozen as the polar ice cap.[3] Factoring thaws out such frozen assets by providing immediate cash to meet working capital requirements. In the instalment credit industry, for example, instalment receivables due from hire-purchase, leasing and credit sale agreements are discounted for immediate cash.[4] Between industries there are considerable variations in patterns of discounting. Block discounting of instalment receivables differs from factoring in many important respects of which only two need be mentioned. The first is that unless a refinement of block discounting called agency block discounting is used, the dealer does not segregate instalments received from hirers or credit buyers, nor is he under any obligation to account for such receipts. He does, however, guarantee that the hirers or credit buyers would perform their obligations and implements this guarantee by issuing a series of instalment notes or bills of exchange to the finance company. Such notes or bills may be security only or conditional payments. In contrast, a factored client is under an accounting obligation and must segregate receipts from buyers from his own general resources. The receipts are held on trust[5] and where they are cheques or other negotiable payment instruments the client is liable in conversion if he misappropriates them.[6] Secondly, the dealer transfers to the finance company the underlying goods whose receivables are being discounted under a block discounting arrangement. This is not necessarily so in factoring, although it is not unusual for the client to assign all his rights under the contracts generating the receivables to the factor.[7] Given the diversity of discounting, it is unprofitable to consider its various forms in any detail. The discussion which follows is confined to invoice discounting of pure as distinct from documentary receivables. The choice of invoice discounting is to stress that we are concerned only with the financial aspect of discounting and would not consider credit protection, ledger administration and debt collection which are optional extras when a full factoring service is used.[8] But the expression "invoice discounting" as used in this chapter is broader than that accepted by most factors.[9] In particular, it does not discriminate against notification discounting, and covers any arrangement whereby receivables locked up in unpaid accounts are sold to a financier at a discount and for immediate cash. Nothing turns on whether the whole cash consideration is advanced upon purchase or only an agreed percentage, nor on whether notice is

---

[3] T. H. Silbert (1952) 30 Harv. B.R. No. 1, p. 39.

[4] J. W. Lewis Lloyd, *A Short Guide to Block Discounting* (2nd ed., 1965), contains an instructive account.

[5] *G.E. Crane Sales Pty. Ltd.* v. *Commissioner of Taxation (Cwth)* (1971) 46 A.L.J.R. 15; *Tay Valley Joinery Ltd.* v. *C.F. Financial Services Ltd.* (1987) 3 B.C.C. 71.

[6] *International Factors Ltd.* v. *Rodriguez* [1979] Q.B. 351.

[7] See F. R. Salinger, *Tolley's Factoring* (1984), App. V, clause 4(2).

[8] For a good discussion of these see Forman and Gilbert, *Factoring and Finance* (London, Heinemann, 1976); Biscoe, *Credit Factoring* (London, Butterworths, 1975); Salinger, *Tolley's Factoring* (1984).

[9] There is a plague of terminological confusion in discounting. Some are maturity factoring, bulk factoring, venture factoring, invoice discounting, direct collection, agency block discounting, etc. For a discussion of the usages of these and other terms, see Salinger, *op cit.*, Chaps. 2 and 3.

given to debtors. Similarly it does not matter for this purpose whether the discounter (who may for convenience be called a factor) collects the receivables directly or allows the client to collect them as his agent.

Legal framework of discounting

3.2   English law provides, and has always provided, a very simple framework for discounting receivables. Where they are embodied in a negotiable paper, discounting is by negotiation. Sale of trade debts at a discount has always enjoyed the facility of assignment. Equitable assignments are of great antiquity,[10] and since 1874 assignments of debts have been possible at law though they have to be written, and written notice has to be given to the account debtors.[11] One constraint on legal assignments from the point of view of the factor is that only existing receivables can be assigned.[12] Although the idea of existing receivables is not as clear cut as in tangible property,[13] and factors may benefit from the somewhat unsatisfactory distinction between existing and future receivables,[14] it must be said that however elastic the idea of existing receivables is, it does not cover debts expected from contracts as yet only in contemplation.[15] Yet discounting is uneconomic if confined to existing receivables. Here equity's more flexible rules provide a solution,[16] enabling the factor and his client to buy and sell receivables some of which are only in contemplation at the commencement of discounting. The result though, is that most, if not all, discounting arrangements where future receivables are covered, are but equitable assignments.[17] There is little, if any, disadvantage in equitable assignments since, on one view, an assignment complying with section 136(1) of the Law of Property Act 1925 gives a title which is only legal in a procedural sense, being treated for priority purposes as if it were equitable only.[18]

---

[10] See Bailey (1932) 48 L.Q.R. 547; Marshall, *Assignment of Choses in Action* (1950), Chap. 1.

[11] Supreme Court of Judicature Act 1873, s.25(6), re-enacted with slight modifications as s.136 of the Law of Property Act 1925.

[12] Common law did not, and still does not, as a general rule, recognise a present transfer of future property: *Lunn* v. *Thornton* (1845) 1 C.B. 379. The only concession made by common law was the inclusion of potential property in the category of existing property. The concession was modest because the potential existence rule was confined almost exclusively to the agricultural field—essentially to crops and livestock. Common law courts never recognised that goods which a company may manufacture tomorrow or receivables expected from their sale, were things in potentia. In the case of receivables the difficulty was compounded by the formal non-recognition of assignments other than of Crown and negotiable debts.

[13] See para. 2.6, *supra*.

[14] See the reasoning in *Walker* v. *Bradford Old Bank Ltd.* (1884) 12 Q.B.D. 511.

[15] *Cf. G. & T. Earle* v. *Hemsworth RDC* (1928) 44 T.L.R. 605.

[16] *Holroyd* v. *Marshal* (1862) 10 H.L.Cas. 191; *Tailby* v. *Official Receiver* (1888) 13 App.Cas. 523.

[17] *Cf. Pfeiffer GmbH* v. *Arbuthnot Factors Ltd.* [1988] 1 W.L.R. 150, where it was conceded (probably wrongly) that the receivables were sold to the factor under a legal assignment.

[18] *Pfeiffer GmbH* v. *Arbuthnot Factors Ltd.* [1988] 1 W.L.R. 150, adopting (without express reference) the argument of Maclauchlan (1980) 96 L.Q.R. 90.

Discounting arrangements are in general carried out within the framework of a master agreement.[19] The choice of an appropriate structure for the master agreement is dictated largely by considerations of stamp duty. Most agreements take one of two forms in order to avoid stamp duty. The first is what might be called an option or unilateral contract by the client to the factor to buy scheduled receivables. In the jargon of factors, this is called a "facultative" agreement. Under it the client agrees to offer and the factor agrees to accept blocks of receivables. The agreement provides that the factor is under no obligation to accept any offered receivables, but that in the absence of an acknowledgment the offer is deemed to be accepted. The assignment offer is thus a unilateral contract capable of acceptance only by conduct.[20] The dispositive act by which the receivables are assigned is the unacknowledged conduct of the factor. The offer document is not dispositive and therefore escapes stamp duty. The second method is an agreement by which every receivable in existence at the commencement date fixed by the agreement or coming into existence subsequently, is assigned to the factor without the necessity for a new formal act of assignment. However, during the currency of the agreement the client is obliged to notify the factor about receivables which have become vested in accordance with the agreement. This type of master agreement is, to use the jargon of factors, a "whole turnover" agreement. Evidently, neither the facultative nor the whole turnover agreement satisfies the requirements of a legal or statutory assignment, and are therefore valid only as equitable assignments. Since these structures are dictated by the need to avoid liability to stamp duty it is necessary to examine the extent to which they can be considered successful.

Conveyances and agreements for the transfer of property are stampable[21] where the certified[22] value of the transaction is more than £30,000.[23] A sale of receivables is ordinarily liable to stamp duty if carried out through a document,[24] but not otherwise. This is because stamp duty is a tax on instruments, not on transactions. Therefore, if a transaction can be carried out without an instrument no duty is payable.[25] Also, not every instrument brought into existence in the course of a transaction of sale and purchase is stampable. Only instruments whereby any property upon a sale thereof is legally or equitably transferred are liable to tax.[26] How, then, do these principles bear on the two types of master agreement? It is convenient to begin with the whole turnover. Here, the master agreement is the very instrument by which equitable assignment of existing and future receivables is effected. As a matter of principle the agreement is stampable. It is usually not stamped because by postponing the commen-

---

[19] See, e.g. Encyclopaedia of Forms and Precedents (5th ed., 1986), Vol. 4, p. 178, Form 45.
[20] Carlill v. Carbolic Smoke Ball Co. [1893] 1 Q.B. 256.
[21] Stamp Act 1891, ss.54, 59(1) and Sched. 1.
[22] Finance Act 1958, s.34.
[23] Finance Act 1984, s.109 (amending Finance Act 1963, s.55).
[24] Measures Bros Ltd. v. IRC (1900) 82 L.T. 689; Lloyds & Scottish Finance Co. Ltd. v. Prentice (1977) 121 S.J. 847.
[25] IRC v. Angus (1889) 23 Q.B.D. 579 at 583; Oughtred v. IRC [1960] A.C. 206 at 227, 238.
[26] IRC v. Angus, supra.

cement date factors make it impossible for anyone to ascertain the consideration for the purchase and hence the amount payable as duty. No rule of law precludes this avoidance of stamp duty. It is not easy to apply the contingency principle to a whole-turnover agreement. The essence of the contingency principle is that where the amount payable under an instrument is uncertain at the date of its execution, *ad valorem* duty is still assessable on the total amount payable under it if the contingency occurs.[27] This principle applies only where there is a minimum, maximum or specified amount payable under the instrument, albeit on a contingency however remote.[28] It is not easy to adapt the contingency principle to a whole turnover agreement, let alone to a facultative agreement. There is neither a specified nor a minimum or maximum amount payable under the agreement on the basis of which *ad valorem* duty may be assessed. Therefore if a whole turnover agreement is liable to *ad valorem* stamp duty it must be on the theory that the written notifications of vested receivables are themselves stampable. This would only be justified on a reasoning similar to that which commended itself to a majority of their Lordships in *Oughtred* v. *IRC*,[29] where it was held that a subsequent conveyance of the dry legal estate in performance of a prior oral contract for sale was liable to *ad valorem* duty. It did not matter that it was a formal act confirming that which in equity, already belonged to the transferee. If that reasoning is relevant in this context, the argument would be that a written notification of receivables vested in the factor pursuant to the whole turnover agreement would be stampable *ad valorem*. It would for this purpose not matter that the debts are already equitably assigned by the master agreement, any more than it mattered in *Oughtred* v. *IRC*,[30] that the beneficial interest had already passed under the oral contract. For many reasons, however, this adaptation is contrived and unconvincing. First, as Lord Jenkins stressed in *Oughtred* v. *IRC*,[31] the reasoning of the majority applies only where the subject-matter of the subsequent conveyance is such that the *full* title to it can only be transferred by an instrument. This is true of land but certainly not of receivables. Second, even assuming that the reasoning applies to a sale of receivables, it is evidently the case that the written notification is not an instrument whereby receivables are sold; it is at best only evidence of a sale and such a document is not liable to *ad valorem* stamp duty.[32] So much for the whole turnover agreement.

The efficacy of a facultative agreement from the standpoint of stamp duty is more debatable. Typically schedules of receivables offered periodically to the factor for purchase are kept below £30,000 so as to enjoy the small transactions relief.[33] Doubts on the efficacy of this structure arise from three sources. The first is whether the judicial anti-avoidance rule applies to such a deliberate attempt to stay outside stamp

[27] *Sergeant and Sims on Stamp Duties* (9th ed., 1988), p. 28.
[28] *Underground Electric Ry. Co. Ltd.* v. *IRC* [1916] 1 K.B. 306.
[29] [1960] A.C. 206.
[30] *Ibid.*
[31] [1960] A.C. 206 at 241.
[32] *IRC* v. *Angus* (1889) 23 Q.B.D. 579, especially at 589.
[33] Finance Act 1958, s.34(4).

duty. In *Ingram* v. *IRC*[34]—a test case, Vinelott J. held that although stamp duty is a tax on instruments and not on transactions, the court must ascertain the substance of the transaction effected by an instrument in order to determine the question of liability to stamp duty. Accordingly where a preordained series of transactions is entered into for the purpose of avoiding stamp duty the court would disregard steps inserted into that series of transactions which have no business purpose and treat the transactions as a single transaction achieving the preordained end. If we apply this to a facultative agreement, the result would be to consider the series of unilateral offers to the factor to purchase as a series of steps inserted into the transaction of sale and purchase, having no business purpose. On this approach the master agreement would be regarded as the dispositive instrument and the subsequent offers the bases for assessing the amount of tax. This is unpromising. For one thing, the exact status and future of the judicial anti-avoidance rule is not yet assured[35]; for another, the reasoning in *Ingram* v. *IRC*[36] is unconvincing. The judicial anti-avoidance rule is incompatible with the structure of stamp duty which is a tax on instruments, and not transactions.[37] This does not conclude the matter, for another well-established rule casts doubts on the efficacy of the facultative agreement. This is the "all one transaction" rule. According to this rule, although a memo or record of a transaction carried out orally or by conduct does not usually attract the duty which is payable on an instrument effecting the transaction, this is subject to the qualification that where it can be shown that the creation of the memo or record and the previous transaction are in fact "all one transaction" then the duty may be chargeable on the memo.[38] It is very likely that whole-turnover and facultative agreements will be liable to *ad valorem* duty under this rule, although the point is undecided.[39]

The final doubt arises from the availability of small transactions relief. By Section 34(4) of the Finance Act 1958, a certificate of value for purposes of stamping, is required to contain a statement certifying that the transaction effected by the instrument (here the master agreement) does not form part of a larger transaction or a series of transactions in respect of which the aggregate value of the consideration exceeds £30,000. What constitutes part of a larger transaction or a series of transactions is not defined by the Act. In *Attorney General* v. *Cohen*[40] Lord Greene L.J., said that the phrase "a series of transactions" is intended to "sweep in cases where the relationship between the transactions is an integral part and not a fortuitous one depending merely on such circumstances as continuity in time or place, but is such that it would not or might not be sufficient to bring them within the phrase "part of a large transaction." From this it is clear that a succession of sales governed by a single master agreement constitutes a series of transactions and each

---

[34] [1985] S.T.C. 835.
[35] See, *e.g. Craven* v. *White* [1989] A.C. 398.
[36] *Supra.*
[37] Sellar, 1985 S.L.T. 93; Nock [1986] B.T.R. 239.
[38] *Sergeant and Sims on Stamp Duties* (9th ed., 1988), p. 27.
[39] *Cf. Lloyds & Scottish Finance Co. Ltd.* v. *Prentice* (1977) 121 S.J. 847.
[40] [1937] 1 K.B. 478 at 490–491.

forms part of a larger transaction regulated by the single master agreement.[41] This is true both of the facultative agreement and of the whole turnover agreement. Hence the better view is that discounting (master) agreements and the subsequent sales effected thereunder are not eligible for small transactions relief.

The security of the factor

3.3   Discounting of receivables may be undertaken on a recourse or non-recourse basis. In the former, the client undertakes to repurchase the receivables sold to the factor in specified circumstances. In the latter, the factor has no formal recourse against the client, at any rate as regards approved receivables. Even here, describing the transactions as a non-recourse purchase is a little misleading. For one thing, by purchasing approved receivables on a non-recourse basis the factor guarantees only the solvency of approved debtors. He neither guarantees performance of the underlying contract nor accepts the risk of non-payment by unapproved debtors. We shall return to the nature of the recourse obligation. For now it is sufficient to say that the recourse obligation is one of the provisions in the master agreement designed to protect the factor. Another "security" of the factor is the imposition of an upper limit on the aggregate indebtedness of any one debtor, the aim being to minimise the risks inherent in the financial transaction. Associated with this is the exclusion of particular non-approved receivables. Even when such receivables are bought, it is almost always on a recourse basis and this is so whether or not the transaction is with or without recourse. Discounting arrangements typically contain a number of warranties.[42] First, there may be a warranty of the value and validity of assigned receivables. Here the client warrants that the goods or services whose receivables are assigned have been delivered or performed according to contract, and that the invoice contains a valid collectible debt of the amount stated, free of contra accounts. Additionally, the master agreement contains a warranty that there will be no variation of the terms of contracts relating to assigned receivables, and that the receivables are free from incumbrances.[43] Like contractual warranties, the above warranties provide personal security for the factor. A breach will, of course, only entitle the factor to damages, but given the invariable practice of exacting an indemnity from the client, a factor will normally find sufficient protection in the retention fund in the sense that he will set off any resulting loss against the fund. Where, however, the retention is insufficient to absorb the resulting loss, the only remedy available is a personal action for breach against a client of doubtful solvency. Most discounting agreements contain an irrevocable power of attorney empowering the factor to perfect assignments, indorse negotiable instru-

---

[41] See also, Monroe and Nock, *The Law of Stamp Duties* (6th ed., 1986), p. 88.
[42] See, *e.g. The Encyclopaedia of Forms and Precedents* (5th ed., 1986), Vol. 4, p. 178, Form 45, clauses 12 & 13.
[43] *Ibid.*, clause 12.

ments, institute and defend proceedings in the name of the client, and to do all the other things necessary to perfect his title to the assigned receivables or the goods from which the receivables are expected. Since the power is given to secure the factor's proprietary interest in the assigned receivables, it is revocable neither by the unilateral act of the donor (client), nor by his death, bankruptcy or liquidation.[44] The power affords the factor some "security" and facilitates the enforcement of the assignment. The trust provision in the master agreement[45] could also afford valuable security. In non-notification discounting of receivables such a provision is invariably a feature of the master agreement, and most notification discounting of receivables contain similar provisions. Apart from the provision, it is plain law that an assignor of receivables receives proceeds as a constructive trustee for the assignee.[46] This is so whether or not a trust provision is inserted, unless the accounting obligation inherent in the assignment is excluded. The insertion of the trust provision is necessary to make assurance doubly sure. In its commonest form, the trust provision is a clause stating that all receipts on account of assigned receivables are held in trust for the factor and must be remitted *in specie* as soon as received. It has been held that the provision is effective to make the client a trustee of the receipts,[47] and where the receipts—in the form of cheques and bills, are misappropriated, the client is liable for conversion.[48] The factor in such cases has a proprietary tracing claim valid against the client and any subsequent administrator or liquidator, and to which the ordinary rules of equitable tracing would apply. But if the receipts are dissipated, there is nothing to trace,[49] and the factor may find himself with only a personal claim against an insolvent client.

The master agreement usually contains provisions for guarantee and indemnity.[50] These afford personal security to the factor although when combined with a right to set off damages and loss against the retention fund, could, no doubt, prove powerful. A guarantee may take a variety of forms. It may be an agreement to pay if the account debtors default. This is in substance an indemnity, save that the client's liability is conditional on default by the debtors. The significance of this type of provision is that if the account debtor's obligation to pay ceases for whatever reason, that of the client as a guarantor automatically comes to an end.[51] A guarantee may, however, take the form of an agreement that the account debtors will not only pay their debts, but also that they will perform their

---

[44] Powers of Attorney Act 1971, s.4. See also, *Sowman* v. *David Samuel Trust Ltd.* [1978] 1 W.L.R. 22.

[45] See *The Encyclopaedia of Forms and Precedents* (5th ed., 1986), Vol. 4, Form 45, clause 11.1

[46] *G.E. Crane Sales Pty. Ltd.* v. *Commissioner of Taxation (Cwth)* (1971) 46 A.L.J.R. 15; *Barclays Bank plc* v. *Willowbrook International Ltd.* [1987] 1 F.T.L.R. 386.

[47] *Tay Valley Joinery Ltd.* v. *C.F. Financial Services Ltd.* (1987) 3 B.C.C. 71.

[48] *International Factors Ltd.* v. *Rodriguez* [1979] Q.B. 351.

[49] *Roscoe* v. *Winder* [1915] 1 Ch. 62; *cf. Re Oatway* [1903] 2 Ch. 356.

[50] See *The Encyclopaedia of Forms and Precedents* (5th ed., 1986) Vol. 17, p. 371, Form 17. In *NRG Vision Ltd.* v. *Churchfield Leasing Ltd.* [1988] B.C.L.C. 625, the guarantee was secured by a floating charge over the client's undertaking.

[51] *Cf. Moschi* v. *Lep Air Services Ltd.* [1973] A.C. 331; *Hyundai Heavy Industries Co. Ltd.* v. *Papadopoulos* [1980] 1 W.L.R. 1129.

obligations under the supply contract. Here if the account debtors fail to perform, there is not only a breach of the supply contract, but also of the contract of guarantee. For this the factor is entitled to damages, but only damages. In *NRG Vision Ltd.* v. *Churchfield Leasing Ltd.*,[52] a discounting agreement of sums due under leasing agreements provided that the client guaranteed the payment by the lessees of all sums due under the leasing agreements and the due performance of all the lessee's obligations thereunder. A number of lessees defaulted in their payments and the discounter who took a floating charge as security for the client's liabilities under the financing transactions, put in receivers. One of the many issues argued was whether the appointment of receivers was good and this turned partly on the construction of the guarantee, since, whatever liability there was on the part of the client arose out of it. For the client it was argued that only performance was guaranteed. Therefore, upon default in performance by the lessees, the client became liable in damages, but as these were unquantified, the demand by the discounter was invalid and so was the appointment of receivers based on it. The discounter argued that the guarantee created a double-barrelled liability and effectively secured two things: payment by the lessees of all sums due under the leasing agreement, and secondly, due performance of all obligations thereunder. In the end, Knox J. found it unnecessary to decide which construction was correct. This was partly because whichever construction was adopted, the conclusion was that the arrears which should have been paid but were unpaid by the lessees—the principal debtors, were the measure of the client's liability as a guarantor, and this was enough to make the appointment valid.

As a practical matter, the question what a guarantee in a master agreement secures is of the first importance since it fixes the measure of the guarantor's liability and hence, at least in some cases, the amount of permissible set-off by the factor against the fund retained. In relations between the factor and his client, the distinction between the two types of guarantee may be but only of marginal significance. But where third-party rights have supervened—garnishors, administrators and liquidators, the distinction assumes central significance as it affects the application of the retained fund.

Apart from the provision for guarantee and indemnity, two other provisions lie at the heart of the factor's security. These are the recourse (sometimes called repurchase) obligation and the retention fund. Each deserves a special treatment and must now be considered.

The nature of the recourse obligation

3.4   A provision that the factor shall repurchase assigned receivables is one of the most important securities at the disposal of the factor. This is a feature of most non-notification discounting agreements. But even with regard to the so-called purchase without recourse, there is invariably an element of recourse. In a formal sense, the latter agreement imposes the

[52] [1988] B.C.L.C. 625.

risk of bad debt on the factor and in so doing, makes the factor an insurer of approved debtors' solvency. But he does not normally underwrite the supply contract under which the receivables arise, nor does he buy unapproved receivables other than on a recourse basis. As we have also seen, the master agreement contains a number of warranties, a breach of which will entitle the factor to call on the client to repurchase assigned receivables. To the extent that these warranties give rise to damages, they give the factor a right of recourse against the client. Their existence sits oddly with the theory that factoring could be without recourse, at least as regards approved receivables. At the minimum, they import limited recourse. A recourse obligation is an obligation to repurchase assigned receivables in certain circumstances specified in the master agreement or any supplemental agreement annexed thereto.[53] The recourse obligation is a put option giving the factor a right to call on the client to repurchase. It is not a unilateral contract in the sense that it does not depend for its efficacy, once exercised, upon acceptance by the client. It does not create any real security because although the put option may be exercised with an eye on the retention fund, it does not, either on its own or taken with the retention fund, create any real rights on assets of the client. Its exercise leads to a debit on the retention fund which reduces the ultimate balance due to the client under the retention. It is, however, a matter, not of set-off, but of account.[54] A set-off presupposes the existence of at least two independent but mutual obligations between two parties. In an accounting situation the existence and amount of one party's liability to the other can only be ascertained by discovering the ultimate balance of their mutual dealings.[55]

The right of retention[56]

The right of retention is a contractual provision entitling the factor to **3.5** pay only a certain percentage of the gross amount of purchased receivables. This varies depending on the riskiness of the debts. In order to implement the retention the factor usually maintains a current account into which is credited:

(i) the purchase price of each receivable before deduction of the discounting charge;

(ii) the amount of any costs or expenses recovered by the factor as a result of any proceedings against or negotiations with any account debtor; and

(iii) any amount paid by the client to the factor under the agreement; and

---

[53] Typically such circumstances would include any disputes as to whether or not a receivable is valid or due in whole or part, or if the account debtor becomes insolvent or bankrupt, or now in the case of a corporate debtor, if it becomes the subject of an administration.
[54] *Re Charge Card Services Ltd.* [1987] Ch. 150.
[55] *Rolls Razor Ltd.* v. *Cox* [1967] 1 Q.B. 552 at 574; *Re Charge Card Services Ltd.* [1987] Ch. 150 at 174.
[56] The factual analysis in this paragraph is based on *Re Charge Card Services Ltd.* at 172.

to which is debited:

   (i) the amount of any payment made by the factor to the client;

  (ii) the amount of any credit note issued by the client to account debtors;

 (iii) the amount of any receivables which the factor has requested the client to repurchase under the recourse obligation;

  (iv) the amount of any liability due under the guarantee;

   (v) all such other sums payable by the client under the agreement including legal costs and expenses incurred in collecting and enforcing payment of assigned receivables;

  (vi) the amount of any payment, cost, damage or liability made or sustained by the factor by reason of any breach of warranty or undertaking by the client;

 (vii) at the end of each calendar month, a discounting charge calculated at a specified rate on the net debit balance of the account plus an administration charge.[57]

In addition the master agreement usually provides for a right of retention as security for any claims or defences which have arisen or may arise against the client, any risk of non-payment by account debtors, and any amount prospectively chargeable to the client as a debit under any of the debitable items. Any credit balance due on the account is called a prepayment, while the client is obliged to make good any debit balance. From the prepayment the client may draw amounts, though he is charged a fee—a few percentage points above the base rate, for sums drawn down before the account debtors remit payment to the factor. In a real sense the retention fund is by far the single most important "security" of the factor. The right to retain is a contractual limitation on the client's right to require payment of the balance on the current account. It does not merely safeguard the factor against overpayment to the client; it constitutes a security against default in performance especially as regards the client's warranties and guarantees. In *Re Charge Card Services Ltd.*[58] it was argued that a factor's right of retention was a registrable charge on book debts of the client and so void for non-registration. Millett J. held that the argument was misconceived, for there was no relevant property capable of forming the subject-matter of the charge. The only asset which the client could charge was its right to sue the factor for any credit

---

[57] Factors say that administration charge is for non-financial services which they provide. This is only partly true because even discounters who provide only finance impose an administration charge. See, *e.g. Re Charge Card Services Ltd.* at 171H, where there was an invoice discounting without any credit protection or ledgering and yet an administration charge was imposed.

[58] [1987] Ch. 150. However, in *Welsh Development Agency* v. *Export Finance Co. Ltd.* (1990) B.C.C. Browne-Wilkinson V.-C. doubted whether he would have reached the same conclusion, as did Millett J., but followed *Charge Card* in the interest of preserving consistency in a matter such as this which is of general commercial importance.

balance due under the discounting agreement, but that right already contained within it liability to suffer a retention. This hardly disposes of the question whether the right so limited was a charge. However, he concluded that the right of retention could not be a charge in favour of the factor for the simple reason that a charge in favour of a debtor of his own indebtedness to the chargor is conceptually impossible. The objection to the charge in these circumstances was not to the process by which it is created, but to the result.[59] A debt is a chose in action—a right to sue the debtor. This can be assigned or made available to a third party, but not to the debtor who cannot sue himself. Once any assignment or appropriation to the debtor becomes unconditional, the debt is wholly or partially released. The debtor cannot, and does not need to, resort to the creditor's claim against him in order to obtain the benefit of the security; his own liability to the creditor is automatically discharged or released. Why the nature of the remedy available for the enforcement of the security created by a right of retention should make this form of security a conceptual impossibility is not at all clear.[60]

The right of retention is not a lien. A lien postulates property of the debtor in the possession or under the control of the creditor.[61] The characterisation of the retention as a debt leads to the conclusion that the right to retain cannot be a lien. To say that the retention is a debt has important consequences. First, as regards liabilities of the client not customarily available to be debited to the current account maintained by the factor, for example, the amount due under the recourse obligation, they may be met by a set-off against the retention fund. Secondly, if the factor becomes insolvent does the retention pass to his estate, giving the client a right to prove for a dividend, or is it to be treated as trust property and so unavailable for distribution among his creditors generally? That the credit balance in the current account is a debt is clear enough. The nature of the retention fund is, however, less clear. If it is treated as money earmarked for a special purpose, then it is not a mere debt and would not form part of the factor's estate in any subsequent insolvency. Accordingly, it would not be available for insolvency set-off,[62] but is returnable to the client, except as regards claims which, by agreement, are matters not of debiting, but of retention.

Problems of discounting receivables

Discounting of receivables meets with many problems, some legal, **3.6** others not. Of the non-legal problems, "kiting" and image stand out. The integrity of discounted receivables may be controlled in two ways[63]—first,

---

[59] *Ibid.* at 176. See also, *Halesowen Presswork & Assemblies Ltd.* v. *National Westminster Bank Ltd.* [1971] 1 Q.B. 1 at 46, aff'd [1972] A.C. 785 at 802, 808 and 810.
[60] See para. 5.8, *infra.*
[61] *Halesowen Presswork & Assemblies Ltd.* v. *National Westminster Bank Ltd.* [1971] 1 Q.B. 1 at 46.
[62] *Re Pollitt* [1893] 1 Q.B. 455; *Re Mid-Kent Fruit Factory* [1896] 1 Ch. 567; *Re City Equitable Fire Insurance Co. Ltd. (No. 2)* [1930] 2 Ch. 293; *Barclays Bank Ltd.* v. *Quistclose Investments Ltd.* [1970] A.C. 567. *Cf. Rolls Razor Ltd.* v. *Cox* [1967] 1 Q.B. 552.
[63] R. W. Burman (1948) 13 J. of Law & Contemp. Probs. 555 at 558 *et seq.*

by original evaluation designed to ascertain the liquidation value of a portfolio of receivables, and secondly, by supervision or policing of receivables. Although both may at times be expensive, they are nevertheless a vital bulwark against loss. One method of valuation is verification. This involves obtaining from account debtors an acknowledgement of the amount due from them by a particular date. In non-notification discounting, this may be difficult. Policing receivables is a detail job and may entail direct collection from the debtors. Where the client collects, as in non-notification discounting, it is preferable if the master agreement requires him to remit payments received from debtors to the factor *in specie*. This is in practice accompanied by a provision that such receipts are held in trust until remitted.[64] *In specie* remittance is advantageous because it assures a valid collection of the receivables; prevents comingling which may have disastrous consequences for the factor if the client becomes insolvent; and usually affords further proof of the genuineness of invoices sent to the factor. This last point requires elaboration. The profitability of bulk discounting of receivables depends in part on effective policing, and *in specie* remittance is a keystone in any policing system because apart from signalling declines in collections to the factor, it enables him to discover whether the client has been supplying him false invoices representing non-existent sales.[65] This is the problem of "kiting,"[66] *i.e.* of the client keeping one step ahead of the factor by presenting to him the appearance of growth in his business operations, making ever-increasing assignments of non-existent receivables, and obtaining larger and larger prepayments, repaying the factor out of his own resources. Kiting may take a number of forms: a client may inflate the value of the invoices sent to the factor; he may falsify accounts in the statements he submits to him. In each case he kites his assignments because he gives the impression that he is assigning receivables of greater value than those he actually possesses. There is no evidence of the scale of kiting in England. What is clear is that this problem is a commercial fraud unlikely to be encountered with solvent clients. When, however, insolvency looms over the client, reputational considerations are, it is thought, insufficient to discourage this species of client misbehaviour. The moral is factor beware!

The image problem is still seen by factors as the most serious non-legal problem. A recent survey[67] shows that the factoring industry, for example, still has an image problem among the business audience. In particular, non-users of the facility and many financial advisers—mainly accountants, do not fully understand its possible benefits and view it as a lender of last resort. This shows that factors have not completely shaken off the image of the old line American factor. In those early years of factoring, advancing money on the strength of receivables was resorted to as a final measure to ward off inevitable bankruptcy.[68] This problem

---

[64] See, *e.g. The Encyclopaedia of Forms and Precedents* (5th ed., 1986), Vol. 4, Form 45, clause 11.1.
[65] As was the case in *Teal Investments* v. *Higham Motors* [1982] 2 N.Z.L.R. 123.
[66] Note (1952), 101 U. Pa. L.R. 392 at 393.
[67] *The Times*, July 4, 1989, pp. 31 *et seq.*
[68] Note, 24 New York Univ. L.Q.R. 598.

survives into modern times, and while it is no longer true that clients go to the factor or other discounter of receivables only when they are on their last leg,[69] it is equally clear that all too often entrepreneurs turn to factors for their first time when their banks, hitherto usually their only providers, refuse an additional loan or increased overdraft.[70] At this stage of their awareness such business people clearly seem to regard using discounting as a near-desperation move. Today, members of the Association of British Factors who account for about 90 per cent. of factoring, are all subsidiaries of larger financial groups, many of them banks.[71] This banking connection certainly helps to improve the image of the factor, though, on one view,[72] this has merely exacerbated the very misconceptions that a wider acceptance of discounting should dispel.

The legal problems of discounting divide broadly into three categories, namely, debtor-related problems, insolvency of the client, and conflicts with third parties claiming discounted receivables under a separate, and probably fraudulent assignment, by the client. Many of these problems are not specific to discounting and arise regardless of the form which receivables financing takes. As general problems they are discussed elsewhere. Debtor-related problems are discussed in Chapter 8. These are essentially problems of set-off, prohibition against assignment, post-contract variation of the underlying supply contract, and the general question of assignability of particular rights. Insolvency of the client is discussed in Chapter 7. The discussion covers the effects of the basic types of insolvency proceedings[73]—administration, administrative receivership and liquidation, on receivables financing. Conflicts with third parties are discussed in Chapter 6, and the problems are all matters of priorities. There is no need to duplicate these discussions. What is proposed is to isolate certain problems on these general themes which are specific to discounting or which have a particular significance to it.

Debtor-related problems

Two problems will be discussed in this section. The first is the liability **3.7** of the factor on a credit note issued to the debtor with his approval. The second is his liability to repay money received from the client who now complains of defective or non-performance. As to credit notes, it is tolerably clear that they may create a valid set-off in favour of the

---

[69] Contrast, *International Factors Ltd.* v. *Streeve Construction* [1984] N.I.L.R. 245, where the client turned to the factor only after it had become hopelessly insolvent partly because of the difficulty experienced in collecting its receivables. The discounting was no palliative as the factor found it no easier to collect the receivables.

[70] *The Times*, July 4, 1989, p. 33 (hereafter referred to simply as *Times Survey*).

[71] *Times Survey*.

[72] Forman and Gilbert, *Factoring and Finance* (London, Heinemann, 1976), preface.

[73] Insolvency proceedings are:

  (i) voluntary arrangement;
  (ii) administration;
  (iii) administrative receivership; and
  (iv) insolvent liquidation;

see Insolvency Act 1986, s.247(1).

account debtor. The extent of such a set-off is a matter of prime concern to the factor particularly where he has paid the client who is now insolvent and his retention is insufficient to recoup the shortfall. As a general rule, notice of assignment fixes the date on which contra accounts against the client crystallise for purposes of set-off.[74] Unmatured accounts at that date are not available for set-off against the debtor's present liability,[75] except where such contra items are inextricably interwoven with the supply contract under which the debtor's obligation to pay arose.[76] The scope of this exception and the degree of connection necessary for it to apply are both undecided and unclear. A credit note issued prior to notice of assignment is a valid set-off; one issued after is also valid if it is a written admission of the client's liability existing before the notice of assignment. But generally post-notice credit notes relating to post-notice liabilities are not available for set-off unless they fall within the exception to the general rule that notice crystallises contra accounts capable of set-off. However, the debtor may not like to rely on set-off for a number of reasons. One may be that nothing is owed to the client against which the latter's liability on the credit note may be set off. Another is that the client may at any rate be insolvent and the debtor may not be content to prove for a dividend. In that and other situations, it is both reasonable and natural to look to the factor to whom his payment was made. Can he do so? Generally he cannot.[77] First, by approving the issue of a credit note the factor does not, without more, assume the obligations of his client under the underlying supply contract. It is elementary that in English law obligations cannot be transferred to a non-contracting party otherwise than by novation.[78] It is not being suggested that in appropriate circumstances a credit note is incapable of being construed as a novation of the underlying contract; the point here is that an ordinary credit note does not, without more, constitute a novation of the supply contract, and it is difficult to see what commercial sense there is in such novation for the factor. Secondly, it may be argued that by approving the issue of a credit note the factor assumes liability under it by virtue of some kind of estoppel. This is certainly a more promising line of attack. But upon consideration this line of attack disintegrates just like the one based on novation. Assuming that by approving the issue of a credit note a factor impliedly warrants that the client is entitled to the amount stated in the note, this does not really advance the argument for his liability on the note. The question, surely, is not whether the debtor is entitled to the amount in the credit note; it is whether he is entitled to it from the factor. Approval of the issue of the note is quite consistent with the view that the factor agrees that the debtor is entitled to the amount from the client. This is the natural inference to be drawn from the approval, and may in fact operate to waive the factor's right to insist that

---

[74] *Young* v. *Kitchin* (1878) 3 Ex.D. 127; *Roxburghe* v. *Cox* (1878) 17 Ch.D. 520.
[75] *Re Pinto Leite & Nephews* [1929] 1 Ch. 221. See also, *Jeffryes* v. *Agra & Mastermann's Bank* (1866) L.R. 2 Eq. 674.
[76] *Government of Newfoundland* v. *Newfoundland Ry. Co.* (1888) 13 App.Cas. 199.
[77] Contrast, Salinger, *Tolley's Factoring*, para. 11.36.
[78] *Tolhurst* v. *Associated Portland Cement Maufacturers (1900) Ltd.* [1902] 2 K.B. 660 at 668.

notice of assignment crystallised the debtor's set-off. But it does not stop him from denying personal liability on the note. A third argument in favour of the factor's liability on the note is based on mistake of fact. The remedy here is of course restitutionary. It is argued[79] that a debtor to whom a credit note is issued in recognition of defective or non-performance by the factor's client, paid the price under a mistake of fact. This must be considered doubtful. Such an expansive view of mistake will threaten the security of recipients of money and unsettle unnecessarily the finality of transactions. A more formidable objection to the argument based on mistake of fact is that the debtor did not pay under a mistake of fact at all. His error is no error at all, buy a misprediction.[80] Lastly, where the credit note is in respect of defective performance not amounting to non-performance, the debtor's claim is based on partial failure of consideration. This has generally never been a sufficient ground for allowing recovery of money paid under such a contract,[81] it being thought that the remedy of damages is adequate even where the payee is insolvent, so that the prospect of a substantial right of proof is rather bleak. So much for credit notes.

The second problem mentioned at the outset is what happens where a diligent debtor has paid his debt to the factor but the client fails to perform under the supply contract. To be meaningful it must be assumed that the client has now descended into insolvent liquidation and that there are virtually no assets available for the satisfaction of unsecured claims. It must also be assumed that the factor has paid the client the discounted amount due under this particular receivable at a time when he had no grounds to believe or suspect that the client will not perform the supply contract. The relationship with the client has ended. The qualification that he has unknowingly paid the client is necessary because if the factor has not paid the client there is in a real sense a true superfluity in his assets for which he ought in all conscience to rid himself by returning the payment to the debtor. Also where he pays the client at a time he knew[82] that he would not perform the supply contract, fairness and justice require that the factor should be held liable to repay the money to the debtor. In such circumstances there is nothing harsh or unconscionable in the conclusion that the factor, and not the debtor, ran the financial risk of non-performance by the client. Outside these two situations it is not easy to say whether a diligent debtor should recover money paid under an unperformed contact. In one sense it could be said that the debtor should not recover on the theory that, by paying in advance of performance (by

---

[79] Salinger, *op. cit.*, para. 11.36. See also, *Sheldon and Fidler's Practice and Law of Banking* (Plymouth, Macdonald & Evans, 11th ed., 1982), p. 602.
[80] Birks, *Introduction to the Law of Restitution* (OUP, 1985), p. 147.
[81] *Whincup* v. *Hughes* (1971) L.R. 6 C.P. 78. The proposals for reform in the *Law Commission Working Paper* (No. 65), Pt. III were later dropped on reconsideration in *Law Commission Report* (No. 121), para. 3.11.
[82] I have deliberately refrained from stating the test of knowledge in the objective terms of "ought to know," although there is no reason of principle why a factor who pays the client when he ought to know from his association with the client that non-performance of the underlying contract between his client and the account debtor is inevitable, should not be liable in restitution.

the client), he, of his own accord, runs the financial risk of non-performance.[83] In this sense the debtor is no worse than a consumer who pays a mail order company, a travel agent or a jobber, in advance of performance and who now seeks to recover because the payee has become insolvent and can no longer perform. In these cases recovery depends on whether or not the advance payment was segregated from the general assets of the payee. If it was, the payor may recover it as on a trust,[84] but not otherwise.[85] Where recovery is denied, it is on the theory that the advance payment created a debt in favour of the payor who in effect extended credit to the payee. So, our debtor, like his consumer friends above, should bear the loss if the credit is misplaced. He should not be able to recover from the factor. After all, if the payment was directly to the client who is now insolvent, he cannot expect to recover it. Why should he be in a better position because an assignee, in the shape of a factor, is interposed between him and the insolvent client? This is more so when it is realised that assignment law neither improves nor worsens the position of the debtor.[86] Considerations of this nature suggest powerfully that the debtor's claim against the factor should be denied. However, these generalisations do not (it is submitted) reflect accurately the debtor's claim. To start with the proposition that assignment law neither improves nor worsens the account debtor's position. This, of course, is very far from the truth. Take the simple example of set-off. Notice of assignment crystallises the debtor's contra claims eligible for set-off against the assigned debt. By cutting off subsequent contra accounts which would have been set off against the assignor, the debtor is prejudiced, and more so as he is powerless to stop the assignment (unless this is prohibited by contract)[87] which does not require his consent.[88] Also claims deemed personal to the debtor and the factor's client may not be set off against the factor notwithstanding that they are valid against the client.[89] It is difficult to assert in the face of these manifest prejudices that

---

[83] This is the view of the INTERNATIONAL INSTITUTE FOR THE UNIFICATION OF PRIVATE LAW (Unidroit) in its *Convention on International factoring, Final Report*, May 1988, Art. 10(1). See also, R. M. Goode [1982] J.B.L. 338 at 339 *et seq.*

[84] *Re Nanwa Gold Mines Ltd.* [1955] 1 W.L.R. 1080; *Re Kayford* [1975] 1 W.L.R. 279; *Re Chelsea Cloisters Ltd.* (1981) 41 P. & C.R. 98; *Re Eastern Capital Futures Ltd.* [1989] B.C.L.C. 371.

[85] See *Moseley* v. *Cressey's Co.* (1865) L.R. 1 Eq. 405, and *Swiss Bank Corp.* v. *Lloyds Bank Ltd.* [1982] A.C. 584 where there was no obligation to segregate the funds and therefore no trust. The problem of consumer prepayment for goods or services to insolvent payees has escaped the zeal of the legal performer. Despite recognition of this problem, neither the Cork Committee, Cmnd. 8558, para. 1052, nor the Office of Fair Trading (OFT) considered legislative imposition of statutory trust on such prepayments appropriate. See, *OFT, The Protection of Consumers' Prepayments: a discussion paper* (1984), paras. 5.11 *et seq.* A private member's Bill titled "Consumers' Prepayment (Protection) Bill 1982" which sought to extend the *Kayford* principle to all prepayments received by suppliers of goods and services, failed to mature into an Act despite an unopposed first reading. For an account of the unsuccessful efforts of the National Federation for Consumer Groups (NFCG) to pursue a reform, see [1984] J.B.L. 105.

[86] R. M. Goode [1982] J.B.L. 338 at 339–341.

[87] *Helstan Securities Ltd.* v. *Hertfordshire CC* [1978] 3 All E.R. 262.

[88] *Ex p. South* (1818) 3 Swans 392.

[89] *Stoddart* v. *Union Trust Ltd.* [1912] 1 K.B. 181.

assignment law does not worsen the debtor's position. If by allowing the debtor a claim for a refund against the factor the law improves his position, this is as it should be.

Secondly, the comparison with the position of consumers' prepayments to insolvent suppliers is not apt. The reason consumers' claims fail is that if a debt only is contemplated, a claim for recovery is in effect an assertion of a total failure of the consideration for the payment. Such an assertion may be rewarded with a restitutionary proprietary claim if the payment can be identified. But having been confounded with the payee's general assets no proprietary remedy is available, the payor being left to prove in the payee's insolvency. Here, however, the debtor is not claiming against the insolvent client, but against the solvent factor and there is no convincing argument of principle or policy why he should not recover if he can make out an appropriate ground for relief. It is to these grounds that we now turn.

There are two main heads of relief which the debtor may invoke. One is that the payment was made under a mistake of fact. The second is a total failure of consideration. Resulting trust might yet be invoked, but since any such claim will be based on a failure of purpose, it is proposed to consider it as a sub-category of failure of consideration. The claim for recovery cannot, of course, be based on the contract between the debtor and the client which, so far as the factor is concerned, is *res inter alios acta*, apart from any objection to a contractual claim on the ground of want of privity.[90] Both mistake and failure of consideration are restitutionary claims independent of contract. With regard to mistake, the debtor's argument would be that he paid the money under a mistaken belief that the client will perform. This belief is now unfounded because of the client's non-performance. If the payment was truly induced by a mistake of fact the debtor ought to be able to recover it from the factor. This is because restitution for mistake of fact rests on the fact that the payor's judgment was vitiated in the matter of the transfer of wealth to the payee. Such true cases of mistake must be distinguished from a payment induced by a misprediction. A misprediction cannot found a claim for restitution.[91] A mistake as to the future is not a mistake of fact, but a mere misprediction. A misprediction does not show that the payor's judgment was vitiated, only that as things turned out, it was incorrectly exercised.[92] A prediction is an exercise of judgment and the mispredicter unilaterally assumes the risk of disappointment if events prove his prediction wrong. Into what category does the debtor's payment fall? In my view it falls into the category of money paid under a misprediction because the debtor's mistake, if any, is as to the purely futuristic possibility of performance by the client. It is not a mistake as to existing facts. Therefore, a restitutionary claim based on mistake is likely to fail.

A restitutionary claim based on failure of consideration is more promising. A person who has paid money pursuant to a contract and receives no part of the consideration paid for is entitled to recover the

---

[90] *Scruttons Ltd.* v. *Midland Silicones Ltd.* [1962] A.C. 446.
[91] Birks, *Introduction to the Law of Restitution* (OUP, 1985), p. 147.
[92] *Ibid.*

payment as on a total failure of consideration.[93] The payment in such cases could properly be seen as conditional[94] in the sense that the payor did not part out and out with his money, but qualified the transfer. One may therefore argue that the payment by the debtor to the factor was originally conditional, the condition of retaining it being eventual performance by the factor's client under the supply contract with the debtor. Accordingly, when the client fails to perform, the condition fails and with it the factor's right to retain the payment.[95] It has, however, been objected that this reasoning is unpersuasive because the doctrine of failure of consideration depends upon the existence of an actual or supposed, but ineffective contract.[96] True it is that cases[97] which have used the language of failure of consideration have almost always involved actual or supposed contracts. But it by no means follows that the doctrine of failure of consideration is incapable of application outside the confines of contract law. Nor, it is thought, is there any reason for supposing that "consideration" here is necessarily limited to that furnished pursuant to a contract.[98] On the contrary, in the *Fibrosa* case[99] Lord Wright used the language of conditional payment in describing money paid under a frustrated contract. If the objection is well founded the same result may be achieved by adopting a resulting trust analysis. In *Essery* v. *Cowlard*,[1] for example, it was held that the trustees of a marriage settlement held the trust property on a resulting trust for the settlor because the settlement was executed in contemplation of a marriage and the contract to marry had definitely and absolutely been terminated so that there was a failure of consideration. If this reasoning is persuasive and relevant to the present discussion, the factor holds the payment from the debtor (who receives no performance under the supply contract) on a resulting trust. However, it now appears that there is a grave objection to the resulting trust analysis. In all the cases applying this reasoning it did not appear on the face of the instrument of disposition that the transferee was intended to take beneficially. This is unlike a payment to the factor who, *ex hypothesi*, is beneficially entitled to the payment, being a purchaser of the receivables in respect of which the payment is made. This is a conclusive answer to the argument founded on resulting trust, but has nothing to do with the wider doctrine of failure of the "consideration" or "purpose" of payment. As regards the latter, the factor may rely on two counter-arguments. The first is that although from the point of view of the debtor there is a failure of consideration, he (the factor) has nothing to do with it. He is merely a conduit pipe through which the payment or

[93] *Hunt* v. *Silk* (1804) 5 East 440; *Rowland* v. *Divall* [1923] 2 K.B. 500; *Butterworth* v. *Kingsway Motors Ltd.* [1954] 1 W.L.R. 1286.
[94] Birks, *op. cit.*, 223–226.
[95] *Fibrosa Spolka Akcyjna* v. *Fairbairn, Lawson, Combe, Barbour Ltd.* [1943] A.C. 32 at 65, *per* Lord Wright.
[96] Goode [1983] J.B.L. 338, 339–341.
[97] *Hunt* v. *Silk, supra*; *Rowland* v. *Divall, supra*; *Butterworth* v. *Kingsway Motors Ltd. supra*; *Rover International Ltd.* v. *Cannon Film Sales Ltd.* [1989] 1 W.L.R. 912.
[98] See Birks, *Introduction to the Law of Restitution* (OUP, 1985), pp. 233 *et seq.*
[99] [1943] A.C. 32 at 65.
[1] (1884) 26 Ch.D. 191.

its equivalent gets to the client who ought to be seen as the ultimate recipient. The second is that since he has paid his client, the debtor has led him detrimentally to change his position by paying in advance and it scarcely lies in his mouth to say that the payment ought to be undone. Although there is as yet no recognised general defence of change of position in English law,[2] there does not seem to be any principled objection to the use of estoppel in this type of situation. After all, the debtor was the cause of the problem by paying in advance and as between two innocent parties the author of a problem ought to bear the loss resulting therefrom. In the light of these, it seems that there is truly no principle of law by reference to which recovery by the debtor can be justified. If he is allowed to recover, such an act of judicial charity can only be accounted for by invoking a Robin Hood policy of redistribution from the wealthy to the poor.

The problems discussed in this paragraph are unlikely to be decided as it is understood that the sums involved are usually so small as not to justify the expense of litigation, and in many cases, the factor would normally be willing to repay the debtor and look to his retention for recoupment.

Insolvency of the client

The insolvency of the factor's client has important consequences for the **3.8** factor. Not only is this the occasion for reopening a number of pre-liquidation transactions (including the discounting), but also specific insolvency rules may operate to avoid certain assignments to the factor. The general impact of the commencement of insolvency proceedings on the receivables financier is discussed in Chapter 7. Some of that discussion is relevant here and would not be repeated. In this section we shall consider only three specific insolvency rules and how they might affect the discounting transaction. These are the provision for the avoidance of dispositions effected after the commencement of compulsory winding up[3]; extortionate credit transactions[4]; and liability for wrongful trading.[5]

Compulsory liquidation relates back to the date of the petition for winding up.[6] Any disposition of the client's property made after the commencement of liquidation is void unless the court orders otherwise.[7] The purpose of this avoidance is to prevent the improper alienation of the property of a company in dire financial straits during the period which must inevitably elapse before a petition for winding up is heard.[8] The

---

[2] *Baylis* v. *Bishop of London* [1913] 1 Ch. 127; *R.E. Jones Ltd.* v. *Waring & Gillow Ltd.* [1926] A.C. 670, and generally, see Goff and Jones, *Law of Restitution* (3rd ed., 1986), pp. 695–699.
[3] Insolvency Act 1986, s.127.
[4] *Ibid.*, s.244.
[5] *Ibid.*, s.214.
[6] Insolvency Act 1986, s.129.
[7] *Ibid.*, s.127.
[8] *Re Wiltshire Iron Co.* (1868) L.R. 3 Ch.App. 433 at 447; *Re J. Leslie Engineers Co. Ltd.* [1976] 1 W.L.R. 292 at 304. In *Ex p. Schwarcz* [1989] B.C.L.C. 424, Hoffmann J. held that there is no need for protection of unsecured creditors if the company is solvent.

courts take a wide view of "disposition." A sale of a company's property is a disposition for this purpose.[9] It follows that, in principle, discounting transactions might be avoided under this provision. However, to be caught, what is disposed of must at the date of the disposition be property of the company. This is an important qualification because where an insolvent company assigns receivables which come into existence after it has descended into insolvent liquidation, the assignment may or may not be avoided. For this purpose a distinction must be drawn between the case where the receivables arise from pre-liquidation performance of an underlying contract by the company on the one hand, and where nothing is earned by the company's performance prior to the commencement of liquidation, so that the receivables arise, if at all, only through post-liquidation performance by the liquidator, on the other. In the former case the vesting of the receivables in the assignee after commencement of liquidation is not a disposition of the company's property. The disposition took place at the date of the assignment and not when the receivables arose. Although this conclusion is undecided,[10] it is thought that the analysis is consistent with the reasoning in *Tailby* v. *Official Receiver*,[11] and the result in some of the cases.[12] In the latter the assignment is open to attack on at least two grounds. The first is that it is a post-liquidation disposition of the company's property since the receivables were unearned both at the date of assignment and when winding up commenced. If this analysis is wrong, the assignment may nevertheless be challenged on the ground that it lacks a subject-matter because, both before and after the assignment, the company never earned the assigned receivables.[13]

How does this analysis affect the factor? It would seem that discounting may be vulnerable given the length of time which may elapse between the filing and the hearing of a petition for winding up. It is possible that both the client and the factor may innocently continue to assign and accept fresh receivables unaware that a petition has been filed. The longer the time gap between the filing and the hearing the greater the risk. The extent of avoidance will depend on the structure of the master agreement. If a whole turnover structure is used the risk is less because the master agreement is the assignment, so that on the face of it the assignments are valid as regards earned receivables, whether or not payable after the commencement of winding up. Of course what is assigned cannot include those receivables earned by the liquidator in performing the client's current contracts.[14] Different considerations arise in the case of a facultative agreement. Here considerations of stamp duty force the parties to structure the transaction as a unilateral contract. The client makes the

[9] *Re Wiltshire Iron Co.*, *supra*; *Re Tramway Building & Construction Co. Ltd.* [1988] Ch. 293.
[10] *Re French's (Wine Bar) Ltd.* [1987] B.C.L.C. 499 and *Re Country Stores Pty. Ltd.* (1987) 11 A.C.L.R. 385, provide rough analogies.
[11] (1888) 13 App.Cas. 523.
[12] *Re Davis* (1889) 22 Q.B.D. 193; *Re Trytel* [1952] 2 T.L.R. 32.
[13] As in *Ex p. Nichols* (1883) 22 Ch.D. 782; *Wilmot* v. *Alton* [1897] 1 Q.B. 17 esp. at 22; *Re De Marney* [1943] Ch. 126.
[14] *Ibid.*

offer to sell by sending schedules of receivables to the factor who may accept or reject the offer. Acceptance constitutes the assignment. The risk here is that the client may make an offer to sell which is accepted by the factor in ignorance of the filing of a petition for the winding up of his client. As compulsory winding up dates back to the filing of the petition, the purported assignment is a void disposition.

The scope for prejudice is, however, reduced by the existence of a discretionary jurisdiction to validate avoided disposition.[15] This aim is furthered in practice by the fact that the courts take a broad view of the width of this discretionary jurisdiction. The statute prescribes no criteria by reference to which the exercise of the discretion is to be informed. This is as it should be and such evidence as is provided by the case law indicates that regard is had to all the relevant circumstances affecting the offending disposition.[16] In general, no validating order will normally be made where the disposition is not for the benefit of the company.[17] But in *ex post facto* applications, it is not relevant to compare what the position of unsecured creditors would be if the disposition is validated and what it would be if it is not.[18] This approach sits oddly with the fact that a disposition which is shown to have reduced the net assets available for the settlement of unsecured claims will not normally be validated.[19] Since the factor will normally pay the net credit in favour of the client to him or his liquidator, it is thought that it will not normally be difficult to demonstrate the case for validation. Difficulties may arise where the existence of a net deficiency (against the client) in the current account between the parties justifies withdrawal of payment to the client or his liquidator. In such a case making a validating order will not benefit the client, and may in any event make the disposition, if validated, an undue preference.[20]

It is to be noted also that where the pre-liquidation assignment to the factor is conditional or voidable at the instance of the client, in the latter case because of a vitiating factor affecting the formation of the contract of assignment, the happening of the contingency or waiver of the right to avoid, is a dispositive act and where either event occurs after the presentation of a petition for winding up, the resulting disposition is void.[21] So much for avoidance of dispositions. Let us now turn to the question whether a discounting transaction is liable to be reopened as an extortionate credit transaction.

One of the two complaints frequently made by clients against discounting of receivables is the expense involved.[22] It is common knowledge that like many other forms of financial accommodation, factors charge com-

---

[15] Insolvency Act 1986, s.127.

[16] *Re Steane's (Bournemouth) Ltd.* [1950] 1 All E.R. 21; *Re Clifton Place Garage Ltd.* [1970] Ch. 477.

[17] *Re McGuinness Bros. (UK) Ltd.* (1987) 3 B.C.C. 571.

[18] *Re Tramway Building & Construction Co. Ltd.* [1988] 2 W.L.R. 640 at 648–649.

[19] *Ibid.*

[20] By s.238(7) of the Insolvency Act 1986, a payment does not cease to be an undue preference merely because it is paid pursuant to a court order.

[21] *Re French's (Wine Bar) Ltd.* [1987] B.C.L.C. 499 at 504.

[22] *Times Survey*, p. 31. The other is that over-zealous debt collection by a factor could jeopardise relationships with customers.

mitment fees, setting up fees, administration charge expressed as a percentage of the turnover of assigned receivables, etc. There is also a finance charge calculated on a daily yield basis in respect of prepayments made to the client before receipt of payment from the account debtors and usually a few percentage points above the base rate.[23] The result of these fees and charges is that discounting is normally more expensive than a banking facility, for example, a term loan or an overdraft. Factors explain that this is justified because some of them perform administrative functions such as ledger administration, debt collection and credit protection, which are absent in a banking financing package.[24] This may indeed be so although it has to be said that there is no evidence that discounters who do not offer the above optional extras have not always imposed an administration charge[25]—or perhaps, they do not know why some discounters impose an administration charge! This is not the place to debate the question whether discounting is cost effective. The concern here is whether the combination of the above fees and charges justifies the conclusion that a discounting transaction is reviewable in certain circumstances as an extortionate credit bargain. Section 244 of the Insolvency Act 1986 gives the court a discretionary jurisdiction to reopen an extortionate credit transaction concluded within three years of the onset of insolvent liquidation. To apply, it is necessary that the transaction involved the provision of credit. On the face of it one may think that "credit" is limited to loans or overdrafts—thus not covering a discounting transaction involving, as it does, the sale and purchase of receivables. Although no statutory guidance is provided, there is no reason why this narrow meaning of "credit" should be adopted. Since this provision is very similar to the provision in the Consumer Credit Act 1974,[26] it is permissible to adopt the statutory definition of "credit" in the latter statute. There, "credit" is defined as including any form of financial accommodation.[27] If this is applicable, it follows that although a discounting transaction may not fairly be described as a loan in law, it is nevertheless a form of financial accommodation. This conclusion disposes of any objection to the applicability of extortionate credit law to discounting transactions based on the meaning of credit. It remains to consider whether other provisions of section 244 will be satisfied. By definition[28] a transaction is extortionate if, having regard to the risk accepted by the factor, (a) the terms of the discounting are such as to require grossly exorbitant payments to be made by the client, or (b) it otherwise grossly contravenes ordinary principles of fair dealing. Any transaction in respect of which a section 244 application had been made is presumptively extortionate unless the contrary is proved.[29] It should be noted that a discounting transaction does not necessarily escape (a)

---

[23] *Times Survey*, p. 31.
[24] *Ibid.*
[25] See, *e.g. Re Charge Card Services Ltd.* [1987] Ch. 150 at 171H where an administration charge was imposed by an invoice discounter not offering credit protection or ledgering.
[26] s.138(1).
[27] s.9(1).
[28] Insolvency Act 1986, s.244(3).
[29] *Ibid.*

above, merely because the client is not required to make payments to the factor. What the factor retains counts as a payment to him by the client, at any rate, for this purpose. Therefore, although there is no prima facie exorbitant rate, and extortionate is not equated with harsh and unconscionable,[30] it is not impossible that the fees, charges and discounts which the factor receives, may, in appropriate circumstances, stamp the transaction with the badge of extortion. Precisely how much is necessary for this purpose is not a matter capable of being stated. Every case will depend on its own facts.

As pointed out earlier, this jurisdiction is discretionary and may not be exercised even where a prima facie case of extortion is made. Where, however, it is exercised, the range of remedies which the court may give is wide, and includes setting aside the whole or part of the obligation created by the extortionate transaction.[31] The last issue for consideration in this section is whether a factor could ever be liable for wrongful trading. A person is liable for wrongful trading if, being a director of a company (now in insolvent liquidation), he allowed it to continue trading at a time when he knew or ought to have concluded that there was no reasonable prospect that the company would avoid going into insolvent liquidation.[32] For this purpose a company goes into insolvent liquidation if it goes into liquidation at a time when the assets are insufficient for the payment of its debts, other liabilities and the expenses of the winding-up.[33] Arguably a company will not be deemed to go into insolvent liquidation if as a result of the barring of claims on some debts a net surplus is produced for the contributories.[34] Nor, it is thought, would there be liability for wrongful trading in the somewhat exceptional situation where a company which has gone into liquidation on the ground of insolvency turns out to have been solvent all along.[35] Knowledge that there is no reasonable prospect of the company avoiding insolvent liquidation is not limited to facts subjectively known to the director because the provisions[36] also postulate an objective test. Therefore, in deciding whether a director knew or ought to have concluded that there was no reasonable prospect of the company avoiding insolvent liquidation, the knowledge which will be imputed to him is not limited to what is ascertainable from existing facts and documents, but also what, given reasonable diligence and an appropriate level of general knowledge, skill and experience, was ascertainable.[37] Assuming all the other ingredients of wrongful trading are present, can a factor be liable? Nobody is liable for wrongful trading who was not a director of the company at the relevant time. Could a factor be liable as a director? This question is a vexed one

---

[30] *Davies* v. *Directloans* [1986] 1 W.L.R. 823.
[31] Insolvency Act 1986, s.244(4).
[32] *Ibid.*, s.214(2).
[33] *Ibid.*, s.214(6).
[34] As in *Re Joshua Shaw & Sons Ltd.* [1989] B.C.L.C. 362.
[35] As in *Re Islington Metal & Plating Works Ltd.* [1984] 1 W.L.R. 14.
[36] Insolvency Act 1986, s.214(4).
[37] *Re Produce Marketing Consortium Ltd.* (1989) 5 B.C.C. 569.

and remains undecided.[38] It is clear that in an ordinary case a factor cannot, without more, be treated as a director and so would not be liable for wrongful trading. But this does not conclude the question of liability because by definition[39] a director includes a shadow director. A person is a shadow director if he is a person in accordance with whose directions the directors of the company are accustomed to act except where advice is given in a professional capacity, for example, as a solicitor or an auditor.[40] Does this mean, then, that a factor is a shadow director? The answer is far from obvious, not least because of the degree of involvement of a factor offering the full service in the day-to-day management of his client's corporate affairs. Whilst no sufficiently precise test of the threshold of unacceptable interference is possible at this stage, it is by no means clear that a factor who knowingly encourages a client to continue trading when he ought to have concluded that there was no reasonable prospect of avoiding insolvent liquidation, would not be liable for wrongful trading. To advise or provide finance and other services is one thing, to instruct and dominate the client's affairs, quite another. Profit motive is very tempting and a factor may encourage an insolvent client to continue trading even when this is at the expense of unsecured creditors. There is nothing inherently just in allowing the factor to escape liability for wrongful trading in such situations. On the contrary the case for liability is as strong as it could possibly be. One result of such liability may be to discourage factors from financing companies out of their difficulties, although at the moment there is no evidence of this. This harmful side effect could be minimised if the courts make a constructive use of the available defence to liability.[41]

Profitability of discounting depends to some extent on the ability of the factor to resist adverse claims to receivables assigned to him. His client may have made a fraudulent assignment of the same receivables to someone else—a fixed charge to a bank; a sale to another financier, etc. The factor may be faced with a tracing claim from a seller of goods whose

---

[38] *Cf. Re a Company (No. 005009 of 1987), ex p. Copp* [1989] B.C.L.C. 13 where Knox J. refused to strike out a claim for wrongful trading against a bank specific chargee because on the material available, ignoring the possibility of further evidence at the trial, the claim was not obviously unsustainable. However, this refusal does not imply that the claim will succeed at the trial. In subsequent proceedings (see *Re M.C. Bacon Ltd.* (1990) B.C.C. 78) the liquidator's claim that the bank was a shadow director was abandoned since it became clear during cross-examination that the bank's directions to the directors of the company were in fact ignored. There could therefore be no finding that the directors were accustomed to act in accordance with the directions of the bank.

[39] Insolvency Act 1986, s.214(7).

[40] *Ibid.*, s.251. However, it does not follow that an adviser could never be a shadow director of a company he advises. On the contrary, an adviser could so dominate a company's affairs as to make the conclusion that he is a shadow director virtually inevitable. To advise is one thing, to direct or instruct, quite another. For a general guidance, see *Re Maidstone Buildings Provisions Ltd.* [1971] 1 W.L.R. 1085.

[41] Insolvency Act 1986, s.214(3) enables a director to escape liability upon showing that once he became aware of the absence of any reasonable prospect that the company will avoid insolvent liquidation, he took every step to minimise the loss to unsecured creditors. This defence is, however, exhaustive: see *Halls* v. *David* [1989] 1 W.L.R. 745 where Knox J. held that the directors of Produce Marking Consortium Ltd. could not plead s.727 of the Companies Act 1985.

sale terms included a property reservation clause.[42] In all these cases and many more, the question is essentially one of priority. It is no comfort to the factor that there is probably no area of the law where the rules of preference among competing claimants to the same property are more confused than in relation to dealings in debts. Where the rule in *Dearle* v. *Hall*[43] applies, priority may go to the factor if he gave the first notice of assignment to the account debtors. The rule, however, does not always apply,[44] and if the argument[45] that the rule is inapplicable to legal or statutory assignments is well founded, the stability of discounting is very greatly imperilled, as most discounting agreements are at best equitable assignments only, and so liable to defeat by a bona fide legal assignee of the same receivables without notice.[46] These and other issues of priority are considered in more detail in Chapter 6 and no more need be said at this stage.

The future of discounting

Discounting is gradually, but steadily, being established as a credible **3.9** alternative source of corporate finance. This process is likely to continue for some time. It is now getting over its initial image problem and gradually taking its place alongside venture capital, bank finance and the finance lease as a source of business finance. Its association with banks and other financial institutions is beneficial both from the standpoint of reputation and access to funds. Although it is a relatively young industry it has demonstrated remarkable adaptability to changing business practices. Few would have considered discounting relevant to the administration procedure[47] or even management buy-outs. But there is evidence that some administrators have turned to factors for funds needed to achieve the statutory purpose(s) of their appointment.[48] Nor is that all. Discounting has been used recently to gear up management buy-outs,[49] and in principle, there is no reason why it cannot be used to facilitate a management buy-in. All these are new areas scarcely contemplated a few years ago as situations where discounting could be useful. How wrong we have been. No doubt, this trend is likely to continue. Four areas of future growth deserve special mention. These are, the computer revolution, venture factoring, intra-group factoring and back-to-back factoring.

Some factors have developed a direct on-line communication for their clients.[50] For example, the computerised system, FacFlow, was designed

---

[42] As in *Pfeiffer GmbH* v. *Arbuthnot Factors Ltd.* [1988] 1 W.L.R. 150.
[43] (1828) 3 Russ 1.
[44] For limits on the rule, see para. 6.5, *infra*.
[45] See Oditah (1989) 9 O.J.L.S. 513.
[46] See paras. 6.14. *et seq.*, *infra*.
[47] Under Pt. II of the Insolvency Act 1986.
[48] See *Administrations under the Insolvency Act* 1986: *The Result of Administration Orders made in 1987*, para. 6.04 (by Mark Homan for the Research Board of the Institute of Chartered Accountants of England and Wales (1989)).
[49] *Times Survey*, p. 31.
[50] *Ibid.*, p. 33.

to give clients rapid access to daily updated information about their own business. Through a custom-designed modem, the client can make quick checks on how much cash is available under a prepayment facility and how much is due from individual account debtors. This system combines an optional printout of information shown on the participating clients' visual display units. The latest development in the range of services offered by one factor[51] through the FacFlow system is the direct input of data. Under it details of invoices and credit notes can be sent directly to the factor's mainframe computer, giving even quicker access to cash, it also avoids all the inconvenience associated with postal services, *e.g.* delays and loss of parcels, and in addition offers a facility for automatic checking of accounts. The implications of this revolution in information technology for the future of discounting can hardly be overstated, and no doubt, the resulting efficiencies will greatly benefit both the discounting industry and participating clients.

Another useful new addition to the range of services provided by discounting is venture factoring.[52] The aim here is to offer linked venture or development funding as well as the usual factoring services, and if this innovation can provide modest amounts for underwriting development or venture funding, it means that discounting is becoming more sophisticated and diverse. Since a venture factor can arrange an invoiced-based financing package, it is able to overcome one disadvantage of traditional venture capital funding where the lender takes a stake in the borrower's business in return for funding. For large groups of companies intra-group discounting could provide for greater efficiency. A group of companies may create a finance company as a subsidiary within the group to buy up receivables of other members of the group in return for immediate cash. The finance company will administer their ledgers and protect them against bad debts and collection problems. To raise the necessary funds the finance company may assign its pool of receivables to a lender as security. It may even raise the money in the capital markets by issuing loan notes secured on its pool of receivables. Alternatively, it may discount its pool of receivables to an outside factor under a back-to-back discounting arrangement. It has been suggested that in years to come a clearing bank may lend to a corporate borrower based on an undertaking of repayment from a factor under an arrangement analogous to a confirmed, irrevocable letter of credit.[53] These innovations in discounting show the adaptability of discounting to the needs of our time.

---

[51] Lombard Natwest Commercial Services: see *Times Survey*, p. 33.
[52] *Times Survey*, p. 34.
[53] Salinger, *Tolley's Factoring and the Lending Banker* (Tolleys, 1986), pp. 15 *et seq.*

CHAPTER FOUR

FINANCING BY OUTRIGHT ASSIGNMENT

The background

Receivables may be assigned outright in discharge or reduction of an **4.1**
existing indebtedness. A creditor who presses his debtor for payment may
be satisfied with an assignment of a debt owed to his debtor by a third
party. In some cases the transaction is essentially of a mercantile nature.
Goods have been supplied or services rendered to a debtor who is unable
to pay. As a last resort the creditor may agree to an assignment in the
hope that the third party debtor of his own debtor is more solvent. In this
way the assignment assures him of payment. Sometimes, however, the
assignment is part of a financing transaction. Where goods or services are
supplied on a 30, 60, or 90 day credit, the supplier may, if this is the
agreement, accept an assignment of a debt owed to his debtor in
satisfaction. More significantly, the consideration for the assignment may
be a loan or overdraft. In this case, if the assignment is in repayment of
the advance, it is in law neither a sale nor a mortgage of receivables: as to
sale,[1] because the consideration is an advance, and not a purchase price;
as to mortgage, because *ex hypothesi* the assignment is calculated to repay
rather than secure the repayment of the advance. Nor is it a secured non-
recourse funding for the borrower has no equity of redemption in the
assigned receivables. Although the documentation of the financing transaction may contain a provision entitling the borrower to a refund of any
excess left after the lender has been recouped, on good authority[2] such a
provision does not disguise an equity of redemption.

Mercantile or financing transaction?

Outright assignment of receivables in discharge or reduction of an **4.2**
existing debt may be either of a mercantile or a financing character.
Whether it is one or the other depends on the factual background known
to the parties as well as the objective aim of the agreement. Where the

---

[1] A sale of receivables involves as its consideration, not the payment of an advance by the
purchaser, but of a purchase price. If the consideration for an assignment of receivables is a
loan or the extension of some other form of credit, it is not a sale transaction whatever else
it may be.
[2] *Re George Inglefield Ltd.* [1933] Ch. 1. See also, *Burlinson* v. *Hall* [1884] 12 Q.B.D. 347.

assignment is the result of pressures for payment, with no prior agreement so to discharge or reduce the debt paid, the assignment is properly described as a mercantile transaction. Acceptance of this mode of payment is a last resort. On the other hand, if credit is extended to the assignor on the basis of an agreement that the resulting debt shall be liquidated by an assignment of a debt owed to the assignor, the transaction is of a financing character. Here, the assignment is the agreed mode of payment. It is not the result of pressures on the assignor after the contractual date for payment has elapsed, so that unlike mercantile assignments, it is not accepted as a last resort.

Mercantile assignments are of great antiquity.[3] The landmark *Twyne's case*[4] was one such assignment. There, a sheep farmer transferred all his property to a creditor by way of an absolute assignment in satisfaction of a debt. The assignment, however, failed because by retaining possession of the assigned property, the Star Chamber concluded that the transaction was a fraudulent conveyance. In *Yeates* v. *Groves*,[5] D sold premises to E and X. When B, a creditor, pressed him for payment of a debt already overdue, D assigned part of the debt due from E to him. This was held to be a good equitable assignment in discharge of D's indebtedness to B. Also, in *Lett* v. *Morris*,[6] a builder directed his employer to pay the amount due to him under a building contract to a timber merchant who had pressed him for payment. There was no prior agreement that the price of timber supplied to the builder was to be discharged by assigning the debt due from the employer. Therefore, although the outright assignment was in discharge of a pre-existing debt, it was not financing in character because it resulted from creditor pressure, and there was no prior agreement to pay by assignment.

In all assignments involving a mercantile transaction, it is possible that if the assignor comes upon cash after the assignment, the assignee may abandon his assignment and insist on cash payment. After all, his primary concern is to be paid. This possibility alone does not suggest that the assignment is intended as security only,[7] unless there are other facts from which the contrary inference can be drawn. Even where such an assignment is expressed "as security," the relationship between the parties and the factual background against which the assignment was made, may indicate that the word "security" is used in the loose sense of indicating that the assignee views the assignment as *assuring* him of

---

[3] *Yeates* v. *Groves* (1791) 1 Ves.Jun. 280; *Ex p. South, Re Row* (1818) 3 Swans. 392; *Lett* v. *Morris* (1831) 4 Sim. 607; *Crowfoot* v. *Gurney* (1832) 9 Bing. 372.

[4] (1603) 3 Co.Rep. 80b, 76 E.R. 809.

[5] (1791) 1 Ves.Jun. 280, 30 E.R. 343.

[6] (1831) 4 Sim. 607, 58 E.R. 227.

[7] *Sandford* v. *D V Building & Constructions Co. Ltd.* [1963] V.R. 317. From the financier's point of view what matters is that he gets paid. Whether the payment is effected by outright assignment of receivables due to the borrower, or is met from his general resources, would seem irrelevant. Departures from the agreed mode of payment are unobjectionable if they do not amount to a variation, waiver, or rescission of the initial agreement: see *Lloyds & Scottish Finance Ltd.* v. *Cyril Lord Carpet Sales Ltd.* (1979) 129 N.L.J. 366 at 372. *Cf.* Gough, *Company Charges* (1978), p. 275, n. 6.

payment. *Siebe Gorman & Co. Ltd.* v. *Barclays Bank Ltd.*[8] is a strong authority in support. There, RHM was indebted to the plaintiffs for safety equipment supplied on credit. They entered into a deed of assignment by which, after reciting the indebtedness and the plaintiffs' request for payment, RHM assigned bills of exchange and letters of credit (including their proceeds) to the plaintiffs. It was argued that the assignment was void as an unregistered charge. Three factors were urged in support: that the assignment was expressed "as security"; that if RHM had discharged its indebtedness to the plaintiffs from another source, it would have been entitled to a reassignment of the bills—this showed that RHM had an equity of redemption; that the assignment had no certificate of value. While this was consistent with a mortgage, it was inconsistent with an outright assignment.

Slade J. held that the deed was an outright assignment of the bills in reduction of RHM's indebtedness to the plaintiffs. The choice of the parties as to stamping was irrelevant; the factual background negatived any suggestion that the assignment was for security. Although it was not without significance that the consideration for the assignment was the extension of credit facilities, this alone was insufficient to turn the assignment into a security. The factual matrix showed that there was an indebtedness, there was pressure for payment; the genesis of the deed was the request for payment of the outstanding debt. The relationship between the parties was that of trade creditor and debtor. There was no business sense in taking the bills as security rather than in reduction of the indebtedness. Therefore, although expressed "as security," the deed in reality effected an outright assignment.[9] In mercantile assignments the pressure for payment and the absence of a prior agreement so to discharge the debt in respect of which it is given are unifying features. The consideration for the assignment is the creditor's forbearance to sue for payment of the debt.[10] Assignments of this kind create no security interests over the corporate assignor's book debts and consequently are exempt from registration.

Problems may, however, arise where the receivables assigned do not exhaust the amount owed to the assignor by the account debtor. Such an assignment must necessarily be equitable, for there can be no legal

---

[8] [1979] 2 Lloyd's Rep. 142. In *Carreras Rothman Ltd.* v. *Freeman Matthews Treasure Ltd.* [1985] Ch. 207, the plaintiffs paid off media creditors and agents who had rendered services to the defendants, and took an assignment of debts owed to them by the defendants. This is similar to an advance by a financier followed by an outright assignment of receivables owed to the borrower by some other third party. See also *G. & N. Angelakis Shipping Co. S.A.* v. *Compagnie Nationale Algerienne de Navigation (The Attika Hope)* [1988] 1 Lloyd's Rep. 439, where one of the assignments was given in reduction of a pre-existing debt.

[9] [1979] 2 Lloyd's Rep. 142 at 162. See also, *Lyon* v. *TY-Wood Corp.*, 239 A 2d 819 (1968).

[10] Generally speaking, the mere existence of an antecedent debt is not consideration for an assignment because such consideration is necessarily past. Equally, it has never been doubted that the discharge or reduction of a pre-existing debt is sufficient consideration: *Currie* v. *Misa* (1875) L.R. 10 Ex. 153 at 161, 162; Bills of Exchange Act 1882, s.27(1)(*b*). In other cases the court will readily infer a forbearance to sue for the pre-existing debt, even where there is no express or implied agreement to forbear: *Sandford* v. *D V Building & Constructions Co. Ltd.* [1963] V.R. 137 at 140, 141; *Re Smyth* [1970] A.L.R. 919; *The Attika Hope* [1988] 1 Lloyd's Rep. 439 at 441.

assignment of part of a debt.[11] In equity the assignment creates a charge on the whole fund pending appropriation and payment of the specific part. But the charge is not registrable because it secures an out-and-out assignment, and not an hypothecation.[12] Besides, it is arguable that the charge arises by the operation of equitable principles, rather than by the conscious acts of the parties. It is settled law that the category of registrable charges is limited to those *created* by the parties.[13] However, in *Re Brush Aggregates Ltd.*,[14] such an equitable charge was held void for non-registration. In that case, the corporate assignor sold its gravel pit. Out of the purchase price it assigned a part absolutely to solicitors for legal and other costs. It was held that the assignment was a present charge on future book debts as and when they arose. Consequently the assignment was void as an unregistered charge. Since the assignment was of part of a debt it necessarily took effect as an equitable charge on the whole fund pending appropriation and payment of the specific part assigned. The report of the case does not disclose whether there were other facts which could support the inference that only a security was intended by the assignment, though, the factual background seems to negative such an analysis. It is submitted that if the sole ground of decision was that assignment of part of a debt created a registrable charge over the whole fund in equity, the case cannot be supported.

The financing aspect

4.3   An outright assignment of receivables in discharge or reduction of an existing debt may be part of a financing transaction. A bank advances money to a customer and takes an assignment of sums due to the customer in repayment. The debts when collected are paid into a special account in reduction of the advance. This technique of financing receivables is suitable for revolving credit, and provided the understanding is that the customer has no management autonomy over the assigned receivables, it cannot be attacked as a mortgage. That the consideration

---

[11] Because such assignments are not absolute within the meaning of L.P.A. 1925, s.136(1): *Forster* v. *Baker* [1910] 2 K.B. 636; *Re Steel Wing Co. Ltd.* [1921] 1 Ch. 349; *Williams* v. *Atlantic Assurance Co.* [1933] 1 K.B. 81 at 100. This conclusion does not rest simply on a literal interpretation of the phrase "absolute assignment" in the statutory language. Before 1873 an assignee was permitted to bring his action at law in the name of the assignor when he was seeking to recover a whole debt assigned to him. If a debt had been broken into parts this procedure was not appropriate. A creditor cannot recover a debt piecemeal in a court of law. Therefore, when part of a debt was assigned, proceedings to enforce the assignment had to be brought in a court of equity. The assignee was the proper plaintiff in the suit, though the assignor and the assignees of the other parts of the debt were all necessary parties, so that all the obligations of the debtor and the rights of all persons interested in the debt might be established in the same proceedings. This was, and still is, the rule of the Chancery Court: *Norman* v. *FCT* (1962) 109 C.L.R. 9 at 29.

[12] *Ashby, Warner & Co. Ltd.* v. *Simmons* [1936] 2 All E.R. 697; *Re Lawson Constructions Pty. Co. Ltd.* [1942] S.A.S.R. 201. Cf. *Re Brush Aggregates Ltd.* [1983] B.C.L.C. 320.

[13] Companies Act 1985, s.395(2); *Brunton* v. *Electrical Engineering Corp.* [1892] 1 Ch. 434; *Capital Finance Co. Ltd.* v. *Stokes* [1969] 1 Ch. 261; *London & Cheshire Insurance Co. Ltd.* v. *Laplagrene Property Co. Ltd.* [1971] Ch. 499.

[14] [1983] B.C.L.C. 320.

for the assignment is a loan does not matter. The assignment is not registrable as a charge on book debts.[15] Financing by outright assignment remains important where off-balance sheet results are desired because the transaction may be structured to improve the corporate borrower's gearing ratio,[16] or where the borrower desires to avoid having the loan taken into account in calculating borrowing restrictions in existing debt instruments.

The analogy of production payments[17]

In oil and gas project finance the "production payment" provides a **4.4** model for financing by outright assignment of receivables. A production payment is an assignment by the licensee of an oil and gas exploration licence to a lender, of a fractional interest of his share of production of any or all of the minerals covered by the licence or the proceeds of sale, until the lender has received an agreed quantity or their proceeds.[18] In other words, money is advanced to the company being financed in return for an assignment of oil and gas to be produced or the proceeds of sale thereof. The correct legal analysis of a production payment is unclear. On the one hand, a production payment could take effect as a promise to assign oil and gas or the proceeds of sale.[19] If this is the meaning of the operative part of the production payment, in law nothing is assigned; the lender has only a contractual right which may, in an appropriate case, be enforced specifically if money has already been advanced.[20] Such a right is distinctly disadvantageous in that it can stand up against neither secured creditors nor the administrator or liquidator of the promisor. Besides, even where the promise is performed, the assignment takes effect not from the date of the original promise but from the date the assignment is executed. This may render it liable to be set aside as an undue preference if it was executed at a relevant time.[21] Cross-claims will also continue to build up against the promisor's interest in the operating agreement.[22]

If the language of "grant" is used in the production payment agreement, there is no reason for giving the transaction the limited effect of a promise to assign.[23] On the other hand, a production payment could

---

[15] *Ashby, Warner & Co. Ltd.* v. *Simmons* [1936] 2 All E.R. 697; *Re Lawson Constructions Pty. Ltd.* [1942] S.A.S.R. 201; *Siebe Gorman & Co. Ltd.* v. *Barclays Bank Ltd.* [1979] 2 Lloyd's Rep. 142.

[16] But See Pt. I of the Companies Act 1989.

[17] See generally, Walker (1942) 20 Tex.L.Rev. 259; Vagts (1965) 43 Tex.L.Rev. 825; Schmidt (1967) 65 Mich.L.Rev. 1206; Marriage (1977) 5 Int'l Bus. Law 207; Lewis & Willoughby (1980) 3 Houston J. of Int'l Law 51; McCormick (1983) 1 J.E.R.L. 21 at 25 *et seq.*; Daintith & Willoughby, *UK Oil & Gas Law* (2nd ed., 1984), paras. 1–420 *et seq.*

[18] Walker, *op. cit.,* 262.

[19] Schmidt, *op. cit.,* 1211.

[20] *Swiss Bank Corp.* v. *Lloyds Bank* [1982] A.C. 584 at 595; Jones & Goodhart, *Specific Performance* (1986), p. 124.

[21] Insolvency Act 1986, ss.239 & 240; *Re Jackson & Bassford* [1906] 2 Ch. 467 at 476; *Re Gregory Love & Co.* [1916] 1 Ch. 203.

[22] For a discussion of these and other problems arising from a promise to assign, see para. 5.10, *infra.*

[23] *Cf.* Marriage, *op. cit.,* 216–217.

operate as a security for the repayment of the sum advanced.[24] In this case it has to be registered in order to be enforceable against assignees, execution creditors and any subsequent administrator or liquidator of the licensee, if the interest of the licensee under an exploration licence is properly described as an interest in land.[25] Whether this is the true analysis depends on the language of the production payment as well as the factual background of the transaction. But it does not necessarily follow that a production payment is a security merely because the consideration for the assignment is a loan; nor does it follow that because repayment is to come only from oil and gas and any proceeds of sale thereof, a production payment is not a security.[26] On the contrary this is normally the position in secured non-recourse loans. Between a promise to assign and a security lie other possibilities. One of these is that a production payment is a purchase of a present property right.[27] However, it seems unlikely that a production payment can bear this meaning. For one thing, the consideration for the assignment is a loan rather than a purchase price; for another, a forward purchase agreement would be required to effect a sale. This objection is not disposed of by saying that the assigment is of a present right to receive deliveries or their monetary equivalent. A forward purchase agreement does give a *present* right to future deliveries. Although the question is not free from difficulties, the better view is that a production payment is an outright non-security disposition of oil and gas or their proceeds in repayment of an advance. The disposition repays rather than secures the repayment of the advance. Since this is the mode of repayment agreed by the parties, the production payment provides a model for financing by outright non-sale and non-security assignments. *Reynolds Bros. (Motors) Ltd.* v. *Essanda Ltd.*[28] provides an analogy. In that case a debtor assigned 10 tractors in reduction of an existing indebtedness. The assignment was not attacked as a charge on the tractors. The conclusion, therefore, is that a company can dispose of its receivables other than by way of sale or security, for the purpose of raising money. This technique of financing on the strength of receivables has enormous potential for growth. At the moment it has been only a little explored. We shall next consider two situations: where a fixed sum is assigned, and where the assignment is of work in progress.

Assignment of a fixed sum

4.5   A borrower may assign debts owed to him to his financier as part of a financing transaction. Where the advance is more than the value of the

---

[24] Schmidt, *op. cit.*, 1211.

[25] This is unclear: see Marriage, *op. cit.*, 216 *et seq.*; *cf.* Daintith & Willoughby, *op. cit.*, para. 1–204; Lewis & Willoughby, *op. cit.*, 55–58. If it is not an interest in land, but an intangible personal property, similar to its interest under the operating agreement, the security interest is not registrable as a charge unless it is a floating security: Companies Act 1985, ss.396(1)(*b*), (*c*), (*f*) and 396(2)(*c*). But it would be subject to the moratorium imposed on enforcement of securities by ss.10 and 11 of the Insolvency Act 1986.

[26] *Cf.* Daintith & Willoughby, *op. cit.*, para. 1–422.

[27] Lewis & Willoughby, *op. cit.*, 59 *et seq.*

[28] (1983) 8 A.C.L.R. 422. At 426 Mahoney J.A. (NSW) said that it was not suggested in argument that the transaction operated by way of security or charge over the tractors.

debts assigned, no question of disguised mortgage is likely to arise. Difficulties may, however, arise if the nominal value of the assigned debts is greater than the sum advanced. Assuming the assignment contains a provision entitling the assignor to the excess, if any, remaining after the lender has been recouped, is the transaction a mortgage? The answer depends on the factual background against which the assignment was made as well as the objective intention of the parties. If the understanding was that the lender should be repaid by an assignment, and the agreement is not otherwise open to attack as a sham,[29] there is no ground in law or equity, upon which the assignment could be construed as a mortgage. It may be objected that this begs the question whether the transaction is a sham. It is, however, difficult to see why an outright assignment should be treated as a sham. It does not give the appearance of creating rights and obligations different from that contemplated by the parties. If it was a purely mercantile transaction no one would attribute falsity to the parties. Why should it make a difference because the aim is financing? In urging recognition of outright non-security assignments one is not necessarily making a case for literalism, nor preferring form to substance. On the surface the transaction bears a striking resemblance to a secured non-recourse lending against receivables. In reality it is not.

Secured non-recourse funding in this context means a transaction which gives the lender a security interest in designated receivables, even though the borrower assumes no personal obligation to repay, and the lender must look exclusively to his security for satisfaction.[30] In this sense a secured non-recourse lending against receivables differs from an outright disposition of receivables in repayment of an advance. In the former, but not in the latter, the assignor has an equity of redemption in the assigned receivables. The provision entitling the assignor to repayment of the excess, if any, in the latter form of financing, does not disguise an equity of redemption. In *Re George Inglefield Ltd*,[31] a case of block discounting, clause 18 of the discounting agreement provided that the financier should account to the assignor for any balance left after he had recouped himself. At first instance, Eve J. held that the clause disguised an equity of redemption. He was reversed by the Court of Appeal. The parties contracted that the financier should be satisfied with so much; clause 18

---

[29] By definition a "sham" is a transaction designed to give the appearance of creating legal rights and obligations different from the actual legal rights and obligations which the parties intended to create: *Snook* v. *London & West Riding Investment* [1967] 2 Q.B. 786 at 802; *Ramsay* v. *I.R.C.* [1982] A.C. 300 at 323.

[30] *Mathews* v. *Blackmore* (1857) 1 H. & N. 762 (action for debt failed though it is clear from the judgments that the transaction was treated as a loan to be repaid out of the trust funds). In *Green* v. *Hertzog* [1954] 1 W.L.R. 1309 at 1311, Lord Goddard C.J. referred to a transaction as a loan by a partner to a partnership, although no common law claim would lie for money lent since liability between partners is joint. See also, *De Vigier* v. *I.R.C.* [1964] 1 W.L.R. 1073.

[31] [1933] Ch. 1. In *Burlinson* v. *Hall* (1884) 12 Q.B.D. 347, T assigned certain debts to the plaintiff, his creditor, to pay himself the cost of collection, plus the sum owed to him, and to pay the surplus, if any, to T. It was held to be a good assignment in discharge of T's indebtedness, even though, as the court observed, the assignor might be entitled to have the subject-matter of the assignment reassigned to him if the debt owed to the assignee was repaid from another source.

merely made clear that which would have been a legitimate inference from the agreement of the parties.

Though the case was concerned with sale of receivables, the same must in principle be true of an outright non-security assignment. This conclusion cannot be affected by the financier's contractual obligation to hand over to the assignor any excess left after he has been repaid. His obligation is to repay the excess, if any, out of his general resources, not to account *in specie* for an equity of redemption. On this basis, a financier who has received more than is contractually due to him is a debtor, rather than a trustee of the excess for the assignor. The financier is not bound to segregate the excess from his own resources, and hand it over as such to the assignor. The contrary would be the case if the provision entitling the assignor to the excess, in truth, disguised an equity of redemption.[32] An analogy is found in *Re Warren*.[33] A builder was financed by W. Under the arrangement W guaranteed the builder's overdraft. It was agreed that any money realised from the sale or other dealing with the buildings should be paid to solicitors, who, after certain deductions, were to pay it into W's account. W was to apply the sums in reduction of the builder's overdraft. The Divisional Court held that the arrangement was a good equitable assignment of the moneys due to the builder according to the terms of the agreement.

Outright assignment of a fixed sum in discharge or reduction of an existing indebtedness is not registrable as a charge on book debts. Consequently, it is unaffected by the law as to avoidance or modification of security interests in any subsequent administration or liquidation of the assignor. This could be important because implicit in any evaluation of the riskiness of a proposed investment is the perceived ease with which the investor could enforce the agreement. Restrictions on his ability to reach the underlying assets affect the quality of the investment and hence returns on the investment.

Assignment of work in progress[34]

4.6   The assignment of work in progress is more likely to be challenged as a mortgage of receivables. In many construction contracts, as indeed in

---

[32] If the assignee is bound to keep the excess separate from his own assets he is a trustee for the assignor and this may throw some light on the nature of the assignor's interest in the excess. See generally, *Fitzgerald* v. *Fitzgerald* (1910) 10 S.R. (NSW) 484 at 488; *Henry* v. *Hammond* [1913] 2 K.B. 515 at 521; *Cohen* v. *Cohen* (1929) 42 C.L.R. 91 at 101. The nature of the assignor's interest in the excess may also bear on the question whether he can trace it into the assets of the assignee: *Lister* v. *Stubbs* (1890) 45 Ch.D. 1 at 15; *Attorney-General's Reference (No. 1 of 1985)* [1986] Q.B. 491.

[33] [1938] Ch. 725. In *Bank of Liverpool* v. *Holland* (1926) 43 T.L.R. 29, the defendant was indebted to W who owed money to the bank. W assigned the debt due from the defendant to the bank, provided that the amount recoverable should not exceed a named amount. It was held that this was an outright assignment, subject to the proviso that the bank must hold the excess as trustee for W.

[34] The details of assignment of work in progress vary greatly. The model described in the text is adapted from Glynis Jones, "Off-Balance Sheet Financing" (1986) 4 Co. Law Digest 62 at 63.

other contracts, the contractor utilises bank finance. Usually the contractor irrevocably assigns to the bank sums due to it under the contract and guarantees performance of the contract by issuing a performance bond. The financing agreement will provide that the bank's receipt is sufficient discharge of the employer who is requested to pay instalments due directly to the bank. The bank makes periodic advances to the contractor to finance the contract. Interest is charged on the amount drawn down. Sums due under the construction contract reduce the overdraft until the bank is fully recouped. This is followed by a reassignment of any balance outstanding under the construction contract to the contractor. In accounting terms the contractor has no direct repayment obligation and consequently no liability is recorded in its balance sheet. The only additional disclosure in the accounts is a note on the contingent liability in respect of the performance bond. The transaction is intended as an outright assignment of receivables in discharge or reduction of the assignor's indebtedness to the bank.

However, the correct legal analysis of the financing arrangement just described is not free from difficulty. One thing is clear. The absence of a direct repayment obligation is not inconsistent with a secured non-recourse lending against receivables.[35] If this is the correct analysis, then, regardless of accounting practice, the transaction is a loan secured by a mortgage of receivables. But can the transaction be described as an outright non-security assignment of receivables in discharge or reduction of the corporate assignor's indebtedness? The fact that the consideration for the assignment is an advance is a circumstance of significance, and rules out any analysis based on sale of the receivables. Also the revolving nature of the credit facility extended by the bank would, at first sight, suggest that the assignment was intended as a continuing security. The provision for reassignment completes the picture. That provision differs from one obliging the assignee to repay any excess to the corporate assignor. But does such terminological difference justify the radically different characterisation of both methods of financing? If the nature of a transaction depends on the intention of the parties, can it not be argued that if an outright assignment was really intended, it should be enforced as such? Some of these questions were answered by Wynn-Parry J. in *Re Kent and Sussex Sawmills Ltd.*[36]

In that case a company, having contracted to supply logs, obtained overdraft facilities from its bank on terms of sending a letter to the debtors directing them to pay all moneys due to the company under the contract into its account with the bank. The direction was irrevocable except with the written consent of the bank, and a receipt from the bank was sufficient discharge. On a summons for directions by the liquidator (the company having gone into liquidation a year later), two questions were argued: was the letter of authority to the debtors an assignment of the sums due to the contractor under the contract? If it was an assignment, was the assignment an out-and-out disposition of the company's interest, or was it merely for security? Wynn-Parry J. held that the

[35] See n. 30, *supra*.
[36] [1947] Ch. 177.

letter of authority was a good equitable assignment. The assignment was to provide continuing security and hence void as an unregistered charge on the company's book debts. This was because:

> when one has to look at a document brought into existence between a borrower and lender in connexion with a transaction of borrowing and lending, one must approach the consideration of that document with the expectation of discovering that the document is intended to be given as security for the borrower's indebtedness.[37]

This approach ignores the possibility that the assignment may have gone to reduce the corporate assignor's overdraft at the bank. The arrangement was designed to provide revolving credit and the debt created by the bank finance was intended to be self-liquidating. This was achieved by the outright assignment of the work in progress in diminution of the assignor's indebtedness to the bank. Yet his Lordship started off on the footing that the transaction was a loan secured by a mortgage of receivables. The assumption that in a lender/borrower relationship, a purported outright assignment of receivables must be viewed as a security does not always hold good.

It is fair to say that the case was not argued on the basis of an outright non-security assignment, no doubt, because it was thought that there was no tertium quid between a sale and a mortgage of receivables. This was a mistake. It was argued that the assignment was a sale to the bank, an argument difficult to square with the evidence. The bank advanced the money, not as a purchase price, but as a loan. There was no subsequent agreement to treat the advance as a purchase price. The true nature of the transaction was that the bank advanced money to the company on the understanding that the assignment would reduce the amount advanced. No mortgage was intended and none was in fact created. Therefore, although the assignment could have been cancelled as soon as the bank was repaid, this alone could not, it is submitted, alter the legal nature of the transaction as an outright disposition of receivables in repayment of the amount advanced. Unfortunately, however, it was this possibility more than any other factor that led Wynn-Parry J. to the conclusion that the assignment was in substance and effect a mortgage.[38] It is to be hoped that as the patterns of corporate finance become more sophisticated the courts would be less astute to characterise a genuine outright assignment of receivables as a mortgage simply because the motive is financing.

To be sure, the argument is not that an assignment of work in progress cannot be given as security only. On the contrary many such assignments are calculated to do just that. The argument is that the existence of a lender/borrower relationship alone should not inexorably lead to the conclusion that an assignment which, in substance and effect, was intended to be outright in discharge or reduction of the corporate assignor's indebtedness, falls to be treated as a mortgage. There is nothing in English law to suggest that a lender/borrower relationship is

---

[37] *Ibid.* at 181.
[38] *Ibid.* at 182.

inconsistent with an outright assignment of receivables. Much of the confusion arises from the common, albeit incorrect, assumption that sale and mortgage are exhaustive of the existing patterns of financing against receivables.

In *Re Row Dal Constructions Pty. Ltd.*,[39] there was overwhelming evidence that the assignment, apparently outright on its face, was intended as security only. The bank asked for it as security, obtained and regarded it as such. The conclusion that it was not an outright assignment in discharge of the corporate assignor's indebtedness to the bank gave effect to the intention of the parties. This case and *Re Kent and Sussex Sawmills Ltd.* highlight the difficulties of financing by outright assignment of work in progress.

[39] [1966] V.R. 249.

SECURITY INTERESTS OVER RECEIVABLES

General

5.1   For the most part security interests over receivables are normally in the form of a charge or mortgage. When receivables become embodied in a negotiable paper, a pledge of the paper could be taken as security for short-term debt obligations. Most retention of title agreements contain a "proceeds clause" entitling the seller to trace the proceeds of authorized sub-sales.[1] The agreement itself performs a security function. Exceptionally, the debtor may, with the consent of the creditor, attorn receivables owed by him to a third party. From this it is clear the security may be taken over receivables in one or more of five ways. However, the bulk of this chapter is devoted to assignments by way of charge and mortgage, although for the sake of completeness it is proposed to consider very briefly, other forms of security.

Pledge

5.2   A pledge of documentary receivables[2] is a bailment of a negotiable instrument as security for the payment of a debt or the discharge of other obligations in respect of which the instrument was given.[3] The pledgee is a bailee whose bailment is of unlimited duration and is not terminable by the pledgor save by tender of the secured amount.[4] Once delivered, the pledgee has superior rights to the instrument as against all claimants. His entitlement extends to the proceeds of the debt embodied in the instrument because his right to enforce payment is co-extensive with possession of the instrument.[5] Unlike a pledgee of tangible personality, a holder of a negotiable debt as security, has not just special property in the instrument and debt embodied therein, but the whole present interest in the receivables. What interest the pledgor has in the instrument is reversionary. The pledgee has an implied power to sub-pledge the

---

[1] See J. Spencer [1989] J.B.L. 220, for a factual analysis of sample standard form retention of title clauses in use.
[2] For the meaning of documentary receivables, see para. 2.5, *supra*.
[3] *Donald* v. *Suckling* (1866) L.R. 1 Q.B. 585; *Halliday* v. *Holgate* (1868) L.R. 3 Exch. 299.
[4] *Ibid.*
[5] Bills of Exchange Act 1882, s.38; *Sutters* v. *Briggs* [1922] A.C. 1 at 20.

instrument, and this does not terminate the pledge.[6] If the sub-pledgee becomes a holder in due course,[7] he can detain the instrument until the face value of the instrument is paid, even if this is larger than the secured amount. The pledge does not suffer from the disadvantages of other possessory securities which may deprive the pledgor of possession and use of a valuable asset. This is because a negotiable debt, unlike tangible personalty, cannot be put to any physical use; it can only be discounted before maturity, or presented for payment on maturity.

From the standpoint of formality, a pledge of documentary receivables is the simplest and most cost-effective security which can be taken. All that is necessary is that possession of the instrument be delivered to the pledgee with the intention that it be held as security. There is no requirement of stamping or registration,[8] as these may destroy the negotiability of the instrument. However, it is absolutely necessary that possession be given to the pledgee. For this purpose, possession must be actual, rather than symbolic.[9] An agreement to give possession in future, even where written, is clearly insufficient to constitute the transaction a pledge,[10] although it may, when taken with other factors, evince an intention to give a security which might take effect as an equitable charge.[11] Such a charge is very inferior to the pledge because it is liable to be defeated by a bona fide legal transferee for value without notice. A pledge of documentary receivables does not normally survive the loss of possession of the negotiable paper, and unlike tangible personalty, it is not clear that the law will recognise a continuation of the pledgee's right simply because it is returned to the pledgor for a limited purpose.[12]

The remedy of a pledgee of tangible personalty is sale; he cannot foreclose.[13] A pledgee of documentary receivables may not only discount them prior to maturity (even where this involves a breach of the contract of pledge), but may wait and foreclose at maturity by presenting it for payment. A pledgee who is a holder in due course has a better security than the assignee of pure receivables. For one thing, he holds the instrument free of defects in the title of his transferor and free of equities which the previous parties have between themselves because the instrument is autonomous of the underlying contract in respect of which it was

---

[6] *Donald* v. *Suckling* (1866) L.R. 1 Q.B. 585.
[7] Within the definition in the Bills of Exchange Act 1882, s.29(1).
[8] Companies Act 1985, s.396(2)(*f*). This provision applies only to negotiable instruments given to *secure* payment of book debts, and would seem (at least on a literal reading) inapplicable to a pledge of a negotiable instrument given as *payment*. However, since the aim of the exception is to preserve the negotiability of such instruments it is hoped that the courts would see their way to apply the exception to instruments given as payment.
[9] *Cf. Official Assignee of Madras* v. *Mercantile Bank of India* [1935] A.C. 53, where the Privy Council held that delivery of railway receipts in respect of some groundnuts entrusted to the railway for carriage, was constructive delivery of the groundnuts on the theory that the receipts were title to the groundnuts. The same is true of bills of lading.
[10] *Re Morritt, ex p. Official Receiver* (1886) 18 Q.B.D. 222 at 232, 234; *Dublin City Distillery Ltd.* v. *Doherty* [1914] A.C. 823 at 843.
[11] *Harrold* v. *Plenty* [1901] 2 Ch. 314.
[12] *Cf. North Western Bank Ltd.* v. *Poynter* [1895] A.C. 56; *Re David Allester* [1922] 2 Ch. 211 (trust receipt in relation to goods released for the purpose of sale did not create a registrable charge on the goods).
[13] *Carter* v. *Wake* (1877) 4 Ch.D. 605.

drawn or accepted.[14] Second, he enjoys other procedural and substantive advantages.[15] Because of the width of the protection afforded to a holder in due course, it is easier to resist an action on the bill by attacking the holder's status as a holder in due course. In Canada, this line of attack was used to protect consumers who issued cheques and other bills of exchange to financiers in circumstances where the consideration had failed.[16] Thus, there developed a line of authority holding that a holder's title to a negotiable instrument is defective where it is shown that before receiving it, he had knowledge or a well-founded suspicion that the consideration anticipated in the underlying transaction by the party liable on the instrument had not been received or had failed in whole or part, or would very likely fail in such a way as to constitute the alienation of the instrument a fraud, or a negotiation a breach of faith.[17] In England there are restrictions on the use of consumer bills of exchange in secured consumer credit transactions.[18]

Clearly, not all contract rights are pledgeable. A simple contract debt is not pledgeable. So also, hire-purchase and credit sale agreements which are frequently deposited as security. On the other hand, negotiable instruments given in payment for goods delivered, or services rendered, or facilities made available, are pledgeable. The test whether or not a document is pledgeable is whether it embodies a debt obligation so that possession of the instrument entitles the holder and no one else, to payment. Many documents evidence title to a debt, but are not pledgeable because although in some cases the obligor/debtor may demand production of the document before he pays, possession of the document does not *ipso facto* entitle the possessor to receive payment. What is not clear is whether negotiable certificates of deposit are pledgeable. One view[19] is that these instruments may be pledged and even taken as security by the issuing bank. Doubts as to the pledgeability of such instruments arise from two sources.[20] The first is the status of the instrument as a negotiable paper. There are dicta in support of the negotiability of certificates of deposit,[21] and the better view is that such certificates are negotiable. This also accords with the practice of bankers. The second is the conceptual difficulty raised by *Re Charge Card Services Ltd.*[22] Can a

---

[14] Bills of Exchange Act 1882, s.38(2).

[15] See E. P. Ellinger, *Modern Banking Law* (OUP, 1987), pp. 506–507.

[16] *Federal Discount Corp. Ltd.* v. *St Pierre* (1962) 32 D.L.R. (2d) 86, discussed by Ziegel, (1970) 48 Can B.R. 309. This line of authority has now been largely, though not entirely, superseded by Pt. V of the Bills of Exchange Act, R.S.C. 1970 (1st Supplement) c. 4 (Canada).

[17] B. Crawford, *Crawford and Falconbridge's Banking and Bills of Exchange* (8th ed., 1986, Toronto: Canada Law Book Inc.), Vol. 2, para. 1461 and the cases there discussed.

[18] Consumer Credit Act 1974, ss.123 and 124.

[19] Cresswell *et al, Encyclopaedia of Banking Law*, para. E2451.

[20] See Ellinger [1989] J.B.L. 64; Goode, *Legal Problems of Credit and Security* (2nd ed., 1988), pp. 129–130.

[21] *Customs & Excise Commissioners* v. *Guy Butler (International) Ltd.* [1977] Q.B. 377 at 382; *Libyan Arab Foreign Bank* v. *Bankers Trust Co.* [1989] 3 All E.R. 252 at 273. If the negotiability of certificates of deposit has been recognised judicially since 1977 there can now be little doubt that such instruments have become truly negotiable.

[22] [1987] Ch. 150.

bank be the pledgee of a negotiable certificate of deposit which it has issued? A similar question arises where an insurer holds a policy which it has issued as security for an advance to the insured. It seems that there is no reason why the bank cannot be the pledgee.[23] The certificate is not discharged, nor is its currency affected because it comes into the hands of the bank at some point before maturity, if it does not remain with the bank at maturity.[24] Moreover, since the money on deposit has no existence separate from the certificate, a pledge of the certificate will give the bank the whole present interest in the deposit, and this is sufficient to defeat the title of an assignee of the deposit from the pledgor, and also that of any subsequent administrator or liquidator of the depositor. There is no analogy between a cheque payable out of funds in a current account and a certificate of deposit. Therefore, although a cheque is no assignment of the funds out of which it is payable,[25] a negotiable certificate of deposit is somewhat on a different footing because the deposit has no existence separate and distinct from the certificate. The right to enforce payment of the deposit is co-extensive with possession of the certificate and the bank can hold the certificate as security before its maturity.

Contractual liens

Liens, though commonly used in a narrow sense to describe rights **5.3** arising by operation of law, are capable of arising, and frequently arise, from consensual agreements. Documentary receivables are normally subject to the bankers' lien when they are deposited with a bank for collection, unless the lien is excluded by agreement between the banker and its customer.[26] However, the banker's lien is not a product of contract. A contractual lien is by definition a mere personal right to detain the subject-matter of the lien as security for the performance of an obligation.[27] It gives the lienee no right of disposal.[28] But in the context of documentary receivables, a contractual lien is much more than a personal right of detention unless by contract the right to proceeds of the document is excluded. Where there is no such exclusion, a contractual lien entitles the lienee to the proceeds because the right of action embodied in the document is concurrent with possession of the document itself. The rule here follows the analogy of the banker's lien.[29] If this is so, it follows that there is no conceptual distinction between a contractual lien over documentary receivables and a pledge. Both give a power of sale, and a power to present the document for payment at maturity.

In time charters, it is not uncommon for the shipowner to be given a contractual lien over sub-freights due from sub-charters, as security for

---

[23] *Cf.* Ellinger [1989] J.B.L. 64 at 65.
[24] *Cf.* Bills of Exchange Act, 1882, s.61.
[25] *Hopkinson* v. *Forster* (1874) L.R. 19 Eq. 74. *Shand* v. *Du Buisson* (1874) L.R. 18 Eq. 283; Bills of Exchange Act 1882, s.53(1).
[26] *Brandao* v. *Barnett* (1846) 12 Cl. & F. 787 at 810.
[27] *Donald* v. *Suckling* (1866) L.R. 1 Q.B. 585 at 604, 610, 612.
[28] *Ibid.*
[29] *Sutters* v. *Briggs* [1922] A.C. 1 at 20; *Re Keever, a bankrupt* [1967] Ch. 182.

the discharge of accrued obligations under the charterparty.[30] The extent of the right is clear: it gives the shipowner the right to intercept the sub-freights before they are paid. There is no right to follow the proceeds once paid.[31] If the extent of the right is any indication of its nature, one would be compelled to characterize the right as a personal right of interception, lying somewhere between the unpaid seller's right of stoppage in transitu,[32] and a floating charge. There is now authority[33] for the view that a shipowner's contractual lien is a charge on the sub-freights and where, as is usually the case, the charterer retains management autonomy over the sub-freights before the shipowner perfects his lien by a notice of claim to the shippers or sub-charterers, the charge is a floating security.[34] The implication is that the lien must be registered in order to be valid against creditors and liquidations. Not only does registration defeat the commercial purpose of the lien, but also, reduces unnecessarily the already limited remedies available to shipowners.[35] Today, the lien is no longer registrable,[36] and this, to some extent, removes the incentive to analyse the lien in terms of a personal right. There are, however, problems with analysing the lien even as a non-registrable charge.[37] First, if the lienee cannot trace the proceeds against the charterer (who for purposes of the charge analysis is the chargor), then the charge created by the shipowner's lien is indeed of a kind unknown to equity jurisprudence. It lacks most of the incidents of a true charge. A true charge gives the chargee rights *in rem*. A chargor who receives debts charged with the discharge of an obligation holds them as a constructive trustee for the chargee.[38] This is not true of the lienor of sub-freights.[39] Further, third parties who receive charged property with notice of the charge are constructive trustees.[40] The same cannot be said of third party recipients of sub-freights before the right of lien is exercised. However, in *Re Welsh Irish Ferries Ltd.*,[41] Nourse J. said that if a shipper made payment to a third party who had notice of the lien, the shipowner could follow the payment into his hands. This would be comforting to the shipowner if it were true that there is this type of tracing remedy. It is difficult to accept Nourse J.'s statement as law because the defeasibility of the right to intercept sub-freights once paid does not depend on the identity of the

---

[30] See, *e.g.* clause 18 of the New York Produce Exchange Form; Baltime Form, clause 18; and Linertime Form, clause 20.
[31] *Tagart, Beaton & Co.* v. *James Fisher & Sons* [1903] 1 K.B. 391 at 395; *Federal Commerce & Navigation Co. Ltd.* v. *Molena Alpha Inc., The "Nanfri"* [1979] A.C. 757 at 784; *Re Welsh Irish Ferries Ltd., The "Ugland Trailer"* [1986] Ch. 471 at 479; *The Annangel Glory* [1988] 1 Lloyd's Rep. 45 at 49. See Wilford [1986] L.M.C.L.Q. 1; [1988] L.M.C.L.Q. 148.
[32] Sale of Goods Act 1979, s.44.
[33] *Re Welsh Irish Ferries Ltd.* [1986] Ch. 471.
[34] *The Annangel Glory* [1988] 1 Lloyd's Rep. 45.
[35] See Wilford, [1988] L.M.C.L.Q. 148.
[36] Companies Act 1985, s.396(2)(g).
[37] Oditah [1989] L.M.C.L.Q. 191 at 194–197.
[38] *International Factors Ltd.* v. *Rodriguez* [1979] Q.B. 351; *Barclays Bank plc* v. *Willowbrook International Ltd.* [1987] 1 F.T.L.R. 396.
[39] *Tagart, Beaton & Co.* v. *James Fisher & Sons* [1903] 1 K.B. 391.
[40] See n. 38, *supra*.
[41] [1986] Ch. 471.

recipient of the payment. What if at that time no monies are due under the charterparty? Nor is the shipowner's inability to trace answered by saying that the lien is a floating charge. Even if this were so, it does not explain why the shipowner cannot follow the identifiable proceeds of the sub-freights in the hands of the charterer or his agent after he has given notice of claim (which for this purpose is the crystallizing event).[42]

The second difficulty with the charge analysis arises if the shipowner's contractual lien is a floating charge. The administrator of an insolvent charterer can deal with the sub-freights freely even where the shipowner has given notice of claim to shippers or sub-charterers, as if the lien did not exist.[43] In addition, preferential claims will be payable out of the sub-freights, in priority to the claim of the shipowner.[44] Being a floating security, the shipowner cannot, by giving prior notice to the shippers, steal a march on specific assignees of the sub-freights who have given no notice.[45] The extreme commercial improbability of these results suggests that the charge analysis must be wrong. It is superficially tempting to suggest that these difficulties can be overcome by a specific security. Seeing, however, the degree of control and policing necessary to establish a specific security over sub-freights, very few charterers would concede such management autonomy to the shipowner. It seems that the charge analysis is an error which crept into the law partly because of the equitable character of the old admiralty jurisdiction, and partly because sub-freights are by their nature insusceptible of possessory security except where they are paid by means of a bill of exchange. It is unfortunate that the equitable nature of the old admiralty jurisdiction should colour the nature of a lien which does not owe its origin to the exercise of that jurisdiction.

The better view is that the shipowner's contractual lien is a *personal* right, *sui generis*, to intercept freight before it is paid. The inability to follow proceeds of sub-freights is not because that is the event which defeats it; rather, the ability to trace is a consequence of an underlying property right,[46] and this, the lien does not give. The personal right analysis suffers from one obvious weakness: it does not explain how the shipowner overcomes the problem of privity when enforcing payment

---

[42] *Tagart, Beaton & Co.* v. *James Fisher & Sons, supra*; contrast *Wehner* v. *Dene SS Co.* [1905] 2 K.B. 92, where Channell J. held that the notice of claim was effective although it was served after the agents had received the sub-freights. In *Molthes Rederi Aktieselskabet* v. *Ellerman's Wilson Line Ltd.* [1922] 1 K.B. 710 at 717, Greer J. left open the question whether such notice was effective, because *Wehner* was on this point apparently in conflict with *Tagart, Beaton & Co.* The reconciliation of both cases might be that, whereas in *Wehner* the bill of lading freight was payable to the owners (so that the charterer's agents were their own, at least for the purpose of collecting the freights), in *Tagart, Beaton & Co.*, no bill of lading contract was made on shipment, so that the contractual right to receive freights passed directly to the charterers.
[43] Insolvency Act 1986, s.15(1) and (3).
[44] Insolvency Act 1986, ss.40, 175, 386 and Sched. 6.
[45] *Ward* v. *Royal Exchange Shipping Co.* (1888) 58 L.T. 174; *Re Ind, Coope & Co. Ltd.* [1911] 2 Ch. 223 at 233; *Canadian Imperial Bank of Commerce* v. *FBDB* [1985] 3 W.W.R. 318 (Alberta QB Ct.).
[46] *Lister* v. *Stubbs* (1890) 45 Ch.D. 1 esp at 15; *Attorney-General's References (No. 1 of 1985)* [1986] Q.B. 491.

against the shippers or sub-charterers.[47] When there is a sub-charter party there is no direct contract between the sub-charterer and the shipowner. How is the shipowner's lien to be accounted for as against the sub-charterer or the holder of a bill of lading? In the latter case, one can start with the proposition that the bill of lading contract is made, as it appears upon its face to be made, with the shipowner.[48] In the case of a sub-charter, since the head charter will normally be incorporated into the sub-charter it is theoretically possible to say that the shipowner is a joint promisee with the head charterer and that the sub-charterer is the promisor (as regards enforceability of the lien).[49] Alternatively, one could say that the charterer holds the benefit of the lien clause in the charterparty on trust for the shipowner. Although the personal right analysis is conceptually purer than other analyses of the nature of the shipowner's lien, there is now no pressure to urge it (rather than say that the lien is an assignment of the sub-freights) since the lien is no longer a registrable charge.[50]

Attornment

5.4   Security over receivables could take the form of an attornment from the debtor to the financier with the consent of both the original creditor and the financier.[51] Today, with the facility of legal and equitable assignments readily available, it is doubtful whether anything can be gained by attornment. Apart from *Shamia* v. *Joory*,[52] most of the cases which developed attornment as a method of transfer of debts are old and obscure.[53] Further, they seem to confuse attornment with novation. For example, some of them insist that the person attorned to, must give up his primary claim against the original creditor.[54] Practically, it will be difficult to persuade a financier advancing money on the strength of receivables to give up his claim in debt against the party being financed. In addition, it is not clear whether consideration is required. It has been suggested that where there is a fund in existence, no consideration is required; but if there is no fund, and the claim of the original creditor rests primarily in debt, consideration must be furnished.[55] However, the suggestion is difficult to accept. For one thing, most of the cases in which

---

[47] The problem of privity was raised in an acute form in *Care Shipping Corp.* v. *Latin American Shipping Corp., The "Cebu"* [1983] Q.B. 1005, where there was a sub-sub-charter.

[48] *Wehner* v. *Dene SS Co.* [1905] 2 K.B. 92 at 98.

[49] *Cf. Coulls* v. *Bagot's Executor and Trustee Co.* (1967) 40 A.L.J.R. 471 at 477.

[50] Companies Act 1985, s.396(2)(g).

[51] As in *Israel* v. *Douglas* (1789) 1 H. Bl. 239, 126 E.R. 139; *Wilson* v. *Coupland* (1821) 5 B. & Ald. 228.

[52] [1958] 1 Q.B. 448.

[53] *Israel* v. *Douglas* (1789) 1 H. Bl. 239; *Wilson* v. *Coupland* (1821) 5 B. & Ald. 228; *Lilly* v. *Hays* (1836) 5 Ad. & E. 548; *Walker* v. *Rostron* (1842) 9 M. & W. 411; *Hamilton* v. *Spottiswoode* (1894) 4 Exch. 200; *Liversidge* v. *Broadbent* (1859) 4 H. & N. 603; *Griffin* v. *Weatherby* (1868) L.R. 3 Q.B. 753.

[54] *Cuxton* v. *Chadley* (1824) 3 B. & C. 50; *Wharton* v. *Walker* (1825) 4 B. & C. 163.

[55] Davies (1959) 75 L.Q.R. 220 esp at 228.

attornment has been recognised involve debts.[56] In *Liversidge* v. *Broad-bent*,[57] for example, Martin B said that the same principle applies to bankers in a position of having the money of another which they are liable to pay on demand. Also, in *Shamia* v. *Joory*[58] attornment was upheld despite argument to the contrary, the "fund" attorned being no more than a debt on account of goods sold. The "fund" in *Walker* v. *Rostron*,[59] consisted of proceeds of goods sold, and in *Hamilton* v. *Spottiswoode*,[60] the fund consisted of the purchase price of goods to be delivered in future. Notwithstanding these authorities, McPherson J. refused to apply the concept of attornment to a simple debt in *Rothwells Ltd.* v. *Nommack*.[61] If the difficulty was whether the party attorned to has to furnish consideration, that would create no problems for the receivables financier since a promise to forbear or actual forbearance suffices.[62] Goff and Jones[63] have, however, argued that the objections to attornment as a method of transferring debts are both historical and practical: historical, because it would have circumvented the common law procedural obstacle to assignment of non-negotiable debts; practical, because by giving the party attorned to a proprietary right in the subject-matter of the attornment, it may give a right to trace which would survive the debtor's insolvency.

Neither objection is compelling. First, the argument founded on circumvention does not stand analysis. Many legal rules are substitutes rather than complements. The plurality of devices available for the achievement of a given legal result means that the well-advised citizen can almost always achieve results denied him by one legal device by using another. This is particularly true of the law relating to transfer of debts. For example, powers of attorney and novation were not objected to on the ground that they were used to circumvent the common law procedural obstacle to assignment of debts. Besides, it is difficult to see how novation can be justified and attornment objected to. Both involve the introduction of the strangers to the original obligation. It is said that novation creates a new contract, but where is the consideration in a novated obligation? If a debt is novated on terms that the same amount remains payable at maturity (which remains the same), and a new creditor is substituted for the old one, where is the benefit to the debtor or the detriment to the new creditor?[64]

Second, the fear of creating a proprietary right surviving the debtor's insolvency is unfounded. Unless the debtor has given security for payment, the party to whom a debt has been attorned has no proprietary

---

[56] *Wharton* v. *Walker* (1825) 4 B. & C. 163 (rent due from tenant); *Walker* v. *Rostron* (1842) 9 M. & W. 411 (price for goods sold); *Hamilton* v. *Spottiswoode* (1849) 4 Exch. 200 (future debts).
[57] (1859) 4 H. & N. 603.
[58] [1954] 1 Q.B. 448.
[59] (1842) 9 M. & W. 411.
[60] (1849) 4 Exch. 200.
[61] (1988) 13 A.C.L.R. 421.
[62] *Hamilton* v. *Spottiswoode* (1849) 4 Exch. 200.
[63] *Law of Restitution* (3rd ed., 1986), pp. 520–521.
[64] *Olsson* v. *Dyson* (1968) 120 C.L.R. 365 at 390.

right enforceable in the debtor's insolvency. So, there is no fear of creating a new category of secured creditors entitled to preferential treatment in the debtor's insolvency. All this is really academic in the context of receivables financing because nothing is gained by framing a security as an attornment rather than an assignment, except that the security is an oral legal mortgage and so incapable of being overreached by a subsequent legal assignee. Like any other security interest over receivables, security by attornment is registrable as a charge.

Reservation of title to proceeds of sale

5.5 A reservation of title clause in a sale, hire-purchase, or rental agreement, is a security device if effective. The problem is with effectiveness. In the present hostile judicial climate, it is difficult to see how such an agreement containing a proceeds clause can ever be effective. The case law is plagued by unnecessary refinements and over-analysis. All this would be welcome if one understood what exactly the courts are doing. My guess is that the courts are looking for the "true" intention of the parties. The statement itself is an admission that their apparent intention would almost certainly be denied legal effect. For the raw deal which has been given to sellers whose sale terms include a reservation of title clause, the courts are wholly to blame. One can only sympathize with the "poor" seller who sits on the horns of a dilemma: the urge to remain competitive requires that trade credit be extended to the buyer; yet the very extension of such credit weakens any argument based on a duty to account for the proceeds of resale or hiring. This, as we shall see, is the assumption in the cases; an assumption very difficult to justify as a matter of principle. It is very hard to see what conceptual difficulty there is in recognising that prior to the authorised disposal by the buyer or hirer, there is, as the credit period shows, a debt relationship but that this is replaced by an accounting obligation immediately upon the disposal. However, it is fair to add that this is usually not the structure of retention of title agreements. The supplier is not usually in the privileged position of a strong financier to exact and enforce provisions requiring the buyer to pay in the proceeds of resale into a special account. Nor is his security advanced by labelling the relationship as financing; active and expensive policing are absolutely essential. A perusal of the clause in *Tatung (UK) Ltd.* v. *Galex Telesure Ltd.*[65] shows the extent of judicial hostility to retention of title agreements. If the clause in that case failed, as it did, one is compelled to conclude that "proceeds" clauses will inevitably be characterized as unregistered charges. If the concern is publicity, a simple solution is to insist on registration.[66] The problem has not attracted the attention of the legal reformer. In the meantime, the clauses have been subjected to the most minute of scrutinies, and not surprisingly, they have not emerged unscathed. There is an alarming failure by the courts to recognise that retention of title agreements are a species of purchase-money security. If

---

[65] (1989) 5 B.C.C. 325.
[66] See S. Wheeler [1987] J.B.L. 180.

hire-purchase agreements and Quistclose trusts are upheld despite their obvious security function, it is not easy to justify the present judicial hostility to retention of title agreements. It is not without significance that purchase-money considerations underlie the pragmatic approach of the House of Lords in *Abbey National Building Society* v. *Cann,*[67] where it was held that in a bank financed acquisition of land, the acquisition of the legal estate and the grant of a legal charge were one indivisible transaction, at any rate where there is prior agreement to grant the charge. Therefore, the purchaser never acquires anything more than an equity of redemption; there can be no *scintilla temporis* between the acquisition of the legal estate and the grant of a legal charge. With these observations, we shall now return to the law. The discussion is limited to proceeds. Two examples of clauses in use are:

" . . . the Customer shall be at liberty to sell the goods in the ordinary course of business on the basis that the proceeds of sale are the property of and held on trust for the Company."[68]
" . . . the proceeds of resale or other dealing shall in any period preceding the payment of the full price as aforesaid be held by the buyer in a separate account as trustee there for the Company."[69]

Both clauses are models of clarity. But to be upheld, it is necessary to show that this reflects truly the intention of the parties. The focus of the debate on the efficacy of "proceeds" clauses is whether the proceeds clause is an ancillary security by which the seller perfects his title to that which in equity already belonged to him, that is to say, the goods, or a substantive assignment of receivables, the legal title to which has already vested in the buyer. If it is the former, the clause is valid and effective and not open to attack as an unregistered charge,[70] although it is liable to be defeated by a bona fide purchaser of the legal title to the receivables without notice.[71] If the latter, the clause is a charge and to be valid, it must be registered as such.[72] It is now no longer disputed that where the proceeds relate to mixed or manufactured goods incorporating other goods, the clause takes effect as a charge, which must, to be valid against other claimants, be registered.[73] The difficulty is with unmixed goods. Here, the result of the cases is that to be effective, the seller must show there is in law and fact, an accounting obligation imposed by the sale terms on the buyer. For this purpose, an ordinary retention of title

---

[67] [1990] 2 W.L.R. 832.
[68] Taken from a sample by Julie Spencer [1989] J.B.L. 220 at 228.
[69] The clause in *Tatung (UK) Ltd.* v. *Galex Telesure Ltd.* (1989) 5 B.C.C. 325 at 328.
[70] *Aluminium Industrie Vaassen BV* v. *Romalpa Aluminium Ltd.* [1976] 1 W.L.R. 676; *Len Vidgen Ski & Leisure Ltd.* v. *Timaru Marine Supplies (1982) Ltd.* (1985) 11 Recent Law (NS) 416 (New Zealand).
[71] For a full discussion, see *post*, para. 6.8.
[72] *Re Bond Worth Ltd.* [1980] Ch. 228; *Pfeiffer GmbH* v. *Arbuthnot Factors Ltd.* [1988] 1 W.L.R. 150; *Tatung (UK) Ltd.* v. *Galex Telesure Ltd.* (1989) 5 B.C.C. 325.
[73] *Borden (UK) Ltd.* v. *Scottish Timber Products Ltd.* [1981] Ch. 25 at 45. This result flows from the fact that a reservation of title in mixed goods will almost always be treated as a charge: *Clough Mill Ltd.* v. *Martin* [1985] 1 W.L.R. 111 at 120, 124 and 125; *Re Peachdart Ltd.* [1984] Ch. 131; *Specialist Plant Services Ltd.* v. *Braithwaite Ltd.* (1987) 3 B.C.C. 119.

agreement does not, without more, impose an accounting obligation.[74] No implication of duty to account will be read into the contract as such a term is not necessary to give the contract business efficacy.[75] A declaration that the buyer is a bailee of the goods is, on its own, insufficient to impose an accounting obligation on the seller because not all bailees are fiduciaries.[76] The fact that the sale was on credit is not without significance. If the buyer can deal with the goods as he pleases and sell them at any price and on such terms as he may choose, it is difficult to see how he can be a fiduciary. In *Tatung (UK) Ltd.* v. *Galex Telesure Ltd.*,[77] the seller sought to overcome this difficulty by inserting a provision that "notwithstanding any agreed terms of payment, the goods are not sold or delivered on credit but on condition that the ownership of the goods remains with the company" until payment of the full price. It was held that this transparent subterfuge was unavailing. The case is interesting partly because Phillips J. virtually "overruled" *Romalpa case*,[78] and partly because the provision that the buyers were fiduciaries was held to exclude equitable tracing, leaving the seller to stand or fall with his contractual tracing right.

Another difficulty in the path of a successful proceeds claim is the defeasibility of the claim upon payment of the purchase price. The root of the difficulty is the dictum of Slade J. in *Re Bond Worth Ltd.*,[79] that any contract which, by way of security for the payment of a debt, confers an interest in property, defeasible upon performance of the obligation is a mortgage or charge. This, of course, is question begging because the whole question is whether title is conferred rather than retained.[80] If title to proceeds is retained rather than conferred, is a registrable charge thereby created? The analysis in *Clough Mill Ltd.* v. *Martin*,[81] would suggest a negative answer. The relevance of this question is in relation to the definition of a charge in the amended Part XII of the Companies Act 1985. Under the new law a charge is any form of security interest over property.[82] It would seem not to matter whether the security is retained or conferred. That the claim is designed to give security is not enough to make it a registrable charge. But where title is retained *until* payment for the goods, the retention contains a built-in temporal and quantitative

---

[74] *Hendy Lennox (Industrial Engines) Ltd.* v. *Grahame Puttick Ltd.* [1984] 1 W.L.R. 485; *Re Andrabell Ltd.* [1984] 3 All E.R. 407; *Re Country Stores Pty. Ltd.* (1987) 11 A.C.L.R. 385 at 395; *Pfeiffer GmbH* v. *Arbuthnot Factors Ltd.* [1988] 1 W.L.R. 150; *Tatung (UK) Ltd.* v. *Galex Telesure Ltd.* (1989) 5 B.C.C. 325; *cf. Aluminium Industrie Vaassen BV* v. *Romalpa Aluminium Ltd.* [1976] 1 W.L.R. 676; *Len Vidgen Ski & Leisure Ltd.* v. *Timaru Marine Supplied (1982) Ltd.* (1985) 11 Recent Law (NS) 416 (New Zealand).
[75] *Ibid.*
[76] *Henry* v. *Hammond* [1913] 2 K.B. 515; *Hendy Lennox (Indusrial Engines) Ltd.* v. *Grahame Puttick Ltd.* [1984] 1 W.L.R. 485 at 497–499; *Re Andrabell Ltd.* [1984] 3 All E.R. 407 at 412–416; *Re Country Stores Pty. Ltd.* (1987) 11 A.C.L.R. 385 at 396.
[77] (1989) 5 B.C.C. 325.
[78] [1976] 1 W.L.R. 676.
[79] [1980] Ch. 228 at 248.
[80] A point forcefully made in *Clough Mill Ltd.* v. *Martin* [1985] 1 W.L.R. 111 at 123, 124 and 125; *John Snow & Co. Ltd.* v. *DBG Woodcroft* [1985] B.C.L.C. 54 at 63.
[81] [1985] 1 W.L.R. 111.
[82] Companies Act 1985, s.395(2).

limitation on the seller's interest. Even if such an interest is described as absolute title, effect cannot be given to it because the title is absolute only to the extent of the unpaid balance of the purchase price, nor does it survive such payment. If this be correct, it would be idle to scrutinize the clause to see whether the interest was granted rather than retained. The result would be a registrable security. It is to be noted also that the concession in *Romalpa case*[83] that the buyers were bailees has now become legendary. In no subsequent case where Romalpa was distinguished was this not considered critical. It seems that despite the liberal approach indicated by the Court of Appeal in *Clough Mill Ltd.* v. *Martin*,[84] trial courts have refused to be sympathetic towards the retention of title seller. The courts have made heavy weather of the requirement of fiduciary as a prerequisite of tracing. In doing so they seem to have forgotten that the fiduciary principle is not a monolithic concept. It is a simple pragmatic concept which could be associated with undertakings arising from contract.[85] Also it is now widely accepted that the requirement of fiduciary relationship in the context of tracing is itself an historical error.[86] The courts could not have limited it to trust and trust-like situations, if the recipient of money paid under a mistake of fact is a fiduciary.[87] Nor would it have been easy to raise a fiduciary relationship from the fact that money has been paid for a consideration which has wholly failed.[88] Yet both are instances of situations where the courts have in the past refused to be hamstrung by the fiduciary principle if the claim to trace was otherwise meritorious. There is no reason of legal theory or policy why the same reasoning should not be applied in tracing claims by retention of title sellers. Such an approach would be consistent with the theory that the existence of a fiduciary relationship is a consequence rather than a pre-requisite of tracing.[89]

As the law now stands, the seller aiming to follow the proceeds of resale or other dealing with unpaid goods supplied by him may try one of three devices. First, he may seek to vest legal title to proceeds in himself. This can be achieved if the buyer resells or deals with the goods as an agent of the seller.[90] This device is of doubtful efficacy and at any rate implausible. It is in neither party's interest to have the buyer resell as a true agent of the seller. From the buyer's point of view, it is a cession of substantial control over his business to the seller. Also, it does not account for the profit expected by the buyer. For the seller, the prospect of liability in contract and possibly tort (as a principal) is unattractive. The second solution is to declare a trust of the proceeds. This must be accompanied by sufficient policing of the proceeds in order to deprive the

---

[83] [1976] 1 W.L.R. 676 at 680.
[84] See n. 81, *supra*.
[85] See Gautreau (1989) 68 Can BR 1.
[86] Oakley (1975) 28 *Current Legal Problems* 64; Pearce (1976) 40 Conv. 277; Goff and Jones, *Law of Restitution* (3rd ed., 1986), pp. 71–72.
[87] *Chase Manhattan Bank NA* v. *Israel-British Bank (London) Ltd.* [1981] Ch. 105.
[88] *Sinclair* v. *Brougham* [1914] A.C. 398; *Neste Oy* v. *Lloyd's Bank plc* [1983] 2 Lloyd's Rep. 658.
[89] *Agip (Africa) Ltd.* v. *Jackson* [1989] 3 W.L.R. 1367 at 1386.
[90] *Benjamin's Sale of Goods* (3rd ed.), para. 386, p. 239.

buyer of management autonomy over the receivables. The policing may also indicate that the buyer is a true fiduciary. Otherwise a declaration of trust, without more, is likely to be disregarded as not representing the parties' intention.[91] There are other difficulties with the trust device. First, it deprives the buyer of essential cash flow and it is open to doubt whether the trust also covers the buyer's profit. Secondly, where there is a credit period, it is difficult to sustain a trust. The concern is not that a debt and a trust cannot co-exist in the same relationship[92]; it is that if the goods are resold during the credit period, the trust cannot take effect because the debt relationship is still on foot and both cannot co-exist at the same time. This difficulty can, of course, be avoided if the contract provides for termination of the credit period upon a disposal of the goods and for a trust to arise *eo instanti*. Such a provision will be resisted by many buyers, for it makes the credit illusory. If it is inserted simply to avoid the difficulty under discussion and is not enforced, the courts are likely to disregard it as an unavailing sham. If the trust arises afterwards, two problems arise. The first is that since some part of the purchase price would have been paid, the seller's interest in the proceeds held on trust is limited to the amount necessary to discharge the debt owed to him. This is unquestionably a registrable security interest. The second problem is that if the goods are resold on credit the subject-matter of the trust may be no more than the obligation of the buyer to the seller. In that case, *Re Charge Card Services Ltd.*[93] requires that we ask whether the buyer could sensibly be said to hold his own obligation on trust.[94] But if we treat the sub-buyer's debt as the subject-matter of the trust, this difficulty disappears. A third solution is to declare a trust of only a part of the proceeds equivalent to the unpaid amount owed to the seller.[95] Apart from the problem of identifying the part of the proceeds appropriated to the trust,[96] there is also the difficulty of establishing a truly fiduciary relationship.

The handwriting is on the wall for retention of title sellers. English trial courts are reluctant to recognise this type of purchase-money security, superior to the charge in that it is immune from the requirement of registration. For all this, one must sympathize with the sellers. The only effective solution is to register the agreement as a charge—this will injure the credit of the buyer and where he retains management autonomy over the resulting receivables, the security is a floating charge with all its disadvantages.

Charge and mortgage

5.6   Security over receivables normally takes the form of a charge simpliciter, or a mortgage. Occasionally, one encounters documents of security

---

[91] *Cf. Tatung (UK) Ltd.* v. *Galex Telesure Ltd.* (1989) 5 B.C.C. 325, where there was a declaration of trust though there was no evidence that it was enforced.
[92] *Barclays Bank Ltd.* v. *Quistclose Investments Ltd.* [1970] A.C. 576 and *Re EVTR Ltd.* [1987] B.C.L.C. 646, show that a debt and a trust relationship can arise out of the same transaction, though not at the same time. *Cf.* Ziegel (1963) 41 Can B.R. 54 at 96, 106.
[93] [1987] Ch. 150.
[94] *Cf.* D. Yates (1977) 41 Conv. 49 at 53.
[95] *Benjamin's Sale of Goods* (3rd ed.), para. 383, p. 237.
[96] *Palmer* v. *Simmonds* (1854) 2 Drew 221 ("bulk" insufficient appropriation of property to a trust).

over receivables purporting to create a first fixed *legal* charge. Conceptually, this is an impossibility. Apart from land mortgages,[97] English law does not recognise a legal charge over personalty. A document expressed as a legal charge creates an equitable security only. As a matter of legal theory, an equitable charge is altogether a different animal from a mortgage. A charge is created when receivables are expressly or constructively made liable, or appropriated to the discharge of a debt or some other obligation.[98] A security given by way of an equitable charge is not one which absolutely transfers the receivables with a condition for reassignment upon redemption, but is a security which only gives the chargee a right of payment out of the fund of receivables appropriated to the security without transferring the fund.[99] But the security is not potential: the chargee has a present right to have it made available even in advance of default.[1] Further, although the chargee gets no legal right of property, absolute or special, or any legal right of possession, he has a right of non-possessory control which is co-extensive with the absence of a right in the chargor to dispose of the receivables without his consent.[2] It is also to be noted that apart from contract, the chargee has no right to foreclose,[3] for he has no estate capable of being made absolute. The remedy of a chargee of receivables is to have it enforced, not by an action against the debtor, but by proceedings against the chargor for an assignment of the receivables.[4] Since the chargee (who has no assignment) cannot proceed directly against the debtor, the question arises whether the debtor's right to set off continues to build-up as if there was no charge. On one view,[5] this is so because there is no change in beneficial ownership of the receivables consequent on the creation of the charge. The better view is that notice of the charge is a cut-off point for purposes of set-off. Upon receipt of notice of the charge, a balance is struck between the chargor and the debtor. Any credits given to the chargor by the debtor after the notice of charge cannot affect the security of the chargee. The charge gives the chargee rights *in rem* against the fund of receivables and though he cannot, in the absence of a contract to that effect, take possession, the debtor cannot deplete the fund by post-notice credits given to the chargor. This is consistent with the result of the cases where set-off was denied in respect of credits given to a company in receivership after the floating charge had crystallized.[6] The reasoning in

---

[97] Law of Property Act 1925, s.87.
[98] *Rodick* v. *Gandell* (1852) 1 De G.M. & G. 763 at 777; *Palmer* v. *Carey* [1926] A.C. 703 at 706–707; *Swiss Bank Corp.* v. *Lloyds Bank Ltd.* [1982] A.C. 584 at 595.
[99] *Tancred* v. *Delagoa Bay & East Africa Ry. Co.* (1889) 23 Q.B.D. 239 at 242.
[1] *National Provincial & Union Bank of England* v. *Charnley* [1924] 1 K.B. 431 at 449.
[2] *Ibid.*
[3] *Tennant* v. *Trenchard* (1869) L.R. 4 Ch.App. 537, but the chargee cannot be compelled to take a mortgage instead of enforcing a sale: *Matthews* v. *Goodday* (1861) 31 L.J.Ch. 282 at 283.
[4] *Burlinson* v. *Hall* (1884) 12 Q.B.D. 347 at 350.
[5] R. M. Goode [1984] J.B.L. 172 at 174.
[6] *Rendell* v. *Doors & Doors Ltd.* [1975] 2 N.Z.L.R. 191; *Leichhardt Emporium Pty. Ltd.* v. *AGC (Household Finance) Ltd.* [1979] 1 N.S.W.L.R. 701. For a more detailed discussion, see para. 8.5, *infra.*

those cases was that a charge creates a partial assignment which is made complete upon crystallization.[7]

The reasoning is important because it shows not only the artificiality inherent in distinguishing a charge from a mortgage created by an assignment, but also, the difficulty of locating precisely where the distinction lies.[8] By definition a mortgage of receivables is an assignment with a proviso for reassignment upon redemption.[9] There need not in fact be such a proviso because once the character of the assignment as a security is established, equity implies an equity of redemption[10] to show that although the security of the mortgagee is title to the receivables, that title is nonetheless limited to the amount necessary to discharge the debt or other obligation for which the assignment was made. However, as a matter of contract, the chargee is usually given the power to execute a legal assignment as attorney of the chargor and to appoint a receiver. These powers diminish to vanishing point, any remaining distinction between a charge and a mortgage.

Cross-over security over receivables[11]

5.7 The problem to be discussed is a fixed charge over existing and future receivables, taken as a continuing security for all amounts owing or which may become owing, but without imposing any corresponding obligation on the bank to make further advances. The commercial background of such a security is clear enough: the lender takes a charge which in economic but not legal terms, is a hybrid incorporating all the advantages of a floating charge with none of the statutory limitations on its operation.[12] The borrower continues to use the proceeds of the receivables (in an indirect way) in the course of its business to its own benefit, and to the benefit of the lender who continues to earn interest on the loan in the comfortable knowledge that if his prospects of ultimate repayment appear in peril, he can at any time enforce his security.[13] It is difficult to see what policy objections can be raised to this form of security.[14] If a

---

[7] *Biggerstaff* v. *Rowatt's Wharf Ltd.* [1896] 2 Ch. 93 at 106; *N.W. Robbie & Co. Ltd.* v. *Witney Warehouse Co. Ltd.* [1963] 1 W.L.R. 1324 at 1333, 1338.

[8] *London County & Westminster Bank Ltd.* v. *Tompkins* [1918] 1 K.B. 515 at 526.

[9] *Tancred* v. *Delagoa Bay & East Africa Ry. Co.* (1893) 23 Q.B.D. 239.

[10] *Durham Brothers* v. *Robertson* [1898] 1 Q.B. 765 at 772.

[11] For a sample of early and current literature, see Brealy [1985] L.M.C.L.Q. 409; Pennington (1985) 6 Co.Law. 9; Pearce [1987] J.B.L. 18; McCormack (1987) 8 Co.Law. 3.

[12] Floating charges are subject to various statutory limitations. First, preferential debts have to be paid out of assets subject to a floating charge: Insolvency Act 1986, ss.40 and 175. Second, floating charges are invalid if created within 12 months of the onset of insolvent liquidation: Insolvency Act 1986, s.245. Third, an administrator can dispose of, or otherwise deal with, assets subject to a floating charge as if the charge did not exist: Insolvency Act 1986, s.15(1) and (3).

[13] See, *Re Keenan Brothers Ltd.* [1985] I.R. 401 at 415.

[14] *Cf. Insolvency Law and Practice: Report of the Review Committee,* Cmnd. 8558, (1982) para. 1586. The recommendation of a statutory reversal of the decision in *Seibe Gorman & Co. Ltd.* v. *Barclays Bank Ltd.* [1979] 2 Lloyd's Rep. 142, was not implemented. See also, Pennington (1985) 6 Co.Law. 9 at 21.

corporate borrower is driven to such financial straits that it is prepared to effect an immediate charge on all receivables which it may ever own, the existence of which is published to the commercial and financial world, an elaborate machinery set up to enable the borrower to benefit by collection of the receivables cannot turn the security into a floating charge, if it is otherwise specific in a theoretical and practical sense.

The efficacy of a cross-over specific security on receivables was first recognised in this country in *Siebe Gorman & Co. Ltd.* v. *Barclays Bank Ltd.*[15] and shows how flexibly equitable principles have been adapted to commercial transactions. In that case, a company created a debenture secured by a first fixed charge on all its present and future receivables. During the continuance of the security, the company was to pay into its current account with the bank, proceeds of the receivables, and was not free to create any additional incumbrances on the receivables without the written consent of the bank. The debenture was silent on the company's right of withdrawals from the account. No notice was given to the debtors. Slade J. held that the security was specific rather than floating. It was implied that even when the account was in credit, the company could not make withdrawals without the bank's consent, and he could see no objection in principle to a fixed charge over present and future receivables. The case has been followed,[16] and distinguished.[17] In principle, there is no difficulty with such a security, and the fact that the company is allowed to continue to trade and to use (by an indirect means) the proceeds of the receivables in so doing, poses no conceptual difficulty. However, in *Hart* v. *Barnes*,[18] Anderson J. said:

> "While the business of the company was a going concern, the aggregate of funds representative of the company's book debts would probably fluctuate between extremes. It is for this reason that, in my opinion, it was not open to the company to create the 'fixed and specific charge' in respect of the company's book debts, each book debt (or many of them) being an evanescent entity to which nothing could attach until the appointment of a receiver."

This statement expresses a doctrinal objection to the possibility of having a fixed charge over an "evanescent entity" represented by existing and future receivables. Such a fluctuating entity is assumed to be insusceptible of a specific security. It is difficult to agree with Anderson J. A charge is not specific because its subject-matter is fixed. The interest of a partner in a firm is a fluctuating entity, the precise content of which is unascertainable prior to dissolution of the firm. Yet it has never been doubted that it is a proper subject-matter for a specific security.[19] On the other hand, a floating charge can be taken over specific property, for example, land.[20]

---

[15] [1979] 2 Lloyd's Rep. 142.
[16] *Re Keenan Brothers Ltd.* [1985] I.R. 401; *Re Permanent Houses (Holdings) Ltd.* [1988] B.C.L.C. 563; *Ex p. Copp* [1989] B.C.L.C. 13.
[17] *Kelly* v. *James McMahon Ltd.* [1980] I.R. 347; *Re Armagh Shoes Ltd.* [1982] N.I. 59; *Re Brightlife Ltd.* [1987] Ch. 200.
[18] (1982) 7 A.C.L.R. 310 at 314.
[19] *United Builders Property Ltd.* v. *Mutual Acceptance Ltd.* (1980) 144 C.L.R. 673 at 688.
[20] *Mercantile Credits Ltd.* v. *Atkins (No. 1)* (1985) 9 A.C.L.R. 757 at 761.

The truth is that the subject-matter has nothing at all to do with the quality of a charge as specific or floating. The confusion arises from the three probanda of a floating charge given by Romer L.J. in *Re Yorkshire Woolcombers Association Ltd.*[21] namely, that it is over a class of assets, present and future; the class is one which, in the ordinary course of business would change from time to time; and the charge contemplates that until some future step is taken to enforce the security, the company is free to use the charged assets in the course of business. Of the three, only the last expresses accurately the true distinction between a fixed and a specific security. The critical inquiry is whether the charge concedes a present management autonomy to the borrower/chargor over the assets subject to the charge, until the chargor's authority is withdrawn. If it does, the charge floats even if expressed as a specific security.

The concept of management autonomy

5.8   It may now be taken as settled law that a charge over present and future receivables could in appropriate circumstances be admitted to the category of specific securities. The focus of modern debate on the efficacy of a cross-over security is on the circumstances in which such a security will be regarded as fixed rather than floating. Labelling a charge as fixed may, when taken with other relevant circumstances, indicate that that truly expresses the intention of the parties. But the fact that a floating charge has been taken over the undertaking of the company, and that nothing more is gained if the charge is not treated as a specific security, is not a circumstance of significance.[22] It must be shown that in law and fact, the chargee, and not the borrower, has management autonomy over the charged receivables. What exactly suffices for this purpose is gradually being worked out by the cases. First, it is inconsistent with the nature of a specific security that the chargor retains the power to dispose of the assets or their proceeds without the consent of the chargee. Otherwise, it would be difficult to say that the assets have been finally and irrevocably appropriated to the security. On the other hand, a specific security is consistent with some form of freedom to deal with the assets covered by the charge.[23] For example, in land mortgages, a mortgagee may be content to allow the mortgagor to create other incumbrances on the property. This has never been held sufficient to convert the security from specific to floating. And even where the authority is exceeded, the question is essentially one of priorities, and does not affect the nature of the first mortgage as a specific or floating security. Why, then, should a different legal régime apply to receivables? It follows from this that the absence of a restriction on the chargor's ability to create other securities over the charged receivables is not such a concession of management autonomy to the borrower as would turn the security into a floating charge. A restriction is a clog on the borrower's equity of redemption, and on its own, insufficient to dispossess the borrower of his dispositive

---

[21] [1903] 2 Ch. 284 at 295, affd. *sub nom. Illingworth* v. *Houldsworth* [1904] A.C. 355.
[22] *Re Armagh Shoes Ltd.* [1982] N.I. 59 at 66.
[23] *Siebe Gorman & Co. Ltd.* v. *Barclays Bank Ltd.* [1979] 2 Lloyd's Rep. 142 at 159.

capacity over the receivables. On the creation of a specific charge, the borrower retains his equity of redemption with which he can deal and pass a good title to junior incumbrancers. The conclusion is that a clog on the chargor's equity of redemption is neither necessary nor sufficient to establish a specific security over existing and future receivables.

Apart from contract, an equitable chargee of receivables has no right to possession. The chargor cannot deal with the receivables, neither can the chargee, in the latter case if the time for enforcement of the security has not arrived. Such an arrangement would virtually paralyse the borrower. To obviate this, charge instruments provide that the borrower shall collect and pay into its account with the chargee, the proceeds of the charged receivables. The proceeds remain within the charge,[24] and it is absolutely necessary that the borrower is not free to withdraw from the account without the consent of the lender, whether or not the account is in credit. If he is free to do so, then, for all the labelling of the document as a fixed charge, only a floating security would have been created,[25] because the borrower would be free unilaterally to release the proceeds from the charge. Such management autonomy does not show a final and irrevocable appropriation of the receivables to the charge, and is inconsistent with a specific security. It is not law that when property which by its nature is required for the borrower's business is charged specifically, a licence to deal with them must be implied.[26] On the contrary, English law does not recognize the concept of a fixed charge over present and future receivables coupled with a licence to collect and use the proceeds in the course of trade. Such a blanket consent is invariably fatal to the existence of a specific security.[27] The objection here is that when one combines a charge on future receivables with the notion of a licence in the debtor unilaterally to release some receivables from the charge under a blanket consent, the resulting amalgam is simply too weak to support the view that there exists a final and irrevocable appropriation essential for the constitution of a specific security.[28] The concept of a fixed charge on property which has as yet no present existence and which can be removed from the scope of the charge by the unilateral act of the borrower, is so chimeric as to deprive the word "fixed" of its ordinary meaning.[29] Where

---

[24] *Barclays Bank plc.* v. *Willowbrook International Ltd.* [1987] 1 F.T.L.R. 386; *cf. Re Keenan Brothers Ltd.* [1095] I.R. 401 at 417.

[25] *Re Armagh Shoes Ltd.* [1982] N.I. 59; *Re Brightlife Ltd.* [1987] Ch. 200.

[26] *National Provincial Bank of England Ltd.* v. *United Electric Theatres Ltd.* [1916] 1 Ch. 132, where an argument to the contrary was advanced and rejected.

[27] *Re Yorkshire Woolcombers Association Ltd.* [1903] 2 Ch. 284 at 289; *Great Lakes Petroleum Co.* v. *Border Cities Oil Ltd.* [1934] 2 D.L.R. 743; *Hart* v. *Barnes* (1982) 7 A.C.L.R. 310; *Waters* v. *Widdows* [1984] V.R. 503; *cf. Evans, Coleman & Evans Ltd.* v. *R.A. Nelson Construction Ltd.* (1958) 16 D.L.R. (2d) 123; *Lettner* v. *Pioneer Truck Equipment Ltd.* (1964) 47 W.W.R. (NS) 343 at 349: "The fact that banking practice in Canada permits the extension of credit and permits the borrower (by licence, as it were) to collect some accounts to pay wages and current creditors does not destroy the fixed nature of the mortgage." English courts have never gone this far, and are unlikely to recognise any such banking practice which permits the borrower under a fixed charge to collect receivables in order to discharge current debts. But see *Re A.H. Masser Ltd.* [1986] I.R. 455.

[28] *R.* v. *FBDB* (1987) 17 B.C.L.R. (2d) 273 at 304.

[29] *Ibid.*

is the finality? Where is the irrevocability? Where, indeed, is the appropriation by the chargee who remains unaware of the charge's demise as he was of its birth? It seems safe to conclude that as English law has not recognised a *tertium quid* between a fixed and floating charge, a specific charge with a licence to deal falls to be treated as a floating security.

In short, whether a purported specific charge over existing and future receivables will be recognised and given effect as such, depends on whether the lender has management autonomy over the charged receivables. Such autonomy must exist in law and fact. In practice the receivables when collected are paid into a special account kept with the lender who releases some of them into the borrower's ordinary account. Once released, the proceeds lie outside the specific charge,[30] although they may well be caught by a floating charge held by the same lender. In *Re Brightlife Ltd.*,[31] although there was a clog on the borrower's equity of redemption and a provision for payment of the proceeds into the borrower's bank account, the charge was held to be a floating security. It was silent on withdrawals, and since the chargee was not the banker of the borrower, there could be no implication that access to the account was restricted, nor was this so in fact. The case shows the difficulty facing non-bank creditors taking a specific security over present and future receivables, but it is not authority for the preposition that such a charge must always be treated as a floating security.[32] Non-bank creditors can establish sufficient management autonomy by opening either in their own names alone, or jointly in the name of the borrower and theirs, a special account. In the former case they would be the only signatories to the account. In the latter they would be joint signatories. In either case the creditor retains effective control over the fund representing the proceeds of the receivables and this is enough to show that the security is specific rather than floating.

It remains to consider the relevance of subsequent conduct and the absence of notice to the account debtors on the existence of a fixed charge over existing and future receivables. To begin with the latter, it is settled law that an assignment is complete between the assignor and assignee without notice to the debtor.[33] If this be so, why should notice to account debtors be considered relevant to the constitution of a specific security over receivables? One answer is that if the debtors are allowed to build up contra accounts against the borrower, there is no final and irrevocable appropriation of the receivables to the charge[34] because the resulting set-off diminishes the fund. This may be so, but it is a misundertstanding of the concept of appropriation to conclude that the set-off makes appropriation revocable. The availability of set-off affects neither the finality nor the irrevocability of an appropriation. Besides,

---

[30] *Re Permanent Houses (Holdings) Ltd.* [1988] B.C.L.C. 563 at 567.
[31] [1987] Ch. 200.
[32] *Cf.* Hanson [1987] L.M.C.L.Q. 147 at 150.
[33] *Gorringe* v. *Irwell India Rubber Works* (1886) 34 Ch.D. 128; *Re City Life Assurance Co. Ltd.* [1926] Ch. 191 at 215, 220.
[34] A similar argument was rejected in *Seibe Gorman & Co. Ltd.* v. *Barclays Bank Ltd.* [1979] 2 Lloyd's Rep. 142 at 159, and *Re Keenan Brothers Ltd.* [1985] I.R. 401 at 425.

even where notice is given to the debtors, such notice cannot affect their accrued rights of set-off. Nor can it affect rights arising from future equities which are inseparably connected with the debt charged and mature out of obligations incurred prior to notice.[35] Indeed, it is possible to say that apart from legal and contractual set-off, the right to set-off in equity is an integral art of the debtor's obligation to pay.[36] Thus we could say that a debtor who has a set-off for defective performance by the creditor, is liable to pay, not the gross contract price, but a net amount after deducting his contra account. In such cases it is proper to say that what vests in the chargee as receivables is not the gross contract price but the debtor's net liability.[37] The receivables arise and vest in the chargee burdened with the debtor's right to set off in equity, on a reasoning similar to that which commended itself to the Court of Appeal in *Re Connolly Brothers Ltd. (No. 2)*.[38]

The relevance of subsequent conduct is more problematic. When, for example, it is said that the evidence shows that the borrower collected and used charged receivables, is that fact alone sufficient to show that the parties intended a floating security only? Much of the practical steps taken by a lender holding a specific security over existing and future receivables to establish management autonomy are usually conduct subsequent to the charge. Are such actions of any probative value? The cases seem to place some weight on such monitoring and policing of receivables, but it is doubtful whether they can be taken as indicating that conduct subsequent to the creation of the charge is admissible in proof of the parties' intention. Just as with negotiations prior to the creation of the charge,[39] it is impermissible to construe a charge by reference to what the parties did after it was created, unless the subsequent conduct is relied upon as evidence of a variation of the charge, or to found an estoppel.[40] The objection to the admission of such evidence is that subsequent conduct is equally referable to what the parties meant to say as to the meaning of what they did say. Besides, the admission of subsequent conduct might imperil third parties since they can no longer rely on the charge as an exhaustive statement of the bargain between chargor and chargee. Nothing would conduce more to uncertainty of commercial transactions if it were open to the courts to admit this species of evidence, for that would lead to the result that an agreement means one thing today and quite another a week or month later. It is therefore suggested that in construing charge documents purporting to create a specific security over existing and future receivables, the courts must limit their inquiries to what the parties contemplated at the time of the charge, unless it is alleged that the parties have by subsequent conduct varied the charge or

---

[35] *Government of Newfoundland* v. *Newfoundland Ry. Co.* (1888) 13 App.Cas. 199.
[36] *Federal Commerce & Navigation Co. Ltd.* v. *Molena Alpha Inc. (The Nanfri)* [1978] Q.B. 927 at 974; *BICC plc.* v. *Burndy* [1985] Ch. 232 at 248–250. *Cf.* Goode, *Legal Problems of Credit and Security* (2nd ed., 1988), pp. 138 *et seq.*
[37] *Rother Iron Works Ltd.* v. *Canterbury Precision Engineers Ltd.* [1974] Q.B. 1 at 6.
[38] [1912] 2 Ch. 25.
[39] *Prenn* v. *Simonds* [1971] 1 W.L.R. 1381.
[40] *Whitworth Estates Ltd.* v. *Miller* [1970] A.C. 583; *F.L. Schuler AG* v. *Wickman Machine Tool Sales Ltd.* [1974] A.C. 235 at 261, 268–269, 272.

waived a right arising thereunder. This is not to say that a charge is fixed because the parties label the document as such.[41]

Management autonomy and wrongful trading

5.9   The concept of a fixed charge over existing and future receivables has greatly enhanced the security of lenders. When applied to current assets financing no better security could be contemplated. The borrowing is self-liquidating as receivables are collected and paid into the borrower's account. By extending to future receivables, the lender sits on a gold mine. The security, which must of necessity be equitable only, is self-executing as soon as the debts come into existence.[42] The borrower receives them as a constructive trustee for the lender whose tracing remedy, in case of misappropriation, is unimpaired.[43] The security is reinforced by appropriate covenants exacted from the borrower. In theory such covenants could affect every aspect of corporate activity. If enforced, they could, when taken with the steps necessary to police and monitor the charged receivables, impinge heavily on the borrower's corporate activities, and on occasion, impair its efficiency. The concern here is, however, not efficiency. It is that when the borrower is in desperate financial straits, the amount of control ceded to the lender may qualify the lender as a shadow director with potential liability for wrongful trading. A person is guilty of wrongful trading if[44]:

(a) the company has gone into insolvent liquidation; and

(b) at some time before the commencement of winding up of the company, he knew or ought reasonably to have concluded that there was no reasonable prospect that the company would avoid going into insolvent liquidation; and

(c) he was a director of the company at that time.

It will be assumed for the purpose of this discussion that requirements (a) and (b) have been established, the only question being whether the lender was a director at the relevant time. Director includes a shadow director.[45] A person is a shadow director if he is a person in accordance

---

[41] In Canada, labelling is all-important provided the charge does not contain any modifier: see *Lettner* v. *Pioneer Truck Equipment Ltd.* (1964) 47 W.W.R. (NS) 345; *Re Westmorland Home Insulators Ltd.* (1981) 35 N.B.R. (2d) 386; *Bank of Nova Scotia* v. *Scott* (1985) 67 B.C.L.R. 143, and compare *Great Lakes Petroleum Co.* v. *Border Cities Oil Ltd.* [1934] 2 D.L.R. 743, *R.* v. *Lega Fabricating Ltd.* (1981) 29 B.C.L.R. 161 where the charge documents contained words modifying the chargee's right to collect charged receivables before default in payment of the secured amount and were held to be floating rather than fixed charges.

[42] *Holroyd* v. *Marshall* (1862) 10 H.L.Cas. 191; *Tailby* v. *Official Receiver* (1888) 13 App.Cas. 523; *Re Lind* [1915] 2 Ch. 345 criticized by Mathews [1981] L.M.C.L.Q. 40; *Re Gillott's Settlement* [1934] Ch. 97 at 109; *Palette Shoes Pty. Ltd.* v. *Krohn* (1937) 58 C.L.R. 1; *Booth* v. *FCT* (1988) 76 A.L.R. 375 at 377.

[43] *International Factors Ltd.* v. *Rodriguez* [1979] Q.B. 351; *Barclays Bank plc.* v. *Willowbrook International Ltd.* [1987] 1 F.T.L.R. 386.

[44] Insolvency Act 1986, s.214(2).

[45] *Ibid.* s.214(7).

with whose directions or instructions the directors of the company are accustomed to act.[46] Clearly, this definition excludes most lenders but, exceptionally, a lender may become a shadow director. Whether or not this occurs depends upon the degree of control, direct or indirect, exercised by the lender over the day to day management of the borrower's corporate activities. What degree of control suffices for this purpose, cannot be precisely or exhaustively stated. One thing is clear: a substantial degree of control over corporate activities can be achieved by loan covenants.[47] The danger of substantial interference is more acute with fixed security over receivables. It is arguable that in the present state of the law, the degree of control and monitoring of receivables necessary to establish the requisite management autonomy, comes very close to establishing the threshold of unacceptable interference with the borrower's corporate activities. To police its security is one thing, to instruct desperate directors on the conduct of the company's business, quite another.

It is worth noting that in *Ex p. Copp*,[48] a bank's application to strike out a liquidator's claim against it for wrongful trading failed. Knox J. refused to strike out the claim because on the material available, ignoring the possibility of further evidence at the trial, the liquidator's claim for wrongful trading was not *obviously* unsustainable. However, the refusal did not carry with it any prognostication that the liquidator's claim will succeed at the trial. Be that as it may, the case is some support for the view that the possibility of holding a bank liable for wrongful trading is not so clearly untenable, and banks will do well to reduce their control over, and interference with, the affairs of financially troubled companies.

Security over cash deposit[49]

The question whether a creditor can take an effective real security over **5.10** funds deposited with him is one which is much discussed but which has produced little unanimity among commentators. All are, however, agreed that such a security, if at all possible, cannot be by way of an assignment. An assignment of the deposit as security for an advance operates as a partial or total release of the amount on deposit.[50] This is not conceptually pure because it fails, first, to account for the fact that for there to be a release, the obligations must be held in the same right, and here one arises from a deposit, whilst the other, from an advance. It may be that

---

[46] *Ibid.*, s.251.
[47] See Douglas-Hamilton, "*Creditor liabilities resulting from improper interference with the management of a financially troubled debtor*" 31 Business Law 343 (1975).
[48] [1989] B.C.L.C. 13. At the trial, the liquidator abandoned his claim for wrongful trading because it emerged during cross-examination that although the bank had indeed instructed the directors on the conduct of the company's business, the instructions were in fact ignored. It was therefore impossible to say that the directors were accustomed to act in accordance with the bank's instructions: see *Re M.C. Bacon Ltd.* (1990) B.C.C. 78.
[49] See generally, Pollard [1988] J.B.L. 138, 219.
[50] *Broad v. Commissioner of Stamp Duties (NSW)* [1980] 2 N.S.W.L.R. 40 at 46; *Re Charge Card Services Ltd.* [1987] Ch. 150 at 175, 176.

the requirement of "same right" means no more than the idea that the obligations are owed in the same capacity, that is to say, in their respective private capacities and not as agent of, or trustee for, someone else. Secondly, the concept of release does not account for the depositor's equity of redemption since the assignment is by way of security rather than a sale. The charge overcomes the problem of release because nothing is assigned; the chargee gets only a right of non-possessory control over the deposit, and is entitled to look to it for repayment of the advance. In *Re Charge Card Services Ltd.*,[51] it was held that a creditor cannot take a charge over an obligation owed by himself. The objection to a charge in this situation is the result. A creditor cannot himself take such a security because a debt is a chose in action—a right to sue; he cannot enforce his security by an action against himself. This may indeed be so, but the question remains, why should the peculiarity of the method available to a creditor to enforce a charge over the amount held by him on deposit affect the question whether such a security is conceptually possible? The answer given is the same circular argument that the creditor cannot sue himself.

This assumed conceptual impossibility is sound or weak depending on the vantage point from which it is viewed. Viewed as an item of property, the debt can be charged to the depositee as security because even if it is accepted that as between depositor and depositee there is only an obligation, this obligation could very well be the subject of property rights in favour of the debtor; once the depositee wears the hat of a chargee, the depositor's right to the deposit becomes a right of property held as security. But seen primarily through the remedy available for the enforcement of the charge, the conceptual impossibility comes into sharp focus. Goode's[52] objection to such a charge is partly that s.136 of the Law of Property Act 1925, contemplates three parties, which is not possible in this situation. Even assuming this to be so, it does not follow that the depositee cannot take a charge on the deposit. For one thing, the charge does not come within the provision, and no one suggests that the statute has in any way impaired the efficacy of equitable charges[53]; for another, it is not unknown for trustees to take an assignment from their beneficiaries. Although the notion that trustees could give notice to themselves seems bizarre, that did not pose any conceptual difficulty. Why should the present situation be treated differently? Such a notice goes, not to the constitution of the security, but to its priority.

It is to be noted also that there are cases in which debtors have been held trustees of the debt owed by them.[54] Nobody was bothered by the conceptual difficulty which perplexed Millett J. in *Re Charge Card Services Ltd.*[55] Moreover, it is not uncommon for insurance companies to take a charge over policies issued by them. On the contrary, such

---

[51] [1987] Ch. 150 at 175, 176.
[52] R. M. Goode, *Legal Problems of Credit and Security* (2nd ed., 1988), p. 125.
[53] *William Brandt's Sons & Co.* v. *Dunlop Rubber Co.* [1905] A.C. 454 at 461. Australian courts may take a different view: *Ollson* v. *Dyson* (1970) 120 C.L.R. 365.
[54] *Moore* v. *Darton* (1815) 14 De G. & Sm. 571; *Paterson* v. *Murphy* (1868) 38 L.J.Ch. 46.
[55] [1987] Ch. 150 at 175–176.

securities are commonplace. Are we to assume that the courts which enforced such securities did not know that insurance policies are conditional debts, or innominate choses in action, payable on the happening of the insured event? Considerations of this nature suggest that the question whether this type of security can be taken by the debtor himself is very much an open one. It is not satisfactory that the peculiarity of the method of enforcing such a security should make its existence a legal impossibility. It may be that the question cannot be answered as a matter of cut and dried law. After all, in the final analysis what interest is sufficient to support a real security is a matter of legal policy. There does not seem to be any policy objection to this form of security. *Ex p. Mackay*,[56] should be considered a strong authority on the conceptual possibility of such a security because the argument that a debtor cannot have a charge on royalties due from him was advanced and rejected.

It has also been suggested[57] that where a person gives his bank a fixed charge over his receivables and undertakes to pay, and later pays the collections into an account controlled by the bank, the bank becomes a debtor of the chargor, and the "charge" asserted by the bank over the proceeds so paid in, becomes in reality a contractual set-off. The suggestion has a prima facie appeal, but cannot be accepted as law. It is true that the ordinary banker and customer relationship creates a debt, but it by no means follows that every business relationship entered into between a banker and his customer creates a debt. Indeed, proceeds of receivables paid into a bank account are held on trust, first, to discharge the amount advanced, and secondly, to give the surplus to junior incumbrancers having a claim on the proceeds.[58] It is naked red herring to suggest that the *Charge Card* analysis can be usefully adapted to this financing relationship. If the suggestion was sound, it would follow that where the security over receivables is taken to secure an advance to a third party and the assignor becomes insolvent, the bank must return the proceeds intact to the assignor's liquidator, deprived of insolvency set-off for want of mutuality. There are good reasons for believing that this is not the law.

A related problem is whether a bank can take a pledge of a negotiable paper covering deposits which it has issued. There is here no conceptual difficulty because the paper has an existence separate and distinct from the debt obligation it embodies. There is no reported authority for the view that if a bank holds a negotiable paper which it has issued prior to its maturity, the currency of the paper is thereby affected.[59] Nor can the depositor confer superior rights on third parties as regards the amount on

---

[56] (1872) L.R. 9 Ch.App. 127, better reported in (1872) No. 42 L.J.Bkcy 68.

[57] R. M. Goode, *Legal Problems of Credit and Security* (2nd ed., 1988), p. 129.

[58] *Ex p. Caldicott, re Hart* (1884) 25 Ch.D. 716. There is nothing in *Space Investments Ltd. v. Canadian Imperial Bank of Commerce Trust Co. (Bahamas) Ltd.* [1986] 1 W.L.R. 1072 to the contrary. There, the Privy Council held that where a bank trustee lawfully deposits trust money with itself as banker pursuant to express authority in that behalf, the beneficiaries have no proprietary interest in the assets of the bank, but are, like other depositors, ordinary unsecured creditors so that in the liquidation of the bank their claims ranked *pari passu* with those of the bank's customers and other unsecured creditors.

[59] *Cf.* Bills of Exchange Act 1882, s.61, and compare Goode, *op. cit.*, pp. 129–130.

deposit while the bank retains possession of the negotiable paper. Its currency is not affected, nor is its effect suspended or held in abeyance.

In practice, security over cash deposits can be effectively taken by a document making the repayment of the debt conditional (flawed asset), prohibiting assignment or other dealing with the amount on deposit,[60] and giving the bank extensive rights of set-off. This will be just as good as a charge if the obligation secured is that of the depositor. The fact that it is contingent is not of moment.[61] Where the obligation is that of a third party any problems envisaged on account of want of mutuality in the depositor's insolvency, can be overcome by taking a guarantee from the depositor, so that the funds on deposit serve as security for the depositor's contingent liability on the guarantee. This is done daily in relation to performance bonds and standby letters of credit.[62] Alternatively the funds could be deposited with a third party followed by an assignment of the debt thereby created to the financing bank.

Forms and effect of mortgage of receivables

5.11   A document purporting to be a mortgage of existing receivables, may assign immediately, a present right to receive payment of the debts in the future. In a tree and fruit metaphor, the assignment is of the tree,[63] rather than the fruits.[64] Or it may assign the receipts rather than the assets which produced them. The latter type of assignment is common in debt subordinations effected by trust.[65] When future receivables are involved, a document purporting to be a mortgage, may be either a present assignment of future receivables, or a mere contract to assign them when they come into existence. Although what has no present existence is incapable of a present transfer at law,[66] such a transfer may take effect in equity as indicating an intention that ownership shall pass automatically when the receivables come into existence.[67] In that case, the assignment is self-executing on the theory that equity regards as done that which ought to be done, provided that the receivables are clearly identified as to make them sufficiently appropriated to the security. In a contract to assign,

---

[60] *Helstan Securities Ltd.* v. *Hertfordshire C.C.* [1978] 3 All E.R. 262.

[61] *Day & Dent Constructions Pty. Ltd.* v. *North Australian Property Pty. Ltd.* (1982) 150 C.L.R. 85; *Re Charge Card Services Ltd.* [1987] Ch. 150. See also, Insolvency Rules 1986 (S.I. 1986 No. 1925), rr. 4.90 and 13.12.

[62] *Re Rudd & Son. Ltd.* (1986) 2 B.C.C. 98, 955.

[63] *Shepherd* v. *FCT* (1965) 113 C.L.R. 385; *Booth* v. *FCT* (1988) 76 A.L.R. 375.

[64] *Glegg* v. *Bromley* [1912] 3 K.B. 474; *Norman* v. *FCT* (1962) 109 C.L.R. 9.

[65] See *post,* para. 6.13 where this is discussed.

[66] *Lunn* v. *Thornton* (1845) 1 C.B. 379. The only concession made by the common law was the inclusion of potential property in the category of existing property. This concession was modest because the potential existence doctrine was confined to the agricultural field, essentially to crops and livestock. The common law courts never recognised that goods which a company may manufacture tomorrow or receivables expected from their sale, were things in potentia. In the case of receivables the difficulty was compounded by the formal non-recognition of assignments other than of Crown and negotiable debts.

[67] *Holroyd* v. *Marshall* (1862) 10 H.L.Cas. 191; *Tailby* v. *Official Receiver* (1888) 13 App.Cas. 523.

further action by the assignor is contemplated, and where the assignor is unwilling to do so, the security of the mortgagee depends on the availability of specific performance. Generally, a contract to give a mortgage will normally be specifically enforceable, on the theory that a claim to damages is obviously less valuable than a security in the event of the mortgagor's insolvency, provided that the consideration is already executed.[68] If the loan contract is executory, the application of the maxim that equity will not decree specific performance where damages would be an adequate remedy, results in the mortgagee being left to his claim for damages because there is no equity to decree specific performance of a contract to take a loan,[69] even if the lender has part performed.[70] This is an important distinction between a present assignment of future receivables, and a contract to assign them in future. The distinction is also important to questions of set-off, priority of competing claimants and the liquidator's avoiding powers in insolvent liquidation. With regard to set-off, it is clear that since there is no assignment, a notice to the debtor, of the contract to assign, does not affect the accumulation of contra accounts. The rule that after an assignment the assignor and the debtor cannot do anything to jeopardize the security of the assignee,[71] has no application. Also third parties taking assignments of the receivables will prevail. The extent to which their priority depends on the absence of notice of the contract to assign, depends on the relevance of the rule in *De Mattos* v. *Gibson*[72] to this enquiry. It has recently been said that the rule is still good law, and that equity has jurisdiction to restrain, as opposed to enforcing affirmatively, a knowing interference with contract rights.[73] The rule is of dubious significance, and at any rate applies, where it does at all, only to actual as opposed to constructive notice.

Where the promisor is in insolvent liquidation, the relevant time is not the date of the contract to assign, but of the actual assignment. This may make the assignment not only an undue preference,[74] but also vulnerable in other respects.

Between a present assignment and a promise to assign in the future lies a conditional assignment. Such a security is made conditionally, that is to say, to take effect on the happening of some future event, such as the institution of insolvency proceedings against the assignor or a default in

---

[68] *Swiss Bank Corp.* v. *Lloyds Bank Ltd.* [1982] A.C. 584 at 595.
[69] *Rogers* v. *Challis* (1859) 27 Beav. 175; *Western Waggon & Property Co.* v. *West* [1892] 1 Ch. 271 at 275; *Loan Investment Corp. of Australasia* v. *Bonner* [1970] N.Z.L.R. 724; *Rothwells Ltd.* v. *Nommack (No. 100) Pty. Ltd.* (1988) 13 A.C.L.R. 421 at 425. For a collection of the few instances where equity may depart from the general rule, see Jones & Goodhart, *Specific Performance* (1986), pp. 123–129.
[70] *Crampton* v. *Varna Railway Co.* (1872) L.R. 7 Ch.App. 562 (prospective borrower part performed).
[71] *Roxburghe* v. *Cox* (1878) 17 Ch.D. 520; *Brice* v. *Bannister* (1878) 3 Q.B.D. 569.
[72] (1859) 4 De G. & J. 276.
[73] *Swiss Bank Corp.* v. *Lloyds Bank Ltd.* [1979] Ch. 548 at 569–575, rvsd. [1982] A.C. 584 (not on this point). For a good general discussion, see Gardner, 98 L.Q.R. 279.
[74] *Re Jackson & Bassford* [1906] 2 Ch. 467 at 476; *Re Gregory Love & Co.* [1916] 1 Ch. 203. For purposes of registration, time runs not from the date of the agreement, but when the promise is fulfilled by the execution of a charge: *Williams* v. *Burlington* (1977) 121 S.J. 424; *The "Annangel Glory"* [1988] 1 Lloyd's Rep. 45 at 48.

performance under any contract, or default in meeting repayment obligations under the loan contract. It seems that such an assignment, although a present security, will be considered as created from the date the contingency supervenes, at least for purposes of determining whether it is avoidable by the liquidator. In any event, if the assignor retains control and use of the receivables before the happening of the contingency, the assignment takes effect, if at all, as a floating security.

A present assignment may pass a legal or an equitable title to the assignee. Such a security will be legal where it takes the form of an attornment from the debtors, or a statutory assignment.[75] In the latter case, the assignment must be absolute and not purport to be a charge only. The fact that the assignment is expressed to be by way of security does not, without more, prevent the assignment from being absolute,[76] but it may, when taken with other relevant circumstances, indicate that a charge only was intended.[77] Also a conditional assignment is not absolute within the section,[78] so that where a notice to the debtor indicates that until some future event happens, the assignor is entitled to payment, the assignment floats in the limbo of equitable securities.[79] The test of absolute assignment is whether the assignee alone has a right of payment against the debtor. If he alone has the right the assignment is absolute, but not otherwise. Apart from being absolute, the assignment must not be of a part of the fund of receivables,[80] although an assignment of the residue could be statutory.[81] Of course, the receivables must have a present existence,[82] and both the assignment and the notice to the debtor must be written. The written notice to the debtor can be given at any time, and by anybody.[83] Its purpose is not so much to secure priority; it goes to the acquisition of the legal assignment. The courts have interpreted the requirement of written notice rather strictly. Thus, a notice which specifies an earlier date as the date of the assignment is bad and ineffectual,[84] but a notice which specifies no date is valid.[85] If the assignment is statutory, the assignee is a legal mortgagee of the receivables, and may not only sue in his own name and give a valid discharge,

---

[75] Within s.136 of the Law of Property Act 1925.

[76] *Tancred* v. *Delagoa Bay and East Africa Ry. Co.* (1889) 23 Q.B.D. 239; *Hughes* v. *Pump House Hotel Co.* [1902] 2 K.B. 190.

[77] *Mercantile Bank of London Ltd.* v. *Evans* [1899] 2 Q.B. 613; *The "Halcyon the Great"* [1984] 1 Lloyd's Rep. 283.

[78] *Durham Brothers* v. *Robertson* [1898] 1 Q.B. 765 at 773.

[79] *Gatoil Anstalt* v. *Omennial Ltd., The "Balder London"* [1980] 2 Lloyd's Rep. 489.

[80] *Forster* v. *Baker* [1910] 2 K.B. 636; *Re Steel Wing Co.* [1921] 1 Ch. 349; *G. & T. Earle Ltd.* v. *Hemsworth RDC* (1928) 44 T.L.R. 605; *Williams* v. *Atlantic Assurance Co.* [1933] 1 K.B. 81 at 100; *Walter & Sullivan Ltd.* v. *Murphy & Sons Ltd.* [1955] 2 K.B. 584.

[81] *Harding* v. *Harding* (1886) 17 Q.B.D. 442.

[82] *Booth* v. *FCT* (1988) 76 A.L.R. 375 at 377.

[83] *Bateman* v. *Hunt* [1904] 2 K.B. 530 at 538.

[84] *Stanley* v. *English Fibres Industries Ltd.* (1899) 68 L.J.Q.B. 839; *W.F. Harrison & Co. Ltd.* v. *Burke* [1956] 1 W.L.R. 419. Equity takes a liberal attitude: *Whittingstall* v. *King* (1882) 46 L.T. 520. However, the requirement of written notice is mandatory, even where the debtor cannot read and clear oral explanation of the assignment has been given to him: *Hockley and Papworth* v. *Goldstein* (1920) 90 L.J.K.B. 111.

[85] *Van Lynn Developments Ltd.* v. *Pelias Construction Co. Ltd.* [1969] 1 Q.B. 607.

but also has all the legal rights and remedies incident to ownership.[86] He takes subject to equities having priority over his assignment. Equities extend to all legal[87] and equitable[88] defences vested in the debtor, but do not include prior assignments.

An assignment which for any reason fails to comply with the statute, is valid and effectual as an equitable mortgage. Like a statutory assignee, the holder of an equitable assignment takes subject to equities vested in the debtor.[89] He cannot, as a general rule, sue in his own name, but has to join the assignor as a co-plaintiff or co-defendant.[90] This requirement of joinder is procedural rather than substantive because although the assignee cannot obtain any relief without joinder of the assignor,[91] the action is not a nullity[92]—a point which may assume wider significance in the context of limitation of actions.[93] Today no action may be defeated for misjoinder or non-joinder of parties,[94] and in an appropriate case, the necessity for joinder may be waived. This may be done, for example, where the debtor for whose benefit the rule as to joinder exists, disclaims any necessity for joinder of the assignor.[95] It is also well settled that there is no need for joinder where the subject-matter of the equitable assignment is a chose in equity, the reason being that assignment transfers every right which the assignor has in the chose.[96] But where opportunity for joinder is given to the equitable assignee and refused, the requirement of joinder may not be waived.[97] So also, where the assignment is disputed.[98]

The inability of the equitable assignee to sue in his own name is one point of distinction between such an assignee and his legal counterpart. Another distinction is that the rule in *Dearle* v. *Hall*[99] applies to successive equitable assignments but not to legal assignments.

Whether the assignment is legal or equitable, there is the need for appropriation of the receivables to the security. Appropriation here means that the purported assignment must be sufficiently imperative as to impose an obligation on the debtor, and must also identify the receivables assigned. For example, a mere intimation to the debtor that a third party

---

[86] LPA 1925, s.136(1). Consequently, the assignor can no longer sue for the receivables: *Read* v. *Brown* (1888) 22 Q.B.D. 128 at 132; *Hughes* v. *Pump House Hotel Co.* [1902] 2 K.B. 190; *Walter and Sullivan Ltd.* v. *Murphy & Sons Ltd.* [1955] 2 Q.B. 584.

[87] *The Raven* [1980] 2 Lloyd's Rep. 266.

[88] *Roxburghe* v. *Cox* (1881) 17 Ch.D. 520.

[89] *Mangles* v. *Dixon* (1852) 3 H.L.C. 702 at 731; *Young* v. *Kitchin* (1878) 3 Ex.D. 127.

[90] *E.M. Bowden's Patents Syndicate Ltd.* v. *Herbert Smith & Co.* [1904] 2 Ch. 86; *Performing Right Society Ltd.* v. *London Theatre of Varieties Ltd.* [1924] A.C. 1; *Central Insurance Co. Ltd.* v. *Seacalf Shipping Corp., The "Aiolos"* [1983] 2 Lloyd's Rep. 25.

[91] *The Aiolos, supra* at 33.

[92] *Ibid.* See also, *Weddell* v. *J.A. Pearce & Major* [1988] Ch. 26, not following *Compania Colombiana de Seguros* v. *Pacific Steam Navigation Co.* [1965] 1 Q.B. 101.

[93] *Weddell* v. *J.A. Pearce & Major* [1988] Ch. 26.

[94] R.S.C., Ord. 15, r. 6.

[95] *William Brandt's Sons & Co.* v. *Dunlop Rubber Co.* [1905] A.C. 454.

[96] *Cator* v. *Croydon Canal Co.* (1843) 3 Swans 593; *Donaldson* v. *Donaldson* (1854) Kay 711.

[97] *Performing Right Society Ltd.* v. *London Theatre of Varieties Ltd.* [1924] A.C. 1.

[98] *The Aiolos* [1983] 2 Lloyd's Rep. 25.

[99] (1828) 3 Russ. 1.

has a claim on the debt is insufficient appropriation.[1] But a direction by an assignor to his debtor, sent to the assignee and notified by the assignee to the debtor, has been held sufficient.[2]

Floating charge over receivables

5.12   A floating charge is a present security[3] over a fund of assets, enabling the chargor to use the constituents of the fund in the ordinary course of its business without the consent of the chargee.[4] Because the charge does not attach to any specific item in the fund until crystallization, it provides an ideal security for lending without paralysing corporate activities. The floating charge is very important in branch banking and for many years has remained at the heart of corporate finance, especially for the small and medium size undertakings. This inherent flexibility of the floating charge provokes continuing debate as to the proprietary of including the floater in the category of equitable real securities. There is no space for entering the debate in this work. Therefore, whether a floating charge is best analysed as a mortgage of future assets,[5] or a contingent but defeasible real security,[6] or as passing no real rights to the chargee prior to crystallization,[7] will wait for another occasion. It is believed that the concept of a "fund of assets" satisfactorily explains the nature of a floating charge.[8] The essential nature of a fund is that the fund retains its identity, although its constituents may change from time to time.[9] This is well illustrated by the assets of a company. The form taken by corporate assets is constantly changing, as receivables owed to the company are paid and others created, as out of date machinery is replaced, and as raw materials are turned into finished goods and sold as stock; yet the assets are regarded as a continuing entity with its identity intact, and over which debenture holders may have a floating charge, and in which shareholders may have shares producing dividends.[10]

   This leads us to the distinction between a specific and a floating security. A floating security need not be over future property[11]; it need

---

[1] *Watson* v. *Duke of Wellington* (1830) 1 Russ & M. 602.
[2] *The Zigurds* (1931) 47 T.L.R. 525.
[3] *Evans* v. *Rival Granite Quarries Ltd.* [1910] 2 K.B. 979 at 999. See also, Farrar (1980) 1 Co.Law. 83 and the authorities there cited.
[4] *Re Panama, New Zealand and Australian Royal Mail Co.* (1870) L.R. 5 Ch.App. 318; *Re Florence Land & Public Works Co., Ex p. Moor* (1878) 10 Ch.D. 530; *Re Hamilton's Windsor Ironworks, Ex p. Pitman and Edwards* (1879) 12 Ch.D. 707; *Re Colonial Trusts Corp.* (1879) 15 Ch.D. 465; *Governments Stock and Other Securities Investment Co. Ltd.* v. *Manila Ry. Co. Ltd.* [1897] A.C. 81.
[5] Pennington, *Company Law* (London, Butterworths, 5th ed., 1985), pp. 480–481.
[6] McLelland in P. D. Finn (ed.), *Equity and Commercial Relationships*, pp. 280–281.
[7] Gough, *Company Charges* (London, Butterworths, 1978), p. 72; Gough in P. D. Finn (ed.), *Equity and Commercial Relationships*, pp. 253–259.
[8] Goode, *Legal Problems of Credit and Security* (2nd ed., 1988), p. 49.
[9] Lawson and Rudden, *Law of Property* (OUP, 2nd ed., 1982), p. 38.
[10] *Ibid.*
[11] *Kelley* v. *James McMahon Ltd.* [1980] I.R. 347 (existing land).

not be over an entire undertaking[12]; the property subject to such security need not be such as will be constantly turned over in the course of business.[13] A security is not a floating charge because its subject-matter is liable to fluctuate in terms of money.[14] It is floating because until some future event occurs, the chargor has management autonomy over the fund of assets charged. The autonomy is inherent in the nature of the security, and independent of contract.[15] Hence a floating charge is not a specific mortgage plus a licence to the mortgagor to dispose of them in the course of business. The chargor's management autonomy may, and frequently is, limited by contract. For example, a provision that the chargor is not free to factor receivables, or create specific charges ranking before or *pari passu* with the floating security, is a contractual restriction on the chargor's management autonomy. Its effect on third parties rests squarely on whether or not they are affected by notice of the restriction.[16] But the fact that they cannot take free of the restriction if they have notice shows that the floating security is a present real security.

The courts take a broad view of the chargor's management autonomy. For example, the autonomy extends to creating subsequent fixed charges over a part of the assets covered by the floating charge which prevail over the floating charge.[17] The autonomy explains why payment of the ordinary debts of the corporate chargor cannot be impugned by the floating chargee.[18] Where a floating charge required consent of the chargee to any new issue of debentures, it was held that this did not cover the issue of a subsequent fixed charge.[19] Despite the floating charge, the chargor can sell any property covered by the charge,[20] even where the sale is in many respects unusual and unprecedented,[21] unless the effect of the sale is that the company ceases to be a going concern.[22] Because of the breadth of management autonomy ceded to the corporate chargor by the Courts, it is common for debentures to limit the chargor's dealing powers, not just

---

[12] *Evans v. Rival Granite Quarries Ltd.* [1910] 2 K.B. 979; *Re Bond Worth Ltd.* [1980] Ch. 228; *The Annangel Glory* [1988] 1 Lloyd's Rep. 45 (floating charge over defined receivables).

[13] *Mercantile Credits Ltd. v. Atkins (No. 1)* (1985) 9 A.C.L.R. 757 at 761.

[14] *Ibid.*

[15] *Wallace v. Evershed* [1899] 1 Ch. 891 at 894; *Evans v. Rival Granite Quarries Ltd.* [1910] 2 K.B. 979 at 999.

[16] *Hamilton v. Hunter* (1982) 7 A.C.L.R. 295; *Re Bartlett Estates Pty. Ltd. (in Liq.)* (1988) 14 A.C.L.R. 512 at 516–517 (floating chargee may intervene to restrain dealings other than in the ordinary course of business and may recover property so mishandled where bona fide third party rights have not intervened).

[17] *Re Hamilton's Windsor Ironworks, ex p. Pitman and Edwards* (1879) 12 Ch.D. 707; *Wheatley v. Silkstone & Haigh Moor Coal Co.* (1885) 29 Ch.D. 715; *Governments Stock and Other Securities Investment Co. Ltd. v. Manila Ry. Co. Ltd.* [1897] A.C. 81; *Re Arauco Co. Ltd.* (1898) 79 L.T. 336.

[18] *Willmott v. London Celluloid Co.* (1886) 34 Ch.D. 147.

[19] *Cox Moore v. Peruvian Corp. Ltd.* [1908] 1 Ch. 604.

[20] *Re Old Bushmills Distillery Co., ex p. Brett* [1897] 1 I.R. 488; *Hamer v. London, City & Midland Bank Ltd.* (1918) 87 L.J.K.B. 973; *Reynolds Bros. (Motors) Pty. Ltd. v. Esanda Ltd.* (1983) 8 A.C.L.R. 422.

[21] *Re H.H. Vivian & Co. Ltd.* [1900] 2 Ch. 654; *Re Borax Co., Foster v. Borax Co.* [1901] 1 Ch. 326, (but see p. 343). Contrast, *Torzillu Pty. Ltd. v. Brynac Pty. Ltd.* (1983) 8 A.C.L.R. 52.

[22] *Hubbuck v. Helms* (1887) 56 L.J. Ch. 536.

to transactions in the ordinary course of business, but to transactions in the ordinary course of the issuer's *ordinary* business.[23] This form of drafting may not deprive the chargor of capacity to create a second floating charge over part of the assets covered by the first.[24] It does, however, prevent the company from creating a second floating charge over the same assets, ranking *pari passu* or ahead of the first charge.[25] While the charge floats, an execution which is complete prevails over the chargee, the reason being that an uncrystallized charge is not an equity subject to which an execution creditor takes.[26] Executions could be forestalled if the chargee appoints a receiver provided he has bargained for this right,[27] or applies to court for the appointment of a receiver.[28] If neither of these steps is taken, the holder of an uncrystallized charge cannot, by giving notice of claim, crystallize his charge over the assets threatened with execution.[29] Nor can he give notice to the debtors in order to secure priority over subsequent specific assignees of the same receivables.[30]

The extent of the chargor's management autonomy impacts on the ability of a third party transferee to take free of the uncrystallized charge. If a restriction on the autonomy is exceeded, does this affect a third party? It seems that the restriction is best analysed as an equity, existing separately from, and logically antecedent to the equitable and real security constituted by the floating charge. The reason for characterizing the restriction in this way is to protect subsequent transferees for value of an equitable as opposed to a legal interest without notice.[31] It is a little contrived to say that it is a mere contractual restriction,[32] for the simple reason that if that characterization was correct, third party transferees would take free of the charge even with notice.[33] It is clear that the restriction is not a naked equity, since it binds third parties with notice.[34]

---

[23] See, *e.g. Fire Nymph Products Ltd.* v. *The Heating Centre Pty. Ltd.* (1988) 14 A.C.L.R. 274 esp. at 278.
[24] *Re Automatic Bottle Makers Ltd.* [1926] Ch. 412.
[25] *Smith* v. *English & Scottish Mercantile Investment Trust* [1896] W.N. 86; *Re Benjamin Cope & Sons Ltd.* [1914] 1 Ch. 800; *Re Household Products Co. Ltd.* (1981) 124 D.L.R. (3d) 325.
[26] *Robson* v. *Smith* [1895] 2 Ch. 118; *Evans* v. *Rival Granite Quarries Ltd.* [1910] 2 K.B. 979; *cf. Re Opera Ltd.* [1891] 3 Ch. 260 (crystallization after seizure but before sale); *Taunton* v. *Sheriff of Warwickshire* [1895] 1 Ch. 734 (crystallization after seizure and sale but before payment of proceeds to execution creditor).
[27] *Cf.*, Gough, *Company Charges*, pp. 156–157.
[28] *McMahon* v. *North Kent Ironworks Co.* [1891] 2 Ch. 148; *Edwards* v. *Standard Rolling Stock Syndicate* [1893] 1 Ch. 574; *Re Victoria Steamboats Ltd.*, *Smith* v. *Wilkinson* [1897] 1 Ch. 158; *Re London Pressed Hinge Co. Ltd.* [1905] 1 Ch. 576.
[29] *Robson* v. *Smith, supra*; *Evans* v. *Rival Granite, supra*; *Re Caroma Enterprises Ltd.* (1979) 108 D.L.R. (3d) 412.
[30] *Ward* v. *Royal Exchange Shipping Co. Ltd.*, *ex p. Harrison* (1887) 58 L.T. 174; *Re Ind, Coope & Co. Ltd.* [1911] 2 Ch. 223.
[31] McLelland, in P. D. Finn (ed.), *Equity and Commercial Relationships*, p. 281.
[32] *Cf.* Gough, *Company Charges*, pp. 156–157.
[33] But see, *Hamilton* v. *Hunter* (1982) 7 A.C.L.R. 295; *Re Bartlett Estates Pty. Ltd.* [1988] 14 A.C.L.R. 512 at 517.
[34] *Ibid.* A naked equity is personal to the parties and does not bind outsiders even with notice: *National Provincial Bank Ltd.* v. *Ainsworth* [1965] A.C. 1175 at 1238, 1253, unless the circumstances are such as to raise a constructive trust.

As regards notice, it is settled that registration of a charge is constructive notice only of the prescribed particulars. Since restrictions are not as yet part of such particulars their registration is not constructive notice.[35] The situation would be different where there is actual notice.

Crystallization of a floating charge[36]

Crystallization is the event which converts a floating security into a **5.13** specific charge. It operates as an equitable assignment to the chargee.[37] The charge then settles on the specific items comprising the fund over which it once floated. It also terminates the company's management autonomy. As Nourse J. put it,[38] "that which kept the charge hovering has now been released and the force of gravity causes it to settle and fasten on the subject-matter of the charge within its grasp. The paralysis, while it may still be unwelcome, can no longer be resisted." The paralysis, while it lasts, does not affect the scope of the charge. Post-crystallization assets of the company continue to be caught.[39] Events of crystallization are not, however, fixed by law.[40] It is now settled that a floating charge will crystallize on winding up of the company,[41] even though only for the purpose of reorganization[42]; on the appointment of a receiver[43]; on the cessation of business[44]; on the happening of an event

---

[35] *Wilson* v. *Kelland* [1910] 2 Ch. 306; *G. & T. Earle Ltd.* v. *Hemsworth R.D.C.* (1928) 44 T.L.R. 605, affd., *ibid.* 758, C.A.; *Siebe Gorman & Co. Ltd.* v. *Barclays Bank Ltd.* [1979] 2 Lloyd's Rep. 142. Contrast, *Re Manurewa Transport Ltd.* [1971] N.Z.L.R. 909, decided under s.4(2) of the Chattels Transfer Act, 1924 (New Zealand), which provides that registration of a security over chattels is notice, not only of the existence of the security, but of its contents. However, in *Dempsey & National Bank of New Zealand Ltd.* v. *Traders' Finance Corp. Ltd.* [1933] N.Z.L.R. 1258, the provision was held inapplicable to a security transfer of hire-purchase agreements because the rentals were not chattels. But now, see Companies Act 1985, s.415(2)(a) inserted by s.103 of Companies Act 1989 under which regulations may be made making restrictions on the creation of other charges ranking in priority or *pari passu* with the existing charge, registrable.
[36] Gough, *Company Charges* (London, Butterworths, 1978), pp. 84 *et seq.*
[37] *Biggerstaff* v. *Rowatt's Wharf Ltd.* [1896] 2 Ch. 93 at 106; *N.W. Robbie & Co. Ltd.* v. *Witney Warehouse Co. Ltd.* [1963] 1 W.L.R. 1324 at 1333, 1338.
[38] *Re Woodroffes (Musical Instruments) Ltd.* [1986] Ch. 366 at 378.
[39] *Wellington Woollen Manufacturing Co. Ltd.* v. *Patrick* [1935] N.Z.L.R. 23; *N.W. Robbie & Co. Ltd.* v. *Witney Warehouse Co. Ltd.* [1963] 1 W.L.R. 1324; *Ferrier* v. *Bottomer* (1972) 126 C.L.R. 597. See also, Milman (1979) 43 Conv. 138.
[40] *Re Brightlife Ltd.* [1987] Ch. 200.
[41] *Re Colonial Trusts Corp., Ex p. Bradshaw* (1879) 15 Ch.D. 465 at 472; *Edward Nelson & Co. Ltd.* v. *Faber* [1903] 2 K.B. 367 at 376. In *Re Obie Pty. Ltd. (No. 2)* (1983) 8 A.C.L.R. 574 at 581, it was held that the appointment of a provisional liquidator did not crystallize the floating charge.
[42] *Re Crompton & Co. Ltd.* [1914] 1 Ch. 954.
[43] *Taunton* v. *Sheriff of Warwickshire* [1895] 2 Ch. 319; *Stein* v. *Saywell* (1969) 121 C.L.R. 529; *George Barker (Transport) Ltd.* v. *Eynon* [1974] 1 W.L.R. 462. In *Re Peter Gabriels Controls Pty. Ltd.* (1982) 6 A.C.L.R. 684, it was held that where a charge is to crystallize on the appointment of a receiver, crystallization is incomplete until the appointee accepts the appointment.
[44] *Hubbuck* v. *Helms* (1887) 56 L.J.Ch. 536; *Re Woodroffes (Musical Instruments) Ltd.* [1986] Ch. 366.

contractually specified as a crystallizing event,[45] whether this be by the giving of a crystallization notice,[46] or automatically without the necessity for any notice.[47] In the absence of contract, a floating charge does not crystallize automatically on the crystallization of another charge over the same assets, whether such other charge be prior[48] or subsequent[49] to the crystallized charge. The reason is said to be that the determination of the corporate chargor's management autonomy by one chargee does not necessarily mean that another chargee would determine it.[50] This reasoning has a prima facie appeal where the charges cover different assets. Where they have the same subject-matter, the reasoning is unappealing. If the chargor's authority is determined by one chargee, the assets can no longer be used in the process of trade. To say that another chargee has not determined it may be true as a matter of theory; practically, the paralysis, while it may still be unwelcome by the other chargee, can no longer be resisted. The cases, by focusing exclusively on the contractual effect of crystallization, overlook its proprietary effects. How can the management autonomy of the company continue after the appointment of a receiver over the self-same assets by another chargee? How can the company pay current debts from such assets? During the receivership the power of the directors is inversely related to the scope and validity of the receivership. These show that the contractual analysis which ordains that the crystallization of one charge does not crystallize another charge has only a superficial appeal. The better view, it is submitted, is that the crystallization of one charge automatically crystallizes other charges over the same assets. This view gives effect to the proprietary consequences of crystallization.

A related question is whether the appointment of an administrator crystallizes a floating charge independently of contract. As a matter of legal theory, the petition for an administration order[51] cannot, in the absence of contract, crystallize a floating charge. First, the petition may be dismissed. Secondly, in relation to the appointment of a receiver by the court, it has been settled for some time that the issue of a writ initiating proceedings for the appointment of a receiver does not crystallize a floating charge.[52] The same reasoning applies to the petition for an

---

[45] *Stein* v. *Saywell* (1969) 121 C.L.R. 529 (it was assumed that the second floating charge crystallized automatically on the appointment of a receiver under the first floating charge, pursuant to a provision to that effect in the second charge. See also *Re Brightlife Ltd.* [1987] Ch. 200 (crystallization by notice).

[46] *Re Brightlife Ltd., supra.*

[47] *Stein* v. *Saywell, supra; Re Manurewa Transport Ltd.* [1971] N.Z.L.R. 909; *Fire Nymph Products Ltd.* v. *The Heating Centre Pty. Ltd.* (1988) 14 A.C.L.R. 274; *Re Permanent Houses (Holdings) Ltd.* [1988] B.C.L.C. 563.

[48] *Cf. Stein* v. *Saywell* (1969) 121 C.L.R. 529 (contract to that effect); *Gatsby* v. *Gatsby Kelowna* (1979) 3 C.B.R.(N.S.) 1.

[49] *Re Woodroffes (Musical Instruments) Ltd.* [1986] Ch. 366.

[50] *Ibid.*; but see Loo Choon Chaiw [1986] L.M.C.L.Q. 519 esp. at 527 *et seq.*

[51] Under Pt. II of the Insolvency Act 1986.

[52] *Re Roundwood Colliery Co.* [1897] 1 Ch. 373; *Re Hubbard & Co. Ltd.* (1898) 68 L.J.Ch. 54. Canadian courts have taken a different attitude: *Industrial Development Bank Ltd.* v. *Valley Dairy Ltd.* [1953] O.R. 70; *Gatsby Enterprises (Kelowna) Ltd.* v. *Gatsby Kelowna (1976) Ltd.* (1979) 30 C.B.R.(N.S.) 1.

administration order. Does it also follow that the making of an administration order does not crystallize a floating charge? The question is not free from difficulty. It is thought that the making of an administration order on the ground that an administration will lead to a more advantageous realisation of the company's assets than is possible in a liquidation or for the approval of a voluntary arrangement or for sanctioning an arrangement or a compromise with creditors under section 425 of the Companies Act 1985, crystallizes a floating charge independently of contract.[53] This is because it is with a view to winding up. After all, while the administration lasts the company exists only for the purposes specified in the administration order, and it is thought that this is sufficient disinvestment to crystallize a floating charge. Also, it would seem that if the company ceases to trade during the administration any existing floating charges would crystallize. So also, if its undertaking is disposed of with a view to cessation of business.[54]

Automatic crystallization of floating charges and priorities

The question whether an automatic crystallization clause is valid can be taken as now settled.[55] In principle, such a question ought never to have arisen once it is conceded that the events of crystallization are not fixed by law. The policy objections may, however, persuade a court to deny effect to an ambiguous or obscure automatic crystallization clause.[56] If the clause is clear, effect must be given to it. The efficacy of such clauses is no longer topical because the sting has been removed from automatic crystallization clauses by the definition of a floating charge as a charge which, as created, was a floating charge.[57] This definition is for certain purposes only,[58] and the wider question remains whether automatic crystallization clauses bear on priority. One view[59] is that they affect the question of attachment of the security to assets charged. Attachment, the argument continues, is primarily and exclusively a matter for the chargor and chargee, and does not affect priorities. One may even go further and say that the right of priority is not a right of the chargee against the chargor, for ex hypothesi every chargee is a stranger to the other's assignment. However, to say that crysallization goes to the question of attachment, and that attachment is a matter for the chargor and chargee, **5.14**

---

[53] Contrast Goode, *Legal Problems of Credit and Security*, (2nd ed., 1988), p. 64.
[54] *Hubbuck* v. *Helms* (1887) 56 L.J.Ch. 536, provides an analogy.
[55] See n. 47, *supra*; contrast A. J. Boyle [1979] J.B.L. 231.
[56] *Governments Stock and Other Securities Investment Co. Ltd.* v. *Manila Ry. Co. Ltd.* [1897] A.C. 81; *R.* v. *Consolidated Churchill Copper Corp. Ltd.* (1979) 90 D.L.R. (3d) 357; *Re Caroma Enterprises Ltd.* (1979) 108 D.L.R. (3d) 412.
[57] Insolvency Act 1986, s.251 and Pt. I, Sched. 13, (substituting a new s.196 for the Companies Act 1985).
[58] The purposes include, the powers of an administrator to deal with assets covered by a floating charge: Insolvency Act 1986, s.15(1), (3); the powers of a chargee to receive notice of a petition for an administration order: s.9(2)(*a*); to veto the making of an order: s.10(2)(*b*); to appoint an administrative receiver: s.29; and the priority of preferential claims: ss.40, 175, 386, 387.
[59] Goode, *Legal Problems of Credit and Security* (2nd ed., 1988), p. 70.

understates the position. Even in the case of a specific charge, one can equally say that attachment affects only questions between the chargor and chargee; yet, it has never been doubted that the nature of the charge bears on the question of priorities. It is thought that crystallization affects priorities in so far as it turns a floating charge into a specific security. Accordingly, once a floating charge crystallizes, whether automatically or otherwise, a third party taking assets subject to the charge will only prevail in circumstances where a specific charge is liable to be defeated. First, execution creditors cannot take free of the charge; the fact that they are unaware of the crystallization of the charge cannot advance their priority. Secondly, where the charge is not over a debt, the transferee who takes an equitable title only is bound by the charge, the rule being *qui prior est tempore potior est jure*. Where such a transfer is to a bona fide transferee of the legal title for value without notice of the charge, he prevails because his legal title is stronger than the equity of the chargee. Automatic crystallization is inefficient because it does not prevent build up of set-off, unless the debtor knows that the charge has crystallized. As regards receivables, crystallization of the charge operates as an equitable assignment to the chargee.[60] An unauthorised assignment by the chargor after crystallization will prevail if the assignee is the first to give notice, provided he did not know that the charge had crystallized when he took his assignment. This is because even after crystallization priority still depends on the order in which notice is given to the debtors and to some extent this reduces the scope for prejudice to assignees.

Automatic crystallization clauses operate harshly when applied to land and tangible personalty because equitable transferees will be postponed to the crystallized charge. To ameliorate this, it has been argued forcefully that automatic crystallization terminates the corporate chargor's *actual* authority to dispose of assets within the charge, but does not affect his *apparent* authority to deal with the assets.[61] There is no policy objection to this line of reasoning which has the merit of protecting innocent transferees of equitable interests in property subject to a charge. The argument is, however, difficult to accept as a matter of principle. First, to uphold it as a general rule is to smuggle in through the back door, an idea similar to the reputed ownership doctrine of bankruptcy law. The doctrine, which has now been expelled through the front door,[62] never applied to registered companies. Second, the priority of charges does not, as a general rule, depend on the concept of authority. The management autonomy which a corporate chargor enjoys over charged assets prior to crystallization is not the result of actual authority from the chargee. A floating charge is not a specific charge plus actual authority from the chargee to deal with the assets in the ordinary course of business.[63] If he has no actual authority from the chargee prior to crystallization, the chargor does not automatically become clothed with

---

[60] *George Barker (Transport) Ltd.* v. *Eynon* [1974] 1 W.L.R. 462 at 467; *Business Computers Ltd.* v. *Anglo-African Leasing Ltd.* [1977] 1 W.L.R. 578 at 582.
[61] Goode, *op. cit.*, p. 70.
[62] Insolvency Act 1986, s.283(3).
[63] *Evans* v. *Rival Granite Quarries Ltd.* [1910] 2 K.B. 979 at 999.

apparent authority as a result of crystallization. Besides, crystallization does not only terminate the chargor's management autonomy, it converts the charge into a specific security. How can non-intervention by the chargee, without more, endow the chargor with apparent authority when the management autonomy enjoyed prior to crystallization was not the result of actual authority? Third, even if the above arguments are wrong, a third party taking an equitable interest in property after crystallization will usually be unable to prove that he relied upon any representation by the chargee, as opposed to his having relied upon his own assumption in relation to the charge.[64] Fourth, the suggestion concentrates on the contractual effect of crystallization without enough attention being paid to its proprietary effects. Finally, the settled rules of priority among chargees depend, first, on the characterization of these interests and second, utilize the concepts of notice and registration, not actual and apparent authority.[65]

It does not follow from the above that estoppel may not, in an appropriate case, be used to postpone the holder of a security which has crystallized automatically upon the occurrence of a specified event. This will be so, for example, if after the event necessitating automatic crystallization, the chargee slept on his rights and took no steps to enforce and realize his security. In such situations, equity will come to the relief of a transferee who has acted to his detriment on the basis of a basic assumption as to the position, in relation to which the chargee, by his inaction, has partly induced. That the chargee did not know of the transferee's assumption is no answer to the raising of an estoppel in such cases. What constitutes sleeping on his rights for this purpose is a question of fact depending on the circumstances. If Parliament considers the operation of automatic crystallization clauses oppressive, a sensible reform would be to provide that automatic crystallization has no effect until notice of the occurrence of the crystallizing event is filed with the Companies Registry.[66] In this respect, it is to be noted that the only alleged evil of automatic crystallization clauses is the secrecy of their operation. Reform along the above lines would remove this evil, though in the comparable situation where a charge crystallizes on the appointment of a receiver, the crystallization is not suspended until the notice of appointment is filed. All that is required is that it be filed within seven days on the pains of a fine.[67]

Partial crystallization

In the absence of contract, a debenture holder cannot crystallize his **5.15** charge over particular assets while allowing the charge to float as to the

---

[64] Mark Hapgood, I.F.L. Rev., May 1983, p. 34.
[65] *Ibid.*
[66] Companies Act 1985, s.410 empowers the Secretary of State to make regulations on the lines suggested in the text.
[67] Companies Act 1985, s.409.

remainder merely because his security is in jeopardy.[68] A charge must float or crystallize as to all assets within its scope. There is, however, no reason why the parties cannot, as a matter of contract, provide for partial crystallization of the charge. Such a device has a double advantage: for the chargee, it protects his security from any threatened jeopardy and is particularly effective against execution creditors; for the company, it reduces the danger of overkill in automatic crystallization of a charge over its whole undertaking. Partial crystallization can be made to occur either automatically or by a form of intervention specified in the charge.[69] A notice of partial crystallization is valid even if it specifies the whole assets covered by the charge.[70]

A crystallized charge can be decrystallized and refloated. If an event of crystallization occurs subsequently, the charge recrystallizes. It is unclear whether decrystallization and refloatation count as a "creation" of a new charge requiring registration from the date of refloatation. The point is not free from difficulty but it would seem that a refloated charge is different from the already crystallized charge and there is no reason in principle why a decrystallization by waiver should not be treated as an act of "creation." This analysis could, if correct, create interesting priority questions.

Lightweight floating charges

5.16   Despite the relatively modest ranking of floating charges in the pecking order, the Insolvency Act 1986, has made the floating charge an attractive security once again. First, only a person entitled to appoint an administrative receiver[71] may receive notice of a petition for an administration order.[72] Secondly, only such a creditor can "block" the making of an administration order, provided he appoints an administrative receiver by the time the petition is heard.[73] The making of an administration order operates as a stay of enforcement of security interests.[74] Also, the duty of the administrator is to carry out proposals aimed at achieving the purpose of his appointment. Since the administrator has a potentially unlimited tenure, his appointment removes two vital rights from the chargee, namely, the ability to control the timing and conduct of realization of his security. The property may have depreciated when the administrator

---

[68] *Robson* v. *Smith* [1895] 2 Ch. 118; *Evans* v. *Rival Granite Quarries Ltd., supra*; *Re Caroma Enterprises Ltd.* (1979) 108 D.L.R. (3d) 412. In *Re Griffin Hotel Co. Ltd.* [1941] Ch. 129, the chargee appointed a receiver over all the charged assets except one, and Bennet J. held that the charge crystallized over the assets covered by the appointment. The case is not an exception to the general rule of no partial crystallization in the absence of contract. The Court allowed this "apparent" partial crystallization because on the facts, there was no equity of redemption left in the excepted asset if the prior specific chargee enforced his security.
[69] *Re Obie Pty. Ltd. (No. 5)* (1984) 9 A.C.L.R. 151.
[70] *Re Brightlife Ltd.* [1987] Ch. 200.
[71] Administrative receiver is defined in s.29(2) of the Insolvency Act 1986.
[72] Insolvency Act 1986, s.9(2)(*a*).
[73] Insolvency Act 1986, ss.9(3) & 10(2)(*b*).
[74] Insolvency Act 1986, s.15.

vacates office. Worse still, the administrator may not even sell the property at all, or for some time. For these reasons, a first mortgagee may insist on taking a first floating charge over the company's undertaking, even where his specific security fully secures his exposure. Such floating charges intended only for protection against the insolvency procedure are called lightweight charges, since they need not contain all the covenants and restrictions typically found in floating charges, but only restrictions on the creation of other floating charges ranking ahead of or *pari passu* with them.[75] Another reason for taking lightweight floating charges is because of the new powers given to an administrative receiver.[76] Under the new law, an administrative receiver may apply to court for leave to sell assets subject to a specific charge.[77] Thus, a lender with only a fixed charge may find that another lender has this potential ability to dispose of property subject to his security. In the event he will lose control over the timing and conduct of realization of his security. Although the scope for prejudice is minimized,[78] it is not eliminated. Lightweight floating charges are intended to be utilised as Insolvency Act expedients, but as we shall see, the emergence of these limited effect floaters raises a number of difficult points of law.

It has been said[79] that the development of lightweight floating charges indicates the extent to which the banking sector intends to remain masters of their own destiny. The immediate impact of this development on patterns of secured financing is unclear. At the minimum, it will discourage subsequent lenders from injecting money into an ailing company if all they can get by way of security is a second floating charge. This may not be too bad if such a lender is a person entitled to appoint an administrative receiver, since he is entitled to receive notice of a petition for an administration order, and could veto the making of the order. It is not, however, clear that he can do so. This area of the law is one of considerable difficulty. The objective of taking a lightweight floating charge is largely as an expedient entitling the lender to appoint an administrative receiver. If there are other lenders with floating charges, who may appoint an administrative receiver? Or do they all have a right to appoint? If a subsequent floating chargee appoints the first administrative receiver, can the appointee be displaced by receivers appointed by senior floating chargees? Can the chargees enter into an agreement whereby whoever appoints an administrative receiver binds his appointee not to exercise the power given by section 43 of the Insolvency Act 1986? The answers to these questions are everything but easy. It is not clear from the Act:

(1) whether there can be more than one administrative receiver;

---

[75] Rumbelow, L.S.Gaz., March 1989, p. 32 at 33.
[76] *Corporate Recovery: The Immediate Impact of the Administrator Scheme, A Report by City University Department of Law*, April 1988, p. 8 (hereinafter referred to as City University).
[77] Insolvency Act 1986, s.43.
[78] By s.43(3), Insolvency Act 1986.
[79] *City University*, p. 20.

(2) assuming there can be only one and there are competing chargees, who has the best right to appoint;

(3) whether a later administrative receiver can displace one already in office;

(4) whether competing chargees can validly contract with each other that an administrative receiver should not exercise the dispositive power in s.43 of the Insolvency Act 1986.

We shall consider these questions in turn, but first, who is an administrative receiver? An administrative receiver is defined in section 29(2)[80] as:

(a) a receiver or manager of the whole (or substantially the whole) of a company's property appointed by or on behalf of the holders of any debentures of the company secured by a charge which, as created, was a floating charge, or by such a charge and one or more other securities; or

(b) a person who would be such a receiver or manager but for the appointment of some other person as the receiver of part of the company's property.

Can there be more than one administrative receiver?

5.17 Apart from joint administrative receivers appointed by the same chargee, it is not clear from the Act if there can be more than one administrative receiver at the same time. Seen primarily as a machinery for the enforcement of security, there is no reason in principle why there cannot be more than one administrative receiver at the same time. Section 29(2)(b) does not really advance the argument that the scheme of the Act is that there can be only one administrative receiver since it refers to receivers of *part* rather than the *whole or substantially the whole* of the company's assets. On the other hand it is a little artificial to see administrative receivership solely from the standpoint of enforcement of security. The truth is that administrative receivership is one of the main forms of insolvency proceedings.[81] An administrative receiver is an office-holder with the same powers as an administrator.[82] It is for these reasons that no administrator can be appointed while an administrative receiver is in office[83] and why an administrative receiver can be removed only by the court.[84] These features show the movement from contract to status and make it inappropriate to treat administrative receivership as exclusively a machinery for the enforcement of security. It is difficult to see how different administrative receivers appointed under different charges can live together and exercise all their powers without reference to one another, and perhaps, inconsistently. Considerations of this nature indi-

---

[80] Insolvency Act 1986.
[81] See Insolvency Act 1986, s.247(1).
[82] *Ibid.*, s.42(1).
[83] *Ibid.*, s.9(3).
[84] *Ibid.*, s.45(1).

cate that the better view is that it is the scheme of the Act that only one administrative receiver can hold office at any one time, except where joint administrative receivers are appointed. It is possible that because of the scramble for, and partition of, the debtor's assets, or a priority agreement, no chargee has security over the whole or substantially the whole of the company's assets. In that event no chargee can appoint an administrative receiver and none would be entitled to receive notice of a petition for the appointment of an administrator. For the same reason none can veto the making of an administration order. It may be argued that the picture painted above is an impossibility because of section 29(2)(*b*). But as each chargee can rely on that provision, the argument creates a circularity and once it is conceded that there can be only one administrative receiver, the conclusion that on such facts no chargee can appoint an administrative receiver is unavoidable. It remains to consider whether the "one administrative receiver argument" can be substantiated under section 29(2) of the Act. It is arguable that if entitlement to appoint an administrative receiver is at bottom a question of priority between competing chargees, there can be only one administrative receiver. This argument rests on the interpretation of "part" in section 29(2)(*b*). Where there is a prior security (containing a floating charge) ranking ahead of other charges in all respects, then the security of other incumbrancers is in reality over the debtor's equity of redemption. This equity of redemption cannot be considered the "whole" of the company's assets. At best it may constitute "substantially the whole" of the company's assets. This in turn would largely be a function of the amount secured by the security package held by the prior chargee. If the equity of redemption is fairly described as "substantially the whole" of the company's assets, then and only then, would the second chargee, assuming he has a floating charge of some description, be a person entitled to appoint an administrative receiver. But even then, since the prior chargee has a better right to the assets, until his administrative receiver vacates office, the second chargee cannot validly take control of the assets and to this extent cannot appoint an administrative receiver, although, no doubt, he can appoint an ordinary receiver who, however, will have no possession of the charged assets. Therefore, unless the prior chargee can be persuaded to "marshall" his security and a receiver appointed by him can be regarded as a receiver of "part" only of the company's assets, the second chargee is not a person entitled to appoint an administrative receiver. It must be stressed that because of the definition of an administrative receiver by reference to a floating charge, a specific chargee of the only asset owned by the company, for example, a single building, or a single ship, or all the assets of the company, who has no floating charge of any description in his security package, is not a person entitled to appoint an administrative receiver. Consequently, he is not a person entitled to receive notice of a petition for the appointment of an administrator, nor, it is thought, can he veto such appointment.[85]

Who can appoint an administrative receiver?

Assuming that all competing chargees have a floating charge in their **5.18** security package and only one administrative receiver can be appointed at

---

[85] *Cf. Re Meesan Investments Ltd.* (1988) 4 B.C.C. 788 at 790.

any point in time, which chargee is entitled to appoint? Apart from the power to veto an administration, there is the vital section 43 power. If a junior incumbrancer can appoint, although his appointee will be bound to hand over the proceeds of sale, the senior incumbrancers would have lost the important right to determine the timing and conduct of realisation of their securities. Therefore, the right to appoint is an important aspect of a security package. There seem to be three distinct possibilities:

(1) the floating chargee who is the first to appoint;

(2) the floating chargee whose security is first in time;

(3) the chargee who has a floating charge of some description and fixed charges and who, by virtue of the fixed and floating charges, has priority over the whole or substantially the whole of the company's assets.

Broadly, the question is essentially one of priorities: priority of appointment; priority of floating charges; overall priority. Each of these will be examined in turn. The argument in support of "first to appoint" or priority of appointment rests on section 45(1) of the Act which provides that an administrative receiver may be removed from office only by a court order. Where, for example, he is appointed by a junior incumbrancer, so the argument continues, *cadit quaestio*. He can neither be removed by his appointer, nor is he liable to displacement by a subsequent receiver appointed by a senior incumbrancer. If this argument is correct, only such a junior incumbrancer could veto an administration and his appointee could, with or without leave of the court, exercise all the powers of an administrative receiver, including the power under section 43 to overreach senior incumbrances. There would then be an unseemly scramble to appoint a receiver since the ranking of incumbrancers is irrelevant to entitlement to appoint. For a number of reasons this argument is wrong. First, the emphasis is on the *right* to appoint. Since only one administrative receiver can hold office at any one time, a receiver appointed by a junior chargee cannot be an administrative receiver because someone else has a better right to the assets. Indeed no receiver is an administrative receiver whose appointer has not the best right to the assets. Factual possession alone is insufficient if not accompanied by a *right* to possess. Since a receiver, administrative or otherwise, has no better title to the assets within the scope of his appointment than his appointer, it would be strange if by the simple expedient of being the first to be appointed, the rights of senior chargees to appoint were barred. Secondly, as it is senior chargees that have a greater interest in having a say over the making of an administration order and the timing of realisation of their securities, it would be bizarre if this right were removed from under their nose by a "strategic" early appointment by a junior chargeholder. This would hold out an incentive to opportunistic junior chargees seeking to make strategic use of the appointment process. Thirdly, it is difficult to see how a receiver appointed by a junior chargee can remain an administrative receiver after the appointment, by a senior chargee, of a receiver who must of necessity have a better right to possession and control of the whole or substantially the whole of the

122

company's assets. There is no reason to believe that the Act divests senior chargees of their rights to assume possession and control against a receiver appointed under a junior security.

Where all chargees have a floating charge and where all charges enable appointments to be made in respect of all the company's assets or substantially all, is it priority of the respective floating charges or overall priority achieved by a combination of fixed and floating charges, that determines entitlement to appoint an administrative receiver? In other words, is it possibility (2) or (3) above, which is correct? The answer is far from clear. We can illustrate the difficulty by considering the following example. Company A, a special purpose company, owns a portfolio of ten real properties. It mortgages one to Bank B by way of a first legal charge and gives that bank a floating charge over the remaining nine. The security contains a prohibition on the creation of other charges, fixed or floating. Bank C advances money and without notice of the prohibition takes a first fixed charge on the nine properties and a floating charge of some description, but not necessarily over the whole or substantially the whole of the portfolio. We can complicate the picture by assuming that Bank D took a second floating charge over the whole portfolio of properties and entered into a priority agreement with Bank C by virtue of which it is entitled to priority in all respects against Bank C. Is it Bank B, C or D that is entitled to appoint an administrative receiver? If it is the priority of floating charges that determines entitlement to appoint an administrative receiver, since Bank B has the senior floating charge over substantially the whole of the company's assets, it alone can appoint an administrative receiver. Apart from the fact that there is nothing in section 29(2) of the Insolvency Act 1986 which makes priority of a floating charge determinative, this approach does not give effect to the fact that Bank C has priority, by virtue of its fixed charge, over substantially the whole of the company's assets. All that section 29(2)(a) requires is that there be a floating charge of some description in Bank C's security package and that Bank C have the right to appoint a receiver over the whole of the company's assets. It does not say that the security by virtue of which control over substantially the whole of the company's assets is asserted be floating. On the contrary the provision contemplates that part of the security by virtue of which the relevant control is established, could be fixed. The test, it is submitted, is not priority of floating charges. Rather, it is overall priority gained through a combination of fixed and floating charges over the whole or substantially the whole of the company's assets. Thus, as between Banks B and C, Bank C has the better right to appoint an administrative receiver. However, the priority agreement between Banks C and D complicates the picture. As a matter of priorities, Bank C ranks above Bank B (because of its fixed charge[86]) which ranks above Bank D (because its floating charge is first in time[87]) which ranks above Bank C (because of the priority agreement[88]).

[86] *Re Automatic Bottle Makers Ltd.* [1926] Ch. 412.
[87] *Smith* v. *English & Scottish Mercantile Investment Trust* [1896] W.N. 86; *Re Benjamin Cope & Sons Ltd.* [1914] 1 Ch. 800; *Re Household Products Co. Ltd.* (1981) 124 D.L.R. (3d) 325.
[88] *Re Woodruffs (Musical Instruments) Ltd.* [1986] Ch. 366.

There is a circular priority problem. Who, then, can appoint an administrative receiver? It is tempting to conclude that since there is no chargee with absolute priority none can appoint an administrative receiver. This conclusion, however, is unsound. The circular priority is more apparent than real. As a matter of general law, Bank C has a better right than Bank B to appoint an administrative receiver. But since he has contracted this right away to Bank D, it is Bank D that has the right to appoint an administrative receiver. It may be objected that this approach does not give effect to Bank B's priority over Bank D. This objection, however, is not well founded. Bank D's right to appoint is by subrogation to the right of Bank C and this is not unfair to Bank B. Bank B only has to blame the present law which does not give him any effective facility to publicising the restriction on the creation of subsequent charges contained in its charge document. Even if regulations are made under section 103 of the Companies Act 1989, making such restrictions registrable particulars, this will only benefit future chargees as the regulations will not be retrospective. The conclusion is that the question who may appoint an administrative receiver resolves itself into a question of priority of charges. Assuming every lender has a floating charge of some description and has a security enabling him to appoint a receiver over the whole or substantially the whole of the company's assets, it is that lender who has overall priority, whether this be by virtue of his fixed charges alone, or by virtue of his floating charge alone, or by a combination of his fixed and floating charges, that may appoint an administrative receiver. It matters little whether this priority be the result of the invalidity of a prior charge or the result of a priority agreement with a lender who, but for the priority agreement, would have had such priority. This approach is to be preferred, for it mirrors the policy underlying the ability to veto an administration, namely, that when there is a creditor with a prior right to appoint a receiver over substantially the whole assets of a company, it is only fair to give him the option of enforcing his security by making the appointment or consenting to the making of an administration order. It is wrong in principle to give this vital option to a creditor merely because he has a prior floating charge which does not, however, give him priority over assets covered by that charge. This being my conclusion, it seems to me that lightweight floating charges could still be utilised as Insolvency Act expedients, but only by those having effective prior ranking charges over the whole or substantially the whole of the company's assets. Like promissory estoppel which, while incapable of founding a cause of action on its own, but can enable an action to succeed which, without it, would have failed, so also, lightweight floating charges while incapable, on their own, of giving a right to appoint an administrative receiver, can, in combination with fixed charges, enable the lender to appoint an administrative receiver which, without the lightweight floater, he could not do.

Displacement of an administrative receiver

5.19   Where a receiver is appointed in respect of a second or subsequent charge, this does not prevent prior chargees from making their own appointments. If a prior chargee appoints someone else, his appointee will take precedence and displace the receiver in situ.[89] But if the sitting receiver is court-appointed, the prior chargee's receiver will need a court order, which will usually be given as a matter of course, to get possession of the charged assets, unless the order making the appointment states that it is "without prejudice to the rights of prior incumbrancers who may wish to appoint their own receivers."[90] In that case no leave is required. This law is clear and undisputed. But is it the same for a sitting administrative receiver? The answer is unclear. On the one hand an administrative receiver can be removed only by a court order.[91] This would suggest that the general law principles of displacement are inapplicable. There are at least two possible replies to this. The first is that there is a world of difference between displacement and removal of an administrative receiver. While neither his appointer nor the chargor can remove him, the power to do so residing only in the court, there is no reason of principle or policy why an administrative receiver appointed by a junior incumbrancer cannot be displaced by one appointed by a senior incumbrancer. However, since he is an office-holder it would seem that leave of court will be required to get possession of charged assets in his possession. Such leave would be given *ex debito justitiae*. Secondly, a receiver appointed by a junior incumbrancer cannot, in any event, qualify as an administrative receiver because he would normally be unable to fulfil the requirements of section 29(2) of the Act. It is only a receiver appointed by the chargee who has overall priority that ranks as an administrative receiver. Unless the security under which he is appointed is vulnerable, he cannot be displaced, although, no doubt, he can be removed by the court. If this argument be correct, there is simply no problem as displacement will arise only in the case of voidable senior charges.

In property finance, it is to be noted that if a junior mortgagee enters into possession or receipt of the rents, the mortgagor's possession is displaced and the junior mortgagee can receive the rents without accounting to any senior mortgagee until that senior mortgagee intervenes. When he intervenes he displaces the junior mortgagee, but until that time the junior mortgagee is entitled to remain in possession of the rents.[92]

Contracting out of section 43 of the Insolvency Act 1986

5.20 The emergence of lightweight floating charges is a response by corporate lenders to the attractions of the floating security under the Insolvency Act. One of the attractions is the power of the administrative receiver to apply to court for leave to dispose of property subject to a senior charge.[93] If a junior incumbrancer's receiver can exercise this power, senior chargees would lose their right to determine the timing and conduct of realisation of charged assets. In the uncertainty which surrounds the

---

[89] Lightman & Moss, *The Law of Receivers of Companies* (London, Sweet & Maxwell, 1986), para. 21–01, pp. 221–222.
[90] *Underhay* v. *Read* (1887) 20 Q.B.D. 209.
[91] Insolvency Act 1986, s.45(1).
[92] *Re Metropolitan Amalgamated Estates Ltd.* [1912] 2 Ch. 497 at 501.
[93] Insolvency Act 1986, s.43(1).

question of entitlement to appoint an administrative receiver, the nerves of senior chargees would be considerably calmed if they can secure the agreement of other chargees whereby an administrative receiver is not to have the power to apply to court under section 43 for leave to dispose of assets subject to senior charges. In other words, the parties will contract out of section 43. Can they do so? In my view they cannot. First, parties cannot contract out of section 43 because that provision does not deal with private rights alone; it embodies the all-important policy of integrating administrative receivership into the mainstream of insolvency proceedings. Second, since an administrative receiver is an office-holder, any contract which excludes his section 43 power is an attempt to fetter his discretion and on that basis contrary to the policy of the Insolvency Act. Put differently, the section 43 power is not the result of contractual negotiation, but is incident to the receiver's status. So, it cannot be excluded.

Registration of charges

5.21   Most security interests over receivables are registrable. A specific security over receivables is registrable.[94] So also, a floating charge.[95] A pledge of documentary receivables is not registrable.[96] Registration would obviously destroy their negotiability. This immunity from registration does not extend to equitable sub-mortgage by deposit of the mortgage document.[97] An attornment is registrable being a legal mortgage. A shipowner's lien no longer requires registration.[98] An invalid retention of title agreement over proceeds of a resale or other dealing with goods sold or hired out, has been treated as a charge granted by the buyer requiring registration.[99] For purposes of registration no distinction is drawn between existing and future receivables[1]; charges over both are registrable. Where there is a purported charge over goods not requiring registration, but at the date of the charge, property in the goods has passed to a purchaser, the charge is in reality over the resulting receivables and must be registered.[2] A fixed charge over debts, other than book debts, is not registrable because the legislation contains an exhaustive list of registrable charges.[3] It has been held that a fixed charge on a contract which

---

[94] Companies Act 1985, s.396(1)(*c*).
[95] Companies Act 1985, s.396(1)(*e*).
[96] Companies Act 1985, s.396(2)(*f*) (applies only to a pledge of negotiable instruments given to secure payment of book debts). The provision does not apply to a pledge of negotiable instruments given as *payment*, rather than to secure payment.
[97] *Cf.* D. Milman 3 *Insolvency Intelligence*, February, 1990, p. 9.
[98] Companies Act 1985, s.396(2)(*g*).
[99] *Pfeiffer GmbH* v. *Arbuthnot Factors Ltd.* [1988] 1 W.L.R. 150; *Tatung (UK) Ltd.* v. *Galex Telesure Ltd.* (1989) 5 B.C.C. 325. See now, the definition of a charge in s.395(2) of the Companies Act 1985.
[1] *Independent Automatic Sales Ltd.* v. *Knowles* [1962] 1 W.L.R. 974; *Contemporary Cottages (NZ) Ltd.* v. *Margin Traders Ltd.* [1981] 2 N.Z.L.R. 114; Companies Act 1985, s.395(2).
[2] *Ladenburg & Co.* v. *Godwin Ferreira & Co. Ltd.* [1912] 3 K.B. 275; *cf. Re David Allester Ltd.* [1922] 2 Ch. 211.
[3] See Companies Act 1985, s.396.

was not a book debt at the date of the charge is not registrable merely because a book debt may arise from it in future, the reason being that registrability must be determined at the date of the charge.[4]

Only consensual securities within the statutory list are registrable. Charges arising by operation of law do not require registration,[5] but charges arising by a presumption of law must be registered.[6] The distinction is not, however, as clear cut as would seem desirable. Where there is an out and out assignment of a part only of a fund of receivables in payment of a pre-existing debt or by way of sale, in equity, the assignment operates as an equitable charge on the fund. Such a charge does not require registration.[7] In borderline cases, it is advisable to register the charge since the requirement of registration entails no more than delivering the charge in the prescribed form for registration.

Charges must be registered within 21 days of creation.[8] Where the charge is created by a written instrument, the date of execution is the date of creation of the charge.[9] In the case of an issue of debentures, time begins to run from the date of sealing, even if the debentures are not issued until some time later.[10] The date on the charge instrument is not necessarily conclusive evidence of its date of execution.[11] Since the date is not an essential part of a deed, the date of execution can be proved aliunde.[12] The parol evidence rule does not apply to the date of an instrument, so that the date shown on the instrument may be contradicted.[13] Where the charge is created orally its date of execution is not the date money was advanced in reliance on it; rather, it is the date an effective agreement for security was reached. This does not affect the rule that there is no equity to enforce specifically a contract to make or take a loan.

It should be stressed that the test of whether or not an assignment is a security is one of substance and not form, and relevant circumstances are admissible evidence to prove the true nature of the transaction.[14] The effect of registration on priorities is discussed in Chapter 6.[15]

---

[4] *Paul & Frank Ltd.* v. *Discount Bank (Overseas) Ltd.* [1967] Ch. 348.

[5] *Brunton* v. *Electrical Engineering Corp.* [1892] 1 Ch. 434; *Capital Finance & Co. Ltd.* v. *Stokes* [1969] 1 Ch. 261 at 278; *London & Cheshire Insurance Co. Ltd.* v. *Laplagrene Property Co. Ltd.* [1971] Ch. 499; Companies Act 1985, s.395(2).

[6] *Re Moulton Finance Ltd.* [1968] Ch. 325 at 332 (deposit of charge certificate by way of sub-mortgage); *Re Wallis & Simmonds (Builders) Ltd.* [1974] 1 W.L.R. 391 (deposit of title deeds).

[7] *Ashby, Warner & Co. Ltd.* v. *Simmons* [1936] 2 All E.R. 697; *cf. Re Brush Aggregates Ltd.* [1983] B.C.L.C. 320.

[8] Companies Act 1985, ss.398(1)(*b*) & 399(1).

[9] *Esberger & Son Ltd.* v. *Capital & Counties Bank* [1913] 2 Ch. 366; Companies Act 1985, s.414(2)(*a*).

[10] *Re Spiral Globe Ltd. (No. 2)* [1902] 2 Ch. 209.

[11] *Anderson* v. *Weston* (1840) 6 Bing. (NC) 296.

[12] *Esberger & Son Ltd.* v. *Capital & Counties Bank, supra.*

[13] *Re Douglas, Ex p. Starkey* (1987) 75 A.L.R. 97.

[14] See para. 2.12, *supra.*

[15] See, para. 6.24.

CHAPTER SIX

PRIORITIES

Introduction

6.1   In no area of the law are the rules of preference among adverse claimants more confused than in relation to dealings in debts. The competing claimants may be equitable assignees; one may be a legal or statutory assignee, while the other, an equitable claimant. Where the contest is between two equitable assignees, there can be little doubt that as a general rule, priority will be governed by the rule in *Dearle* v. *Hall*[1] so that victory goes to the assignee who gave first notice to the account debtor provided that, at the time he took his assignment or gave consideration, he had no notice of any pre-existing assignment. The rule is modified as regards involuntary assignees and others claiming through the assignor. But if the dispute as to priority is between an earlier equitable assignee who gave notice of his assignment first to the debtor and a subsequent legal assignee without notice, it is far from clear what the applicable priority rule is. Although there is now English authority[2] suggesting that *Dearle* v. *Hall* holds the key to the resolution of such a priority problem, there are a good many reasons for doubting whether this is in fact true.[3] The question remains, therefore, an open one. Nor is this the only area of uncertainty. On the contrary, it is also unclear what rule applies to a contest for priority between the holder of a tracing claim, be this legal or equitable, and a subsequent assignee, whether legal or equitable, of the same receivables in circumstances where the assignee has given the only notice.[4] Again, by reference to what rules are we to resolve a dispute as to priority between a superior landlord claiming sub-rentals (arising from a sub-tenancy created by the head tenant) under section 6 of the Law of Distress Amendment Act 1908, and an earlier legal or equitable assignee of the sub-rentals for value, who has given notice of assignment to the sub-tenants before the superior landlord put in his claim?[5] Occasionally, the rules of priority may be varied by priority agreements, subordination agreements, or waivers. The effect of such

---

[1] (1828) 3 Russ. 1.
[2] *Pfeiffer GmbH* v. *Arbuthnot Factors Ltd.* [1988] 1 W.L.R. 150.
[3] Oditah (1989) 9 O.J.L.S. 513 at 518–523.
[4] See McLauchlan (1980) 96 L.Q.R. 90.
[5] This was the issue in *Re Offshore Ventilation Ltd., Rhodes* v. *Allied Dunbar Pension Services Ltd.* [1989] 1 All E.R. 1161, reversing [1987] 1 W.L.R. 1703.

agreements on third party claimants is not as clear as would seem desirable. Besides, there is the difficulty of identifying an appropriate rule by reference to which circular priority problems are to be resolved. As if these problems are not enough, one has always to consider the effect of registration of charges on what would otherwise be the applicable rule. The sum of these problems and uncertainties is that receivables financing is less safe than is usually assumed, and there is scarcely any justification for the "mumbo-jumbo" of rules into which we now descend.

The general rule

At law, as in equity, the general rule of priority is that estates and **6.2** interests rank according to their dates of creation.[6] This is the first in time rule which is expressed at law in the Latin maxim *nemo dat quod non habet*. Its equitable counterpart is *qui prior est tempore potior est jure*. Both maxims express the same idea that he whose estate or interest was created first is stronger in law, as indeed in equity. As Lord Westbury explained over a century ago,[7] the logic of the first in time rule lies in the assumption that every transfer is an innocent conveyance, that is to say, the transferor disposes of only that to which he is justly entitled. When there are two or more transferees, each takes his share less the depletion by the first transfer. To a large extent, this is still the law, though the scope of its application to claims by assignees or other persons claiming to be entitled to receivables, is at present a matter of considerable uncertainty because of the assumption that all claims to receivables must, in the first instance, be resolved by the rule in *Dearle* v. *Hall*. It may be that in resolving claims of tracing creditors not deriving from assignment, the general first in time rule is applicable.[8] The same is probably true of the contest between a mercantile agent and an assignee,[9] legal or equitable, as well as claims for priority between a superior landlord and an assignee.[10]

However, in practice most assignments are equitable only, either because only part of the receivables due from a named account debtor are assigned, or because the receivables have no present existence. In either case, the assignment must of necessity be equitable.[11] This means that for most purposes disputed questions of priority will be resolved in the manner ordained by *Dearle* v. *Hall*. Where, as will often be the case, the assignments are for security only, they would need to be registered in

---

[6] *Snell's Principles of Equity* (28th ed., 1982), p. 47.

[7] *Phillips* v. *Phillips* (1861) 4 De G. F. & J. 208 at 215.

[8] See para. 6.11, *infra*.

[9] See text accompanying n. 70, p. 138, *infra*.

[10] See para. 6.19, *infra*.

[11] As to part of a debt, because it is not absolute within the meaning of s.136(1), Law of Property Act 1925: *Forster* v. *Baker* [1910] 2 K.B. 636; *G. & T. Earle* v. *Hemsworth RDC* (1928) 44 T.L.R. 605; *Williams* v. *Atlantic Assurance Co.* [1933] 1 K.B. 81 at 100. As to future debts, because they are incapable of effectual transfer at law and must take effect, if at all, only in equity: *Holroyd* v. *Marshall* (1862) 10 H.L.Cas. 191; *Tailby* v. *Official Receiver* (1883) 13 App.Cas. 523.

order to be valid against administrators, liquidators, and other persons having an interest in the assigned receivables.[12] Registration (or non-registration) impacts on both the first in time rule and the rule in *Dearle* v. *Hall*. As will appear later, not all priority questions are governed by the rule in *Dearle* v. *Hall*. Therefore, it is proposed to consider first the one area where the rule clearly applies, namely, successive equitable assignments of the same receivables.

Priority of successive equitable assignees

6.3   Priority of successive equitable assignees is governed by the rule in *Dearle* v. *Hall*. Under the rule victory goes to the person who gives first notice to the debtor.[13] Where the rule applies the first in time rule is displaced, thus enabling a junior or subsequent assignee to gain priority by giving first notice. The reasoning behind this priority by notice of claim is not always clear,[14] and before 1828 this was not the law.[15] Although the rule, no doubt, was an anomalous extension of the reputed ownership doctrine of bankruptcy law into equitable priorities, it is now best rationalised as equating notice of claim to possession of a tangible personalty. An assignee who has given no notice can expect to be postponed to a subsequent assignee who gives such notice to the account debtor, on the basis that he had not taken the ultimate step that assures victory. This priority of the junior assignee is independent of whether or not he made inquiries of the debtor before taking his assignment, for the rule in *Dearle* v. *Hall* is independent of diligence on his part or negligence on the part of the earlier assignee.[16] For this purpose, the notice need not be formal, provided it brings to the appreciation of the account debtor the fact that the receivables claimed have been assigned. Accordingly, a notice acquired *aliunde* by the account debtor is sufficient to preserve the priority of a senior assignee,[17] but insufficient to give a second or junior assignee priority over an earlier assignee of whose assignment the debtor knows nothing.[18] Also, oral notice is sufficient, though like notice

---

[12] Companies Act 1985, s.399(1) and (2) (new amendments).

[13] *Foster* v. *Cockerell* (1835) 3 Cl. & F. 456; *Re Dallas* [1904] 2 Ch. 385.

[14] *Ward* v. *Duncombe* [1893] A.C. 369 at 384–393.

[15] In *Cooper* v. *Fynmore* (1814) 3 Russ. 60, Sir Thomas Plumer V.-C. held that priority between successive equitable assignees of an interest under a marriage settlement was governed by the order of creation. Consequently, although the second assignee inquired of the settlement trustees whether there was any existing incumbrance before he took his assignment and gave notice, he was postponed to the earlier assignee who gave a subsequent notice. Sir Thomas Plumer V.-C. said that mere neglect in giving notice by the first assignee was insufficient to disapply the first in time rule. "In order to deprive him of his priority, it was necessary that there should be such laches as, in a court of equity, amounted to fraud": *ibid*. Although this case was decided before his decision in *Dearle* v. *Hall*, and counsel knew of it before the appeal in *Dearle* v. *Hall* was heard, it was not cited in argument. It is now speculative to say what effect this omission has had on the development of the law of equitable priorities.

[16] *Foster* v. *Cockerell* (1835) 3 Cl. & F. 456; *Re Dallas* [1904] 2 Ch. 385.

[17] *Lloyd* v. *Banks* (1868) L.R. 3 Ch.App. 488.

[18] *Arden* v. *Arden* (1885) 29 Ch.D. 702; *Ipswich Permanent Money Club Ltd.* v. *Arthy* [1920] 2 Ch. 257.

acquired *aliunde*, there is always the problem of proof. To rely on these kinds of informal notice, it is absolutely necessary that the mind of the debtor is brought to an intelligent appreciation of the nature of the assignment, so that a reasonable man of business would act on such information and regulate his conduct by such notice.[19] Casual conversations, however, are not to be elevated to the status of notice of an equitable assignment. In view of the serious consequences attaching to notice of an assignment, not only as regards priority, but also in matters of set-off, etc., informal oral notices are to be avoided. For example, an oral notice of assignment given by the assignee's agent to a clerk in an insurance office where the former had gone to pay premiums due on the assigned policy was held too casual to be operative.[20] But it is also the law that once distinct and clear oral notice has been given to the debtor, no degree of amnesia will relieve him from liability to that assignee if he forgets and pays over the receivables to a subsequent assignee.[21]

Equity's flexibility as regards the notice necessary to secure priority may in this respect be compared with the more strict regime applicable to legal assignments. Whereas in equity, a mistake as to the date of an assignment does not invalidate the assignment,[22] the rule at law has been interpreted rather strictly. At law a mistake as to the date of assignment invalidates a statutory assignment,[23] though a notice of assignment which mentions no date is valid.[24] It must be stressed that the strict rule at law relates to the *acquisition* of legal title to assigned receivables, and not to the different question of *priority*. The purpose of notice intended to secure the priority of an equitable assignment is to inform the debtor that the notice giver has acquired title to the receivables. Therefore, although there is no requirement that the notice of assignment should indicate that payment must be made to the notice giver and no one else, the notice must, however, be plain and unambiguous. It is not enough that the notice is capable of being understood as indicating that receivables have been assigned. It must indicate plainly that the receivables have been assigned.[25]

Notice need not be given by the assignee himself. It may in fact be given by a second assignee who did not intend that result.[26] The omission

---

[19] *Lloyd* v. *Banks* (1868) L.R. 3 Ch.App. 488 at 496.

[20] *Ex p. Carbis* (1834) 4 Deac. & Ch. 354; *Re Tichener* (1865) 35 Beav. 317 at 318.

[21] *Burrows* v. *Lock* (1805) 10 Ves. 470 at 475–476. As to when a corporate debtor can be said to forget, see Wedderburn (1984) 47 M.L.R. 345.

[22] *Whittingstall* v. *King* (1882) 46 L.T. 520.

[23] *Stanley* v. *English Fibres Industries Ltd.* (1899) 68 L.J. Q.B. 829; *W.F. Harrison & Co. Ltd.* v. *Burke* [1956] 1 W.L.R. 419; *cf. Denney, Gasquet & Metcalfe* v. *Conklin* [1913] 3 K.B. 177. These cases are discussed by Megarry (1956) 72 L.Q.R. 321. In *Gatoil Anstalt* v. *Omennial Ltd., The "Balder London"* [1980] 2 Lloyd's Rep. 489, the notice suspended payment to the assignee until the happening of some event; before then the account debtor was to make payments to the assignor. Mocatta J. held that owing to the suspensory character of the notice, it did not amount to a notice of assignment to the debtor as is required to validate a statutory assignment. A stronger reason for the judgment would be that the form of the notice indicated that the assignment was conditional rather than absolute: *Durham Brothers* v. *Robertson* [1898] 1 Q.B. 765 at 773.

[24] *Van Lynn Developments Ltd.* v. *Pelias Construction Co. Ltd.* [1969] 1 Q.B. 607.

[25] *James Talcott Ltd.* v. *John Lewis & Co. Ltd.* [1940] 3 All E.R. 592.

[26] *Ipswich Permanent Money Club Ltd.* v. *Arthy* [1920] 2 Ch. 257 at 272–273.

to give personal notice by the assignee to the debtor may not be fatal.[27] To be operative, the notice must be given to the account debtor or his authorised agent. Generally, a solicitor is not a general agent of his client to receive a notice of assignment unless on the facts (which will be rare) such a general authority can be spelt out.[28] He is an agent of the client only in the matter in which he is engaged, so that a notice of an assignment concerning the subject-matter of his retainer is notice to the client.[29] In such circumstances the solicitor is bound to communicate any notice received by him to his client,[30] but if in breach of duty he fails to do so, the client is still bound.[31]

Where a notice of an equitable assignment is sent by post, it does not take effect until it is received by the debtor.[32] This is so whether or not he opens it on that date. But where it is received after business hours, it is deemed to have been received on the next working day.[33] All notices received on the same date rank *pari passu* and are treated as simultaneous notices ranking *inter se* according to the date of creation.[34] In principle, a notice of assignment sent by an instantaneous means of communication, such as telex or facsimile, should take effect when it is received at the other end.

An equitable assignee seeking to gain priority by notice may be disabled from doing so if the second limb of the rule in *Dearle* v. *Hall* applies. This limb requires that the notice giver should have no notice of any earlier assignment at the time he took his assignment or furnished the consideration for the same. Where he does, the general rule of first in time applies and as against the assignee of whose claim he had notice, priority goes to the senior in point of time of creation.[35] Although authority is lacking, in principle, the priority of his claim against other assignees of whose assignments he was unaware should still be governed by the date of notice to the debtor, provided, of course, that the latter assignees hold equitable assignments only. (This may create a circularity where the other assignees gave notice before the first). That he would have known of their assignments if he had inquired is not fatal, for priority by notice is independent of diligence or negligence on the part of assignees. However, in practice the compass within which this liberal attitude assumes significance is narrowed by two factors. First, the disabling notice need not be actual: it could be imputed or constructive.[36] Thus in *Spencer* v. *Clarke*,[37] a fraudulent assured deposited the policy

---

[27] *Magee* v. *UDC Finance Ltd.* [1983] N.Z.L.R. 438 at 442.
[28] *Saffron Walden Second Benefit Building Society* v. *Rayner* (1880) 14 Ch.D. 406 at 409 –410.
[29] *Dixon* v. *Winch* [1900] 1 Ch. 736; *Magee* v. *UDC Finance Ltd.* [1983] N.Z.L.R. 438.
[30] *Ibid.*
[31] *Ibid.*
[32] *Holt* v. *Heatherfield Trust Ltd.* [1942] 2 K.B. 1.
[33] *Re Dallas* [1904] 2 Ch. 385 at 395.
[34] *Calisher* v. *Forbes* (1871) L.R. 7 Ch.App. 109; *Johnstone* v. *Cox* (1880) 16 Ch.D. 571, affd. (1881) 19 Ch.D. 17, C.A.
[35] *Timson* v. *Ramsbottam* (1837) 2 Keen 35; *Warburton* v. *Hill* (1854) Kay 470; *Spencer* v. *Clarke* (1878) 9 Ch.D. 137; *Re Hamilton's Windsor Ironworks* (1879) 12 Ch.D. 707 at 711; *Re Holmes* (1885) 29 Ch.D. 786.
[36] *Spencer* v. *Clarke, supra.*
[37] (1879) 9 Ch.D. 137.

with A by way of equitable mortgage of which no notice had been given to the insurer. Later he borrowed money from B by assigning the same policy, telling him that the policy had been left at home mistakenly. B gave first notice to the insurer. But Hall V.-C. held that B must be taken to have had constructive notice of A's prior equitable mortgage by failing to make inquiries. Therefore, B's notice to the insurer was unavailing. Secondly, where the prior equitable assignment has been registered as a charge, then although such registration would not convey the requisite notice to the account debtor under the first limb of the rule in *Dearle* v. *Hall*, yet it might be sufficient notice[38] to trigger the second limb and thus render any express notice given by a junior assignee after registration inoperative, provided that the second assignee is a chargee. What the result would be where the debtor acquires knowledge accidentally of the second assignment (a) before the first security assignment is registered within 21 days, and (b) after registration, is unclear. *Arden* v. *Arden*[39] suggests that the result would be the same in either case and that priorities cannot be gained any more than they could be displaced by such accidental knowledge.

It is to be noted that the disabling knowledge is one gained before or at the time the subsequent assignee took his assignment or furnished consideration. A notice gained afterwards, even before notice-gaining priority is given to the account debtor, is not disabling[40]; on the contrary, such notice shows the very necessity for taking the ultimate step that assures victory[41]—notice to the debtor. This second limb of the rule in *Dearle* v. *Hall* is intended to prevent sharp practice: people jumping in and taking advantage of a technical failure to give notice.[42] But one does not need to find sharp practice or its equivalent before invoking the second limb. In itself, the rule makes perfect sense: formalities will not be insisted upon; here, the law follows the ordinary morality of the matter, and rightly insists that a man who has provisional priority based on time of creation of his entitlement should not be squeezed out by somebody coming in when that person had knowledge of the first claimant's position.

Dearle v. *Hall* and assignees of expectant receivables

Much of financing against receivables is carried out on the strength of **6.4** future receivables. Such unearned accounts constitute a satisfactory security because every going concern must necessarily generate receivables even where it is trading at a loss. It has also been argued, and somewhat persuasively, that receivables should be seen as sources of

---

[38] Companies Act 1985, s.416(1); *Wilson* v. *Kelland* [1910] 2 Ch. 306; *Siebe Gorman* v. *Barclays Bank Ltd.* [1979] 2 Lloyd's Rep. 142.
[39] (1885) 29 Ch.D. 702.
[40] *Mutual Life Assurance Society* v. *Langley* (1886) 32 Ch.D. 460.
[41] *Taylor* v. *Russell* [1892] A.C. 244 at 259.
[42] *Rhodes* v. *Allied Dunbar Pension Services Ltd.* [1987] 1 W.L.R. 1703 at 1708, rvsd. [1989] 1 All E.R. 1161, C.A. (not on this point).

long-term capital.[43] Taking the ultimate step that assures victory—notice to "debtors," may be difficult, first, because of the sheer number of debtors, and secondly, because the identity of prospective debtors may be unknown at the date of assignment. Simple or difficult, notice must be given. Here, one encounters one of the most absurd refinements of the rule in *Dearle* v. *Hall*. No rule of equity is perhaps better settled, and yet least understood, than the rule that notice which is given by an assignee of expectant receivables to a possible or future debtor is futile for the purpose of securing priority against other assignees who give notice to the actual debtor after the receivables have come into existence. This harsh rule was established by the army agents cases[44] and has since been applied to notice given to a prospective administrator before he was effectually appointed[45] and to a prospective administrator before the grant of letters of administration.[46] The result of these cases is consistent with the principle which lies at the root of *Dearle* v. *Hall*, namely, that notice to the debtor is equivalent to possession. However, the equitable operations cannot be carried out prospectively. An expectancy or possibility can, in equity, be assigned,[47] but even in equity, it cannot be taken possession of until it has materialised. Therefore, where an expectant receivable is assigned, notice to the future debtor is ineffectual for the purpose of disturbing priorities, until there are in existence both a receivable which is owed to the assignor of which possession can be taken, and a debtor to whom, for this purpose, notice can be brought home. It is obvious that this refinement is a most inconvenient rule for the receivables financier advancing money to the client on the strength of expectant receivables. It is not open to the assignee of an expectant receivable to say that the account debtor, when the debt accrued, ought to have remembered the notice he had received the previous day or week. The previous notice is void altogether[48] because it was given to a person who was not a debtor at that time. To such an extent has the refinement been carried that, if a notice is served after office hours on the day next preceding the accrual of the receivable, it will be treated as good notice on the date it accrued, but if it is received the previous day during office hours, it is bad and

---

[43] H. Kpripke (1952) 36 Minn.L.R. 506.
[44] *Buller* v. *Plunkett* (1860) 1 J. & H. 441; *Webster* v. *Webster* (1862) 31 Beav. 393; *Somerset* v. *Cox* (1865) 33 Beav. 634; *Boss* v. *Hopkinson* (1870) 18 W.R. 725; *Calisher* v. *Forbes* (1871) L.R. 7 Ch.App. 109; *Addison* v. *Cox* (1872) L.R. 8 Ch.App. 76; *Johnstone* v. *Cox* (1880) 16 Ch.D. 571 affd. (1881) 18 Ch.D. 17, C.A.
[45] *Re Dallas* [1904] 2 Ch. 385.
[46] *Re Kinahan's Trusts* [1907] 1 Ir.R. 321.
[47] *Re Clarke* (1887) 36 Ch.D. 348 at 351; *Tailby* v. *Official Receiver* (1888) 13 App.Cas. 523 at 543.
[48] *Re Dallas* [1904] 2 Ch. 385 at 395. In *Ipswich Permanent Money Club Ltd.* v. *Arthy* [1920] 2 Ch. 257 at 270, a perplexed Lawrence J. declared:

> "It seems to me to be a somewhat irrational proposition that although a trustee knows and fully apprehends the nature and effect of an earlier incumbrance, yet he must be treated as not having that knowledge and apprehension when the acquisition of his knowledge took place before his appointment."

He thought *Re Dallas* did not decide this question and held such notice operative, although alternatively he concluded that there was in fact an effectual notice after the trustee was appointed.

ineffectual.[49] Even where the assignee posts a notice every day to the future debtor, there is no way he will know the precise date of accrual of the debt, unlike the army agents cases where gazetting (on which the accrual of the debt depended) was a kind of public notice. Even assuming that posting a notice to a substantial number of future debtors was theoretically possible, the expense is bound to be great and this, no doubt, will be reflected in the cost of financing, which will be borne by the assignor. To put assignors and their financiers to such great expense in the service of no useful purpose is anything but efficient.

The hardship and inconvenience engendered by this rule is mitigated by two factors. The first is a generous interpretation of "existing receivables." As we have already seen,[50] English law treats as existing, not only earned receivables whether or not presently payable, and whether or not ascertained, but also unearned receivables expected under existing contracts. Many contractual relationships are of a long-term nature, and individual contracts are usually implemented within a pre-existing framework. Whether the existence of the framework alone is sufficient to stamp the expected receivables with the badge of existing property is unclear. The second is the facility for registration of corporate charges. Where existing and future receivables are assigned as security for a term loan or an overdraft, registration of the security will constitute notice to subsequent chargees[51] and thus disable recourse to priority-gaining by notice to account debtors.

Limits of *Dearle* v. *Hall*

Few generalisations, legal or otherwise, have been more often repeated **6.5** or more devoutly believed in than this: priority between competing assignees (whether legal or equitable) is governed by the order in which notice is given to, and received by, the debtor. As we have seen, this is probably true if limited to successive equitable assignees. However, enthusiasts of *Dearle* v. *Hall* have often represented the rule as being far more pervasive. The truth, though, is that the rule is subject to a number of important limitations. Because the rule is confined to equitable assignments it does not apply to claims which arise by operation of law. For example, a judgment creditor cannot displace the priority of an earlier assignee (obtained under the first in time rule) by being the first to give notice to the debtor.[52] This is so whether he be a garnishor[53] or the holder of a charging order.[54] Where he has served notice on the garnishee before an assignment he may prevail. The same is in principle true of voluntary[55] and involuntary assignees.[56] Thus a liquidator cannot displace

[49] *Re Dallas, supra.*
[50] See para. 2.6, *supra.*
[51] Companies Act 1985, s.416(1); *Wilson* v. *Kelland* [1910] 2 Ch. 306; *Siebe Gorman* v. *Barclays Bank Ltd.* [1979] 2 Lloyd's Rep. 142.
[52] For a full discussion, see para. 6.7, *infra.*
[53] *Holt* v. *Heatherfield Trust Ltd.* [1942] 2 K.B. 1.
[54] *Scott* v. *Lord Hastings* (1858) 4 K. & J. 633.
[55] *West* v. *Williams* [1899] 1 Ch. 132.
[56] *Re Wallis* [1902] 1 K.B. 719, cited with approval in *Re Anderson* [1911] 1 K.B. 896.

the provisional priority of an earlier assignee by being the first to give notice, for, succeeding only to the title of the insolvent assignor, he takes subject to all equities valid against the claim in the hands of the assignor.[57] The position might differ in the case of expectant receivables. In such a case, where at the commencement of liquidation, the receivables are unearned, and result from the post-liquidation efforts of the liquidator, *Dearle* v. *Hall* is displaced and the title of the liquidator prevails even as against an earlier assignee who has given notice to the debtor before liquidation supervened.[58] The reason for this rule is that the insolvent assignor had nothing to assign. This result has nothing to do with the provision[59] which avoids dispositions effected after the commencement of winding up. The result is to be contrasted with the situation where the receivables exist at the date of liquidation, although unascertained or not payable at that date. Here, the title of the pre-liquidation assignee prevails over that of the liquidator because in claiming the receivables after commencement of liquidation, the assignee is merely crystallising a right which survived winding up.[60] The disposition took place at the date of assignment and not when the receivables are collected. Collecting such receivables does not offend against the rule which avoids post-liquidation dispositions by the insolvent,[61] nor does it contravene the principle of equality in the distribution of the insolvent's estate—such receivables never formed part of the estate.

Also, *Dearle* v. *Hall* does not apply to documentary receivables. Where a debt has become embodied in a negotiable paper, the only person with a valid claim is the holder of the paper. Accordingly, notice to the debtor who has issued such a paper is ineffectual for the purpose of gaining priority.[62] This is so even where the assignor is in possession of the paper and has requested the debtor to recognise the claim of the assignee who has given notice. The debtor can safely ignore the request so long as the paper is still outstanding and has not been returned to him. The notice remains ineffectual even after dishonour of the paper upon presentment. Equally, an action on the debt embodied in the paper, as opposed to the paper itself, is bound to fail whilst the paper remains outstanding (even after dishonour). If it is outstanding at the date of commencement of action, the subsequent acquisition of the paper before trial is unavailing to give the action retrospective validity.[63] The reasoning behind this rule is

---

[57] *Ibid.*

[58] *Ex p. Nichols* (1883) 22 Ch.D. 782; *Wilmot* v. *Alton* [1897] 1 Q.B. 17 at 22; *Re De Marney* [1943] Ch. 126.

[59] Insolvency Act 1986, s.127.

[60] *Re Davis* (1889) 22 Q.B.D. 193; *Re Trytel* [1952] 2 T.L.R. 32; *Re Miller, Gibb & Co. Ltd.* [1957] 1 W.L.R. 703; *Re Charge Card Services Ltd.* [1988] 3 W.L.R. 723, C.A.

[61] *Sowman* v. *David Samuel Trust Ltd.* [1978] 1 W.L.R. 22; *Re Margart Pty Ltd. (in liq.)*, *Hamilton* v. *Westpac Banking Corporation* (1984) 9 A.C.L.R. 269. *Cf. Re Clifton Place Garage Ltd.* [1970] Ch. 477 where both at first instance and in the Court of Appeal, dispositions by the receiver after the presentation of winding-up petition, of property covered by the charge, were treated as avoided by s.227 of the Companies Act 1948 (now Insolvency Act 1986, s.127).

[62] *Bence* v. *Shearman* [1898] 2 Ch. 582. It would of course have made all the difference if the notice of assignment was received before the cheque was issued.

[63] *Belshaw* v. *Bush* (1851) 11 C.B. 191; *Davis* v. *Reilly* [1898] 1 Q.B. 1. Nor can the payee petition for liquidation even after dishonour if the bill is outstanding in the hands of a third party: *Re a Debtor* [1908] 1 K.B. 344.

that the issue of a negotiable paper suspends action on the debt whilst the paper is still outstanding in the hands of someone other than the plaintiff. It is also true that an account debtor who has "discharged" his debt by issuing a bill of exchange is under no duty to stop payment on the bill simply because he has received a notice of assignment or garnishment.[64] With this class of receivables, *Dearle* v. *Hall* notice has nothing at all to do.

Outside the above categories, other limits to *Dearle* v. *Hall* remain. Notice to a debtor may be unavailing where the assignee has contracted not to give notice or where he holds a security which from its nature prevents any notice of claim given before the occurrence of a future event from being effective.[65] The paradigm example is an uncrystallized floating charge. The holder may have contracted that the chargor should, notwithstanding the charge, be free to create subsequent entitlements having priority over the charge. In that case, notice given by the chargee before crystallization of the charge cannot prevail over a subsequent specific assignee who gives a later notice.[66] But even where he has not so contracted, the nature of a floating charge is such that even with the now common negative pledge or covenant not to incumber, the chargee is still not entitled to rush in a notice before crystallization. If he does, the notice cannot prevail over a subsequent execution creditor,[67] and *a fortiori*, over a specific assignee having no notice of the covenant. The position would be different where there is a provision for partial crystallization, whether by notice or automatically.[68]

Dearle v. *Hall* depends for its application on the existence of two or more *valid* equitable assignments. Where one of the only two existing claims is invalid, there is no occasion for the application of *Dearle* v. *Hall* because the only valid claim wins the contest by default. However, in *Pfeiffer GmbH* v. *Arbuthnot Factors Ltd.*,[69] this point seemed to have escaped the court. There were only two claims—one from a reservation of title seller and the other from a factor who had purchased his client's receivables. Having concluded that the reservation of title clause was void against the factor as an unregistered charge (very doubtful), the court went on to resolve the claims to priority by invoking *Dearle* v. *Hall*. It is also clear that in a contest for priority between a mercantile agent to whom goods have been consigned for sale and an equitable or legal

---

[64] *Elwell* v. *Jackson* (1885) 1 T.L.R. 454.

[65] *English & Scottish Mercantile Investment Trust Ltd.* v. *Brunton* [1892] 2 Q.B. 1 at 8, affd. *ibid.*, p. 700.

[66] *Ward* v. *Royal Exchange Shipping Co.* (1988) 58 L.T. 174 at 178; *Re Ind, Coope & Co. Ltd.* [1911] 2 Ch. 223; *Canadian Imperial Bank of Commerce* v. *F.B.D.B.* [1985] 3 W.W.R. 318.

[67] *Robson* v. *Smith* [1895] 2 Ch. 118; *Evans* v. *Rival Granite Quarries Ltd.* [1910] 2 K.B. 979. "It is inconsistent with the nature of a floating security that the holder should be able to pounce down on particular assets and to interfere with the company's business while still keeping his security floating; he cannot at once give freedom and insist on servitude": *ibid.* at 998, *per* Fletcher Moulton L.J.

[68] See para. 5.13, *supra*, for a discussion of automatic crystallization.

[69] [1988] 1 W.L.R. 150, criticised in (1989) 9 O.J.L.S. 513 at 518–523.

assignee of the proceeds of sale, the title of the agent will prevail.[70] More importantly, *Dearle* v. *Hall* does not apply where the assignor was never owed the receivables.[71] This is an important qualification on the rule which, if applied literally, could emasculate the rule. An assignor who has ceased to be "owner" by assignment or other dealing is not, for this purpose, considered as never having "owned" the receivables. *Hill* v. *Peters*[72] shows that where the dispute is between the beneficiaries under a trust and assignees of the trust property fraudulently made by the trustee, priority does not depend on the order in which notice is given to the fraudulent trustee. The reasoning is that beneficiaries having no right to call for the trust property are under no duty to give notice of their interest to their own trustee in order to shield themselves from his fraud. This is all very well and in principle, unobjectionable. But when it is remembered that the subject-matter of the trust was a mortgage, and that neither the beneficiaries nor the sub-mortgagee gave notice to the mortgagor—the debtor for purposes of the rule in *Dearle* v. *Hall*, the suggestion[73] of Fry J. that the sub-mortgagee who had no notice of the trust would not have prevailed even by giving first notice to the mortgagor becomes difficult to follow.

Exactly how relevant *Hill* v. *Peters* is to priority conflicts between receivables financiers is difficult to estimate. What seems clear is that a modern judge is unlikely to be persuaded that a sophisticated financier can opt out of *Dearle* v. *Hall* by framing his security as a trust rather than an assignment. To be sure, a financier, no less than anyone else, is perfectly entitled to rely on obscure rules of equity. The objection here does not rest on the identity of the claimant. It is simply this: a trust of receivables, whether or not as security, is, in this context, almost certainly a bare trust giving the beneficiary a right to call for the corpus. This is inconsistent with the reasoning underlying *Hill* v. *Peters*. Besides, where the trust is imposed on receivables, and the debtor agrees to hold them as trustee for the financier, one runs into the same conceptual difficulty which perplexed Millett J. in *Re Charge Card Services Ltd.*,[74] namely, whether a debtor could sensibly hold his own obligation in trust for another. How will he, it may be asked, enforce and get in the trust property? This conceptual difficulty does not arise where the creditor declares himself a trustee of his right to receive payment for the benefit of the financier. It has been argued[75] that *Hill* v. *Peters* holds the key to the

---

[70] A mercantile agent has a common law lien on goods consigned to him for sale, as security for any debts owed to him by his principal. The lien extends to the proceeds of the goods and gives the agent a paramount right (to the resulting proceeds) against assignees of the principal: *Drinkwater* v. *Godwin* (1775) 1 Cowp. 251; *Webb* v. *Smith* (1885) 30 Ch.D.192.
[71] *B.S. Lyle Ltd.* v. *Rosher* [1959] 1 W.L.R. 8. This is a particularly strong authority because the fact that the son (underwriter) was not beneficially entitled to the funds was unknown to Lloyds. The case indicates judicial disenchantment with *Dearle* v. *Hall*. For criticisms, see Elphinstone, (1961) 77 L.Q.R. 69.
[72] [1918] 2 Ch. 273.
[73] *Ibid.* at 279.
[74] [1987] Ch. 150 at 175. See also, *Halesowen Presswork & Assemblies Ltd.* v. *National Westminster Bank Ltd.* [1971] 1 Q.B. 1 at 46; *Broad* v. *Comsr. of Stamp Duties* [1980] 2 N.S.W.L.R. 40; *cf.* Yates [1971] Conv. 49 at 53.
[75] McLauchlan (1980) 96 L.Q.R. 90.

resolution of questions of priority between the holder of a tracing claim (*e.g.* a reservation of title seller claiming the proceeds of sale) and a subsequent assignee of the resulting receivables. *Dearle* v. *Hall* does not apply because the tracing creditor is the beneficiary under an implied trust of the resulting proceeds of sale. The argument, though, is a little overstated. For one thing, if ever the tracing creditor could establish a trust, it would at best be a bare one to which the reasoning in *Hill* v. *Peters* would seem inappropriate; for another, even if it is assumed (in agreement with the argument) that the assignor holds title to the receivables in trust, the assignee may still win the race for one of two reasons. First, it would be idle to split the receivables from the right to receive them on a kind of fruit and tree analogy. The ultimate debtor is for all practical purposes the fundholder to whom notice should be given. Secondly, the claim of the tracing creditor would almost certainly be overreached once payment is received by the assignee. In that event, his title to the payment as a bona fide purchaser for value without notice is complete and on its own sufficient to assure victory.[76]

Different considerations would of course arise where the ultimate debtor has not paid and the matter lies essentially in receivables rather than receipt.[77] In a priority contest between a superior landlord serving a notice of claim of sub-rentals on sub-tenants pursuant to section 6 of the Law of Distress Amendment Act 1908 on the one hand, and an equitable assignee of the same receivables on the other, *Dearle* v. *Hall* would seem to be inapplicable.[78] One reason for this is that the superior landlord does not derive his claim from the intermediate landlord/assignor, and *Dearle* v. *Hall* applies only to successive assignments from the assignor. A second is that the superior landlord's claim is a title paramount overriding any assignments. If this be correct, it sits oddly with the hostile attitude towards purchase-money creditors such as sellers whose credit sale terms include a reservation of title clause.

Finally, *Dearle* v. *Hall* does not apply to a contest between two legal assignees of the same receivables. Although authority in support is lacking, there are two related reasons of principle why this must be so. The first is the theoretical impossibility of having two legal assignments of the same debts at the same time.[79] Where the first is legal, it exhausts the assignor's interest in the receivables leaving nothing for him to assign to a second creditor. Secondly, even where the prior legal assignment is for security only, and the assignor retains an equity of redemption, since written notice is necessary to the acquisition of a legal assignment, that notice would be sufficient to ensure the continuing priority of the legal

---

[76] *Thorndike* v. *Hunt* (1859) 3 De G. & J. 563; *Taylor* v. *Blakelock* (1886) 32 Ch.D. 560; *Thomson* v. *Clydesdale Bank Ltd.* [1893] A.C. 282; *Coleman* v. *Bucks and Oxon Union Bank* [1897] 2 Ch. 242. The question was left undecided in *Pfeiffer GmbH* v. *Arbuthnot Factors Ltd.* [1988] 1 W.L.R. 150 at 163, though Phillips J. indicated that *Taylor* v. *Blakelock* is an authority in favour of the recipient of the payment.

[77] For a fuller discussion, see para. 6.11, *infra*.

[78] *Rhodes* v. *Allied Dunbar Pension Services Ltd.* [1989] 1 All E.R. 1161, C.A. For a full treatment see para. 6.19, *infra*.

[79] *Cronk* v. *McManus* (1892) 8 T.L.R. 449; *Ellerman Lines Ltd.* v. *Lancaster Maritime Co. Ltd., The "Lancaster"* [1980] 2 Lloyd's Rep. 497 at 503.

assignment. The result is the same whether one applies the first in time rule or *Dearle* v. *Hall*. In certain circumstances, however, the junior assignment may prevail.[80] Also, as argued later,[81] in a contest between a prior equitable assignment and a subsequent legal assignment for value without notice, priority falls to be resolved not by the application of *Dearle* v. *Hall*, but by invoking the bona fide purchaser rule. This shows that, far from having a procedural significance only, the characterisation of assignments as legal or equitable may yet be important in resolving priority conflicts.

The poverty of *Dearle* v. *Hall*

6.6 The rule in *Dearle* v. *Hall* was formulated in the context of a competition for priority between three equitable assignees of a trust fund which was insufficient to meet all their claims. It is also undoubted that so far as competing equitable assignments of debts are concerned, the rule applies with equal force.[82] Given the relatively small number of trustees of a trust fund, it may not have been unreasonable to resolve priority disputes by reference to the dates of notices to the trustees. This is especially so where, as in *Dearle* v. *Hall* itself, an assignee had, before taking his assignment, made inquiries of the trustees and no existing incumbrance is disclosed, and given also the lack of any reliable facility for publicising dealings in debts. In such a situation, preferring the assignee who gave first notice was a reward for diligence even when the result was to make the fundholder a kind of public register. From these humble beginnings, *Dearle* v. *Hall* has hardened into an unwavering rule. A hundred and sixty-six years on, the rule has remained unreformed, and has been extended by analogies inexact, if not false, to new areas for which it was hardly designed. The rule is now so antiquated that it belongs to a past generation. For many reasons it ought no longer to be applied outside trust-related priority disputes.

> 1. *Dearle* v. *Hall* is not rooted in any coherent principle. As *Ward* v. *Duncombe*[83] shows, attempts at justification of the rule founder on its unprincipled nature. The application of the rule has produced

---

[80] Such circumstances will include where the prior legal assignee carves out an equitable interest out of his own assignment, or gives the assignor authority to borrow on the strength of an equitable assignment and this authority is exceeded: see *Perry-Herrick* v. *Attwood* (1857) 2 De G. & J. 21 at 39; *Brocklesby* v. *Temperance Building Society* [1895] A.C. 173. Non-registration of the legal assignment (if it is for security only) may also lead to loss of priority, as would also happen where there is a subordination or priority agreement: see *Re Camden Brewery Ltd.* (1912) 106 L.T. 598; *Re Robert Stephenson & Co. Ltd.* [1913] 2 Ch. 201; *Judson* v. *DCT (Victoria)* (1987) 12 A.C.L.R. 91.

[81] See para. 6.14, *infra*.

[82] In *Gorringe* v. *Irwell India Rubber Works* (1886) 34 Ch.D. 128 at 132, Cotton L.J. assumed that the rule in *Dearle* v. *Hall* applied to debts. The rule was also applied to competing equitable assignments of a debt in *Marchant* v. *Morton, Down & Co.* [1901] 2 K.B. 829, though it is not clear why the ineffectual deed could not count as a written assignment rather than a mere contract to assign.

[83] [1893] A.C. 369 at 390–391.

nearly as much, if not more, injustice as its non-application will produce. This in part explains the judicial reluctance to extend the rule to new areas.

2. The refinements on the rule take it close to pure fiction. Since *Foster* v. *Cockerell*,[84] the rule has become independent of diligence or negligence in giving notice. There is neither a duty to inquire nor a duty to answer inquiries.[85] Priority does not depend on whether inquiry precedes notice. The first giver of notice wins the *Dearle* v. *Hall* lottery on a winner takes all basis (subject of course to any remaining equity in the case of security assignments). That there was no debtor to whom notice could be given when the first assignment was made does not advance the ranking of a senior assignee in the pecking order if junior incumbrancers gave first notice.[86]

3. *Dearle* v. *Hall* notice may be uninformative because it need not specify that the debt should be paid to the assignee.[87] The debtor is supposed to infer this from the fact of assignment. The risk of double liability if the debtor pays the wrong assignee is real.

4. *Dearle* v. *Hall* does not require written notice. Even where the assignment is legal, the written notice required by section 136(1) of the Law of Property Act 1925 goes, not to *priority*, but to *acquisition* of legal title. However, equitable assignments of *equitable* interests under a trust must comply with section 137(3) of the Law of Property Act 1925, which requires written notice. It follows that an oral notice suffices for purposes of priority of equitable assignments of legal choses in action. This type of notice could easily be forgotten; but the debtor's amnesia will not relieve him from liability to make a second payment.[88] He may, of course, recover from the wrong assignee on the basis either of mistake of fact[89] or total failure of consideration,[90] and may also trace the payment. Tracing may, however, be an expensive gamble.

---

[84] (1835) 3 Cl. & F. 456.

[85] *Ward* v. *Duncombe* [1893] A.C. 369 at 393–394. *Cf.* s.137(8), Law of Property Act 1925, under which an assignee of an equitable interest in land, capital money and any securities representing capital money is entitled, subject to payment of costs, to require production of notice of any earlier incumbrance from the trustees.

[86] *Re Dallas* [1904] 2 Ch. 385; *Re Kinahan's Trusts* [1907] 1 Ir.R. 321; *cf. Ipswich Permanent Money Club Ltd.* v. *Arthy* [1920] 2 Ch. 257 at 270.

[87] *Cf.* UCC, Art. 9–318(3) which requires that a notice of assignment indicate that the amount due or to become due has been assigned and that payment is to be made to the assignee.

[88] *Burrows* v. *Lock* (1805) 10 Ves. 470 at 475–476 (notice of first assignment had been given 10 years before second assignee inquired). In *Re Montagu's S.T.* [1987] 2 W.L.R. 1192 at 1210, Megarry V.-C. said that apart from statute, a person should not be said to have knowledge of a fact that he once knew if at the time in question he has genuinely forgotten all about it, so that it no longer operates on his mind. On the question when a corporate debtor could be said to have forgotten a fact, see Wedderburn (1984) 47 M.L.R. 345.

[89] *Chase Manhattan Bank* v. *Israel-British Bank (London) Ltd.* [1981] Ch. 105.

[90] *Sinclair* v. *Brougham* [1914] A.C. 398; *Neste Oy* v. *Lloyds Bank plc* [1983] 2 Lloyd's Rep. 658.

5. *Dearle* v. *Hall* is illogical. Whereas notice acquired accidentally by the debtor is sufficient to preserve the priority of an earlier assignee, it is insufficient to secure the priority of a subsequent assignment over a prior assignment of which the debtor is unaware.[91] This arbitrariness is justified on the tenuous basis that priorities could not be obtained, any more than they could be displaced, by mere accident.

6. *Dearle* v. *Hall* is harsh and absurd when applied to expectancies.[92]

7. *Dearle* v. *Hall* is a counsel of perfection where there is an assignment of streams of receivables due from a multitude of debtors. In such cases, compliance with the rule requires expensive and time-consuming notices to each and every debtor. This will normally be reflected in the cost of financial accommodation to the assignor. Apart from the expense, indorsement of notice of assignment on invoices sent to debtors will guarantee priority only if property in the goods, services or facilities passes upon receipt of the invoice, so that it fixes the date of accrual of the debt. This, of course, is not the law[93] unless the parties so agree. The possibility of a *scintilla temporis* between accrual of the debt and receipt of the indorsed invoice may make all the difference to the ranking of assignees. Such a refinement ought no longer to be encouraged.

For these reasons it is thought that *Dearle* v. *Hall* is not only harsh and inconvenient to the receivables financier, but also hard to justify, and in need of reform.

Garnishee and stop orders

6.7   An unsecured creditor whose debt is unpaid may enforce payment by initiating proceedings. He may also petition for a winding up[94] order against the corporate debtor. But unless driven to the latter option, he will, in general, prefer to obtain judgment for his debt and enforce it against the debtor's property, not least because winding up is essentially a collective and compulsory process for the collection and distribution of the insolvent's assets among creditors. No personal advantages are possible, whereas if he can complete execution before the commencement of winding up, he is home and dry,[95] and thus in a superior position to

---

[91] *Arden* v. *Arden* (1885) 29 Ch.D. 702.
[92] See para. 6.4, *supra*, for a discussion of the priority of assignees of expectant receivables.
[93] Passing of property in goods is regulated by Sale of Goods Act 1979, ss.16–19. Under s.17(1) property passes when the parties intend it to pass. Further rules for ascertainment of the parties' intention are detailed in s.18.
[94] Insolvency Act 1986, s.123(1)(*a*) and (*b*).
[95] *Re National United Corporation* [1901] 1 Ch. 950. *Galbraith* v. *Grimshaw & Baxter* [1910] 1 K.B. 339 affd. [1910] A.C. 508. The court will not make absolute a garnishee order nisi if liquidation supervenes before the time has come for the order to be made absolute: *Roberts Petroleum Ltd.* v. *Bernard Kenney Ltd.* [1983] 2 A.C. 192. Also s.183(3)(*b*) of the Insolvency Act 1986 avoids an attachment of receivables which is uncompleted by receipt of the money before the commencement of winding up. For personal insolvency, see s.346(5)(*b*).

other unsecured creditors who have not taken these vital steps necessary to assure victory. To enjoy this superiority, it is necessary that execution be complete before the intervention, either of creditors having security over the debtor's assets, or office-holders[96] appointed pursuant to some insolvency procedure.[97] For this purpose, a final judgment gives the successful party no secured rights[98]; he gets only the purely personal right to have the judgment enforced, although where money has been paid into court to abide the outcome of litigation, to the extent of that money, the judgment creditor is a secured party,[99] and may even successfully resist any claim by a receiver appointed under a pre-existing floating charge.[1]

The form of execution will depend on the nature of the subject-matter sought to be seized. An execution against receivables and other debts due to the judgment debtor is usually by attachment following a garnishee order.[2] The order can only be made on receivables due,[3] even if unascertained[4] or not presently payable. But where the debt is only a future possibility, the order can accelerate neither its accrual nor time for payment.[5] Although the service of a garnishee order nisi creates a charge on the receivables specified in the order,[6] the priority which the garnishor gains at this stage, and even at the later stage where the order has been made absolute, is only provisional. It is no doubt good as between garnishor and the judgment debtor, subject of course to any valid set-offs or counterclaims which the garnishee may have against the judgment debtor[7]; but to be effective against third parties having proprietary claims over the same receivables, the execution must have been completed by receipt of the receivables. The concept of completion is significant to priority conflicts between a garnishor and third parties claiming the same receivables. Three categories of such claimants will be considered, *viz.*: (i) a prior specific assignee of the same receivables; (ii) a prior floating chargee; and (iii) a liquidator of the judgment debtor.

---

[96] These are the administrator, the administrative receiver and the liquidator (including a provisional liquidator).

[97] The Insolvency Act 1986 recognises four types of insolvency procedure. These are the approval of a voluntary arrangement under Pt. I of the first group of Parts, the making of an administration order under Pt. II, the appointment of an administrative receiver under Pt. III and insolvent liquidation: see s.247(1).

[98] *Brace* v. *Duchess of Marlborough* (1728) 2 P.Wms. 491 at 491–492; *Ex p. Knott* (1806) 11 Ves. 609 at 617; but contrast *West Ham* v. *Ovens* (1872) L.R. 8 Ex. 37 where a judgment was held to be a "valuable security" in the context of a statute which equated security with property.

[99] The payment is usually pursuant to R.S.C., Ord. 22. There is no difference in principle between a voluntary payment into court as in *Re Gordon, ex p. Navalchand* [1897] 2 Q.B. 516 and an involuntary payment as in *Re Ford, ex p. The Trustee* [1900] 2 Q.B. 211.

[1] *W.A. Sherratt Ltd.* v. *John Bromley (Church Stretton) Ltd.* [1985] Q.B. 1038.

[2] R.S.C., Ord. 49.

[3] *Dunlop & Ranken Ltd.* v. *Hendall Steel Structures Ltd.* [1957] 1 W.L.R. 1102.

[4] *O'Driscoll* v. *Manchester Insurance Committee* [1915] 3 K.B. 499.

[5] *Webb* v. *Stenton* (1883) 11 Q.B.D. 518, applied in *Re Greenwood* [1901] 1 Ch. 887.

[6] *Rogers* v. *Whiteley* [1892] A.C. 118; *Galbraith* v. *Grimshaw & Baxter* [1910] 1 K.B. 339 at 343–344, affd. [1910] A.C. 508.

[7] *Tapp* v. *Jones* (1875) L.R. 10 Q.B. 591; *Hale* v. *Victoria Plumbing Co.* [1966] 2 Q.B. 746. Because the attachment does not work an assignment of the debt, the garnishee cannot set off a debt owed to him on another account by the garnishor, there being no mutuality: *Sampson* v. *Seaton Railway Co.* (1875) L.R. 10 Q.B. 28.

A prior specific assignee

6.8   A garnishor takes subject to all equities affecting the debt at the date of the service of the order nisi.[8] Equities for this purpose are not confined to valid contra accounts which the garnishee has against the judgment debtor, but include all valid claims to the debt. Accordingly, where before service of the order nisi, the receivables have been made over bona fide to a third party, the title of the assignee prevails.[9] This is so whether or not the assignee has given notice of assignment to the debtor (now the garnishee),[10] for a garnishee order does not effect a transfer of the receivables specified in the order.[11] Hence there is no occasion for invoking the rule in *Dearle* v. *Hall* to priority disputes between the prior assignee and the garnishor. Therefore, where the garnishee, unaware of a prior assignment, pays the garnishor, although he is discharged,[12] the prior assignee can trace the payment against the garnishor who cannot plead bona fide purchase of the payment for value, not being a purchaser for this purpose.

To prevail, the prior assignee must establish the fact of assignment. This will not always be easy. It is settled law that a mandate is no assignment,[13] a rule which assumes some significance in this context. If, upon analysis, a purported assignment turns out to be a mere mandate which has not been acted upon, the service of a garnishee order nisi operates as a revocation of the mandate.[14] The significance of this point is in relation to assignments taking the form of a direction to the account debtor. Unlike tangible personalty title to which passes without the transferee's assent,[15] the relevance of assent of an assignee to a transfer taking the form of a direction is unclear. There is authority for the proposition that if a transfer is intended, a direction to the debtor becomes effective once the direction is posted. This authority, however, has been doubted,[16] and sits oddly with the well-established rule that an

---

[8] *Scott* v. *Lord Hastings* (1859) 4 K. & J. 633; *Arden* v. *Arden* (1885) 29 Ch.D. 702 at 709 –710.

[9] *Holt* v. *Heatherfield Trust Ltd.* [1942] 2 K.B. 1.

[10] *Re General Horticultural Co., ex p. Whitehouse* (1886) 32 Ch.D. 512; *Badeley* v. *Consolidated Bank* (1888) 38 Ch.D. 238; *Sinnott* v. *Bowden* [1912] 2 Ch. 414; *Glegg* v. *Bromley* [1912] 3 K.B. 474. Cf. *Vacuum Oil Co. Ltd.* v. *Ellis* [1914] 1 K.B. 693 where the garnishee prevailed because the equitable mortgagee who gave notice of claim of rent to the tenant was not entitled to possession and the receiver who was entitled gave no notice.

[11] *Holmes* v. *Tutton* (1855) 5 Bl. & El. 65; *Chatterton* v. *Watney* (1881) 17 Ch.D. 259; *Re Combined Weighing and Advertising Machine Co.* (1889) 43 Ch.D. 99. The dicta of James L.J. in *Ex p. Joselyn* (1878) 8 Ch.D. 327 at 330, can no longer (if ever they were) be regarded as authoritative. Because no transfer is effected, the garnishor never becomes a creditor of the garnishee and so cannot petition for the winding-up of the garnishee in the event of non-payment; his only remedy is to bring an action for debt based on the garnishee order and use the judgment as a foundation for a winding-up petition: see *Pritchett* v. *English & Colonial Syndicate* [1899] 2 Q.B. 428. This reasoning is technical and unsatisfactory. It is questionable whether any purpose is served by this use of concept to put the garnishor through the trouble and expense of a second judgment; cf. *Rothwells Ltd.* v. *Nommack (No. 100) Pty* (1988) 13 A.C.L.R. 421 at 425.

[12] R.S.C., Ord. 49, r. 8.

[13] *Bell* v. *London & North Western Railway Co.* (1852) 15 Beav. 548.

[14] *Rekstin* v. *Severo Sibirsko* [1933] 1 K.B. 47.

[15] *Standing* v. *Bowring* (1885) 31 Ch.D. 282.

[16] See *Timpson's Executors* v. *Yerbury* [1936] 1 K.B. 645 at 657.

offer sent by post only becomes effective when received. Besides, it is apparently inconsistent with the reasoning in *Holt* v. *Heatherfield Trust Ltd.* that a notice sent to the debtor takes effect, for purposes of priority, when received. The same is in principle true of the written notice required by section 136(1) of the Law of Property Act 1925 for the acquisition of a legal assignment. On reflection, however, these doubts do not seem to be well founded. The tripartite relationship of assignor, assignee and debtor does not fit neatly or easily into the structure of the postal rule. Besides, it is difficult to analyse a direction as an offer. To whom is such an offer made? By whom is it to be accepted? It is clear law that an assignment does not depend for its efficacy on acceptance by the debtor.[17] How can a direction to the debtor be seen as an offer to the prospective assignee which becomes effective only when accepted? Considerations of this nature suggest that, provided a direction is sufficiently affirmative so as to be incapable of construction as a mere mandate, it ought to take effect as an assignment. If this be so, a garnishee order nisi served on the debtor before notification of assignment to the assignee ought to take subject to the assignment.

It is submitted that the issue is at bottom one of appropriation. The relevant inquiry is not whether the assignee has assented to the transfer; it is whether the direction to the debtor, uncommunicated to the assignee, is sufficiently affirmative to amount to a final and irrevocable appropriation of the receivables to the intended assignment. If the question is answered affirmatively the assignee must prevail. There is no authority inconsistent with this analysis.[18] A direction fails, not because it is uncommunicated to the assignee, but because it fails the appropriation test. Therefore, communication to the assignee is neither necessary to, nor sufficient for, the existence of an assignment. In *Alexander* v. *Steinhardt*[19] the assignment was held good in the absence of communication to the assignee. But in *Percival* v. *Dunn*[20] the written direction assented to by the assignee failed as an assignment because it was not sufficiently affirmative. With the issue under discussion, the postal rule has nothing at all to do. To be sure, the cases[21] thought to deny the efficacy of an assignment uncommunicated to the assignee actually deal with either attornment at common law or novation, both of which require the assent of the assignor, assignee and debtor.[22]

---

[17] *Re Row, ex p. South* (1818) 3 Swan 392; *Gorringe* v. *Irwell India Rubber* (1886) 34 Ch.D. 128.

[18] *Morrell* v. *Wootten* (1852) 16 Beav. 197 (attornment or novation); *Re Hamilton, Fitzgeorge* v. *Fitzgeorge* (1921) 124 L.T. 737 (revocable mandate); *Timpson's Executors* v. *Yerbury* [1936] 1 K.B. 645. In the last two cases the revocability of the mandate showed that there was no final and irrevocable appropriation of the funds. *Cf. Re Kent and Sussex Sawmills Ltd.* [1947] Ch. 177 where the mandate was irrevocable save with the bank's consent and this was sufficient appropriation of the receivables. In *Curran* v. *Newpark Cinemas Ltd.* [1951] 1 All E.R. 295 the Court of Appeal assumed that communication to the assignee was necessary, but since there was no direct evidence of such knowledge or the lack of it, the direction was held good against the garnishor.

[19] [1903] 2 K.B. 208.

[20] (1885) 29 Ch.D. 128.

[21] Such as *Morrell* v. *Wootten* (1852) 15 Beav. 197.

[22] For a discussion of attornment of receivables, see para. 5.4, *supra*.

To say that a garnishor takes subject to equities, and that a garnishee order does not transfer the debt, does not mean that an assignment created subsequent to the service of the garnishee order nisi will prevail over the garnishor. For one thing, it is not an existing equity subject to which the garnishor takes; for another, the opposite conclusion does not give effect to the procedural charge created on the receivables by service of the order. *Geisse* v. *Taylor*[23] is not to the contrary. There, a judgment creditor obtained and served a garnishee order absolute on a company that was indebted to the judgment debtor. The following day the company in good faith borrowed money from W and gave him a debenture secured by a floating charge over all its undertaking. W had notice of the order when he took the debenture, but when the garnishor issued a writ of *fi. fa.* in aid of the garnishee order and goods covered by the charge were seized, W appointed a receiver and claimed the goods. The Divisional Court held that the receiver was entitled to the goods. Although the case has been consigned to that category of decisions explicable on the basis of their own special facts,[24] it is difficult to see how any other conclusion could have been reached. It must be remembered that the dispute did not relate to the garnished receivables, but to goods belonging to the garnishee. That W knew of the garnishee order when he took his charge was not to the point, the garnishee's undertaking being unincumbered. The receivables garnished did not constitute any specific identifiable property in the hands of the garnishee—a point frequently forgotten and no less true even in cases of assignment. The writ of *fi. fa.* may have converted the garnishor into a secured creditor in relation to the goods,[25] at any rate after seizure by the sheriff, but the goods stood as security only subject to the equities affecting them. And though an uncrystallised floating charge is not one of the equities binding an executioner,[26] yet, if the charge crystallises, as it did in *Geisse* v. *Taylor*, before completion of the execution by sale and receipt of the proceeds, the floating chargee must win.[27]

A prior floating charge

6.9 A garnishor attaching receivables belonging to the judgment debtor takes subject to all existing equities, for he can get no better title than the judgment debtor had. It is equally true that these equities do not include an uncrystallised floating charge.[28] It follows, therefore, that an attachment of receivables which is complete by receipt of money before crystallisation of a floating charge over the same assets is good against the chargee.[29] The importance of completion of the attachment can hardly be over-emphasised. If the charge crystallises after the service of the order

---

[23] [1905] 2 K.B. 658.
[24] See *Galbraith* v. *Grimshaw & Baxter* [1910] 1 K.B. 339 at 345.
[25] *Ex p. Williams* (1872) L.R. 7 Ch.App. 314; *Hall* v. *Richards* (1961) 108 C.L.R. 84.
[26] *Evans* v. *Rival Granite Quarries Ltd.* [1910] 2 K.B. 979 at 1002.
[27] *Re Standard Manufacturing Co.* [1891] 1 Ch. 627; *Re Opera Ltd.* [1891] 3 Ch. 260.
[28] *Robson* v. *Smith* [1895] 2 Ch. 118; *Evans* v. *Rival Granite Quarries Ltd.* [1910] 2 K.B. 979.
[29] *Ibid.*

nisi[30] or absolute,[31] but before receipt of the money, the chargee is just in time. It does not matter for this purpose that if the garnishee had not delayed in payment of the debt, the chargee would have been too late. The *if* is a big one, though, this is without prejudice to any recourse the garnishor might have against the garnishee for breach of duty of care! No such duty in fact exists. If, however, there is no provision for partial crystallisation, whether automatically or by intervention, the chargee cannot, whilst the charge is still floating, pounce down on the receivables specified in the order because his security is in jeopardy.[32] Nor can he, in the absence of a provision to that effect in his charge instrument, appoint a receiver over those receivables on the ground of jeopardy.[33] And generally, the power to appoint a receiver in such circumstances cannot be implied into the charge instrument because it is not necessary to give the security business efficacy.[34] The only remedy of a floating chargee in such cases is to apply to court for the appointment of a receiver, and generally, the court will appoint a receiver *ex debito justitiae*.[35]

Administrator[36] or liquidator of the judgment debtor

The concept of "completion" of execution is of critical importance **6.10** where the judgment debtor is an insolvent corporation. This is because the commencement of insolvency proceedings could frustrate the garnishor. First, the petition for,[37] and the making of,[38] an administration order not only operate as a stay on existing proceedings against the company, but also prohibit the commencement of fresh proceedings and enforcement of judgment, in all cases, except with leave of court or permission of the administrator. The commencement of winding-up has the same effect.[39] Although the word "proceedings" has been construed rather strictly in the context of administration,[40] few would disagree that it covers the issue of ordinary process against the company. In doing so, statute has deprived unsecured creditors of their ordinary remedy against the debtor. Jackson[41] has argued very persuasively that the justification for the statutory approach is that it gives effect to the hypothetical "bargain" which the creditors would have entered into if they were able to agree *ex ante* on what would happen if their debtor became insolvent, and that the compulsory and collective régime which the statutory scheme

---

[30] As in *Norton* v. *Yates* [1906] 1 K.B. 112.
[31] *Cairney* v. *Back* [1906] 2 K.B. 746.
[32] *Robson* v. *Smith, supra*; *Evans* v. *Rival Granite, supra*.
[33] *Cryne* v. *Barclays Bank plc* [1987] B.C.L.C. 548.
[34] *Ibid.*
[35] *Re London Pressed Hinge Co.* [1905] 1 Ch. 576.
[36] See Pt. II of the first group of Parts, Insolvency Act 1986.
[37] Insolvency Act 1986, s.10(1)(*c*).
[38] Insolvency Act 1986, s.11(3)(*d*).
[39] Insolvency Act 1986, s.128.
[40] *Air Ecosse Ltd.* v. *Civil Aviation Authority* (1987) 3 B.C.C. 492 (application for revocation of aviation licence by a competitor not a proceeding); *Re Barrow Borough Transport Ltd.* [1989] 3 W.L.R. 858 (application for registration of a charge out of time not a proceeding).
[41] Jackson (1982) 91 Yale L.J. 857.

imposes for the distribution of the assets of the insolvent not only increases the aggregate pool of assets available for distribution, but also reduces strategic costs and makes for administrative efficiencies. By not recognising "incomplete" executions,[42] insolvency law may be said to be effecting an unjust redistribution. If the concern was distributional, there is arguably a better way to achieve that result. This criticism is not answered by appealing to the principle of equality. If the principle has any meaning at all in the present context, it means no more than that *equals* should be treated equally. But it says nothing on the more important question—who are equals, and assumes that an unsecured creditor who has not signed a judgment against the insolvent stands on the footing of equality with his counterpart who has obtained judgment but has not completed execution. Nothing, however, could be further from the truth. The determination of equality for insolvency purposes is eminently a non-insolvency question and should not vary depending on whether or not insolvency has supervened. If it does, insolvency law would not only give some creditors a perverse incentive to make strategic use of the insolvency process, but would create new rights and, on its own, cease to be a forum for the translation of pre-insolvency assets and liabilities of the debtor.[43] It may be that the non-recognition of uncompleted executions furthers the hypothetical "bargain" among the insolvent's creditors, and that the equality accorded by insolvency law to all non-preferential unsecured creditors is justified because neither the creditor who has not obtained a judgment for his debt, nor his counterpart who has obtained judgment but has not completed execution, has taken the ultimate step which assures victory.[44] Therefore, both creditors stand, at the moment of insolvency, in relative positions of equality at least for the purpose of valuing their pre-insolvency rights. In avoiding uncompleted executions, insolvency law does not therefore confer victory upon the unsecured creditors who have not obtained judgment, but assures a tie, especially as they all are assumed to have an equal chance to win this hypothetical race.

When receivables are paid into court, apart from questions of registration and notice, assignees desiring to preserve their priorities must obtain stop orders.[45] Though by granting a stop order the court decides nothing about the question of entitlement,[46] the general rule is that where the assignee is not affected by notice, actual or constructive, of any existing claims against the receivables when he took his assignment,[47] and no notice of claim had been given to the debtor before the fund was paid into court,[48] the priorities of competing claimants are governed neither by the rule in *Dearle* v. *Hall*, nor by the dates of creation, but by the priorities of their respective stop orders. On this basis a junior assignee who obtains an earlier stop order prevails over a senior incumbrancer[49]

[42] See Insolvency Act 1986, s.183(3)(*b*).
[43] See Jackson (1985) 14 J. of Legal Studies 73.
[44] See Jackson (1984) 36 Stan.L.R. 725 at 731.
[45] R.S.C., Ord. 50, r. 10.
[46] *Supreme Court Practice*, para. 50/10/2.
[47] *Mutual Life Assurance Society* v. *Langley* (1886) 32 Ch.D. 460.
[48] *Greening* v. *Beckford* (1832) 5 Sim. 195; *Swayne* v. *Swayne* (1849) 11 Beav. 463.
[49] *Ibid.*

and his title is superior to that of the liquidator or trustee in bankruptcy of the insolvent assignor.[50] The principle is the same where part only of the fund is paid into court, save that the priorities of the assignees will be governed by *Dearle* v. *Hall*, as regards the part not paid in.[51] But an assignee who has given an effectual notice to the debtor before the receivables are paid into court does not lose his priority by being the last to obtain a stop order after the payment-in.[52]

Tracing creditors and the receivables financier

It will not be an infrequent occurrence that the receivables financier **6.11** finds himself caught in a priority dispute with a tracing creditor. The creditor may be an unpaid seller of goods whose sale terms include a reservation of title clause, or another inventory financier, for example, a finance company which has financed goods hired out on hire-purchase, or even the everyday conditional seller. Every inventory financier expects the inventory to be disposed of. The concern is with the resulting receivables, and these are exclusively the subject-matter of receivables financing. In many cases the tracing creditor's claim will fail at a preliminary stage, namely, that there is no "proprietary base"[53] or the absence of the "requisite"[54] fiduciary relationship. The following discussion assumes that the tracer's claim has passed through these preliminary filters and is available in competition with the claim of the receivables financier. The battle may, generally, be fought at two levels—(i) where both parties claim receivables due from a named debtor; (ii) where the receivables have been "discharged" by payment to the assignor and both claim the payment. Although the focus is different, the issue is at bottom the same. If the tracing creditor has a superior claim, the payment by the debtor to the assignor cannot defeat that claim. It is surprising that so

---

[50] *Stuart* v. *Cockerell* (1865) L.R. 8 Eq. 607; *Palmer* v. *Locke* (1881) 18 Ch.D. 381 (assignment took place after the bankruptcy of the assignor, though the assignee took for value without notice).

[51] *Mutual Life Assurance Society* v. *Langley, supra.*

[52] *Brearcliff* v. *Dorrington* (1850) 4 De Gex & Sm. 122; *Livesey* v. *Harding* (1856) 23 Beav. 141; *Re Marquis of Anglesey* [1903] 2 Ch. 727 at 732.

[53] The concept of "proprietary base" is taken from Birks, *Introduction to the Law of Restitution* (OUP, 1985), p. 379 and expresses the idea that a person asserting a tracing right must show that at the beginning of the story he had a proprietary interest in that property and that nothing happened subsequently to deprive him of that interest.

[54] The decision of the Court of Appeal in *Re Diplock* [1948] Ch. 465 is generally believed to have committed English law to the requirement of fiduciary relationship in the context of tracing in equity. But it has not been accepted without criticism: see, *e.g.* Oakley (1975) 28 *Current Legal Problems* 64; Pearce (1976) 40 Conv. 277 at 287–291. In *Agip (Africa) Ltd.* v. *Jackson* [1989] 3 W.L.R. 1367 at 1386 Millett J. said:

> "The only restriction on the ability of equity to follow assets is the requirement that there must be some fiduciary relationship which permits the assistance of equity to be invoked. The requirement has been widely condemned and depends on authority rather than principle. . . . The requirement may be circumvented since it is not necessary that the fund to be traced should have been the subject of fiduciary obligations before it got into the wrong hands; it is sufficient that the payment to the defendant itself gives rise to a fiduciary relationship."

typical a set of facts has not been the subject of any reported litigation in this country.[55] This may indicate either that the preliminary filters have been very effective, or that there is judicial hostility towards tracing creditors. Whatever may be the correct explanation, the question of priority remains very relevant at the practical level, and it is to this that we now turn.

Where debtor "holds" the receivables

6.12   Where the account debtor "holds" the receivables, the primary inquiry must be directed at the question, how did the tracing creditor become entitled? If he claims the receivables as proceeds of goods belonging to him, then the characterisation of his tracing claim as legal (*i.e.* deriving from a common law right) or equitable, depends on the character in which the assignor sold the goods. If he sold as a "true" agent of the tracing creditor, the legal right to payment vests directly in the creditor, and his tracing claim is of a common law origin. The assumption here is that there is no problem with identifying the receivables. If that be so, he will win the race regardless of whether the receivables financier took a legal or an equitable assignment. The priority rule is *nemo dat quod non habet*. Since the receivables financier is not asserting a title derived from an earlier claim to the goods which produced the receivables, he cannot take refuge under any of the recognised exceptions to the *nemo dat* rule.[56] Nor can he claim priority on the basis of being the first to give notice of claim to the debtor. Although this is controversial,[57] the better view is that *Dearle* v. *Hall* does not apply because it is limited in its application to successive equitable *assignments*.[58] This conclusion does not rest on two considerations usually urged in its support.[59] The first is said to be the subordination of assignments to "equities." Equities, so the argument goes, are not confined to legal and equitable contra claims vested in the debtor, but extend to all claims valid against the assignor, whether arising consensually or by operation of law. This will be called the "subject to equities" argument and is dealt with later in the context of an equitable tracing claim. The second is that the tracing creditor is a beneficiary under a trust of the receivables. The argument is not relevant in this context, and is dealt with later.[60]

For a number of reasons the tracing creditor cannot establish a true agency, and would have to fall back on his equitable tracing right. Here priority will depend, first, on the characterisation of the assignment as legal or equitable and, secondly, on notice affecting the assignee. To clear the way for elucidation of the relevance of these two factors, a word or two must at this stage be said on the relevance of *Dearle* v. *Hall*. Two

---

[55] *Cf. Pfeiffer GmbH* v. *Arbuthnot Factors Ltd.* [1988] 1 W.L.R. 150 where the tracing claim was in fact an unregistered charge.
[56] See Sale of Goods Act 1979, ss.21–26.
[57] See McLauchlan (1980) 96 L.Q.R. 90, and contrast Goode, *Commercial Law* (1982), p. 873.
[58] *Snell's Principles of Equity* (28th ed.), p. 65.
[59] *Cf.* McLauchlan, *op. cit.*, 92–95.
[60] See para. 6.14, *Infra.*

theses are topical on this question. The first is inspired by McLauchlan[61] who argues for the irrelevance of the rule in *Dearle* v. *Hall*. This will be called the "irrelevance" thesis. The essence of this thesis is that the contest is essentially between two equitable claimants. For this purpose even a statutory assignment is equitable because section 136(1), Law of Property Act 1925 effects only a procedural reform; so the statutory assignee, like his equitable counterpart, takes subject to equities, which include all equitable claims, whether arising consensually or by operation of law. Accordingly, priorities fall to be decided by the first in time rule, and since there is nothing making the equities of the claimants otherwise unequal, victory goes to the tracing creditor whose claim is earlier in point of time of creation. The second argument is that *Dearle* v. *Hall;* does not apply because the tracing creditor is a beneficiary under trust. This will be called the "trust" argument.

The "relevance" thesis is the second of the two topical theses referred to earlier, and its principal exponent is Goode.[62] The gist of this thesis is that priority will be governed by the rule in *Dearle* v. *Hall*; the winner is the first to give notice. If this is so, priority will almost always go to the assignee who will usually be the first to give notice to the debtor. No argument of principle has been urged in its support, its claim to application resting squarely on policy. The policy argument is that where an equitable tracing creditor chooses to impose an accounting obligation leaving the assignor in apparent ownership of the resulting receivables, he cannot complain, for he ought to have known that they might be the subject of a disposition in favour of a bona fide third party.

It is submitted that neither the "relevance" nor the "irrelevance" thesis holds the key to the resolution of the priority problem under discussion: as to the "relevance" thesis because, first, *Dearle* v. *Hall* applies, as a matter of first principle, to consensual equitable assignments only. Secondly, the policy argument is neither strong nor convincing. It punishes the tracing creditor for what is essentially a structural weakness in the existing legislation for the registration of interests and dealings in receivables. Parliament has given the creditor no facility for publicising and protecting his interest. To subject his claim to *Dearle* v. *Hall* is to reduce unnecessarily the already very limited remedies available for the vindication of his proprietary right. To uphold the "relevance" thesis is also to introduce an idea similar to reputed ownership (which never applied to companies) through the back door. The "irrelevance" thesis, on the other hand, is only partly sound, and that is to the extent that it affirms the view that *Dearle* v. *Hall* has nothing to do with this problem. Beyond that, it is difficult to sustain. First, the "trust" argument. Even assuming the assignor who is a conditional buyer is a trustee, and in breach of trust assigns the resulting receivables, it is not easy to see why a bona fide legal purchaser of the receivables should not take free of the trust. One answer is that the *tabula in naufragio* permitted by the bona fide purchaser rule does not apply where a trustee disposes of trust property in breach of trust.[63] Again, assuming this to be correct, the

---

[61] *Op. cit.*

[62] *Commercial Law* (1982), p. 873.

[63] Donaldson (1977) 93 L.Q.R. 342; *cf.* Goode (1977) 93 L.Q.R. 487.

argument does not carry one far enough. In the first place, it is not at all clear that this disapplication of *tabula in naufragio* applies where the trust is constructive and the transferee took his title unaware of the breach of trust by his transferor.[64] Secondly, even if the disapplication so extends, this will still keep assignees who acquired a legal assignment in the first instance outside the area of non-application. But herein lies the second answer to the trust paradox indicated above. It is said that no assignee in fact acquires a legal assignment for priority purposes because section 136(1), Law of Property Act 1925, effected only a procedural change in the law prohibiting assignments at common law. So, an assignment complying with the statute give the assignee a title which is legal only in the procedural sense that he can sue in his own name. For priority purposes it remains wholly equitable.[65] I have given reasons elsewhere[66] why this cannot be law, and will return to this argument later on.[67] Other objections to the trust argument have been noted earlier.[68]

The "subject to equities" argument is very easily met. The law as to taking an assignment subject to equities has nothing at all to do with priorities of competing claimants.[69] The equities referred to are confined to legal and equitable defences vested in the account debtor, and bind all assignees regardless of notice.[70] If this argument had been well-founded the result in cases like *Thorndike* v. *Hunt*[71] and *Taylor* v. *Blakelock*[72] would no doubt have been different.

Thus far, we have been concerned with the topical theses on this theme, and have shown that neither resolves the priority dispute satisfactorily in a principled manner. The solution may yet lie in a "third" thesis lying somewhere between the two extremes postulated by the other theses. To recapitulate, the "irrelevance" thesis would always give priority to the tracing creditor. The "relevance" thesis would almost always give victory to the assignee, who, if he is an institutional receivables financier, will usually give a first notice to the debtor. The essence of the "third" thesis is that *Dearle* v. *Hall* does not apply because one claimant is not an assignee. In this respect it could be considered a variant on the theme of "irrelevance." But there the similarity ends because priority will then depend on the first in time rule, subject to the application of the bona fide purchaser rule. On this approach, where the receivables financier is an equitable assignee, the tracing creditor will

---

[64] See Oditah (1989) 9 O.J.L.S. 513 at 531–532.

[65] McLauchlan, *op. cit.*, 92–93.

[66] (1989) 9 O.J.L.S. 513 at 521–523.

[67] See para. 6.16 *infra*.

[68] See pp. 138–139, *supra*.

[69] In *G. & N. Angelakis Shipping Co. SA* v. *Compagnie National Algerienne de Navigation, The "Attika Hope"* [1988] 1 Lloyd's Rep. 439 at 442 Steyn J. said:

> "The defendants say that the lien on sub-freights under cl. 18 of the head charter predates the plaintiff's assignment and is an equity to which the plaintiff's assignment takes subject. That . . . is a misconception of the rule regarding taking an assignment subject to equities."

[70] *Chitty on Contracts* (26th ed.), para. 1425, p. 893.

[71] (1859) 3 De G. & J. 563.

[72] (1886) 32 Ch.D. 560.

prevail on the ground that his own claim will usually be the first to arise, and there would seem to be no inequality in their respective equities.[73] Where, however, the assignment is legal, the receivables financier will prevail if when he took his assignment he was not affected by notice of the tracing creditor's claim. For this purpose, the *tabula in naufragio* doctrine applies, so that if possessing only an equitable assignment, the receivables financier becomes aware of the tracing claim, he can take the ultimate step that assures victory, namely, give notice to the debtor, if he already has an absolute assignment. But he cannot at that stage take an assignment complying with the statute, if he did not possess one already. The reason for the latter rule is that he will normally depend on the assignor to assist him by giving another proper assignment, and at that stage he will already have been affected by notice. To improve his position by helping himself to a legal assignment is one thing, to take a fresh assignment, quite another.

In practice most assignments to institutional receivables financiers, be they clearing banks, factors or other financiers, are equitable in character as they would normally cover existing and future receivables. (It may be that as regards those existing at the date of the assignment, the financier can assert a legal claim if the assignment is capable of severance and other formalities for a legal assignment, *e.g.* notice to the debtor, have been complied with). To be on the safe side, some factoring agreements now provide that the assignor warrants that the receivables sold are not subject to any retention of title agreement,[74] or that *it will not* be subject to such an agreement. The warranty is of doubtful relevance to priority conflicts, especially the latter formulation. Where the assignor covenants that the receivables will not be subject to any retention of title agreement, this has been held sufficient to exclude notice of the tracing claim on the part of the factor buying receivables.[75] In that case the point was hurriedly conceded without argument. It is submitted that such a warranty will not protect the receivables financier who in fact had notice of the existence of the tracing claim when he took his assignment. Nor will it always exclude constructive notice where, in all the circumstances, the financier *ought* reasonably to have made inquiries. The "ought" is a big one in that it is difficult to paint a scenario in which such inquiry would be called for. In the average case it would take a financier with exceptional gifts of hindsight, but one which has since disappeared from the financing scene, to inspect the terms on which goods are bought.

Different considerations arise where the debtor has paid over the receivables to the financier before the intervention of the tracing creditor. If that be the case, the financier is in an eminently strong position. If he receives payment before he *first* becomes aware of the tracing claim, his title to the payment is complete—he can plead bona fide purchase of the

---

[73] Equality here does not mean priority in point of time, but refers to the non-existence of any circumstance which affects the conduct of one of the rival claimants, and which may otherwise make it less meritorious than that of the other: *Bailey* v. *Barnes* [1894] 1 Ch. 25 at 36.

[74] See, *e.g. Pfeiffer GmbH* v. *Arbuthnot Factors Ltd.* [1988] 1 W.L.R. 150 at 154.

[75] *Ibid.*

legal title to the cash for value without notice.[76] The situation will be different where he has become aware of the tracing claim at the time of receipt of payment. In that case he may be a bona fide purchaser, but undoubtedly with notice, and can only keep the money if he is also a bona fide assignee of the legal title to the receivables without notice. Of course, if the debtor becomes insolvent and eventually descends into liquidation, neither the tracing creditor nor the receivables financier can trace into its assets. Whoever wins the race for priority becomes entitled to prove for a dividend in the liquidation, but as two claims cannot simultaneously be admitted to proof on account of the same debt—the rule against double proof,[77] the primary question of priority still has to be decided.

Where the receivables have been paid to the assignor

6.13   Here, the assignor is a trustee of the payment for whoever is entitled,[78] and the rules discussed above will govern the question of entitlement. If the payment has been dissipated the question of priority is an idle one. But where it has been invested in identifiable property, the winner of the priority race has a valid proprietary claim to the investment.[79] Usually drafts and other negotiable papers given in payment would have been paid into the assignor's overdrawn account. This raises interesting questions. The bank would defeat both claimants if it can prove two matters. First, it will have to overcome a potential strict liability for conversion of the paper. Liability for conversion is strict, but the bank can rely on section 4 of the Cheques Act 1957 if it can prove that it acted bona fide and without negligence in collecting the proceeds of the paper. This, however, shields the bank from liability; it does not, on its own, assure victory as regards the proceeds of the paper. Therefore, to resist the claims of both the tracing creditor and the receivables financier, the bank must show that as regards the proceeds, it is a bona fide purchaser of legal title without notice that the payment by the assignor into the overdrawn account was in breach of trust.[80] That it knew the payment represents proceeds of receivables is not fatal, if it was otherwise unaware that the disposition was in breach of trust.[81]

Equitable versus legal assignments

6.14   Before the decision in *Pfeiffer GmbH* v. *Arbuthnot Factors Ltd.*[82] it was not clear whether the rule in *Dearle* v. *Hall* governs the question of

---

[76] *Thorndike* v. *Hunt* (1859) 3 De G. & J. 563; *Taylor* v. *Blakelock* (1886) 32 Ch.D. 560. The doctrine has also been applied to tangible personalty: see *Joseph* v. *Lyons* (1884) 15 Q.B.D. 280; *Hallas* v. *Robinson* (1884) 15 Q.B.D. 288.

[77] *Ex p. Macredies, re Charles* (1873) L.R. 8 Ch.App. 535; *Deering* v. *Bank of Ireland* (1886) 12 App. Cas. 20.

[78] *International Factors Ltd.* v. *Rodriguez* [1979] Q.B. 351; *Barclays Bank Ltd.* v. *Willowbrook International Ltd.* [1987] 1 F.T.L.R. 386.

[79] *Re Oatway* [1903] 2 Ch. 356; cf. *Roscoe* v. *Winder* [1915] 1 Ch. 62; *Re Tiley's Will Trust* [1967] 1 Ch. 1179.

[80] *Thomson* v. *Clydesdale Bank Ltd.* [1893] A.C. 282; *Coleman* v. *Bucks and Oxon Union Bank* [1897] 2 Ch. 242.

[81] *Ibid.*

[82] [1988] 1 W.L.R. 150.

priority between a prior equitable assignee and a subsequent legal assignee. Although academic opinions[83] assumed that *Dearle* v. *Hall* applied, and the matter is apparently settled in Canada,[84] I have argued elsewhere[85] that the question is very much an open one notwithstanding the decision in the *Pfeiffer* case. There is no need to rehearse the arguments in detail; it is hoped that a little recapitulation of the main arguments will be sufficient. There are said to be two arguments of principle and one of policy in favour of applying *Dearle* v. *Hall*. For the sake of convenience the two arguments of principle will be called the "subject to equities" argument and the "procedural" argument.

The arguments of principle

The "subject to equities" argument

This argument is founded on section 136(1), Law of Property Act 1925. **6.15** So far as material, the subsection provides that "any absolute assignment by writing . . . is effectual in law (*subject to equities having priority over the right of the assignee*) to pass and transfer . . . (a) the legal right to such debt. . . ." According to the argument, *Dearle* v. *Hall* applies, to the exclusion of the bona fide purchaser doctrine, because section 136(1) makes the legal assignee take subject to equities. The provision thus preserves the rule in *Dearle* v. *Hall* because "equities" are not confined to mere legal and equitable contra accounts vested in the debtor, but extend to equitable interests held by third parties. On this interpretation of section 136(1), a legal assignment remains equitable for purposes of priority, and though the assignment is statutory, the assignee does not become the legal owner of the receivables in a full sense.[86] The argument is at first sight attractive and ingenious, but it cannot be accepted as law. First, section 136(1) does not purport to be a priority provision.[87] It merely preserves equities vested in the debtor and enables such equities to be admitted in diminution or extinction of the legal assignee's claim. The preservation of such equities was necessary because a legal assignee would have taken free of them at law, especially as common law did not recognise set-off[88] except in bankruptcy[89] or pursuant to a contract. Indeed

[83] Biscoe, *Credit Factoring* (1975), pp. 132 *et seq.*; Goode, *Legal Problems of Credit and Security* (2nd ed., 1988), p. 80; Marshall, *Assignment of Choses in Action*, pp. 104 *et seq.*; McLauchlan (1980) 96 L.Q.R. 90; Sykes, *Law of Securities* (4th ed., 1986), p. 804; Ziegel (1963) 41 Can.B.R. 54 at 109, n. 263.

[84] *Pettit* v. *Foster Wheeler Ltd.* [1950] 2 D.L.R. 42 affd. [1950] 3 D.L.R. 320; *Harding Carpets Ltd.* v. *Royal Bank of Canada* [1980] 4 W.W.R. 149.

[85] (1989) 9 O.J.L.S. 513.

[86] *Pfeiffer GmbH* v. *Arbuthnot Factors Ltd.* [1980] 1 W.L.R. 150 at 162.

[87] See *Wolstenholme & Cherry's Conveyancing Statutes* (11th ed., 1925), Vol. 1, p. 358. Mr. Cherry was one of the draftsmen of the Law of Property Act 1925. Although the draftsman of a statute is not always its best interpreter, for he may well confuse what he intended to do with what he has in fact done: *Hilder* v. *Dexter* [1902] A.C. 474 at 477; *Re Ryder & Steadman's Contract* [1927] 2 Ch. 62 at 74, this does not rule out the possibility that an interpretation put forward by him is at least a possible construction of the provision in question.

[88] *William Darcy's Case* (1677) 2 Freeman 28; *Collins* v. *Collins* (1759) 2 Burr. 820 at 825 –826.

[89] *Bailey* v. *Finch* (1871) L.R. 7 Q.B. 34 at 44–45.

it is still the law today that a transferee of a chose in action freely transferable at law before the 1873 Judicature Act takes free of all equities existing between the assignor and the obligor at the date of the transfer.[90] Nothing conduces more to confusion than to mix up "equities" with questions of priority between successive assignees. The equities contemplated by section 136(1) are independent of the competing assignments and prevail over all assignees regardless of notice.[91]

Secondly, the argument based on "subject to equities" involves a massive *petitio principii*. A legal assignee takes only subject to equities *having priority over the right of an assignee*. What these equities are the draftsman has not bothered to elaborate. Even if one were to assume that "equities" include equitable assignments, this will not necessarily cover all equitable assignments of which notice has been given to the debtor. At best, the equities will be limited to perfected equitable assignments which, independently of section 136(1), prevail over legal assignments. Yet the very question at issue is what equitable assignments so prevail. How, then, can one justifiably, and consistently with principle, use *Dearle* v. *Hall* to subordinate a subsequent bona fide legal assignment, for that not only begs the very question in issue, but also assumes that independently of section 136(1), perfected equitable assignments prevail over bona fide legal assignments. It is of course conceded that *Dearle* v. *Hall*, though initially limited to successive equitable assignments of pure personalty, and subsequently extended to equitable interests in land and capital moneys,[92] is capable of extension to legal assignments. The concern here is that it has not been so extended.

The third objection to the "subject to equities" argument is that all the cases[93] usually cited as examples of its application have either been misunderstood or otherwise are patently erroneous. Three such cases are now examined. *Marchant* v. *Morton, Down & Co.*[94] is the first. There, Channell J. treated both assignments as equitable[95] because though the deed of assignment (in respect of the second assignment) was ineffectual as a deed, it was nevertheless valid as a contract to assign and took effect as an assignment in equity. Hence priority fell to be decided by the dates of notice to the debtor, and since the second assignee was the first to give notice, his title was stronger. If one were, however, to treat the second assignment as legal, its priority was consistent with the application of the bona fide purchaser rule.[96] So the result would have been the same whether the applicable priority rule was *Dearle* v. *Hall* or the doctrine of

---

[90] The rule is settled for nearly 300 years: see *Turton* v. *Benson* (1718) 2 Vern. 764 at 765; *Ord* v. *White* (1840) 3 Beav. 357 at 365; *Athenaeum Life Assurance Society* v. *Pooley* (1858) 3 De G. & J. 294 at 296; *Ashwin* v. *Burton* (1862) 7 L.T. 589 (transferee of a bond transferable at law took free of equities between assignor and debtor); *Taylor* v. *Blakelock* (1886) 32 Ch.D. 560 at 567 (transferee of stocks transferable at law before 1874 took free of equities).
[91] *Chitty on Contracts* (26th ed.), para. 1425, p. 893.
[92] Law of Property Act 1925, s.137.
[93] See Goode, *Legal Problems of Credit and Security* (2nd ed., 1988), p. 121.
[94] [1901] 2 K.B. 829.
[95] *Ibid.* at 832.
[96] See also, Thomas [1951] J.S.P.T.L. 480.

bona fide purchaser for value without notice. The second case is from Canada—*Harding Carpets Ltd.* v. *Royal Bank of Canada*,[97] where it was held that a subsequent specific legal assignment prevailed over a prior general assignment (floating charge), not because it was legal, but because notice of it was given to the debtor before the general assignee gave notice. Again, the case is weak as an authority because first, the decision would have been the same whether *Dearle* v. *Hall* or the bona fide purchaser rule applied. What is more, the main authority relied upon by the judge is a passage in *Chitty on Contracts*[98] which is irrelevant to the decision because the editor was discussing the rule that the Judicature Act 1873 did not increase the number of *assignable* contract rights. *Pfeiffer GmbH* v. *Arbuthnot Factors Ltd.*[99] is the third case and an important one because the bona fide purchaser rule was advanced in argument but rejected, Phillips J. preferring to apply *Dearle* v. *Hall*. The case, like the other two, is equally weak. First, the apparent holding on the priority question was in fact a mere *obiter dictum* because having concluded that the claim of the retention of title seller was void as an unregistered charge, there was no occasion to invoke *Dearle* v. *Hall*. The rule of equitable priorities by notice requires for its application at least two valid claims. If one of the only two claims is invalid for whatever reason, the valid one prevails by default. Secondly, even if the seller's claim was valid, the result would have been the same because the factor in whose favour a legal assignment of the receivables was conceded would have prevailed as a bona fide purchaser of legal title to the receivables for value without notice. What is more worrying about *Pfeiffer* is the primary ruling that the seller's charge was invalid against the factor as an unregistered charge. Section 95(1) of the Companies Act 1948, under which the case was decided, avoids charges only against creditors having a proprietary claim against the goods covered by the charge whilst the charge remains unregistered.[1] The avoidance was never in favour of purchasers who are clearly not creditors.[2] A factor purchasing clients' receivables is of course not a creditor for this purpose, even where the purchase is with recourse so that the client is contingently liable if the recourse provision is invoked. Only when the provision is invoked would the factor become a creditor. But even at that stage, he is still not a creditor having a proprietary claim over the receivables which he has bought, for, *ex hypothesi*, they have always been his. In *Pfeiffer* the company was not in liquidation. The result of the case is, however, unexceptionable. Even if the retention of title seller possessed a valid unregistered charge, it was liable to be overreached by a bona fide purchase of the legal title to the receivables without notice of the charge. Since it was conceded that the factor was a legal assignee, he took the receivables free of the charge.

---

[97] [1980] 4 W.W.R. 149.
[98] (24th ed., 1977), p. 561.
[99] [1988] 1 W.L.R. 150.
[1] *Re Ehrmann Bros. Ltd.* [1906] 2 Ch. 697; *Re Ashpurton Estates Ltd.* [1983] Ch. 110 at 123.
[2] The position will be different when the amendments to Pt. XII of the Companies Act 1985 become law because new s.399(1)(*b*) avoids a charge not registered within 21 days against any person who for value acquires an interest in or right over property subject to the charge.

The procedural argument

6.16   The view that section 136(1), Law of Property Act 1925 effects only a procedural change in the law governing assignment of choses in action is the second of the two arguments of principle usually urged in support of the application of *Dearle* v. *Hall* to legal assignments. The substance of the procedural argument may be shortly summarised: section 136(1) is merely machinery. It enables an action to be brought by the assignee in his own name in cases where, prior to the Judicature Act 1873, he could only have sued in the assignor's name. Therefore, an assignee availing himself of the statutory facility gets an assignment which is legal only in this procedural sense. For purposes of priority it remains equitable.[3] The procedural argument is very easily met. First, the disability of an assignee of a legal chose in action prior to 1874 was merely procedural,[4] namely, he could not sue at law in his own name on his own account; he could only sue at law in his own name but as an attorney of the assignor (in cases where the debt was in non-negotiable form)[5] or in equity, in his own name, joining the assignor as a co-plaintiff or co-defendant. But it is equally well known that this procedural obstacle was evaded by letters of attorney, novation and attornment. The result was that by 1874, if not earlier, the development of the law and the facility provided by the evasive devices had pushed the common law objection to legal assignments into history. What section 25(6) of the Judicature Act 1873 did, and was intended to do, was to render these circumlocutions unnecessary.[6]

Moreover, there is no principled support for the view that an assignment which complies with section 136(1) is legal only in a procedural sense. Section 136(1)(*a*) and (*b*) give such an assignee not only the legal right to the debt, but also the *legal and other remedies* for the same.[7] This, surely, must pass all the beneficial and procedural advantages incident to legal ownership of the receivables assigned. It is not easy to see why such an assignment which is legal for every other purpose has to be treated *as if it were* equitable for the purpose of priorities alone, unless one is compelled so to read down the provision. Besides, neither the Judicature Act 1873, s.25(6) nor the Law of Property Act 1925, s.136(1) was intended to destroy the distinction between legal and equitable titles.[8] It is therefore surprising to learn that whereas the significance of the distinction is maintained in respect of dealings in other kinds of property,

---

[3] *Pfeiffer GmbH* v. *Arbuthnot Factors Ltd.* [1988] 1 W.L.R. 150 at 162.
[4] *Master* v. *Miller* (1791) 4 Term.Rep. 320 at 340; *Cartor* v. *Croydon Canal Co.* (1843) 3 Swan. 593 at 593–594; *Balfour* v. *Sea Fire Life Assurance Co.* (1857) 3 C.B.(N.S.) 300 at 308; *Norman* v. *FCT* (1962) 109 C.L.R. 9 at 27; Starke, *Assignment of Choses in Action in Australia* (1972), p. 11.
[5] Negotiable debts, *e.g.* bills of exchange and promissory notes, have always been transferable under the law merchant, though this was, and still is, technically by negotiation rather than assignment. The practice predates the Supreme Court of Judicature Act 1873: see *Ryall* v. *Rowles* (1749) 1 Ves.Sen. 348; Milnes Holden, *History of Negotiable Instruments*, in *passim*.
[6] *Norman* v. *FCT* (1962) 109 C.L.R. 9 at 27.
[7] See also, *Read* v. *Brown* (1888) 22 Q.B.D. 128 at 132.
[8] *Joseph* v. *Lyons* (1884) 15 Q.B.D. 280 at 286.

dealings in receivables are outside the distinction. The concern here is not whether statute could indeed destroy the distinction in relation to dealing in receivables; rather, it is that a more explicit provision than that contained in section 136(1) will be required to justify such an approach.

Thirdly, even assuming that section 136(1) is procedural only, this will not necessarily justify the extension of *Dearle* v. *Hall* to legal assignments. In English domestic law, as indeed in its private international law, priorities have always been treated as a procedural rather than a substantive issue.[9] In the distribution of a limited fund insufficient to pay all assignees in full, the court is not concerned with enforcing against the assignor the individual assignee's original substantive rights against him. The rights of priority are not rights of the parties against the assignor, for, *ex hypothesi*, every assignee is a stranger to the other's assignment. Each assignment ranks according to the incidents attributed to it by law, and generally, the starting point is the characterisation of the assignments as legal or equitable. Therefore, not to extend *Dearle* v. *Hall* to legal assignments is quite consistent with the procedural view of section 136(1).

Finally, if the aim of the reform was merely to remove the procedural obstacle whilst leaving an assignment complying with the statute equitable for every other purpose, nothing could have been easier to draft. In this respect section 25(6) of the Judicature Act 1873 may be contrasted with section 1 of the Policies of Assurance Act 1867, which provides that an assignee of a life insurance policy shall have a right in *equity* to receive the assured amount; a right to give the assurance company an effectual discharge; and shall be at liberty to sue at law in his own name. Section 2 preserves equities vested in the assurance company. The Act, however, does not provide that policies can be *legally* assigned. If it was the intention of section 25(6) to give the assignee the right to sue in his own name whilst confining his assignment to equity, nothing easier to draft can be imagined. Having cosidered the arguments of principle, we shall now examine the arguments of policy.

The policy arguments

Two arguments of policy may be urged in favour of applying *Dearle* v. **6.17** *Hall* to legal assignments. The first appeals to justice. It is argued[10] that the procedural reform effected by section 136(1) was not intended to diminish the efficacy of equitable assignments. If legal assignments are to prevail over prior equitable assignments already notified to the debtor, great injustice will be visited on equitable securities. The injustice of the bona fide purchaser rule in this context is more obvious when viewed against the background that every charge (in the strict sense), every assignment of part of a debt, and every assignment of future debts, will inevitably be equitable and hence lose out always to a subsequent legal assignment. Such a result will be harsh and unfortunate. In my view this is a powerful argument which points compellingly to the overriding need for reform. But it hardly shows why such reform should take the form of

---

[9] *The Colorado* [1923] P. 102 at 108; *The Halcyon Isle* [1981] A.C. 221.
[10] Biscoe, *Credit Factoring*, p. 135.

extending *Dearle* v. *Hall* to legal assignments, and arguably overlooks the great injustice inherent in the application of, and limitations on, the rule itself.

The second argument of policy points to the need to protect the debtor. In essence, it is that uncertainties as to the scope of application of *Dearle* v. *Hall* will inconvenience and prejudice the debtor because if he pays a junior assignee, the debt is not discharged and he will remain liable to pay the senior assignee. Such a risk of double payment ought to be avoided and, so it is argued, applying *Dearle* v. *Hall* to legal assignments will avoid this prejudice because most debtors know about the rule and will ordinarily pay their debt to the assignee who gave the first notice. In any event, how will the debtor know which is a legal assignment and which is equitable? These considerations point to the compelling need to assimilate legal and equitable assignments for purposes of priorities. On reflection, these policy considerations are less compelling than they appear at first sight. First, a notice of assignment may not be informative enough. There is no obligation to specify in the notice that the debtor should pay the assignee and no one else. He is supposed to infer this from the fact of assignment. What if he pays the debt over to a junior assignee? Surely, his obligation to the senior assignee remains—so the risk of double payment is not minimised. Secondly, a debtor who is not sure of the ranking of assignees can play safe by inviting them to interplead.[11] Of course, in such a case the court will almost invariably indemnify him by making the wrongful claimant bear the costs of the interpleader.[12] Thirdly, where the debtor pays a junior assignee he can recover the payment on the basis of total failure of consideration since the debt is not discharged.[13] Thus, the debtor is adequately protected irrespective of the applicable rule.

To be sure, no case is made here for the pre-eminence of legal title. Ideally, the law should protect all bona fide transferees regardless of whether their title is legal or equitable. It is hardly a credit to the law that such a debate as to whether or not *Dearle* v. *Hall* applies should be embarked upon, or that the account debtor should be treated as a kind of public register or, worse still, that an assignee taking receivables as security who has registered his security should be put to the trouble and expense of fishing out account debtors and notifying them that he claims the debt even before time has come for him to enforce the security. The case for reform could hardly be stronger or more patent. What is lacking is the political will. Until reform is effected, the conclusion is, though not without regret, that in a contest between a prior equitable assignee and a subsequent legal assignee without notice, *Dearle* v. *Hall* does not apply. We shall now consider the applicable rule.

The true position

6.18   Two situations will be considered. The first is where a prior legal assignment is followed by a subsequent equitable assignment. Here, the

---

[11] Law of Property Act 1925, s.136(1) proviso (*b*).
[12] *Jones* v. *Farrell* (1857) 1 De G. & J. 208 at 218–219.
[13] Birks & Beatson (1976) 92 L.Q.R. 188; Birks, *Introduction to the Law of Restitution* (OUP, 1985), 219; *Rover International Ltd.* v. *Cannon Film Sales Ltd.* [1989] 1 W.L.R. 912, C.A.

legal assignee will prevail because unless the assignment to him was for security only, it exhausts the entirety of the assignor's interest in the receivables.[14] The result is the same whether one looks at it through *Dearle v. Hall* or through the first in time rule. The prior legal assignee will lose priority in some situations of which only four need be mentioned. One is where the subsequent equitable assignment is carved out of the legal assignee's interest, for example, by way of sub-mortgage. Another is where the legal assignee fraudulently connived at the creation of the subsequent equitable interest. A third is where there is a priority or subordination agreement between the senior and junior assignees. The last is where the legal assignee authorises subsequent dealings by the assignor in the receivables and the authority is exceeded. An equitable assignment created in exercise of the authority will normally prevail against the prior legal assignment,[15] unless the equitable assignee took with notice that his assignment was made in excess or fraud of the authority.

The second of the two situations referred to above is where a legal assignment is created after an equitable assignment has perfected his interest by notice to the debtor. Although this is controversial, it is my view that the legal assignee will prevail and that for this purpose, the *tabula in naufragio* doctrine applies.[16] There are two dicta of high authority and one decision in support of this approach. The first is *Ward v. Duncombe*[17] where Lord Macnaghten said:

> "Apart from the rule in *Dearle v. Hall* an assignee of an equitable interest from a person capable of disposing of it has a perfect equitable title, *though the title is no doubt subject to the infirmity which attaches to all equitable titles. And that infirmity is not and cannot be wholly cured or removed by notice to the trustees.*"[18]

The infirmity to which Lord Macnaghten refers is probably the rule that a prior equitable title is liable to be defeated by a subsequent legal title acquired bona fide for value without notice of the equitable title, and indeed he had referred to this rule a little earlier with approval.[19] Other than this, it is difficult to imagine what other infirmity all equitable titles are subject to. The second dictum comes from *Performing Right Society Ltd. v. London Theatre of Varieties Ltd.*[20] where Viscount Finlay is reported as saying:

> "There may possibly be cases in which a person who has made an equitable assignment might by a subsequent assignment have trans-

---

[14] *Cronk v. McManus* (1892) 8 T.L.R. 449; *The "Lancaster"* [1980] 2 Lloyd's Rep. 497 at 503.

[15] *Perry-Herrick v. Attwood* (1857) 2 De G. & J. 21 at 39; *Brocklesby v. Temperance Building Society* [1895] A.C. 173.

[16] See (1989) 9 O.J.L.S. 513 at 528–532; Sheridan, *Rights in Security*, p. 276.

[17] [1893] A.C. 369.

[18] *Ibid.* at 392. Author's italics.

[19] *Ibid.* at 391.

[20] [1924] A.C. 1.

ferred the legal interest in the same work to a purchaser for value without notice, whose title would prevail over the merely equitable right. . . . "[21]

Admittedly these are mere dicta; but this quality alone does not diminish the statement of principle. Of even greater significance is the decision of Robert Goff J. in *Ellerman Lines Ltd.* v. *Lancaster Maritime Co. Ltd.*[22] There, a charterparty, which was in the New York Produce Exchange Form, provided by clause 18 that the charterers had a lien on the ship for all unearned money paid in advance. The shipowners assigned the insurance policies on the ship to some banks, one of which assignments was legal and the other equitable. Notices of both assignments were given to the insurers. In these proceedings the charterers asserted a lien on the ship and claimed that they were entitled to the proceeds of a hull policy on the ship as derivative security. Robert Goff J. held that, assuming the charterers were entitled to the equitable lien claimed, they could not rank ahead of the financing banks. He said:

> "Turning first to the position of the second defendants, First Dallas Ltd., the assignment of insurance moneys to them must be a legal assignment, which ranks before any equitable interest, even a prior equitable interest, unless the assignee had actual or constructive notice of the equitable interest at the time of the assignment.
>   Turning next to the position of the third defendants, Colonial Bank, I will assume that the assignments to them are equitable. . . . In such a case, on the rule in *Dearle* v. *Hall* priority depends on the date of notice to the debtor. . . . "[23]

It is clear from the approach of Robert Goff J. that he considered *Dearle* v. *Hall* inapplicable to the contest between the lienee and the legal assignee of the insurance moneys, though relevant in resolving the dispute between the equitable claimants. It is a matter of regret that neither the above dicta nor this decision were cited to the court in *Pfeiffer*, an omission which cannot enhance the value of *Pfeiffer* on this point.

For the sake of completeness, it may be added that the effect of acquisition of the legal title to receivables is that all pre-existing equitable interests in the same are forever destroyed, for the plea of bona fide purchaser for value is an absolute, unqualified and unanswerable plea to the jurisdiction of the court.[24] The equitable rights so destroyed cannot thereafter revive even against an assignee who has notice that the equitable rights once existed. Such a purchaser will normally shelter under the legal assignee.[25] There is, however, no sheltering where the

---

[21] *Ibid.* at 19.
[22] [1980] 2 Lloyd's Rep. 497.
[23] *Ibid.* at 503, col. 1.
[24] *Pilcher* v. *Rawlins* (1872) L.R. 7 Ch.App. 259 at 269, 271; *Taylor* v. *London & County Banking* [1901] 2 Ch. 231 at 256.
[25] *Lowther* v. *Carlton* (1741) 2 Atk. 242; *Nottingham Patent Brick & Tile Co.* v. *Butler* (1886) 16 Q.B.D. 778 at 788; *Wilkes* v. *Spooner* [1911] 2 K.B. 473.

subsequent purchaser and the original assignor are one and the same person,[26] the reasoning in such cases being that to allow the assignor so to defeat his own assignment would be not only fraudulent, but turning priorities on their head. In practice the compass within which the bona fide purchaser rule assumes significance is much narrower because of the impact of registration of charges over receivables.

Landlords and the receivables financier

It will not be difficult to find cases where a corporate lessee who has **6.19** created a sub-lease charges the lease by way of mortgage and executes a floating security over its undertaking. In fact this is an everyday affair. Where the sub-tenants remain in possession and the chargee puts in a receiver (who is by contract or statute deemed to be the company's agent), who is the owner of the sub-rentals? Assuming the rent reserved under the head lease is unpaid, can the superior landlord intercept the sub-rentals, without forfeiting the head lease? Some of these questions have now been answered by the Court of Appeal in *Rhodes* v. *Allied Dunbar Pension Services Ltd.*[27] As a background to an understanding of the decision, section 6 of the Law of Distress Amendment Act 1908 must be put in the picture.

The Law of Distress Amendment Act 1908 is the culmination of a series of statutes designed to offer protection to third parties against a landlord distraining for unpaid rent. The interests of lodgers, for example, were first safeguarded by the Lodgers' Goods Protection Act 1871, later incorporated into the Law of Distress Amendment Act 1908, which extends the protection to undertenants and third parties generally. By section 1, a person whose goods have been seized by a distraining landlord may give, in the statutory form, a notice of his interest in the goods, stating the amount of rent, if any, due from him, and undertaking henceforth to pay the rent to the distrainer. In order, however, to avoid the circumlocution of seizure followed by a notice and undertaking in the statutory form, and release of the goods, section 6 gives the distraining landlord a right to serve a notice of claim on the undertenants. The aim, evidently, is to compensate him for the curtailment of his common law right by section 1.[28] The service of a section 6 notice has two effects. First, it establishes a direct tenurial relationship between the superior landlord and the undertenant.[29] Secondly, it effects a statutory assignment of the sub-rentals until the rent owed under the head lease is liquidated.[30] What is not clear is whether the section 6 notice is a paramount right overriding all pre-existing claims on the sub-rentals, or whether it governs merely the triangular relationship between the superior landlord, the head tenant/intermediate landlord and the undertenants, leaving questions of

---

[26] *Barrow's Case* (1880) 14 Ch.D. 432 at 445.
[27] [1989] 1 All E.R. 1161.
[28] *Re a Debtor (No. 549 of 1928)* [1929] 1 Ch. 170 at 175.
[29] Law of Distress Amendment Act 1908, s.3.
[30] *Wallrock* v. *Equity & Life Assurance Society* [1942] 2 K.B. 82 at 84.

priority between the section 6 notice and pre-existing incumbrances to be determined by the general law. A section 6 notice gives the superior landlord a right wider and narrower than distress: wider, because it can be exercised even where no distress is possible, for example, because there are no distrainable goods; narrower, in that it can only be served upon undertenants and other persons from whom rent is due to the intermediate landlord, whereas distress is available in respect of goods found on the premises regardless of their ownership. Does the section 6 notice override pre-existing incumbrances on the sub-rentals?

In *Rhodes* v. *Allied Dunbar Pension Services Ltd.*,[31] Harman J. held at first instance[32] that it did not, only to be reversed on appeal. There, a mortgagee having a legal charge on the intermediate landlord's leasehold interest in property which was in the occupation of undertenants put in receivers who were by contract deemed to be the agents of the company. Whilst the receivers were in possession of the leasehold interest (through receipt of the sub-rentals), the head landlord served a section 6 notice knowing that receivers were in possession. Harman J. gave priority to the chargee because he considered the competing claims as successive assignments to which the rule in *Dearle* v. *Hall* applied, or alternatively, on the basis that the charge was earlier in time. The Court of Appeal overturned his decision, giving two reasons why the superior landlord prevailed. One was that the chargee never went into possession of the lease so that the company remained at all times entitled to the sub-rentals. The appointment of receivers made no material difference. Although appointed by the chargee, the receivers were *deemed* to be the agents of the company. This agency was a real one even though it had some peculiar incidents. Thus, although after their appointment it was the receivers who were entitled to payment of the undertenant's rents, their entitlement was as agents of the company. This was so even though, when they received the rents, they were obliged to deal with the money in accordance with the terms of the debenture. This reasoning may be referred to as the "agency" theory. If this had been the only reason given by the Court of Appeal there would have been some hope for lenders taking sub-rentals as security, provided they are ready to assume the risk of going into possession. However, the court gave a second reason which would have defeated the bank in any event, namely, that section 6 gave the superior landlord a paramount right which is now an incident of the superior landlord/intermediate landlord/undertenant relationship. "A person who takes an assignment of a headlease does so subject to the possibility that if the rent due to the superior landlord is not paid, the superior landlord may garnishee, so to speak, the rent due from undertenants."[33] After all, if the rent is unpaid the head lease may be forfeited and with it, the underlease. This is the "paramountcy" theory.

As a matter of legal policy, this result is unexceptionable—charity must begin at home; a person must be just before becoming generous. For a number of reasons, however, this result is not obvious from a fair reading

---

[31] [1989] 1 All E.R. 1161.
[32] [1987] 1 W.L.R. 1703.
[33] [1989] 1 All E.R. 1161 at 1168.

of the statute. To begin with, the agency theory is weak on many counts. First, a mortgagee places a receiver in control of the mortgaged property for the same reasons that he would normally go into possession himself, namely, to take control and enforce his security. If the reasoning of the Court of Appeal is law, and beneficial ownership remains in the mortgagor even where the secured amount exceeds the value of the security, simply because of the deemed agency of the receiver, then, the mortgagee has no security at all since his security remains forever at the mercy of predators. Such a conclusion can only be justified by invoking the benefit and burden principle—the mortgagee who benefits from the agency by avoiding the liability of a mortgagee in possession should be estopped from avoiding the unpleasant consequences inherent in the agency. Fortunately for the mortgagee, English law is yet to commit itself to such a principle.[34] While such a principle, if it exists at all, can usefully express a *conclusion*, it does not provide a *solution*. Secondly, it would be running the fiction of agency into the ground if a mortgagor having no equity of redemption in the mortgaged property remained beneficially entitled to the property simply and solely because the receiver is deemed to be his agent. True it is that the agency has some real sides to it[35]; but it would distort the agency fiction beyond recognition if one were to say that in all cases where the receiver is in possession, beneficial ownership of the property subject to the receivership remains in the mortgagor. The truth is that before appointment of a receiver, a mortgagor in possession receives rent by leave and licence of the mortgagee who at all times is entitled by virtue of being the reversioner expectant on the underlease.[36] That licence is terminated when the mortgagee takes possession through the receiver even though for certain purposes the receiver is deemed to be the agent of the mortgagor.

The paramountcy theory is more promising but raises some difficulties. It is superficially attractive to say that the intermediate landlord's right to sub-rentals contains an inherent liability to being defeated by a section 6 notice. One problem, however, is that English law has not developed any consistent policy in favour of upholding purchase-money security interests.[37] The conspicuous lack of success of the retention of title clauses bears testimony to this. Yet, the facility of self-help afforded by the section 6 notice is at least akin to a purchase-money security.

The Court of Appeal decision can be better justified on the basis of section 3 of the Law of Distress Amendment Act 1908, which provides that for purposes of recovering any sums payable by an undertenant or lodger to a superior landlord under a section 6 notice, the undertenant or

---

[34] *The Dominique* [1989] 2 W.L.R. 440 at 456. *Cf. Halsall* v. *Brizell* [1957] Ch. 169 at 182; *Tito* v. *Waddell (No. 2)* [1977] Ch. 106 at 302.

[35] *Gomba Holdings UK Ltd.* v. *Homan* [1986] 3 All E.R. 94 at 97–99 (duty to pass information to company if "a need to know" is demonstrated); *Ratford* v. *Northavon D.C.* [1987] Q.B. 357 at 371 (receivers not in rateable occupation of premises since they were there as agents of the company); *cf. Gomba Holdings UK Ltd.* v. *Minories Finance Ltd.* [1989] 1 All E.R. 261 at 263 (company had no proprietary right to all documents concerning it and brought into existence by receivers who were deemed to be its agents).

[36] *Re Ind, Coope & Co. Ltd.* [1911] 2 Ch. 223 at 231.

[37] *Cf. Abbey National Building Society* v. *Cann* [1990] 2 W.L.R. 832.

lodger shall be deemed to be the immediate tenant of the superior landlord, and the sums payable shall be deemed to be rent. By this provision, a section 6 notice terminates any existing underlease, so that from that point there is nothing for the existing charge to bite on, not because it gives a paramount right, but because of the deemed direct tenurial relationship between the superior landlord and the undertenant or lodger, pursuant to section 3.

Cross-over security and the purchase-money lender

6.20 Receivables financing could be self-liquidating. Raw materials are continually being converted into finished goods. These are sold to produce receivables which will in turn support future borrowing, as collections from buyers of the finished goods are deposited into the company's account to reduce current overdraft. Since the process is self-perpetuating, an assignment of existing receivables alone will provide a technically insufficient security to support future borrowing. To overcome this problem and partly also to stay outside the hazard created by the combination of the rules in *Rolt* v. *Hopkinson*[38] and *Clayton's Case*,[39] it is usual for lenders to take an assignment which provides a continuing security for all the borrower's indebtedness. Such a security has two prominent features: first, it extends to all existing and future receivables; secondly, the security is for present and future indebtedness. Both features give effect to the usually long-term relationship inherent in current assets financing. This type of security may be called a cross-over security. For a number of reasons, the borrower may need funding from another source. It may be to purchase a particular item of property, real or personal, or it may be required to perform a one-off contract. The credit rating of the borrower may not command unsecured lending. The new lender would, therefore, naturally desire security and where, as here, the borrower has no unincumbered assets, the only safe harbour is the property sought to be acquired or the contract to be performed. The problem here is how to draft the security agreement so that it is not be caught by the after-acquired property clause in the pre-existing cross-over security. Three settled rules of law complicate this task. The first is that, as a general rule, a borrower can only give away as security property which he owns, and only to the extent of his interest. If the second lender (who may for convenience be referred to as the purchase-money lender) waits until the property is acquired or contract to render services is signed, it may be too late. The after-acquired property clause in the cross-over security would have attached, leaving the borrower with only an equity of redemption. This rule has a beneficial side for the purchase-money lender in that it enables him, if he can, to draft a form of agreement which precludes the borrower from acquiring an interest in the property or contract except subject to the contractual obligation to give

---

[38] (1861) 9 H.L.Cas. 514.
[39] (1816) 1 Mer. 585. For a discussion of the effect of the joint operation of both rules, see para. 6.21 *infra*.

him a senior security. In this event, he will defeat the cross-over security holder.

The second rule is surprising. English law has not developed any coherent or explicit rule in favour of upholding a purchase-money security.[40] Accordingly, it is not the law that where the purchase money or a part of it has been provided by a lender, all the purchaser/borrower acquires is the equity of redemption.[41] It follows that the purchase-money lender cannot expect to prevail over the cross-over security by reason only of having advanced the purchase money, unless prior to the advance the borrower contractually undertook to give him a prior ranking security upon acquisition of the property. It is difficult to see in what circumstances a lender would not exact such an undertaking from the borrower. Indeed it would be quite unrealistic to assume that a commercial lender would ever make money available unconditionally. Thirdly, a composite transaction cannot be regarded as being one transaction, unless it is not only one, but one and indivisible. Accordingly, two transactions, each possessing a legal individuality of its own, do not coalesce into one merely because they are dependent on each other.[42] This rule poses the greatest difficulty to any claim to priority by the purchase-money lender because if the acquisition of the property and the grant of security over it are regarded as individual, albeit dependent transactions, there would be a *scintilla temporis* between the purchase and the mortgage securing the loan with which the purchase was financed, sufficient for the cross-over security to fasten on the property. In that case, he can only prevail if the cross-over security creates a floating charge which has not crystallised. If it has crystallised, for example, because the charge contains a provision for automatic crystallisation in the event of any attempted creation of a senior security, the purchase-money lender may lose out. Where the cross-over security is a fixed charge, the result is the same. The purchase-money lender, even if he has a legal mortgage, cannot plead bona fide purchaser for value without notice. This is because registration of the charge will normally constitute some form of notice.

The question is whether the purchase and the mortgage with which it was financed can be treated as one indivisible transaction, thus not only excluding any scintilla of time between both transactions, but such that in law, as in fact, only the equity of redemption is acquired by the borrower.

---

[40] Other jurisdictions have been more sympathetic towards the purchase-money lender. In New Zealand, for example, s.24 of the Chattels Transfer Act 1924 (as amended), which provides for partial avoidance of unregistered instruments in respect of after-acquired property, does not apply to a purchase-money security interest: see *Broadlands Finance Ltd. v. Shand Miller Musical Supplies Ltd.* [1976] 2 N.Z.L.R. 124 where the section was considered but not applied because the borrower never in fact acquired the property. In America, the Uniform Commercial Code (UCC) (1978 Official Text), Art. 9–312(3) and (4) give a purchase-money lender priority over an interest under an after-acquired property clause.

[41] *Church of England Building Society* v. *Piskor* [1954] Ch. 553 where an argument to the contrary was rejected.

[42] *Church of England Building Society* v. *Piskor* [1954] Ch. 553 at 565.

After a period of doubt and uncertainty,[43] the House of Lords has now ruled that a purchaser of land relying on a bank loan for the completion of his purchase never in fact acquires anything more than an equity of redemption, for the land is, from the inception, charged with the amount of the loan without which it could never have been acquired.[44] In such a case, at any rate where there is a prior agreement to grant a charge on the legal estate when acquired, the transactions of acquiring the legal estate and granting the charge are, in law and in reality, one indivisible transaction. This is a robust approach, thoroughly consonant with the justice of the situation; an example of common law response, in its own ad hoc way, to the need to recognise the priority of the purchase-money lender in the produce of his money. As a matter of legal policy, nothing could be fairer than to give priority to the purchase-money lender whose money produced the property sought to be charged. It is a bad reflection on the law that we have had to wait for so long before the problem is satisfactorily resolved. As the law now stands, a purchase-money lender will almost always have a first charge on the produce of his money, provided he enters into an agreement for such a charge before any interest passes to the purchaser. In the case of the land, for example, it is absolutely necessary that the agreement for security predates exchange of contracts. This will invariably be the case, for it will be difficult to find a commercial lender who will make money available unconditionally. If a similar approach is adopted in relation to other types of property, it would mean that as regards goods, for example, the risk of loss of priority by the purchase-money lender is less because, it would seem, no equitable interest passes before the time agreed for passing of general property.[45] In relation to receivables, the purchase-money security agreement should, where possible, predate the contract out of which the receivables arise. Although this would be difficult, it is the result of the cases which treat as existing receivables all existing contracts from which receivables would arise even where the contracts are still wholly executory. If this is achieved, the purchase-money security prevails, not just

---

[43] In *Wilson* v. *Kelland* [1910] 2 Ch. 306; *Re Connolly Brothers Ltd. (No. 2)* [1912] 2 Ch. 25; *Coventry Permanent Economic Building Society* v. *Jones* [1951] 1 All E.R. 901 and *Security Trust Co.* v. *Royal Bank of Canada* [1976] A.C. 503, the purchase-money lender prevailed because there was no *scintilla temporis* between acquisition of legal title and the grant of security over the property in favour of the lender. But in *Church of England Building Society* v. *Piskor* [1954] Ch. 553 the purchase-money lender failed because the court refused to treat the acquisition and the mortgage securing the loan with which the purchase was completed as one indivisible transaction. There was therefore a scintilla of time between both transactions, sufficient to feed the equitable tenancies created by the purchaser prior to completion. Although this case was overruled by the House of Lords in *Abbey National Building Society* v. *Cann* [1900] 2 W.L.R. 832, it is fair to say that, in *Piskor*, there was no prior agreement to give a security to the lender before completion. Accordingly, even an incumbered legal estate would have been sufficient to feed the estoppel arising from the equitable tenancies. Again, although it is a bit unrealistic to assume that a commercial lender would make money available unconditionally, it remains the case that courts do not imply terms into agreements merely because this may give effect to the intention of one of the contracting parties.

[44] *Abbey National Building Society* v. *Cann* [1990] 2 W.L.R. 832.

[45] *Re Wait* [1927] 1 Ch. 606 at 635–636; *Leigh & Sillavan Ltd.* v. *Aliakmon* [1986] A.C. 785 at 812–813.

because it is earlier in date, but because the receivables never arose except burdened with the equitable charge in favour of the lender. This solution is too risky. A better solution is, where possible, to enter into a priority agreement with the holder of the pre-existing cross-over security before the purchase money is advanced.

In *Rother Iron Works Ltd.* v. *Canterbury Precision Engineers Ltd.*,[46] where the question was whether the defendant could set off against its liability to pay for goods contracted to be purchased before receivership but delivered after it, a pre-receivership debt owed to it by the company, the Court of Appeal held that the defendant's obligation never came into existence, except subject to a right to set off the debt owed to it. That which became subject to the debenture charge was not the gross price of the goods, but the defendant's net liability. This was apparently in spite of the absence of any agreement to this effect, and indicates that the analysis in *Re Connolly Brothers Ltd. (No. 2)* is capable of application to receivables.

Appropriation and tacking of further advances

A debtor paying money to his creditor has the primary right to **6.21** appropriate it to any account, where he owes two or more debts. This may be express or implied,[47] but must be made at the time of payment. Thereafter, the right of appropriation is that of the creditor, and he can do so at any time,[48] although once made, it cannot be altered. However, appropriation by the creditor is not normally final until communicated to the debtor[49] and he can hold up appropriation until as late as possible. As regards form, the law is remarkably flexible. Thus, appropriation could be by issue of proceedings[50]; it can take place in the witness box[51]; even a statement to the jury is sufficient.[52] The creditor's right to appropriate can enhance his security in many ways. First, where two debts are owed, one of which is irrecoverable by suit, and the debtor fails to appropriate the payment to any debt, the creditor can appropriate it to that which is irrecoverable and sue for the other.[53] Similarly, a creditor holding a security for only one debt can apply an unappropriated payment to the discharge of the unsecured debt leaving himself fully secured.[54] An undisclosed intention is not, however, evidence of appropriation.[55] If

---

[46] [1974] Q.B. 1 at 6.
[47] *Manning* v. *Westerne* (1707) 2 Vern. 606; *Young* v. *English* (1843) 7 Beav. 10; *Thompson* v. *Hudson* (1871) L.R. 6 Ch.App. 320.
[48] *Cory Brothers & Co. Ltd.* v. *Owners of Turkish Steamship "Mecca", The "Mecca"* [1897] A.C. 286 at 293.
[49] *Simpson* v. *Ingham* (1823) 2 B. & C. 65.
[50] *The "Mecca", supra.*
[51] *Seymour* v. *Pickett* [1905] 1 K.B. 715.
[52] *Philpott* v. *Jones* (1834) 2 A. & E. 41 at 44.
[53] *Seymour* v. *Pickett* [1905] 1 K.B. 715; *cf. Mills* v. *Fowkes* (1839) 5 Bing (N.C.) 445; *Ashby* v. *James* (1843) 11 M. & W. 542; *Friend* v. *Young* [1897] 2 Ch. 421.
[54] *Ex p. Dickin, Re Foster* (1875) L.R. 20 Eq. 767; *Re William Hall (Contractors) Ltd.* [1967] 1 W.L.R. 948; *cf. Young* v. *English* (1843) 7 Beav. 10; *Thompson* v. *Hudson* (1871) L.R. 6 Ch.App. 320; *Knysh* v. *Corrales Pty Ltd.* (1989) 15 A.C.L.R. 629.
[55] *Leeson* v. *Leeson* [1936] 2 K.B. 156.

neither the debtor nor the creditor exercises the right to appropriate, then one can look at the matter as a question of account and see how the creditor has dealt with the payment in order to ascertain how he did in fact appropriate it. In the case of an active and unbroken current account, the presumption is that the first item on the debit side of the account is the first to be discharged or reduced by the first item on the credit side. The appropriation is made by the very act of setting the two items against each other. This is the rule in *Clayton's Case*.[56] To apply, there must be a current account[57] and it must be unbroken.[58] But even where these requirements are fulfilled, the rule may be excluded, expressly[59] or by implication.[60] The rule is very important in the context of current assets financing effected through the medium of a current account. Four illustrations of its importance merit special mention. First, the rule applies to guarantees. Where a continuing guarantee determines, whether through breach by the beneficiary or death of the guarantor, and an unbroken current account is maintained for the borrower, subsequent deposits into the account will, in the absence of appropriation, redeem earlier items on the account, leaving the fresh drawings unsecured.[61] Secondly, where a bank opens a wages account for a customer in financial distress whilst leaving the existing current account unbroken, the effect of the application of the rule in *Clayton's Case* is to redeem earlier items on the account, leaving the bank a preferential creditor in the subsequent liquidation of the borrower, in relation to fresh drawings.[62] The rule applies even where the intention was not to rank as a preferential creditor; all that is required is that the drawings be actually applied in the payment of wages.[63] Thirdly, a bank which has taken an invalid floating charge within 12 months of the onset of insolvency may end up with a valid security if it maintains an unbroken current account for the chargor. Since payments into the account go to reduce earlier items on the debit side, the result may be to wash out the old debt; the subsequent drawing would then count as new money advanced after the creation of the charge.[64] Here, the rule in *Clayton's Case* defeats the perfectly sensible policy underlying the legislation which avoids floating charges given to secure past indebtedness when the company is in *extremis*.[65] The result is, however, not unjust. A bank which honours cheques drawn on an overdrawn account gives new value and there is no compelling argument based on considerations of fairness for treating payments into the account as redeeming the fresh debts rather than the older ones. If the payor

---

[56] *Devaynes* v. *Noble, Clayton's Case* (1816) 1 Mer. 585 at 608.
[57] *The "Mecca"* [1897] A.C. 286.
[58] *Re Sherry, London & County Banking Co.* v. *Terry* (1884) 25 Ch.D. 692.
[59] *Westminster Bank Ltd.* v. *Cond* (1940) 46 Com.Cas. 60.
[60] *Henniker* v. *Wigg* [1843] 4 Q.B. 792.
[61] *Coulthart* v. *Clementson* (1879) 5 Q.B.D. 42; *cf. Re Sherry, supra*; *Westminster Bank Ltd.* v. *Cond, supra*.
[62] *Re Primrose (Builders) Ltd.* [1950] Ch. 561; *cf. Re James R. Rutherford Sons Ltd.* [1964] 1 W.L.R. 1211.
[63] *Re Rampgill Mill Ltd.* [1967] Ch. 1138.
[64] *Re Yeovil Glove Co. Ltd.* [1965] Ch. 148; *Re Thomas Mortimer Ltd.* [1965] Ch. 186n.
[65] *Re Orleans Motor Co. Ltd.* [1911] 2 Ch. 41 at 45.

passes up his right of appropriation, why should the new rather than the old debts be the ones redeemed by the payments into the account? It is therefore not surprising that although the *Insolvency Law Review Committee*[66] recommended statutory reversal of this particular application of the rule in *Clayton's Case*, this has up to the present day escaped the zeal of the legal reformer. Finally, the rule could, when combined with the rule in *Rolt v. Hopkinson*,[67] embarrass even the most prudent banker. The essence of the latter rule is that a first mortgagee, whose security covers what is then due and further advances, cannot claim the benefit of his security for further advances in priority to a second mortgagee of whose security he had notice before the further advances were made. The principle which underlies this rule is plain and sensible: a first mortgagee should not obtain a security over property which, at the date of the further advance, he knew was no longer that of the mortgagor to deal with as he pleases. In *Rolt v. Hopkinson* itself, the first mortgagee was under no obligation to make the further advances. However, in *West v. Williams*,[68] the Court of Appeal held that the principle was the same whether or not the first mortgagee was under an obligation to make the further advances. The reasoning was that such an obligation was incapable of specific performance, for there can be no specific performance of a contract to make a loan. *West v. Williams* has now been reversed by statute as regards mortgages of land made after 1925,[69] but it continues to apply to mortgages of receivables. The rule in *Rolt v. Hopkinson* has subsequently been extended to the operation of a current account. The result is that where a bank holding a first charge to secure an overdrawn current account has notice of a second mortgage, and permits fresh drawings, it is in effect subordinated to the second mortgagee as regards the fresh advances.[70] This is so whether or not the first mortgage is expressed to be a continuing security.[71] That is not all. If the borrower pays money into the account subsequent to the second mortgage, and there is no evidence of appropriation, the effect of the rule in *Clayton's Case* is to redeem earlier items, so that in time, if payments-in equal the amount of the indebtedness to the bank at the date of notice of the second mortgage, the bank's security automatically becomes a second mortgage ranking after the original second mortgage which now becomes the first mortgage. It was the combination of the rules in *Rolt v. Hopkinson* and *Clayton's Case* that dictated the eventual outcome of the litigation in *Siebe Gorman & Co. Ltd. v. Barclays Bank Ltd.*,[72] so that,

---

[66] *Insolvency Law and Practice: Report of the Review Committee* (Chairman: Sir Kenneth Cork, June 1982), Cmnd. 8558, para. 1562.
[67] (1861) 9 H.L.Cas. 514. See also, *Bradford Banking Co. Ltd. v. Henry Briggs, Sons & Co. Ltd.* (1886) 12 App.Cas. 29.
[68] [1899] 1 Ch. 132.
[69] Law of Property Act 1925, s.94(1)(*c*); Land Registration Act 1925, s.30(3) (where the mortgage imposes an obligation on the mortgagee to make further advances). Such obligation need not be absolute and unconditional. Indeed it would be difficult to imagine under what circumstances an obligation to lend money would be unconditional.
[70] *London & County Banking Co. Ltd. v. Ratcliffe* (1881) 6 App.Cas. 722; *Deeley v. Lloyds Bank Ltd.* [1912] A.C. 756.
[71] *Cf.* J. Tyler, *Fisher & Lightwood's Law of Mortgage* (10th ed., 1988), p. 568.
[72] [1979] 2 Lloyd's Rep. 142.

although the bank's first fixed charge on receivables was upheld, it had however been almost completely redeemed by the payments into the account subsequent to notice of assignment of the bills to the plaintiffs.

In practice, banks overcome this result by taking two steps. The first is to express in the charge document that the charge is a continuing security.[73] Secondly, they strike the debit at the date of notice of the second mortgage and open a new account for subsequent dealings. As the law stands, a lender advancing money on the security of receivables will prevail over a second mortgagee or even an outright assignee of the receivables, as regards further advances, only in three situations. The first is by ruling off the debit on receipt of notice of another claimant. The second is where the junior assignee agrees to subordinate his security to the further advances; the third is where the further advance is made in ignorance of the existence of a junior assignee. What is unclear is whether registration of the second mortgage is notice for this purpose. The writer is not aware of any reported case where the rule in *Rolt* v. *Hopkinson* was applied without actual notice on the part of the first mortgagee, and registration is only constructive notice.[74] Further, where the first mortgage secures a current account, to insist on a duty to search the register before a cheque drawn on the account is honoured would impose an intolerable administrative burden on the mortgagee, and it may be that in such cases the rule applicable to land mortgages securing current accounts[75] may, by analogy, be applied here, with the result that a junior incumbrancer seeking protection should be required to give actual notice of his security. Outside current accounts, there is no reason why registration of the second charge should not be sufficient notice for this purpose.

Waiver, subordination and priority agreements

6.22   The ranking of claims against one another may be varied by the parties. Such a variation may take a variety of forms. An earlier secured creditor may release a particular item of property comprised in his security to another creditor, for example, a bank holding a first floating charge on a company's undertaking may agree to release the receivables so that the company can raise additional finance from other sources and, in particular, by factoring them. Whether this is characterised as a waiver or release of security matters not: the effect is to subordinate the bank's claim to that of the factor, the extent of subordination depending on the precise terms used. Alternatively, two creditors, whether or not both are secured, or one alone is, or neither is, may enter into an agreement by which one (here called the senior creditor) is to rank as to payment of principal and interest above the other (here called the junior creditor). Again, the extent of subordination is a matter for the contract between them. A third example is where two creditors, each holding a valid security interest, agree that, as to particular items comprised in their

---

[73] See, *e.g. 4 Encyclopaedia of Forms and Precedents* (5th ed.), p. 229.
[74] *Cf.* Companies Act 1985, s.416(1).
[75] Law of Property Act 1925, s.94(2).

respective securities, one is to be regarded as the senior creditor whilst as to the remainder, the other is to be the senior creditor.[76] The general problems which such arrangements engender have already been well documented,[77] and no time need now be wasted rehearsing them. What is proposed here is to discuss two problems of enforceability of these agreements (henceforth referred to simply as priority agreements).

The first problem arises commonly in the borrower's insolvency, and is whether the priority agreement contravenes any principle or policy of insolvency law. Two areas of difficulty immediately come to mind. The first is the question of set-off, which can in fact arise outside insolvency. Is the borrower precluded by the priority agreement from setting off any cross-claims it has against the junior creditor? In all but one instance, the borrower can exercise its right of set-off unless this is excluded by the subordination agreement. Insolvency set-off[78] is mandatory[79] if there is the requisite mutuality. It follows that whether the priority agreement is drafted in such a way that the junior debt is expressed not to be due (conditional debt),[80] or that the junior creditor holds the proceeds of his debt or any liquidation dividend on trust for the senior creditor (subordination by trust), set-off is available: in the case of the conditional debt, liquidation accelerates the accrual of the debt obligation; in the case of the subordination trust, the right to receive is not assigned and that establishes sufficient mutuality for insolvency set-off. The one exception alluded to above is where the right to receive, as opposed to the proceeds of the right, is assigned. Here there is no beneficial mutuality and set-off is not available.[81] The moral, in cases where set-off is available, is that careless drafting can make the junior creditor senior in many ways. The second area of difficulty is the *pari passu* principle of insolvency law.[82] As a matter of first principle, no device calculated to defeat the operation of the insolvency laws will be enforced.[83] On the face of it, the priority agreement does not have this as its aim and so does not offend it. But there is a second and more important principle, otherwise known as the *British Eagle*[84] principle, which focuses on the *effect* rather than the *aim* of

---

[76] See *Judson* v. *DCT (Victoria)* (1987) 12 A.C.L.R. 91; *cf. Re Camden Brewery Ltd.* (1912) 106 L.T. 598; *Re Robert Stephenson & Co. Ltd.* [1913] 2 Ch. 201.

[77] Johnston (1987) 15 A.B.L.R. 80 collects citations of relevant discussions, and is itself a very good discussion of the problems.

[78] Insolvency Rules 1986 (S.I. 1986 No. 1925), r. 4.90.

[79] *National Westminster Bank Ltd.* v. *Halesowen Presswork & Assemblies Ltd.* [1972] A.C. 785. The Insolvency Law and Practice Review Committee, Cmnd. 8558, para. 1341, recommended statutory reversal of this decision to enable parties to contract out of insolvency set-off. The recommendation is yet to be implemented.

[80] See Johnston (1987) 15 A.B.L.R. 80 at 117 *et seq.* for a discussion of subordination by conditional debt. *Re Charge Card Services Ltd.* [1987] Ch. 150, shows that even contingent debts are capable of set-off, a principle now affirmed by the Insolvency Rules 1986, rr. 4.90 and 13.12. And, generally, see Wood, *English and International Set Off* (1989), paras. 7–57 *et seq.*

[81] *Bailey* v. *Finch* (1871) L.R. 7 Q.B. 34; *Ex p. Morier* (1879) 12 Ch.D. 491; *Bhogal* v. *Punjab National Bank* [1988] 2 All E.R. 296.

[82] Insolvency Act 1986, s.107; Insolvency Rules 1986, r. 4.181.

[83] *Re Johns, Worrell* v. *Johns* [1928] Ch. 737.

[84] *British Eagle International Airlines Ltd.* v. *Compagnie Nationale Air France* [1975] 1 W.L.R. 758, H.L.

the device or arrangement. The essence of the principle is that where the effect of a contract is that an asset which is owned by a company at the commencement of its liquidation falls to be dealt with in a manner contrary to section 107 of the Insolvency Act 1986, then, to that extent, the contract is void on grounds of public policy.[85] For this purpose, it matters not whether the contract was for value, or was entered into for bona fide commercial reasons, or that the offensive provisions was to take effect only on insolvency. Where it applies, the principle prevents a creditor from enforcing an agreement (otherwise than pursuant to a valid security) for withdrawal of the borrower's unincumbered assets available for distribution among unsecured creditors.[86] The question is whether the enforcement of the priority agreement will be contrary to this principle?

In my view, it cannot be.[87] The principle is not at all a distributional rule. It is a rule of ascertainment of the insolvent's estate and denies effect to agreements which operate to withdraw some assets otherwise unincumbered from the fund of assets available for distribution among all creditors. In *Ex p. Mackay*,[88] for example, if the offensive agreement had been enforced, it would have had the effect that one-half of the royalties which at the beginning of his bankruptcy belonged to the bankrupt would have gone to one creditor alone. Similarly, in *British Eagle* itself, the effect of the clearing house scheme was that, if enforced, it withdrew debts due from Air France from the fund of assets available in *British Eagle*'s liquidation, and, in effect, made Air France and other clearing house creditors, preferred creditors. There can be no objection in principle or policy, and certainly nothing in *British Eagle* requires otherwise, to a priority agreement between two creditors, the effect of which is not to withdraw any asset of the insolvent from the general fund, but to ensure that a senior creditor is paid before a junior creditor. The Australian case of *Horne* v. *Chester & Fein*[89] gave effect to such an agreement, and concluded rightly that nothing in *British Eagle* dictated a contrary result. It has, however, been said[90] that this case will not be followed in England and that English courts will almost certainly consider that priority agreements are within the principle of *British Eagle*, the reason being that *British Eagle* affirms a principle of English public policy and is not based on the narrower point of prejudice to creditors. This will be unfortunate if indeed it is the law. There are good reasons for suggesting that it stretches the *ratio* of *British Eagle* far too wide. First, if a creditor can renounce his right to prove, it is not easy to see why he cannot by contract agree to rank after a particular creditor. Secondly, the Act of Parliament unquestionably says that everybody shall be paid *pari passu*. It does not mean that the court shall look into past transactions,

---

[85] *Carreras Rothman Ltd.* v. *Freeman Matthews Treasure Ltd.* [1985] Ch. 207 at 226.
[86] *Ex p. Mackay* (1873) L.R. 8 Ch.App. 643 at 647.
[87] See also Wood, *English and International Set Off* (1989), para. 5–218; *cf.* Goode, *Legal Problems of Credit and Security* (2nd ed., 1988), pp. 96–97.
[88] (1873) L.R. 8 Ch.App. 643.
[89] (1986) 11 A.C.L.R. 485.
[90] Goode, *Legal Problems of Credit and Security* (2nd ed., 1988), p. 96. *Cf.* Goode, *Principles of Corporate Insolvency Law* (1990), pp. 64–65. However, even r. 11.11(1), Insolvency Rules 1986, recognises the assignment of a right to dividend.

and equalise all the creditors.[91] Thirdly, insolvency law does not have as its aim the dislocation of pre-insolvency agreements where these do not in fact hinder the collective régime which the statutory scheme for distribution substitutes for individual creditor enforcement. Where a priority agreement regulates the relationship between two creditors without affecting the distribution of assets to other creditors or affecting the amount of dividend which they will receive in the absence of the agreement, it is difficult to see on what head of public policy such an agreement will be denied effect. Besides, the contrary assumes that the senior and junior creditors are equals.

The second problem of enforcing priority agreements is as they affect the junior creditor's creditors. Where the senior creditor asserts that, by virtue of the priority agreement, he has a right to the junior debt which is enforceable against, and entitled to priority over, third parties claiming through the junior creditor—subsequent assignees, execution creditors or the junior creditor's liquidator or administrator, the assertion can only be sustained if the priority agreement gives him proprietary rights over the junior debt. For this purpose a distinction must be drawn between the creation in the senior creditor of some equitable rights of a personal nature on the one hand, and the creation in him (by virtue of the priority agreement) of an equitable proprietary right, on the other. If, upon analysis, the priority agreement falls into the former category, it may entitle the senior creditor to an injunction to restrain a threatened breach, but on its own it is insufficient to gain priority over third parties.[92] Secondly, if this is the effect, it will certainly fall foul of the *British Eagle* principle. Again, another distinction must be drawn between a person's agreement to use his rights (or not to use them) in a certain way for the benefit of another on the other hand, and an effective agreement to incumber or part with them in favour of that other person, on the other.[93] A priority agreement which achieves the former, but not the latter, effect, is unenforceable against third party assignees of the junior debt. Of course, it is idle to say whether as a general rule a priority agreement falls into one rather than the other category. The truth is that priority and subordination agreements are not terms of art. They mean exactly what they say and nothing else. If the priority agreement gives the senior creditor proprietary rights, two subsidiary questions must then be answered. The first is over what do the rights exist? Since the alienation is calculated to ensure priority of the senior debt, there is a built-in temporal and quantitative limitation on the interest transferred: it does not survive payment of the senior debt and the extent of alienation is correspondingly limited to the amount necessary to achieve that payment, and no more. In effect, the senior creditor has a security interest. This leads to the second question, does it require registration? If the proceeds receivable on the junior debt are assigned, it will not require registration as a charge on book debts, the reason being that the book debt (if there

---

[91] *Re Smith, Knight & Co.* (1868) L.R. 5 Eq. 223 at 226. And, generally, see T. Jackson (1985) 15 J. of Legal Studies 73.
[92] *National Provincial Bank* v. *Ainsworth* [1965] A.C. 1175 at 1225, 1252–1254.
[93] *Pritchard* v. *Briggs* [1980] Ch. 338.

be one at all) is the loan made by the junior creditor. Therefore, although a charge on book debts will carry through into the proceeds, the reverse process is not possible—a charge on the proceeds does not transform into a charge on the book debts which produced the proceeds. However, it may be that for purposes of registration, no distinction is to be drawn between a charge on book debts and a charge on the proceeds of the book debts. Both should be registrable. That, however, does not conclude the question. It must further be ascertained whether the security interest is a floating charge since registrability does not depend on the subject-matter charged. The answer will depend on the extent of management autonomy which the junior creditor retains over the junior debt, *e.g.* whether the junior creditor is entitled to exercise any voting rights attached to the debt. What degree of autonomy is required to justify treatment of the priority agreement as a floating charge is difficult to say with precision. Every case will depend upon its own facts.

Where the junior debt forms part of a series of debentures it is not to be treated as a book debt for the purposes of the legislation requiring registration of charges on book debts.[94] It must be stressed that, outside such cases, the drafting of a priority agreement so as to make the junior debt a conditional debt or flawed asset, does not, without more, destroy the character of the junior debt as a book debt, a charge on which will require registration.[95] One point which there is no space here to explore is whether a priority agreement can be set aside in the insolvency of the junior creditor as a transaction at an undervalue, or can be disclaimed as an onerous contract. What there is space to consider is the question who may exercise the voting right attached to a subordinated debt—the junior or the senior creditor? On this, one matter is clear: no single answer can be given in terms general enough to cover all the issues and all the circumstances in which this precise question arises. But generally, it will call for a construction of the particular subordinations agreement and the statutory or other provisions involved. It seems that where the subordination is by means of the conditional debt or trust of proceeds technique, only the junior creditor may exercise any voting right attached to the subordinated debt. The reason is that since the subordinated debt is not assigned to the senior creditor, it remains, both at law and in equity, an obligation owed to the junior creditor alone. It may be objected that this conclusion does not give effect, in the case of subordination by trust of the proceeds, to the fact that the senior creditor is the beneficial owner of the proceeds. This objection has a prima facie appeal, but it ignores the fact that the right to vote is incident, not to the proceeds which, in law and fact, have no existence prior to payment of the debt by the debtor, but to the debt itself. And even if the junior creditor is a trustee of the proceeds as and when they arise, it is clear and undisputed law that a beneficiary has no unfettered right to direct the trustee as to the manner of exercise of voting rights attaching to shares which comprise the trust assets.[96] Where, however, the subordination is

[94] Companies Act 1985, s.396(2)(*e*).
[95] *Cf.* Johnston, (1987) 15 A.B.L.R. 80 at 132.
[96] *Re Brockbank* [1948] Ch. 206; *Re Whichelow* [1953] 2 All E.R. 1558. *Cf. Re Butt* [1952] 1 All E.R. 167 at 172; *Hayim* v. *Citibank NA* [1987] 3 W.L.R. 83.

176

by assignment of the junior creditor's rights to receive payment of the subordinated debt to the senior creditor, it is the senior creditor who may exercise such voting rights. In practice this uncertainty can be avoided if the subordinations agreement provides that the junior creditor should do nothing to impair the agreement, and to spell out that it is the senior creditor who may vote on the junior debt.

Circular priority problems

"What should be done when an inadequate fund is to be distributed among competing claimants and under applicable rules of law A is entitled to priority over B, who is entitled to priority over C, who is entitled to priority over A? Or, in a variant, when B and C have claims entitled to equal priority, one of which is superior, the other inferior, to A's claim."[97] **6.23**

Solving these types of circular priority problems is anything but easy. As Gilmore put it, "a judge who finds himself face to face with a circular priority system typically reacts in a manner of a bull who has been goaded by the picadors: he paws the ground and roars with rage. The spectator can only sympathise with judge and bull."[98] For all the sympathy of the spectator, the problem still has to be solved. Circular priority problems typically arise from three sources: subordination and priority agreements; partial invalidity of unregistered charges and those registered out of time; and inconsistent priority rules. Four examples illustrate the difficulty.

Example 1:

Borrower creates a fixed charge over receivables in favour of A, B and C; all register within the time limit; all give requisite notice to debtors in order of creation of their charges. A enters into a priority agreement with C under which C's debt is to be paid before A's. According to normal priority rules A prevails over B who prevails over C. But by virtue of the priority agreement C prevails over A, who prevails over B, who prevails over C, who prevails over A. The circularity here is, however, more apparent than real: the ranking is clear: A-B-C. In order to give effect to the private agreement between A and C, the distributor of the fund will hand over A's claim to C to the extent of C's debt, any balance being handed over to A. B gets nothing when A's claim equals or exceeds the fund, and whether or not A gets anything for himself depends on the size of C's debt. An example, albeit an imperfect one, is the result of the litigation in *Re Woodroffes (Musical Instruments) Ltd.*[99] There, Mrs. W prevailed over preferential creditors who prevailed over the bank which prevailed over Mrs. W by virtue of the fact that she took expressly

---

[97] 2 Gilmore, *Security Interests in Personal Property* (Little, Brown & Co., 1965), para. 39.1.
[98] *Ibid.*
[99] [1986] Ch. 366.

subject to the bank's charge. Hence the bank came first to the extent of Mrs. W's claim, then the preferential creditors, followed by the bank in its own right. Mrs. W came afterwards and received nothing.

Example 2:

Borrower makes three assignments to A, B and C on Monday, Tuesday and Wednesday respectively, none of which requires registration. C gives first notice to the debtor although when he took his assignment he knew of A but not of B. B gives the second notice to the debtor not knowing of A and C. A gives the last notice. The result would be as follows: C prevails over B under the rule in *Dearle* v. *Hall*; B prevails over A under the same rule. But A prevails over C under the second limb of *Dearle* v. *Hall* by virtue of C having known of his assignment when he took his. The fund is of course insufficient to pay all of them. How is the fund to be distributed? It is tempting to subrogate A to C's claim, but when B's claim is large enough to exhaust the whole fund there can scarcely be any justification for bringing in A,[1] because if there was no C, A could not expect to get anything. Why should it make a difference? Moreover, even if subrogation is permissible, the solution ignores the fact that B is entitled to priority over A.[2] Similarly, a distribution B-C-A gives no effect to C's priority over B.

Example 3:

Creditor obtains a garnishee order absolute whilst an earlier charge over the receivables is out of time for registration. The order absolute creates a charge on the receivables; so garnishor prevails over chargee. The charge is subsequently registered, but before the garnishor collects the receivables, the judgment debtor/chargor descends into compulsory liquidation. The execution is incomplete and so invalid against the liquidator, though the registered charge is valid against him. Neither party has overall priority: the garnishor ranks before the chargee, who ranks before the liquidator, who ranks before the garnishor. If all circular priority problems were to be resolved by invoking subrogation, it would follow that the liquidator will step into the shoes of the garnishor and prevail over the chargee. Alternatively, if the subrogation is to be against the party at fault, both the chargee and garnishor are in positions of relative fault, and there is no *a priori* reason for preferring one to the other. Yet there is clear authority[3] that the chargee prevails over both the garnishor and the liquidator. The solution is that the uncompleted execution is invalid and so drops out of contention, leaving the chargee in overall priority.[4]

[1] *Benham* v. *Keane* (1861) 31 L.J.Ch. 129, discussed by Lee (1968) 32 Conv. 325.
[2] *Cf. Re Wyatt, White* v. *Ellis* [1891] 2 Ch. 188 at 208–209, affd. *sub nom. Ward* v. *Duncombe* [1893] A.C. 369.
[3] *Re Payne, ex p. Cross* (1879) 11 Ch.D. 539. See also, *ex p. Blaiberg, re Toomer* (1883) 23 Ch.D. 254.
[4] *Ibid.*

Example 4:

A company creates a valid specific charge over specific goods. A distraining landlord seizes the goods and sells them one month before the company is compulsorily wound up. The execution is good against the chargee who prevails over preferential creditors. By section 176[5] the proceeds of sale of the goods are subject to a statutory charge for the payment of preferential debts of the company, though the landlord ranks as a preferential creditor as to any surplus left after the other preferential creditors have been satisfied. The picture is like this: landlord is senior to chargee, who is senior to preferential creditors, who rank ahead of the landlord. Who is subrogated and to what? To distribute the proceeds among the preferential claimants, to the exclusion of the specific chargee, ignores the fact that the chargee is entitled to priority over them. It may be that, in such a case, excluding the chargee can be explained on the basis that the execution forever destroyed his charge in relation to those goods. Section 176 did not nullify the execution so as to revive the charge, but only directs that the landlord is entitled to the proceeds after preferential creditors. This solution is, however, contrived as it is difficult to see how the landlord's distraint can destroy the pre-existing charge which is valid in all respects. As between the specific chargee and the landlord, the question is one of priorities, not of destruction of the charge.

The impact of registration of charges on priorities

Registration of charges has important consequences for the rules of priority so far considered. So, also, non-registration. It is proposed to examine first the consequences of registration. If all relevant charges are registered within the 21 days required by law, registration goes, not to priority, but to the validity and effectiveness of the charges. Priority will then be determined under the general law. First, registration is notice of the existence of registered prescribed particulars to all other chargees.[6] For this purpose other chargees are charge holders whose securities require registration. They do not include, for example, a shipowner's lien on sub-freight[7] or a fixed charge on debts other than book debts. Such chargees and other persons are not to be taken to have notice of any matter by reason of its being disclosed on the register or by reason of having failed to search the register in the course of making such inquiries as ought reasonably to be made.[8] This will protect a factor buying clients' receivables. For this purpose the distinction between a sale and a charge is important. To this extent constructive notice arising from registration of corporate charges is abolished.[9] This, however, is without prejudice to

6.24

---

[5] Insolvency Act 1986 (applies only in compulsory winding-up).
[6] Companies Act 1985, s.416(1).
[7] Companies Act 1985, s.396(2)(g).
[8] *Ibid.*, s.416(2).
[9] *Cf.* Companies Act 1985, s.711A(2), inserted by s.142(1) of the Companies Act 1989.

any other enactment imposing such a notice.[10] Registration is not notice of assignment to the debtor for purposes of the rule in *Dearle* v. *Hall*.[11] However, where the debtor in fact inspects the register and discovers charges on his obligation, such notice would be sufficient to preserve the priority of a prior assignment, but would, on the authority of *Arden* v. *Arden*,[12] be insufficient to gain priority for a subsequent assignee, even if at that date the prior assignee has given no notice to the debtor. A second consequence of registration is that for chargees whose securities require registration, registration would be notice for the purposes of the second limb of the rule in *Dearle* v. *Hall*. This means that they cannot steal a march on a prior assignee by being the first to give notice to the debtor. The actual notice arising from registration is sufficient to disable recourse to gaining priority by notice to the debtor. Thirdly, although the position is unclear, it would seem that in cases where the security is taken to secure a term loan rather than a current account, registration will be sufficient notice of a second assignment for purposes of the rule in *Rolt* v. *Hopkinson*. More importantly, registration of a charge will prevent a subsequent chargee from being able successfully to advance the plea of bona fide purchaser for value without notice. Registration is only notice of registered prescribed particulars. Nothing is gained by registering optional extras,[13] although a person who inspects and finds such extras cannot take free of them. The issue of a certificate of registration is no longer conclusive evidence that all requirements of the Companies Act have been complied with.[14] The reasoning that, in order to discover the *extent* of the charge, one must look at the charge instrument is now obsolete.[15] Where, therefore, the registered particulars of a charge are not complete and accurate, the charge is void to the extent that rights are not disclosed by the registered particulars which would be disclosed if they were complete and accurate.[16] For this purpose "right" includes any provision or circumstance affecting the priority of the right. A person who has registered incomplete or inaccurate particulars may apply to court for a declaration of priority over certain rights acquired whilst the registered charge remained incomplete or inaccurate. To found jurisdiction, it must be proved to the satisfaction of the court that the omission or error was unlikely to have misled any unsecured creditor materially to his

---

[10] *Ibid.*, s.416(3).

[11] (1828) 3 Russ. 1.

[12] (1885) 29 Ch.D. 702.

[13] *Wilson* v. *Kelland* [1910] 2 Ch. 306; *Siebe Gorman & Co. Ltd.* v. *Barclays Bank Ltd.* [1979] 2 Lloyd's Rep. 142. It should be noted that the actual decision in both cases may not be good law for a much longer time if, as is contemplated by s.415(2)(*a*) of the Companies Act 1985, registrable prescribed particulars include whether the company has undertaken not to create other charges ranking in priority to or *pari passu* with the registered charge.

[14] New s.397(5) of the Companies Act 1985 provides that the certificate shall be conclusive evidence that the specified particulars or other information were delivered to the registrar *no later than* the date stated in the certificate. See also s.402 (effect of omissions and errors in registered particulars).

[15] *Cf. National Provincial & Union Bank of England* v. *Charnley* [1924] 1 K.B. 431; *Re Eric Holmes (Property) Ltd.* [1965] Ch. 1052; *Re Mechanisations Eaglescliffe Ltd.* [1966] Ch. 20; *Re C.L. Nye Ltd.* [1971] Ch. 442; *R.* v. *Registrar of Companies* [1986] Q.B. 1114.

[16] Companies Act 1985, s.402(1).

prejudice, or that no person became an unsecured creditor at a time when the registered particulars remained incomplete or inaccurate.[17] As a result, no order will normally be obtained against a secured creditor, but exceptionally, the court may order that the incompletely registered charge is effective as against a person acquiring an interest in or right over the property subject to the charge if it is satisfied that he did not rely, in connection with the acquisition, on registered particulars which were incomplete or inaccurate.[18]

It will be rare for a memorandum of satisfaction to be filed where the debt is still owed. But where this is done under mistake, the drive to make the register of charges more reliable requires that the chargee bear the cost of the error. In such cases, the charge is void as against an administrator or liquidator of the company and any person who for value acquires an interest over the property subject to the charge, where the relevant event occurs after the filing of the memorandum of satisfaction.[19] What is not so clear is what happens where a memorandum of satisfaction is fraudulently filed by a third party. To apply the above rule in favour of the integrity of the register is to penalise the chargee for a fraud which he has not induced. In such situations, it may be that the above consequence will not follow the filing, on the theory that a fraudulent memorandum of satisfaction is not one which is *duly* signed within the meaning of the statute.

The consequences of non-registration of a charge are more profound, and it is in relation to these that it may fairly be said that registration is a priority point, although the rule would be conceptually more accurate if framed in terms of non-registration. The general rule is that where a charge is created and no prescribed particulars in the prescribed form are delivered for registration within 21 days of creation, the charge is void against an administrator or liquidator of the company creating the charge, and any person who for value acquires an interest over the property, in both cases, if the relevant event occurs after the creation of the charge, whether before or after the end of the 21 day period.[20] This is important because it extends the old law in two respects. First, it confirms the practice adopted after the decision of Templeman J. in *Watson* v. *Duff, Morgan and Vermont (Holdings) Ltd.*[21] In that case it was held that where a second charge is created and registered within the 21 day period required for the registration of an earlier charge, the earlier charge does not lose its priority over the second charge. Not only did this make the register of charges significantly less reliable, but also it made questions of priority depend on the purely fortuitous circumstance of whether the second charge is created within or outside the 21 day period. The result of the new provision is that where a second charge is created within the 21 day period required to register a first charge, the first charge retains

---

[17] Companies Act 1985, s.402(4).
[18] Companies Act 1985, s.402(5).
[19] Companies Act 1985, s.403(5).
[20] Companies Act 1985, s.399(1). Relevant event is defined in s.399(2).
[21] [1974] 1 W.L.R. 450, criticised by R. R. Pennington in *Company Law in Change*, B. G. Pettet (ed.), (1987), pp. 115–116.

provisional priority which becomes permanent if registered within 21 days. But if it is not, then it loses its provisonal priority, and to that extent is but a second charge.[22] Also where neither charge is registered within 21 days of creation, priority goes to the first to register. To this extent registration is a priority point. Where neither is registered, their relative priorities will be determined by the order of creation, on the general first in time principle. An unregistered charge does not, however, lose priority as against a person acquiring an interest in or right over the property subject to the charge, if the acquisition was expressly subject to the charge.[23] One problem, however, remains, namely, what happens where the second chargee knew of the existence of the unregistered first charge at the time he took his own security but did not contract to take subject to it. The solution is straightforward where registration is a priority point. Here, it is only partially so. It seems that in such cases the second chargee would normally prevail because there is no additional requirement of good faith. To introduce such a requirement would constitute an unjustified gloss on the statute, quite apart from the fact that it would necessitate an inquiry into the second chargee's motive. In taking advantage of the registration provisions, the second chargee is neither acting in bad faith nor fraudulently since all he would be doing would be taking advantage of legal rights, the existence of which may be taken to be known to both parties.[24]

A second innovation in the new section 399(1) of the Companies Act 1985 is that it extends the benefit of the partial invalidity to all persons acquiring an interest in the property charged. This is a welcome extension which, no doubt, will be relished by purchasers, especially factors buying receivables. The old law was interpreted as invalidating unregistered charges only against creditors and liquidators.[25] The new provision does not in terms limit protection to purchasers alone. But exactly who else is covered in the expression "person who for value acquires an interest in or right over" property charged is unclear. Does this cover an execution creditor? That execution creditors are not purchasers is clear enough. That they cannot advance the plea of bona fide purchase for value even clearer. But do they acquire a right over the subject-matter of their execution for value? One view is that they are in fact protected by the new provision. To the extent that their debt is discharged by realisation of the goods or collection of the receivables attached, they cannot be regarded as voluntary transferees. At what point, then, do they acquire their interest? If their claim to having given value rests on discharge of the judgment debt, it would seem that they are not transferees for value until the debt is discharged. An attachment does not have this effect. If the out-of-date charge is registered before the execution is complete by receipt of the money, although the execution creditor would have

[22] Companies Act 1985, s.404(1).
[23] Companies Act 1985, s.405(1).
[24] Re Monolithic Building Co. [1915] 1 Ch. 643; Midland Bank Trust Co. Ltd. v. Green [1981] A.C. 513.
[25] Re Ehrmann Brothers Ltd. [1906] 2 Ch. 697; Re Ashpurton Estates Ltd. [1983] Ch. 110 at 123.

acquired a right over the property, he would not at that stage have given value; the charge, earlier in date, might then displace it and thus prevent the execution from being a relevant event for purposes of section 399(1). A way out of this difficulty is to say that by executing judgment the executioner implicitly promises to release his debt and that this promise is sufficient to support the interest acquired before the charge was registered. If this analysis be correct, then the execution, though uncompleted before the registration of the charge, would still rank as a relevant event. There is no argument of legal policy against such a result, except, perhaps, the need for certainty which argues for fixing the relevant date at the time of completion of execution. The analysis based on implied promise is artificial. The better view is that an execution is not a relevant event unless it is completed whilst the charge remains unregistered. For the sake of completeness it may be added that a person who acquires an interest in or over the property charged during a relevant time may nonetheless be outside the protection of section 399(1), for example, if he took his interest as security for payment of a pre-existing debt. In such a case, a recital that the chargee forbears to enforce payment of the debt, would, it is thought, be sufficient value.

The invalidity of an unregistered charge does not, however, avoid the obligation secured. On the contrary, it is enacted that where a charge becomes void, the debt secured becomes repayable on demand.[26] Since the underlying obligation is valid and the charge remains valid between the chargee and the company, it was possible under the old law to seize the security and use it to liquidate the debt secured and this despite the non-registration. *Mercantile Bank of India Ltd.* v. *Central Bank of India*[27] exposed the gap in the provision for partial invalidity. There, a charge over goods was unregistered. The chargee perfected his security by seizing the goods charged before the company went into liquidation. Porter J. held that the seizure crystallized the charge and was good against the liquidator. In *Re Row Dal Construction Pty Ltd.*,[28] an Australian decision, a bank which had an unregistered charge over receivables collected them and repaid itself before the company went into liquidation. The liquidator could not recover the payment because, first, invalidation of unregistered charges was prospective rather than retrospective, and secondly, only security on the company's property was avoided. If, as was the case, the debt is repaid by the chargee helping himself to charged receivables, the security is released, leaving nothing for the liquidator to avoid. The result of both cases made registration something of an optional pastime.

Section 406 of the Companies Act 1985 contains a new provision aimed at discouraging creditors like the bank in *Re Row Dal Construction Pty Ltd.*,[29] and applies where the chargee has disposed of the property subject to the unregistered (and hence) invalid charge. As a matter of construction, the section applies only to "dispositions." Therefore, on a

---

[26] Companies Act 1985, s.407(1).
[27] [1937] 1 All E.R. 231.
[28] [1966] V.R. 249.
[29] [1966] V.R. 249.

literal interpretation, it would not cover the collection of receivables subject to the invalid charge. On the other hand, it cannot be doubted that, as a matter of policy, such a collection is within the spirit of the provision, and it is hoped that the courts will not find it unduly difficult to conclude that collection of receivables is within the provision.[30] Where the section applies, the money received by the chargee shall be held on trust by him and applied, first, in discharge of any sum *effectively* secured by prior incumbrances as well as costs of the disposition (including any previous abortive attempt at disposition); secondly, in discharge of any sum *effectively* secured by the charge and incumbrances ranking *pari passu* with the charge; thirdly, in discharge of any sum effectively secured by incumbrances ranking after the charge. The residue shall be paid to the company or to a person authorised to give a receipt for the proceeds of the disposition of the property.[31] It is not clear why the residue should not be kept by the holder of the invalid charge, if for nothing else, at least to compensate him for the trouble he took in effecting a disposition. It should be noted that "disposition" includes a disposition by a receiver appointed by him.[32] Also, no sum is effectively secured by a charge to the extent that it is void against an administrator or liquidator of the company.[33] It follows that where an unregistered charge is void because of the acquisition of an interest by a third party in the charged property, for purposes of section 406, the invalid charge effectively secures the sum for which it was originally given as security. It is to be noted that nothing in section 406 affects cases like *Mace Builders (Glasgow) Ltd.* v. *Lunn*[34] where it was held that the invalidity of a floating charge under what is now section 245 of the Insolvency Act 1986 did not prevent the chargee from appointing himself a receiver to enforce his security, and repaying his debt from the proceeds. The provision is prospective rather than retrospective, so that once the sum secured by the invalid charge has been repaid there is nothing left for the liquidator to avoid. Nor could he recover the repayment: the charge, not the obligation secured, is avoided. The case remains authoritative because section 406 of the Companies Act 1985 is limited in its operation to charges which have become void to any extent by virtue of the provisions of that Part. That Part deals with consequences of non-registration, whereas section 245 assumes that the invalid charge is not open to attack on the ground of non-registration, and is not contained in the Companies Act, let alone *that* Part. In order to avoid prejudice to purchasers[35] of the property subject to the invalid charge, it is enacted that the sale is not impeachable, nor is the purchaser concerned to see or inquire whether the charge has become void.[36] Where

---

[30] *Cf. Re Brightlife Ltd.* [1987] Ch. 200 at 209 ("a credit balance at the bank cannot sensibly be 'got in' or 'realised.' ").

[31] Companies Act 1985, s.406(2).

[32] Companies Act 1985, s.406(4)(*a*).

[33] *Ibid.*, s.406(3)(*b*).

[34] [1987] Ch. 191, C.A., affirming [1986] Ch. 459. See also, *Re Parkes Garage (Swadlincote) Ltd.* [1929] 1 Ch. 139.

[35] Companies Act 1985, s.406(4)(*c*) defines a purchaser as a person who in good faith and for valuable consideration acquires an interest in property.

[36] *Ibid.*, s.406(1).

the purchaser has actual knowledge of the voidness of the charge over the property, he cannot plead the provision.[37]

No leave of court is now required to register a charge out of time. The new provision simplifies the procedure for registration of a charge out of time but is materially more stringent than considerations applied by the courts in applications for registration of a charge out of time. Where a charge is registered out of time and the company is at that date unable to pay its debts, or subsequently becomes unable to do so in consequence of the transaction under which the charge is created, and insolvency proceedings begin before the end of the relevant period beginning with the date of delivery of the particulars, the charge is void as against the administrator or liquidator.[38] For this purpose, the relevant period is, in the case of a floating charge, two years if the chargee is a connected person, and one year in any other case, and for any other security, six months.[39] The provision adopts the statutory definition of insolvency in section 123 of the Insolvency Act 1986. Establishing that at the date of late registration the chargor was unable to pay its debts is not difficult. The same cannot, however, be said of the chargor becoming unable to do so "in consequence" of the late registration. The latter introduces difficult questions of causation of insolvency. Insolvency may result from many factors: the market for the chargor's goods may be misjudged or decline; it may be caught in a major rescission; its business may depend heavily on that of a third party, in which case the chargor is unlikely to survive the collapse of that party; it may be mismanaged. Ordinarily it will be difficult to see how late registration of a charge *per se* can make the chargor unable to pay its debts. The new provision is an uneasy transplantation of the provisions on avoidance of vulnerable transactions at the onset of corporate insolvency into the somewhat different topography of out of time registration of charges. Be that as it may, it remains true that chargees will fare worse under the new regime. This may be contrasted with what is commonly called the *Re Charles*[40] order under the old regime in applications for extension of time for registration where there has been a notice of meeting to propose a resolution for winding-up, or when a petition for compulsory winding-up is pending. In such cases, time will be extended on terms that the chargee be bound by any subsequent decision of the court setting aside the registration on the application of the liquidator. In *Re Charles* itself, the order was allowed to stand on a rehearing at the instance of the liquidator. So, also, in *Re Braemar Investments Ltd.*[41] Under the new law even such a rare victory for the chargee is no longer possible.

---

[37] *Ibid.*, s.406(6).
[38] Companies Act 1985, s.400(2).
[39] *Ibid.*, s.400(3)(*b*).
[40] *Re L.H. Charles & Co. Ltd.* [1935] W.N. 15; *Re Braemar Investments Ltd.* [1989] Ch. 54.
[41] *Supra.* See also *Re R.M. Arnold & Co. Ltd.* [1985] B.C.L.C. 535 where a chargee agreed that a subsequent unregistered charge, created with his agreement, should be registered at a time the chargor was on its last leg so as to give it priority. The contest was essentially between two secured creditors. No unsecured creditors were prejudiced. *Cf. Re John Bateson & Co. Ltd.* [1985] B.C.L.C. 259. Under the new law this is not possible.

CHAPTER SEVEN

CHALLENGE TO ENFORCEMENT OF SECURITY

A security interest over receivables is normally enforced by getting in the amount owing from the account debtors. For an institutional financier, it will be easier to appoint a receiver to gather in the receivables particularly where the security covers other assets of the debtor. The ease with which a security can be liquidated and turned into cash affects the quality of that security. Whatever form the enforcement takes, it may be challenged on several grounds. Broadly, these grounds divide into two groups—the first group comprises grounds of challenge to security independent of the insolvency of the corporate borrower; the second consists of grounds of challenge which are insolvency-specific. Both groups are examined in this chapter. The first group will be called general challenge, whilst the second is referred to as avoiding powers.

General challenge

7.1   Security over receivables can be challenged, as a matter of general law, on several grounds. First, on the ground that its creation is vitiated by corporate incapacity (including lack of authority by the directors), or mistake, misrepresentation, illegality or duress, or that its creation was induced by fraud. If the security is upset on any of these grounds, any act done under it exposes the secured creditor and any receiver appointed by him to liability in tort, unless the company adopts the tortious acts.[1] Even if the company has capacity, the power to create security may have been exercised for a purpose not beneficial to the company to the knowledge of the secured creditor.[2] Although companies now have very wide, if not unlimited, capacity,[3] the legislation will not cloak fraud. Secondly, the

---

[1] *Re Goldburg (No. 2), ex p. Page* [1912] 1 K.B. 606; *R. Jaffe Ltd. (in liq.)* v. *Jaffe (No. 2)* [1932] N.Z.L.R. 195; *Re Simms, ex p. Trustee* [1934] Ch. 1, citing with approval, *Ex p. Vaughan, re Riddenough* (1884) 14 Q.B.D. 25. By s.34 of the Insolvency Act 1986, the court may order the chargee who appointed the receiver to indemnify him against any liability which arises solely by reason of the invalidity of the appointment. But if the receiver is an administrative receiver, his acts are valid notwithstanding any defect in his appointment: *ibid.*, s.232. For the meaning of "defect" in appointment, see *Morris* v. *Kanssen* [1946] A.C. 459.
[2] *Rolled Steel Products (Holdings) Ltd.* v. *British Steel Corp.* [1986] Ch. 246.
[3] See, *e.g.* s.108 of the Companies Act 1989, inserting a new s.35 and s.35A into the Companies Act 1985.

enforcement of a security may be challenged on the ground that the right to enforce has not arisen, or that although it has arisen, a technical requirement has not been fulfilled, *e.g.* mode of appointment. Thirdly, though the right to enforce has arisen, a particular exercise of the powers given by the charge instrument may be challenged. This may be on the ground that the chargee or his receiver cannot do what he has done, or that he ought to do what he has neglected to do. Challenge on the grounds that the security is vitiated by factors affecting its formation will not be elaborated. An assignment of receivables as security is liable to be set aside or denied legal effect if it was induced by fraud, mistake or misrepresentation. Also an assignment which for any reason is illegal, or unauthorised, may be denied effect. These are matters of general law, a detailed discussion of which is outside the scope of this book.

Conditions precedent to enforcement

The enforcement of a security over receivables may be challenged on **7.2** the ground that the conditions for enforcement have not arisen or, though they have arisen, the right to enforce has not become exercisable. This challenge has been mounted frequently in the context of on-demand loans. In this context, two questions have arisen: what is the meaning of "demand" in a loan repayable on demand? What duty, if any, is owed by the lender? As regards the first, where a charge secures a loan repayable on demand, the debtor is entitled once demand is made, to a reasonable opportunity to implement the mechanics of payment, but not to raise the money if it is not available.[4] The test is not "reasonable time," but "mechanics of payment." Given the modern facilities for transferring funds, for example, electronic fund transfer, the time allowed under the mechanics of payment test could be very short.

In *Bank of Baroda* v. *Panessar*,[5] a time gap of one hour was held sufficient to implement the mechanics of payment. In Australia[6] and Canada,[7] the courts apply the reasonable time test. Since the solvency of the borrower is an important factor in calculating what is reasonable time,[8] in many cases the mechanics of payment test produces the same result as the reasonable time test, since the borrower will in many cases be insolvent.[9] However, in principle, it is not easy to see why the court should read down an on-demand money obligation as merely requiring

---

[4] *R.A. Cripps (Pharmaceuticals) Ltd.* v. *Wickenden* [1973] 1 W.L.R. 994; *Bank of Baroda* v. *Panessar* [1987] Ch. 335.

[5] [1987] Ch. 335. See also, *Cripps* v. *Wickenden, supra* (two hours held sufficient).

[6] See *Bunbury Foods Pty. Ltd.* v. *National Bank of Australia Ltd.* (1984) 153 C.L.R. 491.

[7] See *Ronald Elwyn Lister Ltd.* v. *Dunlop Canada Ltd.* (1982) 135 D.L.R. (3d) 1; *Minster Broadloom Corp. (1968) Ltd.* v. *Bank of Montreal* (1984) 4 D.L.R. (4th) 74 (creditors may not lay down arbitrary requirements which must be satisfied before the question of reasonableness of time allowed for meeting an on-demand money obligation can be objectively considered).

[8] *Minster Broadloom Corp. (1968) Ltd.* v. *Bank of Montreal* (1984) 4 D.L.R. (4th) 74 at 80.

[9] In *ANZ Banking Group (NZ) Ltd.* v. *Gibson* [1981] 2 N.Z.L.R. 513, although the "reasonable time" test was applied, a time gap of approximately two hours was held sufficient.

reasonable time. Fidelity to the parties' intention requires that an on-demand debenture should be given effect as such, and this at most requires giving the borrower time to put the mechanics of payment in motion. If he needs reasonable time to raise the money, he should bargain for this in the first place. Also, the reasonable time test introduces an unacceptable measure of uncertainty. Invariably, some of the factors going to "reasonable" will be unknown to the creditor. Finally, the speed with which security is enforced could be critical in many circumstances. Adopting the mechanics of payment test avoids the obvious prejudice to the financier inherent in the reasonable time test. This is particularly true because in most cases the debtor is insolvent and not in a position to comply regardless of the applicable test.

The right to enforce an on-demand money obligation is a matter of contract. Therefore, where finance is provided on normal banking terms and conditions, the court will not imply into the security document, a right to enforce the security on demand, simply because the security is in jeopardy.[10] Such a term is not necessary to give the security business efficacy, and less so when the bank could apply to the court for the appointment of a receiver. What is unclear is the effect of a misstatement of the amount owing in the notice of demand. Must a demand for payment specify the precise amount owing or is it sufficient if it indicates that the demand is for all sums owing? It would seem that a notice of demand which does not specify the amount owing is valid,[11] though this may be taken into account in deciding whether the time allowed the borrower is sufficient to implement the mechanics of payment. Upholding the validity of the demand in such cases does not, it is thought, prejudice the borrower who is in as good a position as the lender to know the amount owing. Besides, if a precise amount is insisted upon, enforcement may be delayed for a long time in the not uncommon situation where there are current transactions. On the other hand, a solvent debtor may be prejudiced if a precise amount is not specified. It may be that in such cases the lender ought to name a specific figure. If the enforcement is against a guarantor, there is a stronger case for insisting that the notice should specify the amount owing because he is not in a position to know the true state of account between the lender and the borrower.[12]

The cases establish that if the right of enforcement has arisen, the lender is under no duty of care to consider all the relevant circumstances

[10] *Cryne* v. *Barclays Bank plc* [1987] B.C.L.C. 548 at 552.
[11] *Bunbury Foods Pty. Ltd.* v. *National Bank of Australia Ltd.* (1984) 153 C.L.R. 491; *Bank of Baroda* v. *Panessar* [1987] Ch. 335.
[12] In *Bunbury Foods Pty. Ltd.* v. *National Bank of Australia Ltd.*, *supra* at 504, the High Court of Australia left this question open. In *NRG Vision Ltd.* v. *Churchfield Leasing Ltd.* [1988] B.C.L.C. 625, it was argued that a demand for an excessive amount is good as a matter of law, at any rate so long as it makes clear in the particular circumstances what it is that is being sought from the person who receives the demand. Knox J. declined to decide this difficult question which became unnecessary since there was in fact a valid demand for a smaller amount and that was enough to support the appointment of receivers. See also *Byblos Bank SAL* v. *Al-Khudhairy* [1987] B.C.L.C. 232, where it was held that a chargee could rely on facts which existed at the date of an invalid appointment of a receiver (because the demand was premature) but which were unknown to him at that date, to validate retrospectively the appointment.

before enforcing his security. Timing of the exercise of the right is not subject to any restrictions if the right to enforce has arisen.[13] Since no such qualification can be implied into the security as a matter of contract, a wider duty cannot exist in tort. Also, the secured creditor is not bound to refrain from enforcing his security and, for this purpose, appointing a receiver because to do so would diminish the amount available for the settlement of unsecured claims.[14]

Manner of enforcement

Generally, most security interests in favour of institutional lenders are **7.3** enforced by the appointment of a receiver who, by contract, is the agent of the company. Today if such a receiver is an administrative receiver,[15] the agency is implied by statute.[16] It has been said that this agency is a real one,[17] and extends, for example, to the right of the company to require any information in the possession of the receiver if a need to know is shown.[18] But this does not mean that the company, as principal, can assert a proprietary right to all documents brought into existence in the course of the receivership.[19] The agency explains the authorities which deny that receivers are in rateable occupation.[20] The agency raises difficulties and is in many respects nominal only. It is elementary that, though the receiver is the agent of the company, he is concerned primarily for the benefit of the lender to realise the security. That is the whole purpose of his appointment, and his powers are really ancillary to the main purpose which is the realisation of the property subject to the receivership.[21] Thus, the receiver has power to affect the company's

---

[13] *ANZ Banking Group (NZ) Ltd.* v. *Gibson* [1981] 2 N.Z.L.R. 513 (no duty of care in calling up loan and appointing receivers, beyond the terms of the contract); *Shamji* v. *Johnson Matthey Bankers Ltd.* [1986] F.T.L.R. 329 (no duty of care to consider all relevant circumstances before appointing a receiver, for instance, so as to enable the borrower to refinance its business from a new source). See also, *Nash* v. *Eads* (1880) 25 Sol.Jo. 95, and *Belton* v. *Bass* [1922] 2 Ch. 449, which show that a mortgagee can sell even if his aim is to spite the mortgagor. This is still the law, except that he must obtain the true market value of the property at the time of sale.
[14] *Re Potters Oils Ltd.* [1986] 1 W.L.R. 201.
[15] Administrative receiver is defined in s.29(2) of the Insolvency Act 1986, as a receiver and manager of the whole or substantially the whole of the company's property or who would have been such a receiver and manager but for the appointment of someone else as a receiver over part of the company's property. For a discussion of who is an administrative receiver, see para. 5.14, *supra*.
[16] Insolvency Act 1986, s.44(1)(*a*).
[17] *Ratford and Hayward* v. *Northavon D.C.* [1987] Q.B. 357 at 372. In *Rhodes* v. *Allied Dunbar Pension Services Ltd.* [1989] 1 All E.R. 1161, the reality of the receiver's agency led the Court of Appeal to the conclusion that the company remained beneficially entitled to rents charged to the receiver's appointor. This, however, runs the fiction of agency into the ground.
[18] *Gomba Holdings UK Ltd.* v. *Homan* [1986] 1 W.L.R. 1301.
[19] *Gomba Holdings UK Ltd.* v. *Minories Finance Ltd.* [1988] 1 W.L.R. 1231.
[20] *Re Marriage, Neave & Co.* [1896] 2 Ch. 663 (court-appointed receivers); *Ratford and Hayward* v. *Northavon D.C.* [1987] Q.B. 357 (receivers appointed out of court and deemed to be agents of mortgagor).
[21] *Re B. Johnson & Co. (Builders) Ltd.* [1955] Ch. 634 at 644.

position by acts which, though done for the benefit of the lender, are treated as if they were acts of the company. His agency is independent of the wishes of the company; the company pays his fees but lacks power to dismiss him.[22] Nor can the company instruct him on how he should act in the conduct of the receivership. All this is far removed from an ordinary agency.

The agency of the receiver continues until the company goes into liquidation and becomes incapable of having an agent.[23] The power of the receiver to continue realisation of the assets is, however, not affected. Accordingly, he can initiate,[24] or continue[25] an action, and execute documents in the company's name. Where by the deed of charge, a power of attorney is given to the receiver, liquidation does not, without more, terminate that power, though the company can no longer act as principal.[26] If the liquidator is in possession of assets subject to the receivership, a distinction must be drawn between a liquidator who is an officer of the court, and one who is not. In the former case, the receiver has a better right to possession but he cannot exercise the right as it will amount to a contempt of the court. In such a case he requires leave which will usually be given *ex debito justitiae*.[27] But where a liquidator in a voluntary liquidation is in possession, it seems that no leave is required.

It is not clear whether a receiver can continue to trade after the company has gone into liquidation. There are early dicta against post-liquidation trading[28]; on the other hand it has been held that where the right to trade is part of the security over which the receiver was appointed, this power is not affected by windingup.[29] The position is that liquidation terminates the agency of the receiver. This means no more than that the receiver can no longer pledge the credit of the company. He may also be liable personally for contracts entered into by him.[30] He does not, however, automatically become the agent of the lender who appointed him.[31] He will become his agent only when the lender directs or interferes with the conduct of the receivership.[32] Precisely what constitutes direction and interference for this purpose is unclear. First, inaction or passive conduct showing acquiescence is not sufficient inter-

---

[22] *Cf. Kerr on Receivers and Administrators* (17th ed., 1989), p. 375, n. 71.

[23] *Gosling* v. *Gaskell* [1897] A.C. 575; *Thomas* v. *Todd* [1926] 2 K.B. 511; *Gough's Garages Ltd.* v. *Pugsley* [1930] 1 K.B. 615; *cf. Re Northern Garage Ltd.* [1946] Ch. 188. The statutory deemed agency of the administrative receiver is terminated if the company goes into liquidation: Insolvency Act 1986, s.44(1)(*a*).

[24] *Re Northern Garage Ltd.* [1946] Ch. 188.

[25] *Gough's Garages Ltd.* v. *Pugsley* [1930] 1 K.B. 615.

[26] *Sowman* v. *David Samuel Trust Ltd.* [1978] 1 W.L.R. 22. See also, Powers of Attorney Act 1971, s.4.

[27] *Re Henry Pound, Son & Hutchins* (1889) 42 Ch.D. 402; *Re Potters Oils Ltd.* [1986] 1 W.L.R. 201; *cf. Re Landmark Corp. Ltd.* (1968) 88 W.N. (Pt. 1) (NSW) 195 at 196.

[28] *Re Henry Pound, Son & Hutchins, supra* at 421.

[29] *Mercantile Credits Ltd.* v. *Atkins (No. 1)* (1985) 9 A.C.L.R. 757 at 763.

[30] The point was left open in *Gosling* v. *Gaskell* [1897] A.C. 575 at 579. See, however, Insolvency Act 1986, ss.37(1)(*a*) and 44(1)(*b*).

[31] *Gosling* v. *Gaskell, supra; Re Wood's Application* [1941] Ch. 112 at 116.

[32] *Standard Chartered Bank Ltd.* v. *Walker* [1982] 1 W.L.R. 1410 at 1416; *American Express International Banking Corp.* v. *Hurley* [1985] 3 All E.R. 564.

ference.[33] If anything, it is evidence of non-interference. Second, ordinary liaison with the lender does not seem sufficient, otherwise the enforcement of the security and the discharge of the receiver's duties may become well nigh impossible. It is not, however, necessary that the receiver should abandon the initiative to the lender before the latter becomes liable as principal.[34] Thus, it was held that where there was constant communication between the lender and the receiver, such that the receiver sought the lender's approval to such actions as he proposed to take, the lender was liable as principal.[35] The case, though, cannot be generalised and whilst it is undoubtedly correct on its own facts, it does not indicate the level of interference which will make a lender liable for the acts of his receiver.

Even where liquidation has not supervened, it is possible for the receiver to become the lender's agent if the latter interferes substantially with the conduct of the receivership. In such a case, although the receiver remains the general agent of the mortgagor company, he will be treated as the agent of the lender for certain purposes. It is important that the threshold of unacceptable interference is set fairly high to permit efficient flow of information between the receiver and his appointor. For the sake of completeness, it is worth stressing that the appointment of a provisional liquidator does not terminate the receiver's agency.[36] Also, liquidation does not affect the exercise of the power of realisation—the power is not open to challenge as a void disposition.[37] It remains to consider, first, whether the receiver is under any duty to continue the mortgagor's business; second, the extent of his power to disclaim existing contracts; and third, the duty of care owed to the mortgagor and any guarantor of the secured debt.

The question whether a receiver appointed out of court is under a duty to continue the mortgagor's business is not free from difficulty. Some of the difficulty arise from his anomalous agency. With regard to a court appointed receiver, there is no doubt that his duty to hold the scales evenly between all those having claims on the insolvent company may require him to continue trading, provided there are sufficient funds.[38] But generally, he will not be required to perform onerous contracts involving depletion of money available for distribution among unsecured creditors.[39] The position of a receiver appointed out of court cannot be so clearly stated. In *Re B. Johnson & Co. (Builders) Ltd.*,[40] the Court of

[33] *Gosling* v. *Gaskell* [1897] A.C. 575; *National Bank of Greece S.A.* v. *Pinios Shipping Co. (No. 1), "The Maira"* [1989] 3 W.L.R. 185 esp. at 194–196, revsd. [1990] 1 W.L.R. 78, H.L. (not on this point).
[34] *American Express International Bank Corp.* v. *Hurley* [1985] 3 All E.R. 564, discussed by Prentice [1985] All E.R. Rev. 51.
[35] *Ibid.*
[36] *Re KVE Homes Pty. Ltd.* [1979] 1 N.S.W.L.R. 181, qualified in *Mercantile Credits Ltd.* v. *Atkins (No. 1)* (1985) 9 A.C.L.R. 757 at 764–765 (not on this point).
[37] *Sowman* v. *David Samuel Trust Ltd.* [1978] 1 W.L.R. 22; *Re Margart Pty. Ltd., Hamilton* v. *Westpac Banking Corp.* (1984) 9 A.C.L.R. 269.
[38] *Re Newdigate Colliery Ltd.* [1912] 1 Ch. 468.
[39] *Re Thames Ironworks, Shipbuilding & Engineering Co. Ltd.* [1912] W.N. 66; *Re B. Johnson & Co. (Builders) Ltd.* [1955] Ch. 634 at 662.
[40] [1955] Ch. 634.

Appeal denied that there was any duty to trade. This was the decision of a strong Court of Appeal, but it cannot be pressed too strongly because the court also denied that a mortgagee or his receiver owed any duty of care to the mortgagor company. Both rulings were dependent or at least mutually supportive.[41] The decisive rejection of the latter ruling by cases affirming the duty principle (the Cuckmere principle), undermines the authority of that case. More recently, Graham J. held[42] that where the refusal to continue trading will not adversely affect the realisation of the assets or affect the trading prospects of the company, if it is possible to trade in the future, the receiver can refuse to perform current contracts. It is doubtful whether some of the restrictions and qualifications which appealed to Graham J. can be accepted as true fetters on the power of a receiver appointed out of court to stop trading. The qualifications more accurately describe the position of a court-appointed receiver. It is thought that the better solution is to consider the question whether the receiver must continue trading as a sub-category of his duties to the mortgagor and mortgagee.[43] On this anlalysis, the receiver will be bound to continue the mortgagor's business where this is beneficial to the realisation of the mortgaged assets, and where not to do so would be a breach of his duty of care to the mortgagor. Of course, if such a duty to continue the business of the mortgagor was recognised as part of the duties of receivers, this may, on occasion, prolong the realisation of the mortgaged assets and arguably diminish the quality of the lender's security.

The extent of a receiver's power to disclaim current contracts is one of the most disputed issues in relation to his powers. A receiver appointed out of court has no statutory power to disclaim onerous contracts.[44] Even where such a receiver is an administrative receiver, the statutory power to do all things necessary to discharge his duties, does not, it is thought, licence him to repudiate all existing contracts of the company.[45] Of course, where the contract is not binding on the company, for example, because it is conditional, etc., there can be little doubt that the receiver can disclaim it. The difficulty is with cases where the contract is binding on the company. Sometimes, the issue is framed as involving the question whether the receiver is in a better position than the company.[46] However framed, the extent of the receiver's power to disclaim current contracts of the company is an important aspect of the mortgagee's security and, in principle, the same rule ought to govern the question of the extent of the

---

[41] Lightman and Moss, *Law of Receivers of Companies* (London, Sweet & Maxwell, 1986), p. 95, para. 8–14.
[42] *Airlines Airspares Ltd.* v. *Handley Page Ltd.* [1970] Ch. 193.
[43] *Cf.* Lightman and Moss, *op. cit.*, p. 96, para. 8–14.
[44] Receivership does not terminate the corporate mortgagor's current contracts: *Parsons* v. *Sovereign Bank of Canada* [1913] A.C. 160; *George Barker (Transport) Ltd.* v. *Eynon* [1974] 1 W.L.R. 462; *Re Diesels and Components Pty. Ltd.* (1985) 9 A.C.L.R. 825. Notwithstanding the extensive powers of an administrative receiver (Insolvency Act 1986, Sched. 1), there is no statutory power of disclaimer. The position is otherwise as regards a liquidator: see s.178 of the Insolvency Act 1986.
[45] *Cf.* Insolvency Act 1986, s.42 and Sched. 1.
[46] *Airlines Airspares Ltd.* v. *Handley Page Ltd.* [1970] Ch. 193 at 198.

mortgagee's power to repudiate current contracts. Since neither the mortgagee nor the receiver is a party to the contract sought to be disclaimed, they cannot be made liable for breach.[47] But if they are liable for inducing a breach of contract, this would be a fundamental derogation from the rights of the secured lender. The proper approach ought to be to treat the question as essentially one of priorities, and to recognise that the receiver or his appointor can disclaim current contracts of the company where the charge gives the lender a superior right to the assets of the borrower, including the current contracts provided that in doing so he does not cause the company avoidable loss. The existence of such superior rights has always been considered as an answer to the tort of inducing a breach of contract.[48] On this approach, we can state the rule thus: a receiver can disclaim current contracts of the company where, as a matter of priority, the charge under which he was appointed ranks ahead of the contract rights of the other party to the contract, and where such disclaimer does not constitute a breach of his duty to the company and any guarantor of the sum secured by the charge. This formualtion recognises only one limit to the receiver's right of disclaimer, namely, the question of duty of care, and has the merit of focusing on the real issue. Most of the cases are consistent with this formulation. Where the receiver or his appointor has been able to disclaim onerous contracts without becoming liable for inducing a breach of contract, it is because the chargee had superior rights.[49] To do otherwise would turn priorities on their head and advance an unsecured claim ahead of the real rights of the secured lender. In such cases, the contract gave the other party personal rights only which ranked behind the secured lender. On the other hand, where the contract produces superior possessor or equitable proprietary rights in the other party to the contract, there can be no disclaimer.[50] The reason is partly that the receiver cannot disclaim the contract without disclaiming the equitable interest. The disclaimer of the contract will, of

---

[47] *Re Diesels & Components Pty. Ltd.* (1985) 9 A.C.L.R. 825 at 827; *Lathia v. Dronsfield Bros. Ltd.* [1987] B.C.L.C. 321; *Edwin Hill & Partners v. First National Finance Corp. plc* [1989] 1 W.L.R. 912, C.A.

[48] *Edwin Hill & Partners v. First National Finance Corp. plc* [1989] 1 W.L.R. 912; Lightman and Moss, *Law of Receivers of Companies* (1986), p. 81, para. 7-14. See also, *Astor Chemicals Ltd. v. Synthetic Technology Ltd.* [1990] B.C.L.C. 1 at 11.

[49] *Lathia v. Dronsfield Bros. Ltd.* [1987] B.C.L.C. 321; *Edwin Hill & Partners v. First National Finance Corp. plc* [1989] 1 W.L.R. 912, *cf. George Barker (Transport) Ltd. v. Eynon* [1974] 1 W.L.R. 462, and *Re Diesels & Components Pty. Ltd.* (1985) 9 A.C.L.R. 825, where the other contracting party had a superior right based on possession of the goods in question.

[50] *Freevale Ltd. v. Metrostore (Holdings) Ltd.* [1984] Ch. 199; *Telemetrix plc v. Modern Engineers of Bristol (Holdings) plc* [1985] B.C.L.C. 213. In *Astor Chemicals Ltd. v. Synthetic Technology Ltd., supra* at p. 11. Vinelott J. said:

> "It does not follow that a receiver [appointed out of court] can otherwise always act in disregard of contractual obligations binding on the company. He may not be so entitled to do so if, for instance, there is a doubt whether there will be a surplus of assets available to the company and the other creditors after meeting the debt due to the mortgagee and if the breach would seriously damage the reputation of the company and impair its goodwill, or if the charge does not extend to all the assets of the company and the breach might affect the ability of the company to continue to trade with other assets."

course, vest the equitable interest in the other party.[51] Such contracts almost always involve land, and the availability of specific performance is always a factor of some weight. Here, the maxim "equity treats as done that which ought to be done", applies to confuse the distinction between property and obligation. It should be stressed that the issue under discussion is not resolved by invoking agency principles. An agent is not liable for inducing a breach of the principal's contract.[52] This, though, is limited to cases of true agency, and would seem inapplicable to the somewhat unusual agency of a receiver. The authority indicating that the receiver might be liable[53] considered the slightly different position of a court-appointed receiver, and is irrelevant to the case of a receiver appointed out of court.

Thus, unless a receiver "adopts" pre-receivership contracts, he can repudiate them with impunity. Because his appointor has the benefit of a security over the company's assets, the consequences of rendering the company liable in damages are in practice felt only by the company and, through it, the unsecured creditors. The secured amount will be paid in priority to the claim for damages of the other party to the broken contract. In this way, the receiver may strip the company of its assets, leaving only the liabilities—"the lemon may, so to speak, be squeezed dry."[54] Apart from the question of priority, and duty of care, a receiver's power to disclaim current contracts is unfettered. In *Airline Airspares Ltd.* v. *Handley Page Ltd.*,[55] Graham J. held that a receiver could repudiate the company's current contracts only when to do so is beneficial to the realisation, and would not damage the company's goodwill. In my view, the qualifications do not represent the true extent of the receiver's power of disclaimer. However, in *Schering Pty. Ltd.* v. *Forrest Pharmaceutical Co. Pty. Ltd.*,[56] Helsham C.J. in Eq., denied the assumption implicit in *Handley Page*, that a receiver appointed out of court and as an agent of the company, could repudiate onerous contracts. In his view, the receiver could not repudiate contracts which attract equitable remedies, such as specific performance and injunction. This assertion may at first sight seem attractive. On reflection, however, the proposition is too wide to be accepted as law. Equitable remedies in aid of enforcement of contractual obligations are generally of three kinds: specific performance, injunction and rectification. It is difficult to accept that wherever any of these equitable remedies is available, and damages would not be an adequate remedy, the court will injunct a receiver from disclaiming

---

If the receiver's power to disclaim is considered as a matter of priority, subject only to any duty of care owed to the mortgagor and guarantor to act reasonably, it is difficult to accept all these qualifications as true fetters on the receiver's power of disclaimer. Vinelott J.'s statement of principle very accurately reflects the position of a receiver appointed by the court, but cannot be accepted as the law governing receivers appointed out of court, unless his qualifications express the duty of care owed to the mortgagor. At any rate, they mean no more than this: the receiver must not cause the company avoidable loss.

[51] *Re Bastable* [1901] 2 K.B. 518.
[52] *Said* v. *Butt* [1920] 3 K.B. 497.
[53] *Re Botibol* [1947] 1 All E.R. 26 at 28.
[54] *Re Diesels & Components Pty. Ltd.* (1985) 9 A.C.L.R. 825 at 828.
[55] [1970] Ch. 193.
[56] [1982] 1 N.S.W.L.R. 286.

onerous contracts. Indeed, where the company is insolvent, damages are almost always likely to be an inadequate remedy since there would be no assets out of which damages could be met. If Helsham C.J. was right, it would follow that in the great majority of cases, the chargee, through his receiver, will remain bound to an unsecured contract creditor. This is simply not the law. One can sympathise with judges attempting to mark out the limits of the receiver's power; but the proposition cannot be put higher than this: a receiver may be unable to disclaim an executory contract, onerous or otherwise, which, because of the availability of specific performance, is capable of generating a present equitable interest. This question is not affected by the availability of restorative or mandatory injunction.

It is also to be noted that not all contracts involving land can be specifically performed. Where the insolvent company is the vendor, and equitable interest has passed before appointment of a receiver, the receiver cannot disclaim the contract. The effect of disclaimer is to vest an absolute interest in the purchaser.[57] If, however, the insolvent company is the purchaser, as a general rule, specific performance is not available because completion requires the receiver to pay money over to the vendor.[58] The court will not compel the receiver to borrow money in order to complete the purchase.[59]

The last question for consideration is the extent of the receiver's duty of care. It is now settled law that although a mortgagee is not a trustee of his power of sale for the mortgagor, he owes the mortgagor a duty of care in the manner in which the power is exercised.[60] The mortgagee can sell at any time once the power has arisen, and need not consider all the circumstances before exercising his power.[61] He is not obliged to wait on a rising market or for a market to recover.[62] Nor is he bound to postpone sale in the hope of obtaining a better price, or to adopt a piecemeal method of sale which could only be carried out over a substantial period.[63] Similarly, where the security is an asset of unstable value, there is no duty to realise the security before it becomes worthless.[64] For the same reason there is no duty of care to ensure that the security is fully insured even where the mortgagor suffers loss as a result.[65] But the mortgagee must take steps to obtain the best price available at the time he exercises his power of sale.[66] A receiver is under a like duty, and the duty is owed to the mortgagor and any guarantor of the secured debt.[67] As yet, the duty

---

[57] *Re Bastable* [1901] 2 K.B. 518.
[58] *Holloway* v. *York* (1877) 25 W.R. 627.
[59] *Re B. Johnson & Co. (Builders) Ltd.* [1955] Ch. 634 at 662.
[60] *Cuckmere Brick Co. Ltd.* v. *Mutual Finance Ltd.* [1971] Ch. 949; *Bishop* v. *Bonham* [1988] 1 W.L.R. 742; *cf. Expo International Pty. Ltd.* v. *Chant* [1979] 2 N.S.W.L.R. 820.
[61] *Shamji* v. *Johnson Matthey Bankers Ltd.* [1986] F.T.L.R. 329.
[62] *Bank of Cyprus (London) Ltd.* v. *Gill* [1980] 2 Lloyd's Rep. 51.
[63] *Tse Kwong Lam* v. *Wong Chit Sen* [1983] 1 W.L.R. 1349 at 1355.
[64] *China and South Sea Bank Ltd.* v. *Tan* [1990] 2 W.L.R. 56.
[65] *National Bank of Greece SA* v. *Pinios Shipping Co. (No. 1), The "Maira"* [1989] 3 W.L.R. 185, C.A. rvsd. [1990] 1 All E.R. 78, H.L. (not on this point).
[66] *Bishop* v. *Bonham* [1988] 1 W.L.R. 742.
[67] *Standard Chartered Bank Ltd.* v. *Walker* [1982] 1 W.L.R. 1410; *American Express International Banking Corp.* v. *Hurley* [1985] 3 All E.R. 564.

has not been extended to unsecured creditors,[68] though in practical terms this may not cause any injustice since unsecured creditors claim through the mortgagor. It will not be rare to find charge documents modifying this duty of care. Such modifications will, of course, be subject to the same common law and statutory controls on exemption clauses as apply to contracts. Thus, where the charge instrument empowers the chargee to exercise the power of sale in such manner as he thinks fit, this will be construed as authorising the chargee to sell in such manner as he thinks fit, within the limits of the duty of reasonable care imposed by the general law.[69] Such subjective words as "think fit" do not give the chargee or his receiver a carte blanche to act as he thinks in disregard of the duty of care imposed by law. Therefore, an authority given to a mortgagee to sell the mortgaged property in such manner, upon such terms and for such consideration as he may think fit, must normally be read as subject to the implicit limitation that it is to be exercised properly within the limits of the general law, that is to say, with the exercise of reasonable care to obtain a proper price.[70] Again, where the charge instrument excludes liability on the part of the chargee or his receiver, howsoever arising, whether this is sufficient to excuse a loss arising from a negligent exercise of the power of sale, depends on the context in which the exclusion appears. In *Bishop* v. *Bonham*,[71] the Court of Appeal, construing a similar expression, held that the exclusion did not cover a sale effected without reasonable care. This indicates a strict approach to the construction of clauses exempting the mortgagee or his receiver from liability for a negligent exercise of the power of sale. It may be that a more explicit clause would be upheld as a matter of construction. This, though, is without prejudice to the controls imposed by the Unfair Contract Terms Act 1977. Where the Act applies, an exemption clause would be enforced only if it passes the test of reasonableness.[72] But the exemption clause cannot exclude the operation of the Act, or prevent a duty of care from arising.[73]

Where a receiver seeks protection under an exemption clause, different considerations arise. The privity rule poses a substantial problem because, as a general rule, the receiver, not being a party to the mortgage, can take no benefit from the exemption clause, unless he can bring himself within one of the exceptions to the privity rule.[74] It has been said that there is no policy objection to a third party benefiting from an

---

[68] *Cf. Latchford* v. *Beirne* [1981] 3 All E.R. 705, overruled as to guarantors in *Standard Chartered Bank Ltd.* v. *Walker, supra*. In *Parker-Tweedale* v. *Dunbar Bank plc* (1990) 14 O.N.L.J. 169, the Court of Appeal held that no duty was owed to third parties to the mortgage, even though they may have beneficial interest in the proceeds of sale and the mortgagee is aware of their rights to a share of the proceeds. There the third parties were equitable beneficial owners under a trust, but the mortgagee's duties were owed to their trustee, the mortgagor.
[69] *Bishop* v. *Bonham, supra* at 753–754.
[70] *Ibid.*
[71] [1988] 1 W.L.R. 742.
[72] *Smith* v. *Eric S. Bush* [1989] 2 W.L.R. 790.
[73] *Harris* v. *Wyre Forest D.C.* [1989] 2 W.L.R. 790, H.L.
[74] *Scruttons Ltd.* v. *Midland Silicones Ltd.* [1962] A.C. 446. See also, Treitel, *Law of Contract* (London, Stevens & Sons, 7th ed., 1987), pp. 477–481.

exemption clause; the only question is one of construction, namely, does the clause cover the event or loss which has occurred?[75] The receiver may rely on it where the mortgagee contracts expressly as his agent in relation to the exemption clause,[76] but even here, there is still the difficulty of showing that the mortgagee contracted with the authority of the receiver or that there was a subsequent ratification. Where the identity of the receiver is unknown at the date of the mortgage, such an authority will be difficult to establish and there can be no ratification unless the principal was capable of being ascertained at the date the deed of mortgage was executed.[77] That the receiver was in the contemplation of the mortgagee or indeed of the mortgagor as well, at the date of the mortgage, is insufficient.[78] Another way out of the privity barrier is for the mortgage to provide that the mortgagor shall pay over to the mortgagee any sums recovered from the receiver.[79] All this may seem acceptable when limited to the tripartite relationship between the mortgagor, the mortgagee and the receiver. But there remains the question how far third parties, such as a guarantor of the mortgage debt, or junior incumbrancers interested in the equity of redemption, will be bound by the exemption clause. Generally, such parties are not bound,[80] and the receiver cannot therefore plead the exemption clause as against them.

Receivership causes a divestment of the powers of the company's directors. This means that although it does not dissolve or annihilate the corporate mortgagor, or affect its internal procedures, it supersedes the directors in the conduct of the company's business, deprives the directors of all power to enter into contracts in relation to that business, or to deal with assets subject to the receivership. In relation to these matters, the powers of the company and its directors are entirely in abeyance.[81] During the receivership, the capacity of the directors to act bears an inverse relationship to the validity and scope of the receivership.[82] The directors, however, retain residual powers which they can exercise so long as this does not unfairly interfere with or prejudice the conduct of the receivership. The residual powers include the power to institute proceedings against the receiver's appointor for breach of contract.[83] Consent of the receiver is not required, provided he is unwilling to bring the action, and

---

[75] Treitel, *op. cit.*, p. 479.

[76] *New Zealand Shipping Co. Ltd.* v. *A.M. Satterthwaite & Co. Ltd. (The Eurymedon)* [1975] A.C. 154; *Port Jackson Stevedoring Pty. Ltd.* v. *Salmond & Spraggon (Australia) Pty. Ltd. (The New York Star)* [1981] 1 W.L.R. 138. At the moment there is reluctance to extend this evasive device outside shipping transactions: see *Southern Water Authority* v. *Carey* [1985] 2 All E.R. 1077. There are other difficulties: *Raymond Burke Motors Ltd.* v. *Mersey Docks & Harbour* [1986] 1 Lloyd's Rep. 155.

[77] *Expo International Pty. Ltd.* v. *Chant* [1979] 2 N.S.W.L.R. 820 at 946; *Southern Water Authority* v. *Carey* [1985] 2 All E.R. 1077 at 1084–1085.

[78] *Southern Water Authority* v. *Carey, supra* at 1085.

[79] Treitel, *op. cit.*, pp. 479–481.

[80] *Scruttons Ltd.* v. *Midland Silicones Ltd.* [1962] A.C. 446; *Leigh & Sillavan Ltd.* v. *Aliakmon Shipping Co. Ltd., The "Aliakmon"* [1986] A.C. 785. See also, Treitel, *Law of Contract* (7th ed., 1987), pp. 482–483, for a discussion of suggested exceptions.

[81] *Moss Steamship Co. Ltd.* v. *Whinney* [1912] A.C. 254 at 263.

[82] *Hawkesbury Developments Co. Ltd.* v. *Landmark Finance Pty. Ltd.* [1969] 2 N.S.W.L.R. 782 at 790.

[83] *Newhart Developments Ltd.* v. *Co-operative Commercial Bank Ltd.* [1978] Q.B. 814.

the company in whose name the proceedings must be brought, is indemnified against any liability for costs.[84] If the mortgagee could be sued, *a fortiori* the receiver may also be sued by the directors since he is unlikely to sue himself.[85] It is no objection in such cases to say that the mortgagee is the beneficiary as the right of action is charged to him. Since there are persons interested in the equity of redemption, the directors are under a duty to such persons to bring the necessary proceedings. It would of course be different where assets are sold to a purchaser against whom the company has a right of action. If the right of action is part of the assets sold, neither the company nor its liquidator can sue the purchaser, unless the sale has been set aside.[86]

Lastly, a receiver appointed under a charge which, as created, was a floating charge, owes duties to the preferential creditors. By statute, he is required, where the free assets of the company are insufficient to pay unsecured claims, to pay them out of assets covered by a charge which started life as a floating security.[87] This is a positive duty[88] and the receiver cannot hand over property to the company where this would be passed on to the debenture holder. A debenture holder who receives property in such circumstances, knowing the facts, is liable to the preferential creditors as a constructive trustee.[89] But where a receiver is appointed under a debenture secured by a fixed and a floating charge, without any separation of the fixed and floating charge assets, the priority of preferential creditors is limited to assets subject to the floating charge.[90] As preferential creditors do not prevail over specific mortgagees, it follows that where a receiver is appointed under a debenture secured by a fixed and floating charge, and he realises property subject to the fixed charge at more than enough to pay off the debenture holder in full, the surplus must be returned to the company or whoever else is entitled to the equity of redemption, and not to the preferential claimants.[91]

Insolvency-related challenge

7.4   English law recognises four types of insolvency proceeding.[92] These are a voluntary arrangement under Part I of the Insolvency Act 1986; an administration under Part II; an administrative receivership under Part III; and insolvent liquidation. Each of these affects the receivables financier, though the extent of impact depends very much on the pattern

---

[84] *Ibid.*
[85] *Watts* v. *Midland Bank plc* [1986] B.C.L.C. 15, where it was held that the action could not be derivative in form. See also, *Hawkesbury Developments Co. Ltd.* v. *Landmark Finance Pty. Ltd., supra.*
[86] *Re Park Gate Waggon Works Co.* (1881) 17 Ch.D. 234.
[87] Insolvency Act 1986, s.40; Companies Act 1985, s.196 as amended by Insolvency Act 1986, s.439(1) and Sched. 13, Pt. 1; *cf. Re Griffin Hotel Co. Ltd.* [1941] Ch. 129; *Re Christonette International Ltd.* [1982] 1 W.L.R. 1245; *Re Brightlife Ltd.* [1987] Ch. 200.
[88] *Westminster Corp.* v. *Haste* [1950] Ch. 442; *IRC* v. *Goldblatt* [1972] Ch. 498.
[89] *IRC* v. *Goldblatt, supra.*
[90] *Re Lewis Merthyr Consolidated Collieries Ltd.* [1929] 1 Ch. 496.
[91] *Re G L Saunders Ltd. (in liq.)* [1986] 1 W.L.R. 215.
[92] Insolvency Act 1986, s.247(1).

which the financing took. In this section, we shall consider the forms of challenge to the enforcement of security which are insolvency-specific, that is to say, which can only be raised in the context of insolvency. Administration itself is a serious challenge because it deprives the secured creditor of two important rights, namely, the right to determine the time to enforce his security, and control over the conduct of realisation of the charged assets. Administration raises several difficult issues, but only those which may affect the receivables financier will be considered.

A court may appoint an administrator if it is satisfied that the company is insolvent or is likely to become insolvent, and considers that the making of an order appointing an administrator would be likely to achieve any of the purposes listed in section 8(3) of the Insolvency Act 1986.[93] The expression "likely to achieve" is now construed as meaning that there is a real prospect of achieving the purpose of the order,[94] although earlier authority indicated a stricter test.[95] The petition may be presented by directors[96] or creditors of the company. Once the petition is presented, a moratorium is imposed on the enforcement of security interests, except with leave of court.[97] No proceedings or execution may be commenced or continued against the company, except with leave of court.[98] The prohibition continues after the order has been made.[99] The courts have construed "proceeding" fairly strictly. Thus it does not cover an application by a competitor to revoke the company's aviation licence.[1] Nor is an application to register a charge out of time a proceeding requiring leave of court.[2] The advertisement of a winding-up petition is a step in the petition and therefore prohibited, except with leave of court.[3] The appointment of a receiver other than an administrative receiver is a step in the enforcement of a security, and is equally prohibited once a petition for an administration is presented.[4] This does not cover the

---

[93] *Ibid.*, s.8(1)(*a*) and (*b*). Under s.9(4), the court may make an interim order, but the court has no jurisdiction to appoint an interim administrator: *Re a Company (No. 00175 of 1987)* (1987) 3 B.C.C. 124.

[94] *Re Harris Simons Construction Ltd.* [1989] 1 W.L.R. 368; *Re Primlaks (UK) Ltd.* (1989) 5 B.C.C. 710; *Re SCL Building Services Ltd.* (1989) 5 B.C.C. 746.

[95] *Re Consumer & Industrial Press Ltd.* [1988] B.C.L.C. 177.

[96] In *Re Equiticorp International plc* [1989] 1 W.L.R. 1010, Millett J. in considering the meaning of directors in s.9(1) of the Insolvency Act 1986, was prepared to follow *Re Instrumentation Electrical Services Ltd.* (1988) 4 B.C.C. 301, where it was held that directors in s.124(1) meant *all* directors. However, he held that once a resolution of a properly convened board of directors to present a s.9(1) application had been passed, any director had authority to make the application on behalf of them all. In *Instrumentation*, the s.124(1) application was presented without any formal resolution of the board of directors.

[97] Insolvency Act 1986, s.10(1)(*b*). In *Re Paramount Airways Ltd.* [1990] B.C.C. 130, the Court of Appeal held that a statutory right to detain an aircraft for non-payment of airport charges under the Civil Aviation Act 1982 was a security within Pt. II of the Act. The exercise of the right, therefore, required the consent of the administrator or the leave of court.

[98] *Ibid.*, s.10(1)(*c*).

[99] *Ibid.*, s.11(3).

[1] *Air Ecosse Ltd.* v. *Civil Aviation Authority* (1987) 3 B.C.C. 492.

[2] *Re Barrow Borough Transport Co. Ltd.* [1989] 3 W.L.R. 858.

[3] *Re a Company (No. 001992 of 1988)* (1988) 4 B.C.C. 451; *Re a Company (No. 001448 of 1989)* (1989) 5 B.C.C. 706 (advertisement of winding-up petition restrained despite the fact that the petition for administration had not been presented).

[4] Insolvency Act 1986, s.10(1)(*b*).

appointment of an administrative receiver. However, uncertainty surrounds the question who is entitled to appoint an administrative receiver. Does this include second and subsequent floating chargees? What of a fixed security over the only property owned by the company?[5] This is undesirable in view of the power to veto the making of an administration order given to the person who is entitled to appoint an administrative receiver.[6] Also, it is not clear whether the moratorium on enforcement of security extends to the exercise of a right of set-off available against the company, or the enforcement of other self-help remedies, such as the right to forfeit a deposit, or the ability of a superior landlord to serve a notice of claim under section 6 of the Law of Distress Amendment Act 1908.

As regards set-off, the question is whether its exercise is an enforcement of a security, or otherwise some form of proceeding or execution against the insolvent. The uncertainty arises from the vagueness of the Insolvency Act 1986 on the effect of the approval of the administrator's proposals, and whether this affects the rights of set off of approving creditors. Security is defined as "any mortgage, charge, lien or other security."[7] Clearly, a set-off, even one given by contract, is neither a lien, nor a charge, nor a mortgage. Whether it is "other security" is more debatable, and the answer would turn on whether one adopts a conceptual or a functional view of the meaning of security.[8] Since a set-off does not rest on any underlying right of property it is not a security at all. But if one were to adopt a functional view by asking what purpose a set-off serves, the answer would be that a set off is at least a commercial security. On balance, it seems preferable to say that "other security" does not include a set-off; it is limited to securities *ejusdem generis* with mortgage, charge and lien. On this view, a debtor of the insolvent company will continue to exercise his right of set-off notwithstanding administration. This result may defeat the purpose of administration, especially in the case of banks holding a credit balance for the insolvent company. However, to deny set-off will be unjust unless the creditor entitled to exercise the right of set off is provided with an alternative security. The exercise of a right of set off is not a "proceeding" or an "execution" and so does not require leave of court.[9] A counter claim is on a different footing[10] because a true counter claim operates not merely as a defence, as does a set off, but in all respects as a weapon of offense, an independent action by the defendant against the plaintiff.[11] The question whether creditors can approve proposals for deferment of the

---

[5] *Cf. Re Meesan Investments Ltd.* (1988) 4 B.C.C. 788 at 790. For a full discussion of these questions see para. 5.14, *supra*.
[6] Insolvency Act 1986, s.9(3)(a). For a discussion of these and other uncertainties surrounding administrative receivership, see para. 5.14, *supra*.
[7] Insolvency Act 1986, s.248(b).
[8] For a discussion of the meaning of real security, see para. 1.2, *supra*.
[9] This follows the analogy supplied by liquidation: see *Peat* v. *Jones* (1881) 8 Q.B.D. 147; *Mersey Steel & Iron Co.* v. *Naylor, Benson & Co.* (1882) 9 Q.B.D. 648, affd. (1884) 9 App.Cas. 434.
[10] *Langley Constructions (Brixham) Ltd.* v. *Wells* [1969] 1 W.L.R. 503.
[11] *Stooke* v. *Taylor* (1880) 5 Q.B.D. 569 at 575–577.

maturity of debts owed by the company, and the effect of such deferment are beyond the scope of this discussion.

The question whether a superior landlord can serve a notice of claim pursuant to section 6 of the Law of Distress Amendment Act 1908, after the presentation of a petition for an administration order, or the making of such order, is undecided. The service of the notice would be prohibited if it amounted to the enforcement of a security, or the issue of a proceeding or an execution on the property of the company. That the notice is not a proceeding is clear enough, for the remedy is essentially self-help and does not require intervention of the court. Whether the right is a form of execution or security is less clear. It seems that it is not an execution, since it is a self-help remedy not dependent on obtaining a judgment for a debt. Nor is it a distress, since the section 6 remedy is given as an alternative to distress. It is arguable that the notice is analogous to distress and therefore within the spirit, if not the letter, of the legislation. If that be so, it follows that the service of the notice of claim is analogous to distress, more so as the aim is to recover unpaid rent. If this analysis is wrong, the service of a section 6 notice can be prevented by treating the right to serve the notice as a form of security. That it arises by statute should not matter since there is no indication that the statute prohibits only the enforcement of consensual security interests.[12] On this approach, the right to serve a section 6 notice would be "other security" within the statutory definition of security.

One of the most important features of an administration is the power of the administrator to deal with charged assets. If the charge started life as a floating security, the administrator may dispose of, or otherwise deal with, the property comprised in it as if the charge did not exist.[13] In the case of a fixed charge, the administrator has no power to deal, but only power to dispose of the property with leave of court, in which case the net proceeds of the disposal, including any shortfall between the realised and the realisable open market value, are to be paid to the chargee.[14] This provision raised serious concerns particularly in relation to fixed charges over receivables. Some of the concerns were whether the administrator could collect and use proceeds of charged receivables, whether his power was limited to factoring the receivables, how he could raise money for the statutory purposes if he was not free to deal with the charged receivables. A recent report[15] shows that this has not raised many problems in practice. In the cases covered by the report, only one administrator used receivables covered by a fixed charge to fund his administration on the

---

[12] See *Re Paramount Airways Ltd.* [1990] B.C.C. 130 (a statutory right of detention of aircraft for non-payment of airport charges a security).

[13] Insolvency Act 1986, s.15(1) and (3).

[14] Insolvency Act 1986, s.15(2), (3) and (5). Insolvency Rules 1986 (S.I. 1986 No. 1925), r. 2.51 requires the administrator to inform the chargee of the date, time and venue of the hearing of the application. A similar power is given to, and a duty imposed on, an administrative receiver: s.43 and r. 3.31.

[15] See Mark Homan, *Administrations under the Insolvency Act 1986: The Result of Administration orders made in 1987*, for the Research Board of the Institute of Chartered Accountants of England and Wales (1989), paras. 5.25 *et seq.* (hereinafter referred to simply as *Homan Report*).

grounds that section 15(2) of the Insolvency Act 1986 did not cover such assets. The matter became the subject of a negotiated settlement.[16] In other cases, the practice emerged, in relation to fixed charge assets generally, that where the chargee's consent has been received or assumed, administrators have not hesitated to dispose of the assets and pay over the net proceeds to the chargee without recourse to the courts.[17] There is as yet no reported case in which an administrator sought leave of court to collect receivables subject to a fixed charge.[18] The practice has been for the administrator to pay over the proceeds to the chargee where there is no dispute as to the chargee's entitlement, his consent being implied.[19] This has the merit of saving time and money involved in an application for leave of court. It is not, however, clear that this practice is supported by law, although it is possible to say that it is within the power of the administrator to do all such things necessary to achieve the purpose of the administration. This is debatable, though the scope of creditor prejudice is rather narrow if the charge is valid and not open to objection on any ground.

Both the chargee and the administrator can apply to court to realise the security.[20] In *Re Meesan Investments Ltd.*,[21] Royal Trust Bank which held a fixed charge on the only property owned by the company in administration, applied for leave to enforce its charge. The administration order was made because the court was satisfied that administration will lead to a more advantageous realisation of the assets of the company than would be possible in a winding-up. The attempt to sell the property as a fully let accommodation had failed substantially; the secured debt was increasing daily so that the security was being eroded, and the administrator had been in office for 10 months. Peter Gibson J. declined leave to enforce the charge. He noted that the administration had gone on for a long time and the bank was justifiably worried especially as its debt was rising whilst its security was depreciating. In the circumstances, the administrator was given two months within which to secure a binding contract, and to report to the court at the end of that time, so that the bank might then proceed with whatever application or submission it considers appropriate.

The case is also important for indications on how the courts may approach applications for leave by the secured creditor. Generally, the court is given a wide discretion which is not circumscribed by any particular considerations. Regard will be had to all the relevant circumstances, not just to the conduct of the administrator, although such conduct is material. In considering whether to grant leave, the court will try, where possible, to hold the scales evenly between all creditors. This may justify postponing sale on a rising market so that some surplus over the secured amount would be left to meet unsecured claims. Where the security is sufficient to satisfy the secured creditor, the court will be

[16] *Homan Report*, para. 5.26.
[17] *Ibid.*, para. 5.25, p. 36.
[18] *Ibid.*
[19] *Ibid.*
[20] Insolvency Act 1986, ss.11(3)(c) and 15(2).
[21] (1988) 4 B.C.C. 788.

reluctant to give leave, not least because to allow the secured creditor to enforce his security, for example, by appointing a receiver, would create costs which will increase unnecessarily the secured debt, with the result that there would be a reduction in the net proceeds of the sale effected by such a receiver.[22]

Under section 15(2) of the Insolvency Act 1986, an administrator may apply to court for leave to dispose of property subject to a fixed charge, but it is a pre-condition to the granting of such leave that the net proceeds of sale realisable on an open market sale by a willing vendor should be paid to the chargee.[23] In *Re Consumer and Industrial Press Ltd. (No. 2)*,[24] joint administrators applied for leave to dispose of a magazine, the title of which was the company's principal asset. The magazine was subject to two fixed charges, and no proposals had been put to the creditors as required by section 23. The administrators argued that the need for a section 23 proposal should be dispensed with because the net proceeds of sale would be insufficient to discharge the fixed charges, so that there would be nothing left for the unsecured creditors.[25] Peter Gibson J. refused leave as that would render meaningless any subsequent meeting of the creditors. The scheme of Part II of the Act is to enable creditors to have a say *before*, not after, the administrator carries out the purposes of his appointment. Leave will be granted before a proposal is put to creditors only in very exceptional circumstances, and where the disposals are really the only sensible course to adopt.[26] A hard pressed administrator may enter into a contract conditional on approval by creditors, though where speed is essential, this is unlikely to be useful.

A potential difficulty with section 15(2) applications is the question of valuation. Leaving aside the question whether leave would be granted, it is provided that it shall be a condition of granting leave to the administrator to dispose of the charged property that the net proceeds of the disposal, and any shortfall on the realisable open market sale by a willing vendor, shall be applied towards discharging the sums secured by the charge.[27] The expression "sums secured by the charge" covers not only the capital sum secured by the charge, but also interest properly payable thereunder and any costs which the chargee is entitled to add to his

---

[22] See n. 72 at the end of this chapter.

[23] Insolvency Act 1986, s.15(5).

[24] (1988) 4 B.C.C. 72. However, in *Re NS Distribution Ltd.* [1990] B.C.L.C. 169, where the administrator sought leave to dispose of the company's leasehold property before the s.23 meeting was held, Harman J. held that this was not a case where the administrator needed leave under s.14(3) of the 1986 Act. The lease was only one of the company's assets and the meeting of creditors would have serious matters before it despite the sale of the lease.

[25] Under the Insolvency Rules 1986 (S.I. 1986 No. 1925), r. 2.24, secured creditors can vote at creditors' meetings only to the extent of their unsecured claim.

[26] See also, *Re Smallman Construction Ltd.* [1989] B.C.L.C. 420, where the scheme approved by creditors proved impracticable, and there was no time for a s.25 meeting. Knox J. held that the court has residual jurisdiction under s.14(3) to authorise an alternative scheme in exceptional circumstances. The case itself was sufficiently exceptional, though he stressed that he was not being asked to override positively proposals approved by creditors. In his view, he would "hesitate long" before adopting such an approach.

[27] Insolvency Act 1986, s.15(5).

security in accordance with the general law and the terms of the charge.[28] There is as yet very little guidance on how the court would exercise the jurisdiction and discretion given by section 15(2). More importantly, the concept of open market sale by a willing vendor is not free from difficulty. Does this indicate a going concern value or a break up value? To be sure, there is always an element of forced sale in an insolvency. In *Re ARV Aviation Ltd.*,[29] Knox J. indicated how the court will exercise its jurisdiction. First, an order under section 15(2) must necessarily be final—once made, the security is gone. There is no jurisdiction to make an interim order.[30] Second, section 15(2) and (5) allow for a two-stage process: the first allows the court to decide whether to make an order authorising the administrator to dispose of the property subject to the specific charge; the second allows the court to direct an enquiry to establish the proper figure for the deficiency between the net proceeds of disposal and the open market value which would be obtained by a willing vendor.[31] On the first stage, the court will assume jurisdiction even where there is no dispute between qualified valuers as to the value of the security. The existence of such a dispute is sufficient but not necessary to found jurisdiction or call for the exercise of the court's discretion.[32] In every case, the court will strive to balance the prejudice that would be felt by the secured creditor if the order were made, against the prejudice to the unsecured creditors who are interested in the promotion of the purposes specified in the administration order. On the stage two enquiry, Knox J. said that the intention of section 15(5) should be the protection to the maximum possible extent of the rights of the secured creditor. The provision did not contemplate as the amount which would be realised on the sale of the property in the open market by a willing vendor anything which is significantly less than what a secured creditor himself would realise.[33] Since valuation is of critical importance to the exercise of the discretion to permit a disposal of charged assets, where practicable, valuation evidence should be submitted to the administrator, though valuation goes not to the existence of jurisdiction, but to the exercise of the discretion.[34] To some extent, this useful guidance does not address fully the question whether an open market sale by a willing vendor is a

---

[28] *Re ARV Aviation Ltd.* [1989] B.C.L.C. 46 at 51. Where mortgagees take action to enforce their security, they are entitled to add their costs to the amount owing under the mortgage. Costs in actions against third parties may only be added to the mortgage if the action is for the protection of the mortgagee's title or the equity of redemption, but not if the action relates to alleged duties of care by the mortgagee in favour of strangers to the mortgage. Accordingly, in *Parker-Tweedale* v. *Dunbar Bank plc (No. 2)* [1990] E.G.C.S. 19, a bank which had successfully defended an action by a beneficiary (whose trustee was the mortgagor) alleging that the bank owed him a duty of care was not allowed to add the costs of its defence to the secured amount. This case could seriously prejudice lenders, although in practice the scope for prejudice is considerably reduced by the fact that an amply drafted clause would certainly bring such expenses within the secured amount.

[29] [1989] B.C.L.C. 46.

[30] *Ibid.* See also, *Re a Company (No. 00175 of 1987)* (1987) 3 B.C.C. 124.

[31] *Re ARV Aviation Ltd., supra* at 51.

[32] *Ibid.* at 50.

[33] *Ibid.*

[34] *Re ARV Aviation Ltd., supra* at 52.

going concern sale or a break up sale. As there is always some element of forced sale in an insolvency, it is undesirable to approach the question of valuation always on the basis of a going concern value, nor is it fair to treat it as if it were always a break up sale. Some measure of flexibility is called for. In the context of receivables financing, there are likely to be few or no problems of valuation because, (i) receivables are unlikely to be included in a sale of the undertaking subject to an administration, and (ii) the value of receivables depends on the solvency of debtors, and their collectible value can be ascertained after proper discounts.

Funding was one of the primary concerns of those who viewed administration with reservations. In practice, this problem has not been insuperable. In nearly half of the cases surveyed by Mark Homan,[35] no external funding was required. In cases where funding was needed, bank finance and factoring have been used.[36] Bank finance is usually by way of a secured term loan or an overdraft. It is not clear where the administrator will find security to support his borrowing. Two solutions suggest themselves. The first is section 19(5) which creates a statutory charge on property subject to a floating charge, for the payment of debts or liabilities incurred by the administrator. Bank finance may qualify as a liability of the company and so be payable out of floating charge property. There remains, however, the problem of enforceability of the statutory charge. On balance, it seems that there is no reason why the bank or any other beneficiary of the statutory charge should not be able to enforce it. The second solution is for the creditor or bank to take a fresh charge to cover his lending. This would not be difficult as the administrator has power to do all things necessary to carry out his functions. This includes power to execute documents in the name of the company.[37] Where factoring had been used by administrators to raise working capital, there was no pre-existing fixed charge on the receivables. But if there are other charges on the company's property, interesting questions of priority will arise on vacation of office by the administrator.

It will not be uncommon for an administrator to find that the company has current onerous contracts which may have to be disclaimed if the purposes of his appointment are to be achieved. Can he disclaim such contracts? The answer is not obvious, and probably is incapable of being stated in terms general enough to apply to every case. What is however clear is that, unlike a liquidator,[38] an administrator has no statutory power to disclaim onerous contracts, even where this is necessary to achieve the purposes of his appointment. An administrator is not in a position analogous to a receiver, or an administrative receiver, as regards pre-administration contracts.[39] Receivers can disregard the company's current contracts and thus expose the company to damages provided they do not

---

[35] *Homan Report*, para. 6.04, p. 46.
[36] *Ibid.*
[37] Insolvency Act 1986, s.42(1) and Sched. 1, para. 9. See also, paras. 3, 14 and 23.
[38] *Cf.* Insolvency Act 1986, s.178(3)(*a*).
[39] *Astor Chemicals Ltd.* v. *Synthetic Technology Ltd.* [1990] B.C.L.C. 1 (injunction granted against administrator threatening a breach of contract because no evidence that injunction would frustrate purpose of administration and damages would have been an inadequate remedy for the other contracting party).

thereby cause the company avoidable loss. They will be personally liable neither for breach of contract nor for the tort of inducing a breach of contract unless the other party to the contract has equitable rights of property arising therefrom.[40] This power of disclaimer, and the limits on its exercise, show that the question is essentially one of priorities. Administrators are not in a like position, and their power of disclaimer is exactly equal to, and co-extensive with, the company's power of disclaimer. However, this does not mean that administrators will always be bound by pre-administration contracts of the company. It may be that the court will permit a disclaimer where it is necessary for the achievement of the purpose of the administration. If this approach is adopted, the right of the other party to the contract to claim damages may be protected by the statutory charge imposed by section 19(5). Also where a party to a contract involving the company has joined in the approval of proposals inconsistent with completion of that contract, it may fairly be assumed that he has implicitly released the company from its obligations under the contract, or at the minimum, agreed to suspend his right to call for performance.

Although the provision for meetings of creditors is one of the safeguards against abuse by the administrator, it affords little protection to secured creditors who can vote only to the extent that they are unsecured.[41] For such creditors the remedy for unfair prejudice is likely to be more useful. Section 27 of the Insolvency Act 1986 gives a creditor power to apply to court for relief where the affairs of the company have been managed by the administrator in a manner which is unfairly prejudicial to his interests, or where he alleges that any actual or proposed act or omission of the administrator is or would be so prejudicial. On such application, the court may make an order[42] to regulate the future management by the administrator, or may direct the administrator to refrain from doing the acts complained of. The court may also make an order directing the calling of a meeting of creditors to consider such matters as the court may specify. Exceptionally, the court may remedy an unfair prejudice by discharging the administration order. This provision for unfair prejudice is modelled on section 459 of the Companies Act 1985.[43] There is, however, no statutory definition of unfair prejudice, and it is not clear whether the applicant should show discrimination against himself.[44] Intent to injure is not necessary, though the conduct complained of must be both prejudicial and unfair.[45] The jurisdiction to remedy unfair prejudice is a very important remedy from the point of view of all creditors. At the moment, there has been very little indication of the principles which will inform its exercise. In one case[46] a creditor with a fixed charge on book debts was to apply for

---

[40] *Freevale Ltd.* v. *Metrostore (Holdings) Ltd.* [1984] Ch. 199; *Telemetrix plc* v. *Modern Engineers of Bristol (Holdings) plc* [1985] B.C.L.C. 213.
[41] Insolvency Rules 1986 (S.I. 1986 No. 1925), r. 2.24.
[42] Insolvency Act 1986, s.27(4).
[43] As amended by Companies Act 1989, Sched. 19, para. 11.
[44] *Cf. Re Carrington Viyella plc* (1983) 1 B.C.C. 98, 951; *Re London School of Electronics* [1986] Ch. 211.
[45] *Re RA Noble & Sons (Clothing) Ltd.* [1983] B.C.L.C. 273.
[46] *Homan Report*, para. 5.39, p. 42.

redress against an administrator who used the book debts to fund his administration. The matter was settled out of court, thus depriving us of an opportunity to see precisely how the remedy against unfair prejudice would work in practice. Cases decided under section 459 of the Companies Act 1985 are not very relevant because many of them involve exclusion of the applicant from management or an allegation of breach of fidiciary duties. One of the interesting questions under section 27(4) is whether the court has jurisdiction to award restitutionary damages against the administrator, or whether the remedies specified in that provision are exhaustive. This question was raised but left undecided in *Re Charnley Davies Ltd.*[47] There, eleven insurance companies applied to court alleging that the administrator had, with the direction of the court, disposed of three insurance brokerage businesses of the company within 13 days of his appointment, without putting any proposals to creditors or calling a creditors' meeting as required by section 23. The unfair prejudice was the undue haste with which the disposals were effected. One of the remedies sought was an inquiry into the damages which the applicants had suffered because of the prejudicial acts. The administrator denied that the court had jurisdiction to make a declaration as to damages. Peter Gibson J. held that the matter was one of construction, and that the administrator's argument may or may not be correct as a matter of construction. It seems, however, that the phrase "as the court thinks fit" in section 27(2) gives the court a wide jurisdiction to award restitutionary damages if that would give relief in respect of the unfair prejudice. In particular, the remedies enumerated in section 27(4) are not exhaustive of the range of reliefs available to the court in redressing unfairly prejudicial conduct. The question, who benefits from such restitutionary damages—secured creditors, unsecured creditors who suffered from the acts complained of, or all unsecured creditors, may not be easy to answer.

Avoiding powers

The commencement of insolvent liquidation[48] is a day of reckoning for all creditors having claims on the insolvent corporation. The company becomes disinvested and the powers of directors to bind it are entirely gone.[49] Creditors are deprived of their ordinary remedies against the company, as proceedings against the company are sisted,[50] and uncompleted executions avoided.[51] Insolvent liquidation is also the occasion for the re-opening of a number of pre-liquidation transactions.[52] The value of security lies in its ability to insulate the creditor from the insolvency of the debtor. Any security that will not stand up on the insolvency of the debtor is undesirable. Yet, of all the tests to which a security transaction

7.5

---

[47] [1988] B.C.L.C. 343.
[48] Insolvency Act 1986, ss.86 and 129 define the time a liquidation commences.
[49] Insolvency Act 1986, ss.91(2) and 103.
[50] *Ibid.*, ss.128 and 130(2).
[51] *Ibid.*, s.183.
[52] See Prentice in B. G. Pettet (ed.), *Company Law in Change*, p. 69.

can be put, insolvent liquidation is the most exacting. This is as it should be, provided the aim of insolvent liquidation is kept in mind. Jackson[53] has argued very persuasively that insolvency law is a set of distributional rules by which the assets of the insolvent are distributed to its creditors primarily according to their pre-liquidation entitlements. In this way insolvent liquidation is no more than a forum for the translation of the pre-liquidation assets and liabilities of the insolvent.[54] In England, secured creditors are outside the statutory scheme imposed by the Insolvency legislation[55] for the payment of creditors,[56] though they might find themselves participating in the scheme to the extent that they are unsecured, or if their security is avoided. The avoidance should neither be arbitrary nor capricious, but should reinforce the standards of sound credit practice and commercial morality. It follows that insolvent liquidation should not be the occasion for dislocating and readjusting pre-liquidation transactions, unless the dislocation or re-adjustment is dictated by a superior insolvency policy. Jackson[57] demonstrates that avoidance powers divide broadly into two categories. On the one hand, there are those that act to implement the collective proceeding by preserving the reasons for its existence. As such these powers inherently diverge from pre-liquidation rights for they are part and parcel of the substitution of a collective set of rights for the individualised rights that exist outside liquidation.[58] Examples in this category include the avoidance of vulnerable floating charges,[59] undue preferences[60] and post-liquidation dispositions.[61] On the other hand, as represented by avoidance of transactions at undervalue,[62] extortionate credit bargains,[63] and transactions defrauding creditors,[64] there are avoidance powers that act to protect against debtor or creditor misbehaviour. In this way they are but a part of the system of rights that should exist both inside and outside insolvent liquidation. It is fair to say that if at all avoidance powers in English insolvency law are informed by any policy considerations, the latter, rather than the former, more accurately reflects the operation of insolvency avoidance powers. The search for policy is even more confused by the uncertainty surrounding the question of who benefits from the existence and exercise of avoidance powers. This question of entitlement is considered later.[65] Now we shall examine in brief the main avoidance powers which are insolvency-specific.

---

[53] (1982) 91 Yale L.J. 857.
[54] See Jackson (1985) 14 J. of Legal Studies 73.
[55] See Insolvency Act 1986, s.107; Insolvency Rules 1986, r. 4.181(1) and (2); r. 4.88.
[56] *Sowman* v. *David Samuel Trust Ltd.* [1978] 1 W.L.R. 22; *Re Obie Pty. Ltd. (No. 2)* (1983) 8 A.C.L.R. 574.
[57] (1984) 36 Stan.L.R. 725.
[58] See Prentice, *op. cit.*, pp. 70 *et seq.* for the application of this thesis to U.K. corporate insolvency law.
[59] Insolvency Act 1986, s.245.
[60] *Ibid.*, s.239.
[61] *Ibid.*, s.127.
[62] *Ibid.*, ss.238, 240 and 241.
[63] Insolvency Act 1986, s.244.
[64] *Ibid.*, ss.423–425.
[65] See para. 7.6, *infra.*

Compulsory liquidation relates back to the date of the petition for winding-up.[66] Any disposition of the company's property after the commencement of the liquidation is void unless the court orders otherwise.[67] The purpose of this avoidance is to prevent the improper alienation of the property of a company in dire financial straits during the period which must inevitably elapse before a petition for winding-up is heard.[68] The courts take a broad view of "disposition." Sales,[69] security assignments,[70] and even payment of money into the company's overdrawn account,[71] are all forms of dispositions avoided by the Act. But only dispositions of the "property" of the company are avoided. Two illustrations of the importance of this limitation on the extent of avoidance must now be considered. The first is where a company assigns future receivables which do not come into existence before the company descends into insolvent liquidation. In this case, a distinction must be drawn between the situation where the receivables arise from pre-liquidation performance by the company on one hand, and where they arise from the post-liquidation efforts of the liquidator on the other. In the former case, the vesting of the receivables in the assignee is not a disposition of the company's property. The disposition took place at the date of the assignment and not when the receivables arose. Although this particular point is undecided, it is thought that it is consistent with the reasoning in *Tailby* v. *Official Receiver*,[72] and the result in some of the cases.[73] In the latter situation the assignment is open to attack on at least two counts. First, it will be avoided as a post-liquidation disposition of the company's property since it was unearned before commencement of compulsory liquidation. Second, if the above reasoning is wrong, then the assignment will be ineffective because there is nothing on which it can operate as the receivables never belonged to the insolvent.[74] A second illustration is that the provision does not avoid the exercise by a receiver or his appointor of the power to realise the property comprised in the security after the commencement of winding-up.[75] The reason for this is that the charged property is not property beneficially owned by the company at the commencement of winding-up. For the same reason completion of a pre-

---

[66] Insolvency Act 1986, s.129.

[67] *Ibid.*, s.127.

[68] *Re Wiltshire Iron Co.* (1868) L.R. 3 Ch.App. 433 at 447; *Re J Leslie Engineers Co. Ltd.* [1976] 1 W.L.R. 292 at 304; *Ex p. Schwarcz* [1989] B.C.L.C. 424 (no need for protection if company is solvent).

[69] *Re Wiltshire Iron Co.*, *supra*; *Re Tramway Building & Construction Co. Ltd.* [1988] Ch. 293.

[70] *Re International Life Assurance Society* (1870) L.R. 10 Eq. 312.

[71] *Re Webb Electrical Ltd.* (1988) 4 B.C.C. 230. However, there is no recovery against a bank which honours cheques drawn in favour of third parties after the commencement of winding up of which the bank was unaware: *Re Loteka Pty. Ltd.* (1989) 15 A.C.L.R. 620. Query whether the exercise of a right of set-off is a disposition.

[72] (1888) 13 App.Cas. 523.

[73] *Re Davis* (1889) 22 Q.B.D. 193; *Re Trytel* [1952] 2 T.L.R. 32.

[74] *Ex p. Nichols* (1883) 22 Ch.D. 782; *Wilmot* v. *Alton* [1897] 1 Q.B. 17 at 22; *Re De Marney* [1943] Ch. 126.

[75] *Sowman* v. *David Samuel Trust Ltd.* [1978] 1 W.L.R. 22; *Re Margart Pty. Ltd.*, *Hamilton* v. *Westpac Banking Corp.* [1985] B.C.L.C. 314; *cf. Re Clifton Place Garage Ltd.* [1970] Ch. 477.

liquidation contract capable of specific performance after the commencement of winding up is not avoided.[76]

Only dispositions by the company are avoided. Dispositions to the company are valid, although in compulsory liquidation, the payor might be able to recover the payment either on the ground of total failure of consideration, or on the basis of the rule in *Ex parte James*.[77] The rule, restricted to officers of the court, is anomalous and probably will not be extended. It has been held inapplicable to a liquidator in a voluntary liquidation, since he is not an officer of the court.[78] The rule does not create new rights, but where it applies it derogates from the rights of the parties interested in the assets available for distribution.

The courts take a broad view of their discretionary jurisdiction to validate offending dispositions. There are criteria which guide, but do not circumscribe, the exercise of the discretion to validate and the court will have regard to all the circumstances.[79] No order will normally be made where the disposition is not for the benefit of the company.[80] In *ex post facto* applications, it is not relevant to compare what the position of unsecured creditors would be if the disposition were validated and what it would be if it were not.[81] But if the disposition is shown to have reduced the assets available for distribution, then to that extent at least, the disposition will not normally be validated.[82]

Where an administration order is made or the company goes into insolvent liquidation, the court has power to re-open a transaction at an undervalue, and for this purpose to make such order as it thinks fair for restoring the position to what it would have been had the company not entered into that transaction.[83] In addition to gifts,[84] a company enters into a transaction at an undervalue if the consideration provided by the other party is significantly less than that furnished by the company.[85] What is "significantly less" in this context is a question of fact depending on the circumstances. The court will not reopen such a transaction if it can be shown that the company entered into it in good faith and for the purpose of carrying on its business, and that at the time it did so there were reasonable grounds for believing that the transaction would benefit the company.[86] The provision requires not just the existence of reasonable

---

[76] *Re French's Wine Bar Ltd.* [1987] B.C.L.C. 499; *Re Country Stores Pty. Ltd.* (1987) 11 A.C.L.R. 385; *cf. Site Preparations Ltd.* v. *Buchan Development Co. Ltd.* 1983 S.L.T. 317, where a floating charge was created four months after the presentation of winding-up petition. It may also be that if a pre-liquidation contract is conditional or voidable at the instance of the company, waiver or confirmation of the contract may constitute a post-liquidation disposition.

[77] (1874) L.R. 9 Ch.App. 609.

[78] *Re John Bateson & Co. Ltd.* [1985] B.C.L.C. 259 at 264; *Re T H Knitwear (Wholesale) Ltd.* [1988] 2 W.L.R. 276.

[79] *Re Steane's (Bournemouth) Ltd.* [1950] 1 All E.R. 21.

[80] *Re McGuinness Bros. (UK) Ltd.* (1987) 3 B.C.C. 571.

[81] *Re Tramway Building & Construction Co. Ltd.* [1988] 2 W.L.R. 640 at 648–649.

[82] *Ibid.*

[83] Insolvency Act 1986, s.238.

[84] *Ibid.*, s.238(4)(*a*).

[85] *Ibid.*, s.238(4)(*b*).

[86] Insolvency Act 1986, s.238(5).

grounds for belief, but also the fact of belief on such grounds. Both are questions of fact. The grounds on which the other party acted must be sufficient to induce in a reasonable person the required belief, and this is a matter of law. If no reasonable grounds for belief exist, mere honest belief in the existence of such grounds is insufficient.[87]

Section 239 of the Insolvency Act 1986 avoids preferences given at the relevant time[88] by an insolvent corporation. Undue preference is given where the recipient is a creditor and the company does or omits to do something which has the effect of putting the creditor in a better position in any subsequent insolvent liquidation than he would have been in if the preference were not given.[89] The preference is undue and therefore liable to be reopened if the company was influenced in deciding to give it by a desire to prefer.[90] It is no longer necessary to establish a dominant intention to prefer; it is sufficient that the decision is influenced by the requisite desire. There is no longer any need to establish an intention to prefer; there must be a *desire* to put the creditor or surety in a better position than he would have been in if the preference were not given. Intention is not desire, for intention is objective whereas desire is subjective. A man can choose the lesser of two evils without desiring either.[91] Undue preference presupposes knowledge of insolvency on the part of the company.[92] The law, however, contemplates that the inability to pay debts as they arise should co-exist with the payment attacked as a preference. The fact that the debtor will be able to pay its debts in future is irrelevant.[93] The primary desire need not be to prefer. It is sufficient if the desire to prefer is one of the factors inducing the payment, even though the dominant motive was to keep open a line of credit, etc.[94] Mere presence of the requisite desire will not be sufficient by itself; it must have influenced the decision to enter into the transaction. But it is not necessary to prove that, if the necessary desire had not been present, the company would not have entered into the transaction. The requisite intention may be proved by direct or circumstantial evidence.[95] A payment which results from creditor pressure is unlikely to be attacked as an undue preference. Where a company agrees to execute a security agreement in future, the execution of that agreement at a time when the company is insolvent, is presumptively an undue preference, whether or not it was executed pursuant to an existing obligation to do so.[96] The execution of a legal charge pursuant to an existing equitable charge is a

---

[87] *Nakkuda Ali* v. *Jayaratne* [1951] A.C. 66 at 77; *Registrar of Restrictive Trading Agreements* v. *W.H. Smith & Son Ltd.* [1969] 1 W.L.R. 1460 at 1468.
[88] Relevant time is defined in s.240 of the Insolvency Act 1986.
[89] See s.239(4).
[90] See s.239(5). This intention is presumed in the case of preferences given to connected persons: s.239(6).
[91] *Re M. C. Bacon Ltd.* (1990) B.C.C. 78.
[92] *Re Sarflax Ltd.* [1979] Ch. 592.
[93] *Re F P & C H Matthews Ltd.* [1982] Ch. 257.
[94] *Re M C Bacon Ltd., supra.* Cf. *Re FLE Holdings Ltd.* [1967] 1 W.L.R. 1409.
[95] *Re M Kushler Ltd.* [1943] Ch. 248; *Re M C Bacon Ltd.* (1990) B.C.C. 78.
[96] *Re Jackson & Bassford Ltd.* [1906] 2 Ch. 467; *Re Gregory Love & Co.* [1916] 1 Ch. 203.

different matter.[97] But where security is given for a past debt, not influenced by a desire to prefer, but by genuine commercial considerations, the giving of the security is not a preference.[98] Also where value is given for the security, there is no preference. Difficulties might arise in the case of transactions on a current account. Are the deals to be treated as isolated transactions requiring fresh value? Or would they be regarded as entries in a continuous account, which indeed they are, and so not requiring to be supported by fresh value? It seems that the latter more accurately reflects the real nature of current account transactions. Payment to a secured creditor of the amount of his debt may or may not constitute a preference. Where the security is a valid specific security, a payment not exceeding the value of the security is not a preference because, to the extent of the payment, the security is released and falls into the pool of assets available for the payment of unsecured debts.[99] If the security is a floater, such payment may be a preference since it would enable the creditor to rank above the preferential creditors, contrary to the statutory priority of preferential creditors. The fact that something has been done under a court order does not, without more, prevent the doing of that thing from constituting the giving of a preference.[1]

In the insolvent liquidation of a company, the court has a discretionary jurisdiction to reopen extortionate credit transactions entered into within three years of the onset of insolvency.[2] A credit transaction is extortionate if, having regard to the risks accepted by the financing creditor, the terms of credit are such as to require grossly exorbitant payments to be made by the company, or otherwise grossly contravene ordinary principles of fair dealing.[3] This provision is modelled on section 138(1) of the Consumer Credit Act 1974. Credit is not defined in the Insolvency Act 1986, but would cover all forms of receivables financing as they all involve some form of financial accommodation.[4] In the context of secured consumer loans, it has been held that extortionate does not mean harsh and unconscionable.[5] There is no prima facie exorbitant rate, but it has been suggested that whilst "grossly exorbitant" in the first limb imposes primarily a substantive control, "grossly contravened ordinary principles of fair dealing" in the second limb imposes a procedural control by focusing on the process by which the transaction is concluded.[6] This is doubtful. It seems that both limbs impose substantive controls. The range of remedies which the court may give is wide and includes setting aside the whole or part of the obligation created by the extortionate credit transaction.[7]

---

[97] *Re FLE Holdings Ltd.* [1967] 1 W.L.R. 1409.

[98] *Re M C Bacon Ltd., supra.*

[99] *Cf. National Australian Bank K D I Construction Services Pty. Ltd.* (1988) 12 A.C.L.R. 683.

[1] Insolvency Act 1986, s.239(7).

[2] Insolvency Act 1986, s.244.

[3] *Ibid.,* s.244(3).

[4] Consumer Credit Act 1974, s.9(1) defines "credit" as including a cash loan and any form of financial accommodation.

[5] *Davies* v. *Directloans* [1986] 1 W.L.R. 823.

[6] Bentley and Howells [1989] Conv. 164 at 167.

[7] Insolvency Act 1986, s.244(4).

Floating charges created within 12 months[8] of the onset[9] of insolvency are invalid except to the extent of any money paid or goods or services supplied to the company at the same time as, or after the creation of the charge, or the value of so much of that consideration as consists of a reduction or discharge of any debt of the company, or any interest discharged or reduced.[10] Where the chargee is not a connected person, the time of creation of the charge is not relevant unless the company was insolvent or became insolvent as a result of the transaction under which the charge was created.[11] This provision is not as draconian as it may at first sight appear. First, the courts take a liberal view of the meaning of money paid "at the time" of the creation of the charge. The provision does not mean simultaneously with the creation of the charge. Thus, a floating charge created 11 days after money was paid to the company and in consideration of that payment was held valid.[12] So also where the charge was created 54 days after money was paid.[13] Here there was no acquiescence or collusion to defraud creditors of the company. To amount to money paid to the company, it is not necessary that the payment be absolute and unconditional.[14] Money is still paid for the benefit of the company creating the charge even where it is advanced on the specific understanding that part of it will be paid to a creditor firm of which the lender is a partner.[15] This, however, was found to be beneficial to the company. Where money paid was calculated to benefit the directors rather than the company, so that the company was no more than a conduit pipe through which the payment was passed to the directors, it was held that the floating charge was not created for any consideration.[16] The result was the same where the cheques in consideration of which a floating charge was created were applied in reduction of the company's overdraft so as to release the directors from their guarantee.[17] In *Re W.G. M'Cleave & Co. Ltd.*,[18] three directors secured the company's bills of exchange and took a floating charge as security for the counter-indemnity from the company at a time when the company was insolvent. It was held that the charge was invalid for want of consideration. The directors' assumption of personal liability on the bills ought to have been held to be sufficient consideration. It is not clear whether the new definition[19] of

---

[8] The prohibited period is two years in the case of connected persons: see s.245(3)(*a*).
[9] Defined in s.245(5).
[10] Insolvency Act 1986, s.245(2).
[11] *Ibid.*, s.245(4).
[12] *Re Columbian Fireproofing Co. Ltd.* [1910] 2 Ch. 120.
[13] *Re F & E Stanton Ltd.* [1929] 1 Ch. 180.
[14] *Re Matthew Ellis Ltd.* [1933] Ch. 458.
[15] *Ibid.*
[16] *Re Destone Fabrics Ltd.* [1941] Ch. 319.
[17] *Re Orleans Motor Co. Ltd.* [1911] 2 Ch. 41.
[18] (1913) 47 Ir.L.T. 214.
[19] Insolvency Act 1986, s.245(2).

consideration will now cover such a case. In particular, it is not clear what exactly is meant by reduction or discharge of any debt of that company.[20]

Second, as regards bank creditors, the operation of the rule in *Clayton's case*[21] may turn past indebtedness into fresh advances[22] provided there is an unbroken current account, and no specific appropriation of payments into the account.[23] Although this particular application of the rule in *Clayton's Case* has been criticised,[24] it may be justified on the basis that, by honouring cheques, the bank provides new money which is used to pay creditors to whom the bank was not liable. The statutory invalidation of floating charges is prospective rather than retrospective. The charge on the company's property, but not the amount secured, is avoided. Consequently, if the company repays the secured amount to the creditor before the charge is attacked, the liquidator cannot recover the payment.[25] To the extent that the debt is paid, the charge is released leaving nothing for the liquidator to avoid. Also, where the creditor enforces the security before the appointment of a liquidator, there is nothing left to avoid, and the liquidator cannot recover the net proceeds realised on the enforcement.[26]

The avoidance powers considered so far apply only when the company descends into insolvent liquidation. They would not apply where the claims of unsecured creditors are statute-barred thereby leaving a surplus of assets for distribution among contributories.[27] Nor would they apply to the somewhat exceptional situation where a company which has gone into liquidation on the ground of insolvency turns out to have been solvent all along.[28] However, the jurisdiction to set aside transactions defrauding creditors does not depend on whether or not the company is insolvent, or even in liquidation, and may be exercised at any time.[29] It is not clear that there is any unifying thread running through all the avoidance powers which are available for the modification of transactions valid outside insolvent liquidation. A consideration of the question, who benefits from the avoidance powers, shows the embarrassing absence of any coherent or explicit insolvency policy.

Who benefits from avoiding powers?

7.6   Various policies are often urged to explain the incidence of avoidance powers in insolvent liquidation. One policy is said to be the need to

---

[20] *Cf.* Stewart, *Administrative Receivers and Administrators*, para. 1016, p. 203, for the suggestion that this provision reverses *Re G T Whyte & Co. Ltd.* [1983] B.C.L.C. 311. This is doubtful because the courts are unlikely to allow a creditor to transmute an unsecured into a secured debt.
[21] *Devaynes* v. *Noble* (1816) 1 Mer. 572.
[22] *Re Yeovil Glove Co. Ltd.* [1965] Ch. 148; *Re Thomas Mortimer Ltd.* [1965] Ch. 186n.
[23] *Re Hayman, Christy & Lilly Ltd.* [1917] 1 Ch. 283.
[24] *Report of the Review Committee on Insolvency Law and Practice*, Cmnd. 8558 (1982), paras. 1561–1562.
[25] *Re Parkes Garage (Swadlincote) Ltd.* [1929] 1 Ch. 139.
[26] *Mace Builders (Glasgow) Ltd.* v. *Lunn* [1987] Ch. 191, C.A.
[27] *Re Joshua Shaw & Sons Ltd.* [1989] B.C.L.C. 362.
[28] *Re Islington Metal & Plating Works Ltd.* [1984] 1 W.L.R. 14.
[29] Insolvency Act 1986, s.425.

further the hypothetical bargain which creditors would have entered into if it were possible for them to negotiate *ex ante* with each other. The powers exist to frustrate any last minute attempt to opt out of the statutory scheme imposed by insolvency law for the distribution of the insolvent's assets.[30] Another alleged policy is the need to discourage debtor or creditor misbehaviour.[31] All this is well if avoiding powers truly further any explicit goal of insolvency law. The doubt arises from uncertainty as to who benefits from the exercise of avoiding powers. If the result of the exercise of the power is to increase the pool of assets distributable among unsecured creditors, some will see this as a promotion of the policy of insolvency law. This itself is problematical. For one thing, such an approach is evidently inspired by a redistributional goal in favour of unsecured creditors. It is debatable whether such a policy is a worthy insolvency goal. The concern, however, is not just distributional. If avoiding powers are exercised solely for the benefit of unsecured creditors, insolvency law would hold out an incentive to unsecured creditors to make strategic use of the insolvency process even where this will not be in the best interest of creditors as a whole. In English law, whether such an incentive exists is problematical since the answer to the question, who benefits from the exercise of avoiding powers, is unclear. As a matter of principle, the question admits of a fairly simple answer. Most of the provisions[32] empower the court to make such order as it thinks fit for restoring the position to what it would have been if the company had not entered into the avoided transaction. They do not authorise the court *always* to declare that property recovered in consequence of the exercise of avoiding powers should be distributed among unsecured creditors. The sort of inquiry called for is the simple one of ascertaining what the position would have been in the absence of the avoided transaction. If the position would have been that the property would be within the scope of an existing charge, then that chargee alone should benefit from the recovery. This approach sees avoiding powers as glosses superimposed by Parliament on the autonomy of private bargains. If property is clawed back for whatever reason, it is not validly alienated, and it is not to the point to ask whether the alienation would, but for the avoiding powers, be valid as against the chargee. This simple straightforward approach has not yet been used to determine the destination of property recovered in exercise of avoiding powers. For purposes of analysis, avoiding powers may be divided into three groups: (i) transactions defrauding creditors,[33] and misfeasance proceedings against directors, receivers and liquidators[34]; (ii) unregistered[35] and vulnerable[36]

---

[30] Jackson (1984) 36 Stan L.R. 725 at 731 ("at bottom, bankruptcy overrides non-brankruptcy rights because those rights interfere with the group advantages associated with creditors acting in concert").
[31] Jackson, *op. cit.* at 778–780.
[32] This is true of provisions avoiding transactions at undervalue, undue preferences and transactions defrauding creditors: see Insolvency Act 1986, ss.238(3), 239(3), 423(2)(*a*).
[33] Insolvency Act 1986, ss.423, 424 and 425.
[34] *Ibid.*, s.212.
[35] Companies Act 1985, s.399.
[36] Insolvency Act 1986, s.245.

charges, and unregistered assignment of book debts by unincorporated associations[37]; (iii) transactions at an undervalue, undue preferences and extortionate credit bargains.

With regard to avoiding powers in Group I, it is clear who benefits from property recovered in exercise of such powers. Under the old law, the courts had settled that recovery in misfeasance proceedings belonged to the debenture holder secured by a general floating charge.[38] So certain were the courts about the correctness of this mode of application of the recovery that, rather than put the debenture holder to the expense and delay of proceedings for misfeasance, the court allowed him, where possible, to auction the right of action.[39] This was not just an act of judicial charity; the court lacked, and still lacks, jurisdiction to deprive the debenture holder of the benefit of the recovery.[40] Although the action is normally brought by the liquidator, title to sue is also vested in any creditor of the company.[41] Misfeasance proceedings are purely procedural,[42] and afford those with title to sue a procedural short cut for recovering the company's property. That which is misapplied is, *ex hypothesi*, not validly alienated, and the reason why a general floating charge catches the proceeds of misfeasance proceedings is not because the right of action for misfeasance is a chose in action. Rather, it is because the chose in action constituted by the right of action is vested in the company, and that which was misapplied was until its misapplication, validly charged by the floating security. Since the misapplication does not count as a disposition in the ordinary course of business, the property in fact never left the charge. The same reasoning will apply to misfeasance actions today. As for transactions defrauding creditors, the court is empowered to make such order as it thinks fit for restoring the position to what it would have been if the transaction had not been entered into, and protecting the interests of persons who are victims of the transaction.[43] An order under this provision enures primarily for the benefit of such persons on whose behalf the application for the order is treated as made.[44] Applications could be made by the administrator, liquidator, or victim of the impugned transaction. If the application is made by the victim, whatever is recovered goes to him. But where the application is made by the administrator or liquidator, it is treated as made on behalf of every victim of the transaction.[45] Accordingly, the recovery will benefit such victims, to the exclusion of other creditors. The victim could be a secured creditor whose charge covers property subject to the fraudulent transaction. Since the aim of this avoiding power is not distributional, and the

---

[37] *Ibid.*, s.344.
[38] *Re Anglo-Austrian Printing and Publishing Union* [1895] 2 Ch. 891; *Wood v. Woodhouse & Rawson United* [1896] W.N. 4; *Re Asiatic Electric Co. Pty. Ltd.* (1970) 92 W.N.(NSW) 361.
[39] *Wood v. Woodhouse & Rawson United* [1896] W.N. 4.
[40] *Re Asiatic Electric Co. Pty. Ltd.* (1970) 92 W.N.(NSW) 361.
[41] Insolvency Act 1986, s.212(3).
[42] *Re Etic Ltd.* [1928] Ch. 861; *Re B. Johnson & Co. (Builders) Ltd.* [1955] Ch. 634.
[43] Insolvency Act 1986, s.423(2).
[44] *Ibid.*, s.425(1)(*a*) and (*b*).
[45] *Ibid.*, s.424(2).

court is directed to restore the status quo, it is only on very rare occasions that recovery will benefit the generality of unsecured creditors.

The beneficiaries of property recovered in the exercise of Group II powers are not difficult to identify. The avoiding powers in this group define the extent of avoidance and against whom. For example, property comprised in an unregistered charge which is void against the liquidator does not fall to be distributed among unsecured creditors merely because the liquidator acts on behalf of unsecured creditors. Where, therefore, there is a second charge which is valid against the liquidator, property comprised therein becomes enlarged to the extent of the avoidance.[46] It is not open to the liquidator to argue that as the avoided charge was valid against the second charge, he (the liquidator) ought to step into the shoes of the avoided charge and rank ahead of the second charge.[47] It is not easy to see how this mode of application justifies the view that avoiding powers promote the collective nature of insolvency proceedings, or increase the aggregate pool of assets available for distribution among creditors. Also, where a floating charge is invalid because it is created within the relevant time before the onset of insolvent liquidation, the benefit of the avoidance goes to junior incumbrancers whose securities cover property hitherto comprised in the invalid charge. The provision does not say that unsecured creditors are to benefit—in fact it avoids, without prescribing the consequences of avoidance on other creditors. There is no argument of principle or policy why the recovery should not be given to junior incumbrancers, even where the result is to enlarge their securities. The same is true of the avoidance of an unregistered general assignment of book debts.

The problem of determining who benefits from property recovered in the exercise of avoiding powers is more serious in Group III, particularly in relation to undue preference. Two questions will be addressed here. The first is whether there is any compelling reason for giving property recovered as undue preference to unsecured creditors. The second is whether the same approach ought to be adopted in relation to transactions at an undervalue and extortionate credit bargains. It is tempting to say that recovery for undue preference belongs to the unsecured creditors because the right of recovery is vested in the liquidator for the benefit of the unsecured creditors. Indeed there is authority in support of such a conclusion.[48] In *Ex parte Cooper*,[49] it was held that the liquidator ought

---

[46] *Sanguinetti* v. *Stuckey's Banking Co.* [1895] 1 Ch. 176; *Re Farnham (a lunatic)* [1895] 2 Ch. 799; *Re Parry, ex p. Salaman* [1904] 1 K.B. 129; *Capital Finance Co. Ltd.* v. *Stokes* [1968] 1 W.L.R. 1158 at 1165.

[47] *Ex p. Payne, re Cross* (1879) 11 Ch.D. 539; *Ex p. Blaiberg, re Toomer* (1883) 23 Ch.D. 254.

[48] *Re Yagerphone Ltd.* [1935] Ch. 392; *Re Quality Camera Pty. Co. Ltd.* (1965) 83 W.N. (Pt. 1) (NSW) 226.

[49] (1875) L.R. 10 Ch.App. 510; *cf. Albert Gregory Ltd.* v. *C. Niccol Ltd.* (1916) 16 S.R. (NSW) 214, where it was argued that the liquidator (who was otherwise willing) should be debarred from bringing proceedings financed by a debenture holder, because the recovery will not benefit unsecured creditors. The argument was rejected.

not to lend his name to an action by a secured creditor to recover goods transferred by the company in circumstances amounting to an undue preference. The reasoning was that the unsecured creditors would not benefit from such an action since the goods were claimed by the secured creditor as part of his security. It is easy to see why the court declined to assist one creditor against another in what was essentially a contest for priority. Without the facility for recovering fraudulent preferences the transferee's title was superior, he having acquired a bona fide legal title to the goods without notice of the applicant's security. Ten years later, Bacon V.-C. and the Court of Appeal held[50] that the doctrine of fraudulent preference was entirely for the benefit of unsecured creditors. In their view, it was a total misapprehension of the law to suppose that a mortgagee, however ample the terms of his security, can obtain the benefit of property recovered as a fraudulent preference. To do otherwise would offend the principle of equality which lies at the heart of insolvency law—in retaining his security, the mortgagee would be acting against the principle of distribution: he would be retaining a part of the insolvent estate and asking to take a part of what remained after it had been diminished by his retention.[51] This is a powerful argument of policy in favour of using insolvent liquidation as a forum for achieving redistribution of wealth from secured creditors (who are assumed for this purpose to be rich) to poor unsecured creditors. Whether this is a worthy goal for insolvency law to pursue is very debatable.[52] Apart from this, the policy argument does not explain why this mode of application of property recovered in exercise of this avoiding power should be confined to fraudulent or undue preferences. Arguably, it may fairly be said that the law as to misfeasance proceedings, unregistered assignments, and invalid floating charges, exists for the benefit of unsecured creditors. Yet property recovered in the exercise of such powers goes to a creditor who holds a charge wide enough to cover such property. The answer may be that both cases were decided under section 164 of the Companies Act 1862, which avoided transfers which would be fraudulent preferences against creditors of the transferor. Hence the provision was thought to exist for the benefit of all creditors. Subsequent legislation,[53] except the Insolvency Act 1986, adopted this language of preferences against creditors. It was under this legislation[54] that *Re Yagerphone Ltd.*,[55] was decided. In that case, joint liquidators in the voluntary winding-up of a company recovered a sum of money alleged to have been paid to a creditor by way of fraudulent preference. A debenture holder secured by a general floating charge claimed that the money formed part of his recovery. Bennett J. rejected the claim primarily because at the time— the time the floating charge crystallized the money was not the property

---

[50] *Willmott* v. *London Celluloid Co.* (1886) 31 Ch.D. 425, affd. (1886) 34 Ch.D. 147, C.A.
[51] *Ibid.* at 436.
[52] See Jackson (1984) 36 Stan L.R. 725 at 741; Jackson (1985) 14 J. of Legal Studies 73 at 75.
[53] See, *e.g.* Companies Act 1929, s.265; Companies Act 1948, s.320.
[54] Companies Act 1929, s.265.
[55] [1935] Ch. 392.

of the company. This is hardly sufficient since there was nothing in that charge which prevented it from catching assets acquired after crystallization. Crystallization is not a cut-off point for determining the assets caught by a general charge, only that henceforth the charge is fixed.[56] If this had been the only reason for the rejection one would be compelled to doubt whether the case was rightly decided. However, Bennett J. gave a second reason: when the money was paid, it ceased to be the property of the company. The payment to that creditor could not have been attacked or impeached, unless the company descended into liquidation within three months (now 12 months). After the payment, the company had no interest in the money, contingent or otherwise. Again, this does not carry one far enough since it is arguable that this avoiding power is a statutory gloss on the autonomy of the private bargain between the company and the creditor. On this basis, it would be irrelevant whether the payment was valid against the debenture holder.[57] Bennett J. gave a third reason: the right to recover a sum of money from a creditor who has been preferred is conferred for the purpose of benefiting the general body of creditors. The money, when recovered, did not form part of the general assets of the company, but was impressed in the liquidators' hands with a trust for those creditors among whom they had to distribute the assets of the company. This seems correct because section 265 of the Companies Act 1929, on which the case was decided, avoided preferences against creditors generally. In this way, even if in bringing an action to avoid a preference, the liquidator was only asserting a procedural title to sue that was sufficient to ensure that recovery swelled the fund of assets available for distribution among creditors generally. The liquidator sued by succession, not to a right of action vested in the company, but vested in the general body of creditors, as against whom the preference was fraudulent and therefore avoided.[58] If this analysis is wrong and the primary question of entitlement remains, it is nevertheless thought that it is now too late to call the correctness of *Re Yagerphone* into question. The principle of *Yagerphone* has been applied to payment recovered in a compromised suit,[59] and to goods recovered by a receiver appointed by a debenture holder before liquidation.[60]

In *N A Kratzmann Pty. Ltd.* v. *Tucker*,[61] the Australian High Court indicated that the principle of *Yagerphone* was confined to money, and did not extend to specific tangible personalty recovered as a fraudulent preference. The reason was that:

" . . . although the moneys paid as a preference were at the time of the payment subject to the charge, the moneys so recovered . . . are not the same moneys . . .

---

[56] *Wellington Woollen Manufacturing Co. Ltd.* v. *Patrick* [1935] N.Z.L.R. 23; *N. W. Robbie & Co. Ltd.* v. *Witney Warehouse Co. Ltd.* [1963] 1 W.L.R. 1324; *Ferrier* v. *Bottomer* (1972) 126 C.L.R. 597.

[57] *Sanguinetti* v. *Stuckey's Banking Co.* [1895] 1 Ch. 176; *Re Farnham (a lunatic)* [1895] 2 Ch. 799.

[58] *Cf.* Sellar, 1983 S.L.T. 253.

[59] *Re Masureik & Allan Pty. Ltd.* (1981) 6 A.C.L.R. 39.

[60] *Re Quality Camera Pty. Co. Ltd.* (1965) 83 W.N.(Pt. 1) (NSW) 226; *cf. Ross* v. *Taylor* 1985 S.L.T. 387.

[61] (1968) 123 C.L.R. 295.

The case would be otherwise . . . where a preference consists of the disposition of specific and identifiable property subject to a charge validly created in relation thereto.''[62]

There is no case where this distinction has been applied, although in *Ross* v. *Taylor*[63] where a receiver persuaded a creditor to return stocks alleged by him to be a fraudulent preference, the Court of Session held that the reacquired stocks were subject to the floating charge; they were therefore not available for distribution among unsecured creditors. The reasoning indicates that if money had been repaid instead of goods, the result would have been the same. This may be contrasted with *Re Quality Camera Pty. Co. Ltd.*[64] where it was held that the principle was the same whether the recovery be in respect of money or goods. In the case itself, money and goods recovered by a receiver appointed out of court before liquidation, on the basis that they were fraudulent preferences, were held to belong not to his appointor, but to the general creditors. The decision in *Ross* v. *Taylor*[65] is apparently inconsistent with this conclusion, though that case was not cited in the latter. It seems that *Ross* v. *Taylor* is preferable as a matter of principle.

It is difficult to see how the question whether recovery for fraudulent preference belongs to a general floating chargee or unsecured creditors can depend on the nature of property recovered. The reasoning in *Kratzmann*[66] proceeds on the basis that where a payment is avoided, the declaration does not affect the title of the payee to any specific or identifiable property, whereas in the case of tangible personalty, the declaration relates to a specific property.[67] This, however, confuses the question of entitlement with the slightly different issue of the remedy available for the recovery of a fraudulent preference. The question of entitlement is logically precedent, and in itself, not affected by the type of remedy available for the vindication of the right to recover. That money paid does not represent any specific asset in the hands of the payee, is too general to be accepted as law. After all, the money may still be identifiable, either in specie or in a new form into which it has been converted. Besides, whatever is recovered from the payee stands exactly in the shoes of the original payment to him. It is not easy to see why the possibility that the payee may not be able to hand over the same coins or notes given to him by the insolvent should answer the question of entitlement in favour of unsecured creditors. If *Kratzmann* is correct, it would follow that where the initial payment has ben invested in specific property, the chargee should get the benefit of that property, since the declaration avoiding the payment can relate to title of the payee in the specific property. Considerations of this nature suggest that *Kratzmann* cannot be considered authoritative on this point.

---

[62] *Ibid.* at 301.
[63] 1985 S.L.T. 387.
[64] (1965) 83 W.N. (Pt. 1) (NSW) 226.
[65] 1985 S.L.T. 387, *supra*.
[66] (1968) 123 C.L.R. 295 at 301.
[67] *Ibid.* at 299–301.

Does *Re Yagerphone Ltd.*,[68] compel us to distribute recovery for undue preference under section 239 among unsecured creditors? There are material differences between the language of section 239 and the earlier legislation, in particular section 265 of the Companies Act 1929, under which *Yagerphone* was decided. For one thing, section 239 contains no references to a preference being void as against creditors. Second, section 239(3) directs the court to make such order as it thinks fit for restoring the position to what it would have been if the preference had not been given.[69] This direction does not clearly require that the recovery be given to unsecured creditors. The purpose of an order under that provision is to restore the property to its position immediately before the impugned transfer. Therefore, if immediately before the transfer it was part of a charge, specific or general, the order can only return the property to the charge. There is no jurisdiction to make any order which does not have as its aim the restoration of the position immediately before the preference was given. To this extent (it is thought) *Re Yagerphone* is no longer law. The result is the same for property recovered in consequence of the setting aside of a transaction at an undervalue. Section 238(3) requires the court to make such order as it thinks fit for restoring the position to what it would have been if the company had not entered into that transaction. In both cases the court has no discretion whether or not to make an order: it is bound to make an order for restoring the status quo *ante* the impugned transaction. Extortionate credit bargains are on a different footing. The decision whether to make an order is for the court and the range of orders is prescribed by statute.[70]

Where property is recovered by an administrator in exercise of an avoiding power and the company does not go into liquidation *immediately* after the administration,[71] there may be a *scintilla temporis* between the conclusion of the administration and the onset of liquidation, sufficient to vest the recovered property in the company. Such vesting is enough to feed any existing charge.

---

[68] [1935] Ch. 392. In the U.S., this question has been resolved by s.551 of the Bankruptcy Code 1978, which provides that any avoided transfer is preserved for the benefit of the estate. This provision gives statutory force to the Supreme Court decision in *Moore* v. *Bay* 284 U.S. 4 (1931), and is apparently justified by the need to prevent junior incumbrancers from improving their position at the expense of the estate when a senior incumbrance is avoided.

[69] The range of orders which the court might make are listed in s.241 of the Insolvency Act 1986. However, in *Re MC Bacon Ltd. (No. 2)* (1990) B.C.C. 430 at 434, Millett J. said *obiter*, that *Re Yagerphone* is still the law notwithstanding s.239(3) which empowers the court on finding a voidable preference proved to make such order as it thinks fit for "restoring the positions to what it would have been if the company had not given that preference" and s.241(1)(c) which empowers the court to release or discharge any security given by the company. In his view those powers are not intended to be exercised so as to enable a debenture holder to obtain the benefit of the proceedings brought by the liquidator. It is submitted that this approach is doubtful and does violence to the language of s.239(3).

[70] Insolvency Act 1986, s.244(2) & (4).

[71] Insolvency Act 1986, s.240(3)(a). Where there is a time gap, it is the date of commencement of the winding up.

[72] In *Re Atlantic Computer Systems plc, The Independent,* September 5, 1990, the Court of Appeal gave practice guidelines on the principles to be applied on applications, under section 11(3) of the Insolvency Act 1986, for leave to exercise proprietary rights against a company during its insolvency administration. First, the burden is on the applicant to demonstrate the case for leave to enforce his right. As the object of section 11(3)(c) is to facilitate achievement of the purposes of administration, leave should normally be given if the exercise of proprietary rights is unlikely to impede achievement of those purposes. Each case calls for an exercise of judgment, and the court should have regard to the parties' interests and all the circumstances of the case. The purpose of the power to give leave is to enable the court to relax the section 11 prohibitions if it would be inequitable for it to apply. In carrying out the balancing exercise, great weight is to be given to the proprietary interests of the applicant. An administration for the benefit of unsecured creditors should not be conducted at the security-holders expense, save to the strictly limited extent that this might be unavoidable. The conduct of the parties might be relevant in some cases. Secondly, it would normally be sufficient ground for granting leave that a refusal would cause significant loss to the applicant. Loss here means financial loss, whether direct or indirect, provided it is not too remote. Thirdly, these considerations might be relevant, not only to the granting or refusal of leave, but also to the decision whether to impose terms if leave was granted or refused. However, although sections 11(3)(c) does not in terms provide for the imposition of terms, the court could achieve under sections 14(3) or (7), or indirectly, by ordering that the applicant should have leave unless the administrator was prepared to follow the suggestion of the court. Finally, where the existence, validity or nature of the security sought to be enforced or was in dispute, the applicant will have to satisfy the court that he has a seriously arguable case. Always, an important consideration is whether the applicant is fully secured. These considerations, naturally, are not exhaustive. There is the need for flexibility, and there is no occasion, therefore, for construing these guidelines as if they are statutory criteria.

CHAPTER EIGHT

EQUITIES AFFECTING ASSIGNED RECEIVABLES

Introductory

The value of receivables lies in the ability and willingness of debtors to **8.1** pay. But even where they are able and willing, the amount collectible is very often not the same as the invoice of assigned receivables. The debtors may have valid and enforceable cross-claims and defences against the assignor. The extent to which such cross-claims and defences can be pleaded against the financier buying or taking receivables as security is of critical importance. The law is thus confronted with two contradictory policies: on the one hand, there is the need to give effect to the increasing use of receivables either as a basis for secured lending or for raising other forms of corporate finance by making them quasi-negotiable; on the other, there is equally the need to protect the debtor by preserving his cross-claims and defences against the assignor and making them available as a defence to a claim for payment by the receivables financier. Which policy is more deserving of protection by the law is beyond conclusive demonstration, for cogent arguments could be advanced in support of either. In favour of limiting cross-claims that may be raised against the receivables financier, one may argue, first, that the needs of modern lending and other financing practices require that non-negotiable debts be given the quality of quasi-negotiability by limiting the number of cross-claims which may be raised against a financier advancing money on the strength of receivables. Limiting the permissible cross-claims which may be raised protects the marketability of receivables as well as their value. Permitting wider scope for the debtor's cross-claims and defences diminishes the value of receivables and the amount of money which the assigning creditor can raise on the basis of this species of personal property.[1] Secondly, permitting a wide variety of cross-claims may unjustly punish the receivables financier who has no control over relations between assignor and debtor. Thirdly, cross-claims may enable the debtor to enjoy a preference over the assignor's other creditors. This argument has, on occasion, been used to limit the scope of cross-claims which a debtor may plead against a receiver appointed by a chargeholder in enforcement of his security.[2] In support of a wider scope for the debtor's

---

[1] *Law Reform Commission of British Columbia: Report on Set Off* (1988), pp. 35–38.
[2] *West Street Properties Pty Ltd.* v. *Jamison* [1974] 2 N.S.W.L.R. 435 at 440; *Leichhardt Emporium Pty Ltd.* v. *AGC (Household Finance) Ltd.* [1979] 1 N.S.W.L.R. 701 at 705.

cross-claims and defences a number of arguments can be raised. In the first place, it may be said that assignment law is already harsh enough on the debtor: the assignment to the financier does not require his consent and he is powerless to stop it[3]; the financier may be less indulgent than the assignor with whom the debtor contracted[4]; if the debtor mistakenly pays the assignor after receiving notice of assignment, the debt is not discharged and he must pay again to the receivables financier.[5] These are inconvenient and there is scarcely any good reason why he should be deprived of the right to raise all his cross-claims. Secondly, since the title of the financier is derivative it ought not to be better than that of the assignor.[6] Indeed it is difficult to see why the commercial value of an assignment should be enlarged at the expense of the debtor. Were it otherwise, receivables would be more valuable in the hands of the financier than in those of the assignor. This may give the assignor a perverse incentive to assign his claims against the debtor.

English law has not embraced any one of these policies to the total exclusion of the other. The solution which the law has settled for is an unsatisfactory compromise between recognising and giving effect to the title of the financier on the one hand, and preserving some of the debtor's cross-claims and defences, on the other. The result, of course, is that this area of the law is one of the most complex and confused heads of equity. It is to the rules working out the compromise that we now turn.

Financier takes subject to "equities"[7]

8.2   No rule of law is perhaps more often repeated than the rule that an assignee of receivables, be the assignment legal[8] or equitable,[9] takes subject to equities having priority over his right. The rule itself is of great antiquity[10] and dates as far back as historical records of assignment go. At the core the rule is reasonably clear but its outer limits have never been defined with anything nearing precision. What constitute equities for this purpose is unclear[11] nor is it easy to discern which equities are entitled to

---

[3] *Ex p. South* (1818) 3 Swans 392.
[4] See *Gordon* v. *Street* [1899] 2 Q.B. 641 (a vicious moneylender masquerading under an alias); *Fitzroy* v. *Cave* [1905] 2 K.B. 364 (assignee took assignment in order to bankrupt debtor and make him unfit to act as a company director).
[5] *Jones* v. *Farrell* (1857) 1 De G. & J. 208; *Brice* v. *Bannister* (1878) 3 Q.B.D. 569.
[6] *Cf. Stoddart* v. *Union Trust Ltd.* [1912] 1 K.B. 181; *Provident Finance Corporation Ltd.* v. *Hammond* [1978] V.R. 312.
[7] Derham, *Set Off* (1987) Chap. 12; Wood, *English and International Set Off* (1989) Chap. 16.
[8] Within the meaning of s.136(1), Law of Property Act 1925.
[9] *Roxburghe* v. *Cox* (1878) 17 Ch.D. 520.
[10] *Peters* v. *Soames* (1701) 2 Vern. 428; *Turton* v. *Benson* (1718) 2 Vern. 764.
[11] For attempts at definition of equities, see Everton, (1976) 40 Conv. 209; Neave and Weinberg [1979] U. of Tasmania L.R. 24, 115; Meagher, Gummow and Lehane, *Equity: Doctrines and Remedies* (2nd ed., 1984), pp. 111 *et seq.* In *Young* v. *Kitchin* (1878) 3 Exch.D. 127 at 130, Cleasby B. said that equities in this context refer to equities which would be enforced in a court of equity. See also *Provident Finance Corp. Ltd.* v. *Hammond* [1978] V.R. 312 at 319 ("equity" is a transaction or event or circumstance which entitles the debtor to say that it is unjust that the debt should be enforced against him without bringing into account his cross-claim arising from the transaction, event or circumstance).

priority over the right of the assignee. The truth is that the expression "equities" is a loose concept not too happily chosen.[12] A few generalisations may, however, be attempted. First, the assignee takes no better right than the assignor had, the rule being *nemo dat quod non habet.*[13] Accordingly, the assignee's claim is subject to all proper contra claims, defences and remedies which the debtor has against the assignor at the date of notice of the assignment.[14] If the underlying contract from which the assigned receivables emanate is vitiated by any factor affecting its formation, for example, mistake, misrepresentation, fraud, duress, undue influence, etc., the assignee takes his assignment subject to the debtor's equity to rescind.[15] In this connection, it is to be noted that, unlike in transfers of tangible personalty,[16] the intervention of the assignee's right does not bar the debtor's right to rescind, even where, as will often be the case, the assignee acquired his right bona fide and for valuable consideration. This is because the equitable rule which bars rescission once innocent third party rights intervene is confined to property rights acquired in the goods, the subject-matter of the vitiated contract, and does not apply to the seller's transfer of his right to receive payment. Put differently, the rule protects transferees of the goods from the buyer and not transferees of the seller's right to receive payment.[17] The result is that the seller cannot transfer his right to receive payment free of the buyer's equity to rescind. One reason for this preservation of the buyer's equity to rescind, it has been said,[18] is that the law gives more protection to proprietary than to contractual rights; and this is justified because the assignee of a receivable takes a greater business risk than the transferee of tangible personalty or land. This may in fact be so, though, strictly speaking, the assignee's right is not purely contractual; it is also proprietary.[19] Another reason is that the seller who has transferred a voidable title has a weaker case for protection from the buyer's disposition than innocent third parties who acquire the goods in good faith and for value from the buyer, whereas the rule preserving the buyer's equity to rescind reflects the stronger interest of the buyer as against an assignee relying on the assignor's (seller's) assurance that there is a collectible debt. At the heart of this justifiction lies the pre-eminence of possession as a basic indicium of title to goods.

---

[12] *Stoddart* v. *Union Trust Ltd.* [1912] 1 K.B. 181 at 188, *per* Vaughan Williams L.J.

[13] Spry (1969) 43 A.L.J. 265 at 269 *et seq.*; Spry, *Equitable Remedies* (3rd ed., 1984), pp. 175–176 (arguing that the rule stated in the text is wider than equitable set-off and that the failure to keep the rule of taking an assignment subject to equities distinct and separate from equitable set-off has led to the over-inclusive approach of English courts to the question of equitable set-off).

[14] *Stephens* v. *Venables* (1862) 30 Beav. 625; *Watson* v. *Mid Wales Ry. Co.* (1867) L.R. 2 C.P. 593; *Christie* v. *Taunton, Delmard, Lane & Co.* [1893] 2 Ch. 175.

[15] *Turton* v. *Benson* (1718) 2 Vern. 764; *Athenaeum Life Society* v. *Pooley* (1858) 3 De G. & J. 294; *Wakefield & Barnsley Banking Co.* v. *Northampton Local Board* (1881) 44 L.T. 697.

[16] *White* v. *Garden* (1851) 10 C.B. 919. *Cf. Car & Universal Finance Co. Ltd.* v. *Caldwell* [1965] Q.B. 525.

[17] Treitel, *Law of Contract* (7th ed., 1987) p. 284.

[18] *Ibid.*

[19] See para. 2.7, *supra*, where this is developed.

Also, it is now settled[20] that an assignee of receivables takes subject to an arbitration clause in the contract between the assignor and the debtor.[21] Since an arbitration clause imposes mutual obligations on the parties,[22] the assignee cannot insist on payment whilst the debtor has a genuine dispute which he desires to arbitrate and which may extinguish or diminish his liability to the assignor. However, monetary cross-claims dominate the debtor's equities. The assignee takes subject to the state of account between the debtor and the assignor at the date of notice of the assignment.[23] From this it follows that if the debt is paid[24] or released[25] before notice, the assignee has no claim against the debtor. Similarly, if the assigned debt is only one item in a running account between the debtor and the assignor, the debtor's liability is not for the gross amount of the debt assigned, but only for the ultimate balance found due at the date of the notice.[26] The assignee takes subject to the debtor's right of abatement at common law for defective performance.[27] This right, confined to contracts for the sale of goods with a warranty and to certain contracts for work and material,[28] is essentially a plea that by reason of the assignor's defective performance, the debt owed is so much less. Where the debt assigned is rent issuing from land, the assignee takes subject to the debtor's common law defences (in the nature of payment) and to his equitable set-off. At common law a debtor (tenant) who expends money on repairs to the demised premises which the landlord has covenanted to carry out, but in breach has failed to carry out, can set off the sum so expended against the landlord's claim for rent.[29] This set-off is an equity subject to which an assignee of the rent takes.[30] Also, where the tenant has paid money at the request of the landlord in respect

---

[20] Although there were initial doubts created by *Cottage Club Estate* v. *Woodside Estate Co. Ltd.* [1928] 2 K.B. 462.

[21] *Rumput (Panama) SA* v. *Islamic Republic of Iran Shipping Lines (The League)* [1984] 2 Lloyd's Rep. 259, applying s.1 of the Arbitration Act 1975.

[22] *Bremer Vulkan* v. *South India Shipping Corp.* [1981] A.C. 909; *Paal Wilson & Co. A/S* v. *Partenreederei (The Hannah Blumenthal)* [1983] 1 A.C. 853.

[23] *Mathews* v. *Wallwyn* (1798) 4 Ves. 118; *Norrish* v. *Marshall* (1821) 5 Madd. 475; *Dixon* v. *Winch* [1900] 1 Ch. 736; *Turner* v. *Smith* [1901] 1 Ch. 213; *De Lisle* v. *Union Bank of Scotland* [1914] 1 Ch. 22; *Parker* v. *Jackson* [1936] 2 All E.R. 281.

[24] *Williams* v. *Sorrell* (1799) 4 Ves. 389; *Re Lord Southampton's Estate* (1880) 16 Ch.D. 178; *Dixon* v. *Winch, ibid.*; *cf. Magee* v. *UDC Finance Ltd.* [1983] N.Z.L.R. 438.

[25] *Stocks* v. *Dobson* (1853) 4 De G.M. & G. 11, but a purported release after notice of assignment is invalid: *De Pothonier* v. *De Mattos* (1858) 27 L.J.Q.B. 260.

[26] On the nature of the debtor's liability on a running account, see *Halesowen Presswork & Assemblies Ltd.* v. *National Westminster Bank Ltd.* [1971] 1 Q.B. 1 at 46.

[27] On common law abatement, see *Mondel* v. *Steel* (1841) 8 M. & W. 858; *Gilbert-Ash (Northern) Ltd.* v. *Modern Engineering (Bristol) Ltd.* [1974] A.C. 689, enacted as s.53(1)(a), Sale of Goods Act 1979.

[28] *Gilbert-Ash (Northern) Ltd.* v. *Modern Engineering (Bristol) Ltd., supra* at 717.

[29] *Taylor* v. *Beal* (1591) Cro.Eliz. 222; *British Anzani (Felixstowe) Ltd.* v. *International Marine Management (UK) Ltd.* [1980] Q.B. 137 at 147.

[30] *Cf. Alloway* v. *Steere* (1882) 10 Q.B.D. 22; *Kitchen's Trustee* v. *Madders* [1950] Ch. 134 which applied the analogy of an assignee of a lease. Both cases seem doubtful especially after *British Anzani (Felixstowe) Ltd.* v. *International Marine Management (UK) Ltd.* [1980] Q.B. 137.

of some obligation of the landlord connected with the property demised, he has a valid set-off for the amount of the payment in extinction or diminution of the rent payable,[31] and this plea is equally available against the assignee of rent. Both defences apply only to the tenant's cross-claims in the nature of liquidated money demands. Where, therefore, the tenant's cross-claim is unliquidated, it can only be an equity subject to which an assignee of rent takes if it is very closely connected with the claim for rent as to be eligible for equitable set-off against the landlord, if the claim for rent had been made by him.[32]

The debtor's rights of set-off constitute the single largest of his enforceable equities. At one level, it is clear that the assignee takes subject to the debtor's rights of legal[33] and equitable set-off.[34] It is not necessary to attempt a detailed discussion of these rights.[35] A few illustrations will do. A debtor who has a liquidated cross-claim against the assignor at the date he receives notice of assignment can set it off against the assignee.[36] The cross-claim need not be of the same pedigree as the debt owed[37]; it need have no connection whatever. On the contrary, it may in fact be acquired for the very purpose of defeating the claim based on the debt.[38] As between the debtor and the assignee there is no requirement of mutuality for purposes of the rule that an assignee takes subject to equities.[39] But where there is no sufficient connection between the debt assigned and the debtor's cross-claim, and the cross-claim arises after notice of assignment, the absence of beneficial mutuality between the debt and the cross-claim is a convenient way of expressing the conclusion that this post-notice cross-claim is not an equity subject to which the assignee took.[40] Where the debtor's equity comprises a right of

---

[31] *Taylor* v. *Beal* (1591) Cro.Eliz. 222; *British Anzani (Felixstowe) Ltd.* v. *International Marine Management (UK) Ltd., supra.*

[32] *British Anzani (Felixstowe) Ltd.* v. *International Marine Management (UK) Ltd.* [1980] Q.B. 137.

[33] *Banco Central SA* v. *Lingoss & Falce Ltd. (The Raven)* [1980] 2 Lloyd's Rep. 266, where the argument that the expression "subject to equities" allowed equitable but not legal set-off was rejected.

[34] *Government of Newfoundland* v. *Newfoundland Ry. Co.* (1888) 13 App.Cas. 199, as explained in *Bank of Boston Connecticut* v. *European Grain & Shipping Ltd. (The Dominique)* [1989] 2 W.L.R. 440.

[35] For a good discussion of the nature of the various types of set-off and analogous doctrines, see Meagher, Gummow and Lehane, *Equity: Doctrines and Remedies* (2nd ed., 1984), Chap. 37; Derham, *Set Off* (1987); Goode, *Legal Problems of Credit and Security,* (2nd ed., 1988), Chap. 6; Wood, *English and International Set Off* (1989).

[36] *Roxburghe* v. *Cox* (1878) 17 Ch.D. 520; *Young* v. *Kitchin* (1878) 3 Exch.D. 127.

[37] *Bennett* v. *White* [1910] 2 K.B. 43, but not where the cross-claim is acquired after notice of assignment: *N.W. Robbie & Co. Ltd.* v. *Witney Warehouse Co. Ltd.* [1963] 1 W.L.R. 1324; *Lynch* v. *Ardmore Studios (Ireland) Ltd.* [1966] I.R. 133.

[38] As in *Tony Lee Motors Ltd.* v. *M.S. MacDonald & Son (1974) Ltd.* [1981] 2 N.Z.L.R. 281.

[39] *Cf. CIBC* v. *Tuckerr Industries Ltd.* [1983] 5 W.W.R. 602 at 604.

[40] *N.W. Robbie & Co. Ltd.* v. *Witney Warehouse Co. Ltd.* [1963] 1 W.L.R. 1324 at 1339. See also *Felt & Textiles of New Zealand Ltd.* v. *R. Hubrich Ltd.* [1968] N.Z.L.R. 716 at 717–718, where the alternative analysis based on lack of mutuality was considered and preferred to expressing the rule in terms of post-notice equities.

"true" equitable set-off,[41] it is necessary that the cross-claim impeach title to the debt such that it would be unjust to allow full payment of the debt without credit being given for the cross-claim. Sometimes, the rule is expressed in terms of the necessity for the cross-claim to flow out of, and be inseparably connected with, the dealings and transactions which also give rise to the debt.[42] It is unclear whether this latter formulation is merely an alternative test of equitable set-off, or a different version of the same test,[43] or even relevant only when determining what post-notice cross-claims rank as equities having priority over the right of the assignee.[44] Occasionally, it is said[45] that whereas the test of "impeach-ment" of title to the legal demand is relevant when considering permiss-ible equitable set-offs between the immediate parties, that is to say, between the assignor and the debtor, the test of "inseparable connection" is used for ascertaining the equities subject to which an assignee takes. For this purpose, the rule of taking subject to equities is but a specific application of the doctrine that a person cannot take the benefit of an obligation without assuming the burdens attaching thereto.[46] If, however, this means that an assignee is subject to the burdens of an assigned contract, the statement is contrary both to principle and authority.[47] Besides, the rule is not that the assignee takes subject to *all* equities; it is that he takes subject only to those equities having priority over his assignment. The approach based on benefit and burden may be a convenient expression of the conclusion that the assignee cannot take free of some equities, but on its own it does not illuminate the category of equities entitled to priority over the assignee.

The truth, probably, is that there is no difference between the "impeachment" and the "inseparable connection" tests. A cross-claim

---

[41] Set-off is recognised in equity in three situations. The first is where a right of set-off exists at law. Its existence will be recognised in equity unless circumstances make reliance on it unjust, *e.g.* because one party is a trustee: *Re Whitehouse* (1878) 9 Ch.D. 595 at 597. The second is that where a debt is equitable only, equity would allow a set-off provided that had it been legal, a set-off would have been allowed at law. Here equity allows set-off by analogy to legal rules: *Clark* v. *Cort* (1840) Cr. & Ph. 154; *Cochrane* v. *Green* (1860) 9 C.B.(N.S.) 448; *Thornton* v. *Maynard* (1875) L.R. 10 C.P. 695; *Tony Lee Motors Ltd.* v. *M.S. MacDonald & Son (1974) Ltd.* [1981] 2 N.Z.L.R. 281. Thirdly, in cases where no question arises, whether of recognising legal rules or of acting by analogy to legal set-off, equity will allow a set-off if the cross-claim impeaches the title to the legal demand or, what is the same thing, if the cross-claim flows out of, and is inseparably connected with, the transaction out of which the claim arose: *Rawson* v. *Samuel* (1839) Cr. & Ph. 161 at 179; *Hanak* v. *Green* [1958] 2 Q.B. 9 at 18 *et seq.*; *Government of Newfoundland* v. *Newfoundland Ry. Co.* (1888) 13 App.Cas. 199 at 212–213. See also, Spry, *Equitable Remedies* (3rd ed., 1984), pp. 173–174. References to "true" equitable set-off are to cases in the third category.

[42] *Government of Newfoundland* v. *Newfoundland Ry. Co.* (1888) 13 App.Cas. 199.

[43] In *Bank of Boston Connecticut* v. *European Grain & Shipping Ltd.* [1989] 2 W.L.R. 440 at 448, Lord Brandon treated it as a different version of the relevant test.

[44] *Business Computers Ltd.* v. *Anglo-African Leasing Ltd.* [1977] 1 W.L.R. 578 at 585 seems to treat inseparable connection as relevant only where the cross-claim sought to be set off arises after notice of assignment.

[45] *Aries Tanker Corporation* v. *Total Transport Ltd. (The Aries)* [1977] 1 W.L.R. 185 at 193, *per* Lord Simon.

[46] *Ibid.* For a similar attempt to apply a generalised principle of benefit and burden, see *Tito* v. *Waddell (No. 2)* [1977] Ch. 106 at 307.

[47] *Young* v. *Kitchin* (1878) 3 Ex.D. 127.

which impeaches the assignee's title to the assigned debt will no doubt be inseparably bound up with the debt. Conversely, a cross-claim which flows out of, and is inseparably connected with, the dealings and transactions which gave rise to the debt is, more than likely, one which impeaches title to the debt. Thus to an action by an assignee against the debtor, the debtor can set up a cross-claim for unliquidated damages arising from breach of the very contract from which the debt arose.[48] An assignee of a simple contract debt cannot take free of unliquidated damages arising from a repudiatory breach of the self-same contract out of which the debt arose, even where the repudiation is accepted after notice of assignment.[49] Where the contract between the assignor and debtor provides that the debtor may deduct from the debt sums due to him from the assignor, the assignee takes subject to the agreement and is bound by a deduction for a post-notice cross-claim provided, it seems, the deduction is in respect of a pre-notice obligation of the assignor.[50] Here, it is not necessary to show that the cross-claim in respect of which the deduction is made has any connection with the debt assigned, the reason being that the debt and the contract of set-off arise from the same transaction and the assignee cannot take the debt without complying with the terms of the contract which qualify the debt obligation. In relations between the debtor and the assignor, it is not all cross-claims which qualify for equitable set-off. For example, unliquidated damages unconnected with the contract from which the debt arose cannot, in the absence of a contrary agreement, be set off against the debt.[51] So also, liquidated claims arising from unsettled accounts between debtor and assignor.[52] Since the debtor cannot assert against the assignee what he cannot set off against the assignor,[53] it follows that such unrelated and unconnected cross-claims, even where they exist at the date of notice of assignment, are not equities having priority over the right of the assgnee.[54] What equities have priority over the assignee's right is a question which has never been explored, let alone conclusively determined. One solution is to say that they are all forms of equitable set-off. This is unsatisfactory because the boundaries of equitable set-off are unmapped[55] and one cannot justifiably make rights of assignees depend on the confused law of equitable set-off.[56] What degree of connection, for instance, need exist

---

[48] *Ibid.*

[49] *Coba Industries Ltd.* v. *Millie's Holdings (Canada) Ltd.* [1985] 6 W.W.R. 14.

[50] *Mangles* v. *Dixon* (1852) 3 H.L. 702; *Rolt* v. *White* (1862) 3 De G.J. & S. 360; *First National Bank of Chicago* v. *West of England Shipowners Mutual Protection & Indemnity Association (Luxembourg) (The Evelpidis Era)* [1981] 1 Lloyd's Rep. 54.

[51] *Bayview Quarries Pty. Ltd.* v. *Castley Development Pty Ltd.* [1963] V.R. 445; *Aboussafy* v. *Abacus Cities Ltd.* [1981] 4 W.W.R. 660.

[52] *Rawson* v. *Samuel* (1839) Cr. & Ph. 161; *Phipps* v. *Child* (1857) 3 Drew 709; *Hill* v. *Ziymack* (1908) 7 C.L.R. 352.

[53] *Bank of Boston Connecticut* v. *European Grain & Shipping Ltd. (The Dominique)* [1989] 2 W.L.R. 440 at 455–456, where a contrary argument was rejected.

[54] *Aboussafy* v. *Abacus Cities Ltd.* [1981] 4 W.W.R. 660.

[55] Despite attempts to do so in *Hanak* v. *Green* [1958] 2 Q.B. 9 at 18 *et seq.*; *Federal Commerce & Navigation Co. Ltd.* v. *Molena Alpha Inc. (The Nanfri)* [1978] Q.B. 927 at 974–975.

[56] See generally, Tettenborn [1987] Conv. 358 at 363 *et seq.*

between a claim and cross-claim before the debtor can be sure of equitable intervention? At one extreme, it is clear that this cannot mean that performance of the obligation on which the cross-claim is based must be a condition precedent to the obligation sued upon,[57] for in such a situation the common law would provide a remedy and there would be no need for equity to intervene.[58] At the other, the fact that the claim and the cross-claim arise from the same contract is neither sufficient nor necessary: insufficient, because some cases stress that something more than the "accident" of the contract being a source of both claim and cross-claim is required[59]; unnecessary, because there are many cases in which claims and cross-claims arising out of separate contracts have been allowed as equitable set-off.[60] Between both extremes lies a long stretch of an intermediate no-man's land where the availability of equitable set-off is unpredictable. This uncertainty is not overcome by saying that we no longer have to dig into old books to find out where the old masters of equity allowed an equitable set-off, being content instead with asking whether it would be unjust to allow the claim without admitting the cross-claim.[61] Such an approach would suggest that equitable set-off is a discretionary relief, the availability of which is to be measured by the length of judges' feet. Clearly, this is not openly admitted to be the law.[62]

Another difficulty with defining permissible equities by reference to the criterion of equitable set-off is the extent to which cross-claims in the nature of counterclaims (not susceptible of equitable set-off) are equities subject to which an assignee takes. In disputes between the assignor and the debtor, the court may in its discretion allow the debtor to enforce a true counterclaim[63] as a procedural set-off and if there is a balance in favour of one of the parties, give judgment for that balance.[64] Should the assignee also take subject to such procedural set-offs? The answer is by no means clear and arguments can be advanced both ways whether or not he should be bound by them. For one thing, factors relevant to the exercise of this discretion in disputes between the assignor and debtor are not necessarily relevant in disputes between the assignee and the debtor; for another, if the discretion is exercised, it may be wrong and unjust as it would involve using rules of procedure to bring about a result contrary to the rights of the parties under substantive law.[65] That would be incon-

---

[57] On the seventeenth century idea of dependency and independency of mutual covenants, see *Nichols* v. *Raynbred* (1615) Hobart 88; *Pordage* v. *Cole* (1669) 1 Wms. Saunders 319h.
[58] *Colonial Bank* v. *European Grain & Shipping Ltd. (The Dominique)* [1988] 3 W.L.R. 60 at 76, rvsd. [1989] 2 W.L.R. 440, H.L. (not on this point).
[59] *Rawson* v. *Samuel* (1839) Cr. & Ph. 161 at 179.
[60] *Bankes* v. *Jarvis* [1903] 1 K.B. 549; *British Anzani (Felixstowe) Ltd.* v. *International Marine Management (UK) Ltd.* [1980] Q.B. 137; *Holt* v. *Telford* [1987] 6 W.W.R. 385.
[61] Cf. *Federal Commerce & Navigation Co. Ltd.* v. *Molena Alpha Inc. (The Nanfri)* [1978] Q.B. 927 at 974.
[62] *BICC plc* v. *Burndy* [1985] Ch. 232 at 248.
[63] A true counterclaim operates not merely as a defence, as does a set-off, but in all respects as a weapon of offence, an independent action by the defendant against the plaintiff: *Stooke* v. *Taylor* (1880) 5 Q.B.D. 569 at 575–577.
[64] R.S.C., Ord. 15, r. 2(4). For a collection of cases showing how this discretion has been exercised in practice, see Wood, *English and International Set-Off* (1989), paras. 6–49 *et seq.*
[65] *Bank of Boston Connecticut* v. *European Grain & Shipping Ltd. (The Dominique)* [1989] 2 W.L.R. 440 at 455.

sistent with the principle that the Judicature Acts, while making important changes in procedure, did not alter, and were not intended to alter, the rights of the parties under substantive law.[66] This is more so in cases where under substantive law the debtor has no set-off against the assignor, whether this be because of the absence of the relevant connection[67] or because the debt assigned is a claim insulated from set-off.[68] Further, to allow such counterclaims as procedural set-offs in all cases where the assignee sues for the debt would undermine the fundamental principle that the assignee ought not to be in a worse position than the assignor. Yet this would be the result since, even as between the assignor and debtor, this form of procedural set-off is available only in some cases and at the discretion of the court. There is obviously something to be said against making the collectible value of an assigned debt depend on the vagaries of judicial charity. This, however, is only one side of the story. In support of permitting the debtor to plead a true counterclaim as a procedural set-off, and hence an equity against the assignee, it may be said that assignment law ought not to prejudice the debtor who is powerless to stop the assignment. If procedural set-off is always denied, then those cases where it may be invoked against the assignor will be forever foreclosed. There is no *a priori* reason why a debt should be worth more in the hands of the assignee than in those of the assignor whose title the assignee asserts. Were it otherwise, the law will be departing from its commitment to the principle that the debtor should fare no worse with the assignee than he would have with the assignor, unless, of course, it can be shown that there is no such unequivocal commitment on the part of the law.[69] Considerations of this nature suggest that the law has yet to tackle satisfactorily the question of how best to treat matters affecting the performance of the contract from which the debt assigned arises. Unlike matters affecting the formation of the contract which are equities subject to which an assignee takes, the treatment of matters affecting the performance of the contract is unclear.

There are *dicta* in support of the view that the rule by which an assignee takes subject to equities has nothing at all to do with equitable set-off.[70] Academic support is not lacking.[71] These dicta can be defended if they mean that "equities" cover more ground than equitable set-off, since equities could include the debtor's substantive right to rescind the contract where it is vitiated by a matter affecting its formation, which cannot be a matter of set-off. But how much more is unclear. Nor is there

---

[66] *Stumore* v. *Campbell & Co.* [1892] 1 Q.B. 314 at 316, 318.

[67] As in *Aboussafy* v. *Abacus Cities Ltd.* [1981] 4 W.W.R. 660.

[68] As in *Bank of Boston Connecticut* v. *European Grain & Shipping Ltd. (The Dominique)*, *supra*.

[69] *Cf. Stoddart* v. *Union Trust Ltd.* [1912] 1 K.B. 181; *Provident Finance Corp. Ltd.* v. *Hammond* [1978] V.R. 312.

[70] *McDonnell & East Ltd.* v. *McGregor* (1936) 56 C.L.R. 50 at 60; *Provident Finance Corp. Ltd.* v. *Hammond, supra* at 320; *Aries Tanker Corp.* v. *Total Transport Ltd. (The Aries)* [1977] 1 W.L.R. 185 at 193.

[71] Meagher, Gummow and Lehane, *Equity: Doctrines and Remedies* (2nd ed., 1984), para. 3710; Spry, (1969) 43 A.L.J. 265 at 269 *et seq.*; Spry, *Equitable Remedies* (3rd ed., 1984), pp. 175–176; *cf.* Derham, *Set Off* (1987), p. 315.

any case, so far as I am aware, where a true counterclaim was enforced as an equity binding on an assignee. The cases[72] usually cited for the opposite view did not, however, involve cross-claims in the nature of counterclaims at all, but merely cross-claims in the nature of true equitable set-offs, albeit the language of counterclaim was used.[73] In this state of the law the only safe conclusion is that the assignee takes his assignment subject to all legal and equitable defences which the debtor has to liability, for example, that the contract is voidable because of a matter affecting its formation, or that a condition precedent to the debt obligation has failed, or that the debtor has accepted a repudiatory breach committed by the assignor, or again, that the debt assigned is only an item in the running account with the assignor. The assignee also takes subject to the debtor's common law defences in the nature of payment,[74] common law abatement, and all legal and equitable set-offs which would have been available against the assignor. These are all equities having priority over the right of the assignee. But how much of true counterclaims is included in the debtor's equities remains at best a matter for speculation.

However, not all equities of the debtor are entitled to priority over the assignee's right. In some cases the ineligible categories of equities are treated as personal to the assignor and debtor and therefore not binding on the assignee.[75] In others, the equities, although impersonal, were not enforced against the assignee either because the debtor had contracted not to assert them against the assignor and the benefit of the agreement passed to the assignee,[76] or because the nature of the contract insulated

---

[72] *Young* v. *Kitchin* (1878) 3 Ex.D. 127; *Government of Newfoundland* v. *Newfoundland Ry. Co.* (1888) 13 App.Cas. 199.

[73] This is the explanation of the *Newfoundland Case* adopted by Sellers L.J. in *Hanak* v. *Green* [1958] 2 Q.B. 8 at 31, and by Lord Brandon in *The Dominique* [1989] 2 W.L.R. 440 at 449.

[74] See *British Anzani (Felixstowe) Ltd.* v. *International Marine Management (UK) Ltd.* [1980] Q.B. 137 at 147 *et seq.*

[75] *Stoddart* v. *Union Trust Ltd.* [1912] 1 K.B. 181; *Provident Finance Corp Ltd.* v. *Hammond* [1978] V.R. 312.

[76] The agreement not to enforce equities may be express as in *Higgs* v. *Northern Assam Tea Co. Ltd.* (1869) L.R. 4 Exch. 387, *Re Goy & Co. Ltd.* [1900] 2 Ch. 149, *Phoenix Assurance Co. Ltd.* v. *Earl's Court Ltd.* (1913) 30 T.L.R. 50; or implied from the nature of the debt instrument, as in *Re Agra & Masterman's Bank* (1867) L.R. 2 Ch.App. 391, *Re Blakely Ordnance Co.* (1867) L.R. 3 Ch.App. 154, *Re General Estate Co.* (1868) L.R. 3 Ch.App. 758, *Hilger Analytical Ltd.* v. *Rank Precision Industries Ltd.* [1984] B.C.L.C. 301. Generally, debentures are payable to bearer or to registered holder: see Companies Act 1985, s.183. Bearer debentures are treated as negotiable securities transferable free of equities: *Bechuanaland Exploration Co.* v. *London Trading Bank Ltd.* [1898] 2 Q.B. 658. Whether other types are so transferable is a matter of construction and where the language is not explicit enough to exclude equities, the courts lean in favour of the rule that the transferee of a debt transferable only in equity before the Judicature Act 1873, s.25(6), takes subject to equities: *Re Natal Investment Co.* (1868) L.R. 3 Ch.App. 355; *Re Palmer's Decoration & Furnishing Co.* [1904] 2 Ch. 743. Unlike insolvency set-off, there is no overriding policy which prevents solvent parties from contracting not to plead equities. Early case law denying this possibility (*Lechmere* v. *Hawkins* (1798) 2 Esp. 626; *Taylor* v. *Okey* (1806) 13 Ves.Jun. 180; *M'Gillivray* v. *Simson* (1826) 2 C. & P. 320) can no longer be regarded as authoritative: see *Hong Kong & Shanghai Banking Corp.* v. *Kloeckner & Co. AG* [1989] 2 Lloyd's Rep. 323.

the assignee from such equities.[77] In the case of negotiable debts, the quality of negotiability insulates some holders[78] of the instrument embodying the debt from cross-claims arising from the contract in respect of which the instrument was issued.[79] Here the equities are treated as collateral to the contract evidenced by the instrument[80] or denied effect on the ground that the instrument is autonomous of, and independent from, the underlying contract in respect of which it was issued.[81]

It is sometimes said[82] that the equitable doctrine of bona fide purchaser for value without notice has no application to choses in action. This, however, is only partly sound and to this extent: the assignee of a chose in action transferable only in equity cannot invoke the bona fide purchaser rule so as to override the obligor's equities entitled to priority over his assignment.[83] The rule in question, however, is a great deal narrower. For one thing, it is unclear whether it applies to a statutory assignee of a legal chose in action[84]; for another, the rule has no application to the assignee of a chose in action transferable at law before

---

[77] This is certainly true of the assignee of freight since freight is insulated from cross-claims whether arising from short delivery and damage to cargo, as in *Henriksens Rederi A/S* v. *THZ Rolimpex (The Brede)* [1974] Q.B. 233, *Aries Tanker Corp* v. *Total Transport Ltd. (The Aries)* [1977] 1 W.L.R. 185; or failure to prosecute a voyage with reasonable dispatch, as in *A/S Gunnstein & Co. K/S* v. *Jensen (The Alpha Nord)* [1977] 2 Lloyd's Rep. 434; or otherwise: *Cleobulus Shipping Co. Ltd.* v. *Intertanker Ltd. (The Cleon)* [1983] 1 Lloyd's Rep. 586, *Elena Shipping Ltd.* v. *Aidenfield Ltd. (The Elena)* [1986] 1 Lloyd's Rep. 425. In *Bank of Boston Connecticut* v. *European Grain & Shipping Ltd. (The Dominique)* [1989] 2 W.L.R. 440, the House of Lords extended the rule against deduction from freight to advance freight due under a charterparty which the shipowner repudiated before the freight became payable. See also *Freedom Maritime Corp.* v. *International Bulk Carriers SA (The Khian Captain) (No. 2)* [1986] 1 Lloyd's Rep. 429. However, a line of cases appears to treat hire as different from freight, so that the rule against deduction from freight does not insulate hire from cross-claims: *Federal Commerce & Navigation Co. Ltd.* v. *Molena Alpha Inc. (The Nanfri)* [1978] Q.B. 927, C.A.; *Santiren Shipping Ltd.* v. *Unimarine SA (The Chrysovalandou-Dyo)* [1981] 1 Lloyd's Rep. 159. Despite attempts to confine deduction from hire to cross-claims arising from deprivation of, or prejudice to, the charterer's use of the vessel (*Leon Corp.* v. *Atlantic Lines & Navigation Co. Inc. (The Leon)* [1985] 2 Lloyd's Rep. 470), it cannot be taken as settled that there can be deduction for hire. For one thing, the distinction between hire and freight is not, it is thought, sufficient to justify the widely varying treatment accorded to both, probably more so as hire and freight are both rewards for services. Now that the rule against deduction from freight is well established it is better to assimilate hire into the rule against deduction. See, generally, Rose [1982] L.M.C.L.Q. 33. For a good general survey of claims insulated from cross-claims, see Wood, *English and International Set-Off* (1989), Chap. 12.

[78] The original payee of a negotiable debt cannot be a holder in due course: *R.E. Jones Ltd.* v. *Waring & Gillow Ltd.* [1926] A.C. 670.

[79] *Nova (Jersey) Knit Ltd.* v. *Kammagarn Spinneri GmbH* [1977] 1 W.L.R. 713. The rule is the same for letters of credit: *Hong Kong & Shanghai Banking Corp.* v. *Kloeckner & Co. AG* [1989] 2 Lloyd's Rep. 323. Failure of consideration is not a defence or a set-off if the holder of the instrument is a holder in due course: *Archer* v. *Bamford* (1822) 3 Stark 175.

[80] The rule is the same for indorsees of overdue instruments: see *Burrough* v. *Moss* (1830) 10 B. & C. 558; *Stein* v. *Yglesias* (1834) 1 C.M. & R. 565; *Whitehead* v. *Walker* (1842) 10 M. & W. 696; *Oulds* v. *Harrison* (1854) 10 Exch. 572.

[81] See cases cited in n. 79, *supra.*

[82] Derham, *Set Off* (1987), p. 246, n. 7.

[83] *Peters* v. *Soame* (1701) 2 Vern. 428; *Turton* v. *Benson* (1718) 2 Vern. 764 at 765; *Ord* v. *White* (1840) 3 Beav. 357 at 365; *Athenaeum Life Society* v. *Pooley* (1858) 3 De G. & J. 294 at 296.

[84] See para. 6.14, *supra.*

the Judicature Acts. Such an assignee takes free of the debtor's equities against the assignor.[85] This is still the law and provides theoretical explanation for the immunity of a transferee of a negotiable debt from equities arising from the contract in respect of which the negotiable instrument was issued, at any rate, in the case of transfers effected before the instrument is overdue.[86] The rule also explains the preservation in section 25(6) of the Judicature Act 1873 of equities vested in the debtor when the possibility of legal assignments was enacted in that statute.

As indicated above, equities personal to the assignor and the debtor are not included in the category of equities entitled to priority over the assignee. The scope of such equities is unclear. One category for which there is rather slender support is damages for the fraudulent misrepresentation of the assignor inducing the contract with the debtor. In *Stoddart* v. *Union Trust Ltd.*[87] the debtor bought a football magazine from the assignor induced by a fraudulent misrepresentation as to the value and weekly circulation of the paper, and sold it to a third party. The assignor assigned the unpaid balance to the plaintiff. In an action by the plaintiff the debtor pleaded that as a result of the fraud and consequential loss arising therefrom, nothing more was due under the contract. The Court of Appeal held that the damages could not be set up as equities against the plaintiff assignee. One reason for this was that the debtor's cross-claim for damages was not sufficiently connected with the plaintiff's claim.[88] In this respect the decision is consistent with the denial (as equities) of unliquidated damages unconnected with the contract. This, however, is not too convincing, for it is difficult to see how much more connection is required, and the case may in fact conceal a judicial discretion not to disappoint the legitimate expectations of bona fide assignees in borderline and doubtful cases. Another reason for the decision may be the reluctance of the court to permit a debtor to repudiate his obligation under a contract in the name of equities, without setting the contract aside.[89] If this be the true explanation, it may be that this has ceased to be so after the Misrepresentation Act 1967,[90] at any rate in cases of innocent misrepresentation. A further explanation is that the debtor's cross-claim for damages for the fraud which induced the contract

---

[85] *Ashwin* v. *Burton* (1862) 7 L.T. 589; *Taylor* v. *Blakelock* (1886) 32 Ch.D. 560 at 567.
[86] Bills of Exchange Act 1882, ss.29(2) and 38(1). See generally Ellinger, *Modern Banking Law* (1987), pp. 506–510.
[87] [1912] 1 K.B. 181. See also *Provident Finance Corp. Ltd.* v. *Hammond* [1978] V.R. 312. *Cf. Re Palmer's Decoration & Furnishing Co.* [1904] 2 Ch. 743.
[88] [1912] 1 K.B. 181 at 191.
[89] *Ibid.* at 192. The right to set aside the contract for fraud was not asserted, no doubt, because it was thought not to be available after the buyer had sold the newspaper to a third party. For the argument that the victim of a criminal fraud can rely on it by way of defence without making restitution, see Treitel, *Law of Contract* (7th ed., 1987), pp. 286–287. *Berg* v. *Sadler & Moore* [1937] 2 K.B. 158, relied upon for the argument turned, however, on illegality and involved a claim by the fraudulent buyer. Therefore it seems a weak authority for the view that the victim of a criminal fraud can rely on it as a defence against an assignee of the purchase price without making restitution.
[90] Under s.2(2). This is unlikely because where a buyer has lost the right to rescind, *e.g.* because restitution is impossible, he does not come within s.2(2): Treitel, *op. cit.*, p. 275. *Cf.* Tettenborn [1987] Conv. 358 at 362–363.

was strictly a personal claim against the wrongdoer, *i.e.* the assignor, and so was something *dehors* the contract.[91] This is curious for many reasons. First, it has never been the law that cross-claims arising outside the contract giving rise to the debt sued upon cannot be set off against the debt.[92] Secondly, it is not easy to distinguish it from cases where the debtor's allegation is breach of a warranty collateral to the contract out of which the debt arose and in which damages for the breach were allowed as equities enforceable against the assignee.[93] Thirdly, it makes an assignment more valuable in the hands of an assignee than in those of the assignor.[94] For these reasons it is thought that *Stoddart*[95] is best explained as a decision based on its own facts, and not an authority for the view that damages for a misrepresentation inducing a contract are equities personal to the assignor and debtor.

Equities enforceable against the assignee are confined to those valid against the assignor whose title the assignee asserts. Where, therefore, an assignee indebted to the debtor assigns his claim to a third party (the second assignee), the debtor cannot set off the debt owed by the first assignee against the second assignee's claim based on the assigned debt.[96]

Temporal aspect of "equities"

One of the most confused aspects of the rule as to taking an assignment **8.3** subject to equities is the ascertainment of the date after which the debtor's equities are not binding on the assignee. The cases are replete with statements that after notice of an assignment the debtor cannot do anything to diminish the assignee's claim.[97] For this reason, notice of assignment fixes the date for ascertaining the debtor's equities subject to which the debtor takes although, exceptionally, the rule grudgingly allows post-notice equities if they flow out of, and are inseparably connected with, the contract which gave rise to the assigned debt.[98] If this exception

---

[91] [1912] 1 K.B. 181 at 194.

[92] *Bankes* v. *Jarvis* [1903] 1 K.B. 549; *British Anzani (Felixstowe) Ltd.* v. *International Marine Management (UK) Ltd.* [1980] Q.B. 137; *Holt* v. *Telford* [1987] 6 W.W.R. 385.

[93] *Lawrence* v. *Hayes* [1927] 2 K.B. 111; *Sun Candies Pty. Ltd.* v. *Polites* [1939] V.L.R. 132. Although *Stoddart* was cited in argument in both cases, in neither was it followed. In the first, there was no reference to it in the judgment of the Divisional Court. In the second, it was distinguished on the tenuous ground that in *Stoddart* the assignee was the claimant, but in the instant case it was the assignor.

[94] Cf. *Jack* v. *Kipping* (1882) 9 Q.B.D. 113, where the trustee in bankruptcy of a vendor who had induced the defendant to buy shares by fraudulent misrepresentation was held subject to the defendant's set-off for unliquidated damages for the fraud. The argument that the defendant's equity was a personal tort was rejected, and the contract of purchase was not rescinded. See also *Re Palmer's Decoration & Furnishing Co.* [1904] 2 Ch. 743.

[95] [1912] 1 K.B. 181.

[96] *Re Milan Tramways Co., ex p. Theys* (1883) 25 Ch.D. 587; *Banco Central SA* v. *Lingoss & Falce Ltd. (The Raven)* [1980] 2 Lloyd's Rep. 266.

[97] *Roxburghe* v. *Cox* (1878) 17 Ch.D. 520 at 526; *Brice* v. *Bannister* (1878) 3 Q.B.D. 569 at 577; *Colonial Bank* v. *European Grain & Shipping Ltd.* [1987] 1 Lloyd's Rep. 239 at 252, 258 (Hobhouse J.).

[98] *Smith* v. *Parkes* (1852) 16 Beav. 115; *Government of Newfoundland Ry. Co.* (1888) 13 App.Cas. 199; *Coba Industries Ltd.* v. *Millie's Holdings (Canada) Ltd.* [1985] 6 W.W.R. 14; *Business Computers Ltd.* v. *Anglo-African Leasing Ltd.* [1977] 1 W.L.R. 578 at 585.

is well-founded, it could emasculate the so-called general rule denying that the debtor's post-notice equities could be enforced against the assignee. This is because the "inseparable connection" rule is the test of true equitable set-off, and equitable set-off constitutes the bulk of the debtor's equities. It would therefore be preferable to say that the debtor can, as a general rule, assert post-notice equities which are true equitable set-offs, provided that where the equities are statutory set-offs or common law defences of abatement and payment, notice of assignment fixes the date after which they may not be enforced against the assignee. This is in fact the law.[99]

At law, before the Judicature Acts, where an assignee of a debt brought an action in the name of the assignor, the debtor was originally entitled to set up all such legal defences and rights of set-off as he had against the assignor at the date the assignee's action was brought.[1] This is understandable since the common law courts looked to mutuality at law. As the debt remained at law the property of the assignor, this was sufficient to establish the requisite mutuality. The result was unjust and on occasion enabled the debtor to extinguish the assigned debt by liquidated cross-claims arising after notice of assignment. For this reason, a court of equity would restrain the debtor from making use of any defence or statutory set-off which he could not have made use of against the assignor if the action had been brought at the time when notice of the assignment was given.[2] This approach gave effect to the assignee's beneficial ownership. From this the rule became established that notice of assignment crystallises the debtor's equities enforceable against the assignee. In proclaiming the rule the courts were not careful to limit it to statutory set-offs and common law defences of abatement and payment which were purely procedural defences designed to avoid circuity of action. But even so limited, there remains the difficulty of ascertaining what liquidated cross-claims are enforceable equities. Two areas of difficulty will be considered. The first is the treatment of cross-claims which are contingent at the date of notice. The second is the question whether the crystallisation of the debtor's equities at the date of notice applies where what is assigned is an executory contract under which nothing is due, or is a pure expectancy.

With regard to contingent cross-claims, the rule is often represented to be that a cross-claim which is not *due* at the date of notice of assignment is not an equity subject to which the assignee takes,[3] even if it arises from the same contract as the debt assigned. A refinement of the rule is said to be that not only must the cross-claim be due at the date of notice of assignment, it must also be payable before the assigned debt becomes payable.[4] One reason for not recognising contingent cross-claims is that if the debt assigned has become payable it is unfair to ask the assignee who

---

[99] *Ibid.*
[1] *Ashburner's Principles of Equity* (2nd ed., 1933), p. 241.
[2] *Ibid.*
[3] *Jeffryes* v. *Agra & Masterman's Bank* (1866) L.R. 2 Eq. 674; *Christie* v. *Taunton, Delmard, Lane & Co.* [1893] 2 Ch. 175; *Re Pinto Leite & Nephews* [1929] 1 Ch. 221.
[4] *Jeffryes* v. *Agra & Masterman's Bank* (1866) L.R. 2 Eq. 674 at 680.

may have given value to wait until the cross-claim asserted as an equity matures into an actual debt and becomes payable. Another reason is valuation. Where the debtor's equity depends on a contingency which may or may not occur, valuation becomes no more reliable than a simple guess. This, however, is not always true particularly where, as is often the case, the contingency has since occurred. The problem here is the rather incautiously wide statement of principle found in the cases asserting the rule of exclusion. An examination of these cases reveals that the rule is not as wide as is often represented. Besides, there is a confusion of contingent liabilities strictly so called, with debts due but payment of which is subject to a contingency bound to occur. The loose use of the words "accruing due," "owing," "accrued due," etc., does not help to clarify the distinction between accrued obligations performance of which is contingent on a future event which is bound to happen, and truly contingent obligations where both the obligation and its performance are contingent.[5] Nowhere else is this confusion more pronounced than in relation to accruing debts which accumulate gradually over time.

In *Jeffryes* v. *Agra and Masterman's Bank*,[6] a bank indebted to a customer sought to set off against an assignee of the debt the customer's contingent liability as an indorsee of certain bills of exchange of which the bank was the holder for value. It was held that the bank could not do so as the customer's liability was contingent on dishonour by the acceptor. It is clear that the bank was asserting a procedural set-off under the Statutes of Set Off,[7] and that the customer was merely a surety guaranteeing payment of the amount of the bills if the acceptor did not pay.[8] In this sense the bank's cross-claim was wholly conditional. If the acceptor paid on maturity there would be nothing due from the customer. Not only was the time of payment of the cross-claim contingent, the customer's obligation was also contingent. It is easy to see why the court was reluctant to allow a claim for payment of the debt not to be unduly held up because the assignor guaranteed payment of other bills of which the bank was a holder. This reasoning also explains *Re Pinto Leite & Nephews*[9] where a statutory set-off of the debtor's contingent cross-claim based on accomodation bills indorsed by the assignor was held not to be an equity subject to which the assignee took. In *Christie* v. *Taunton, Delmard, Lane and Co.*[10] an assignee was held not bound by the assignor's contingent liability to the debtor arising from calls made on the assignor's shares after notice of the assignment. Today, liability for calls is

---

[5] *Mortimer* v. *IRC* (1864) 2 H. & C. 838 at 851. See also para. 2.6, *supra*, for a discussion of the distinction between existing, future and contingent obligations.
[6] (1866) L.R. 2 Eq. 674.
[7] These are the Insolvent Debtors Relief Act 1729, s.13 and Set Off Act 1735, ss.4 and 5. Both were repealed by the Civil Procedure Acts Repeal Act 1879, s.2, but the power to allow set-off which they conferred was preserved first, in s.4(1) of the same statute, and later by ss.38 and 39(1)(*a*) of the Supreme Court of Judicature Act (Consolidation) Act 1925. Today the same power is exercised by virtue both of the Supreme Court Act 1981, s.49(2) and R.S.C., Ord. 18, r. 17.
[8] *Rowe* v. *Young* (1820) 2 Bligh's Reports 391 at 467.
[9] [1929] 1 Ch. 221.
[10] [1893] 2 Ch. 175.

by statute made a present debt payable in future[11] and it may be that if *Christie's* case is decided now the result may well be different unless, perhaps, the dictum[12] suggesting that the cross-claim must have become payable before the assigned debt is due for payment is good law. So explained, the result in the cases is perfectly sensible. But when one considers cross-claims, not based on bills of exchange, which are contingent only in the sense that performance is conditional on counter-performance by the assignor, or on some other event which is bound to happen, it is not easy to see how the reasoning in the above cases can be relevant. In all but *Christie* the performance of the cross-claim was not just contingent; the very existence of the obligation itself was contingent. Yet in *Business Computers Ltd.* v. *Anglo-African Leasing Ltd.*,[13] Templeman J. considered these cases relevant in denying (as an equity binding on a floating chargee whose security had crystallized) the debtor's cross-claim for damages for a breach committed by the chargor before notice of assignment. In his view it would have been different if the debtor had exercised his right to accelerate the cross-claim when the chargor defaulted. But how can one accelerate an obligation which is not owed? The idea behind an acceleration clause is that the obligation is presently due but time for performance is deferred, so that the period of deferral is in effect a credit period.[14] *Holt* v. *Telford*[15] shows exactly how far this confusion has been carried. There, A and B made mutual secured loans to each other on terms that B was to repay A (when time for repayment came) only the amount by which A's loan to B exceeded B's loan to A. A assigned his loan to C who now claimed payment from B. The Supreme Court of Canada held that as B's loan was contingent (it had not become repayable), it was not an equity subject to which C took. The agreement between A and B for set-off was unenforceable against C because B's loan was still contingent. However, as the two loans were closely connected, B could assert an equitable set-off against C. The court reached the right conclusion, but was apparently led astray by failing to distinguish between a present debt payable in future and a debt whose existence and time of payment are both contingent. Also, it is not easy to see how a set-off agreement can be held to be unenforceable simply because time for payment of the cross-claim is postponed. Such agreements should be enforceable even where the cross-claim is truly contingent.[16]

It has been argued[17] that the better rule is one which allows, as enforceable equities, cross-debts which are in existence at the date of the

---

[11] Insolvency Act 1986, s.80.

[12] *Jeffryes* v. *Agra & Masterman's Bank* (1866) L.R. 2 Eq. 674 at 680.

[13] [1977] 1 W.L.R. 578.

[14] *Wallingford* v. *Mutual Society* (1880) 5 App.Cas. 685 at 696; *Re Emerald Christmas Tree Co.* (1979) 105 D.L.R. (3d) 75.

[15] [1987] 6 W.W.R. 385.

[16] *Cf.* Wood, *op. cit.*, para. 16–36. Where there is a contractual right to set off a contingent cross-claim, although the question remains one of construction, the agreement may in fact be two rights rolled into one: first, a right to suspend payment of the assigned debt, and secondly, when the contingent cross-claim becomes a liquidated existing liability, to set it off against the assigned debt: Goode, *Legal Problems of Credit and Security* (2nd ed., 1988), p. 173.

[17] Derham, *Set Off* (1987), p. 312; Wood, *op. cit.*, para. 16–47.

assignee's action to recover the assigned debt, provided they arise out of obligations incurred before notice. The argument is presumably limited to equities in the nature of statutory set-off, abatement and payment at common law, and some hybrid set-offs where equity acts by analogy to statutory set-offs in cases where, had the debt and cross-claim been legal interests, set-off under the statute would have been available.[18] In all these instances the set-off is merely procedural and in disputes between assignor and debtor the cross-claims would have been allowed if they arose before commencement of the action to recover the debt.[19] Where the equity asserted by the debtor is a cross-claim inseparably connected with the assigned debt, it is binding on the assignee even if it arises only after notice of assignment[20] provided it was in existence at the date of commencement of the action to recover the debt.[21] The same is true where the equity asserted is based on a contractual set-off.[22] A fair rule is one which allows the debtor to set off all his cross-claims based on the contract irrespective of whether they arise before or after notice of assignment.[23] The justification for such an approach is that in many cases there is no way in which the debtor could have avoided giving effective credit to the assignor[24] short of cancelling the contract and possibly exposing himself to damages for breach. This suggestion should not apply to equities based on legal or statutory set-off which are designed to avoid circuity of action.

Where what is assigned is an executory contract out of which debts may arise in future, English law treats the future debts as existing choses in action.[25] If the assignee gives notice of his assignment before the debt arises, can the debtor raise as equities cross-claims based on the contract which arise afterwards, albeit before the assigned debt arises? This point is undecided, but it seems that in principle the cross-claim should be enforceable against the assignee. One way of expressing this conclusion is to say that the debt from an executory contract does not arise except subject to the debtor's cross-claim.[26] This is so whether or not the cross-claim would have been eligible for equitable set-off. Where expectant debts[27] are assigned and notice is given to the prospective debtors, the notice is ineffectual for the purpose of securing the priority of the assignee.[28] Is the notice similarly ineffectual for purposes of the rule that

[18] See p. 228, n. 41, *supra.*
[19] *Richards* v. *James* (1848) 2 Exch. 471.
[20] See p. 235, n. 98, *supra.*
[21] *Edmunds* v. *Lloyds Italico SpA* [1986] 1 W.L.R. 492. See also R.S.C., Ord. 18, r. 9 (a party may plead any matter which had arisen at any time whether before or since the issue of the writ).
[22] *The Evelpidis Era* [1981] 1 Lloyd's Rep. 54.
[23] This is the position under American Law: see UCC Art. 9–318.
[24] Tettenborn [1987] Conv. 358 at 364.
[25] See para. 2.6, *supra*, where this is discussed.
[26] On a reasoning similar to that used in *Rother Iron Works Ltd.* v. *Canterbury Precision Engineers Ltd.* [1974] Q.B. 1 at 6.
[27] Expectant debts are those which have no present existence. The contract from which they will arise exists only in contemplation. See para. 2.6, *supra.*
[28] *Calisher* v. *Forbes* (1871) L.R. 7 Ch.App. 109; *Johnstone* v. *Cox* (1880) 16 Ch.D. 571 affd. (1881) 19 Ch.D. 17, C.A.; *Re Dallas* [1904] 2 Ch. 385; *Re Kinahan's Trusts* [1907] 1 Ir.R. 321.

notice of assignment crystallises the debtor's equities enforceable against the debtor? On one view[29] the notice is effectual and no cross-claim arising after the notice can be enforced as an equity against the assignee. This view is curious. True it is that a notice ineffectual for priority purposes is not useless altogether. But it does not follow that an assignee of expectant receivables can take free of the debtor's equities (howsoever arising) which come into existence after the notice of assignment. For one thing, the purported assignment is an empty shell devoid of content before the debt arises; for another, the notice is ineffectual because it was given to a person who was not a debtor at the date of the notice. The rule which crystallises some of the debtor's equities at the date of notice of assignment assumes that at that date there were both a debt and a debtor from whom the debt is due and to whom for this purpose notice of an assignment may be brought home. That rule, however, has no application where what is assigned is an expectancy and where the cross-claim arises either before the debt arises, or simultaneously with the debt, or even afterwards, provided in this case the cross-claim is eligible for true equitable set-off. In *Canadian Admiral Corp. Ltd.* v. *L.F. Dommerich & Co. Inc.*,[30] an assignor factored his receivables. Sales invoices sent to customers were stamped with notice of the assignment and payments were for some time made to the factor. Subsequently, one customer sold goods on credit to the assignor and later purchased goods from the assignor, the invoice containing the usual notice of assignment. The customer refused to pay for the goods, claiming a legal set-off of the debt owed by the assignor. Both the trial judge and the Ontario Court of Appeal denied the set-off principally on the ground that the customer knew that the factor was the assignee not only of existing debts, but also of future debts, and the customer's cross-debt was unconnected with the dealings giving rise to the debts assigned to the factor. The Supreme Court of Canada was not persuaded by this reasoning and (rightly, it is submitted) allowed an appeal by the customer. The factoring agreement was not itself an assignment. Only the specific assignments in respect of which invoices were sent to the debtor were operative. The customer, therefore, received notice of assignment of each debt for the first time when the invoice was submitted to the factor in accordance with the master agreement. Although the factoring here utilised the structure of a facultative agreement,[31] it is submitted that the same reasoning should apply to a "whole turnover" agreement in so far as it involves an assignment of expectant receivables.

Debtor's right to modify or rescind underlying contract

8.4   The problem which we are about to discuss is the extent to which the debtor and assignor can modify or rescind the contract from which the

---

[29] Wood, *op. cit.*, para. 16–117.
[30] (1964) 43 D.L.R. (2d) 1 (Sup.Ct. of Canada).
[31] For the distinction between facultative and whole turnover agreements, see para. 3.2, *supra*.

assigned debt arises after notice of assignment. Put differently, is the debtor's right to modify or rescind the contract an equity subject to which an assignee takes? On the surface, this question admits of an obvious answer: there can be no modification or rescission after notice of assignment. James L.J.[32] affirmed this conclusion when he denied that, after notice of assignment, the debtor can do anything, by payment or otherwise, to diminish the assigned debt. This is the general rule but it needs some qualification. It is suggested that a distinction must be drawn between modification or rescission of an executory contract on one hand and modification or rescission of an executed contract on the other. As a statement of principle governing the modification or rescission of an executed contract, James L.J.'s proposition is unexceptionable. Where the assigned debt has become earned by performance, any purported modification or rescission of the underlying contract is a thing writ in water. In *Brice* v. *Bannister*,[33] a contractor assigned £100 to a creditor at a time when £500 was already earned under the building contract with his employer. Notice of this assignment was given to the employer. Shortly after that the contractor ran into difficulties and the employer advanced money to him to enable him to complete the contract. This was in effect a prepayment in disregard of the notice of assignment. A majority of the Court of Appeal held that the employer was liable to pay the assignee again. The assignment operated as an equitable charge on the £500 which the builder had earned at the date of notice of the assignment. This result is consistent with principle but seems unduly harsh on the employer. The employer might have terminated the building contract when the builder ran into difficulties and engaged someone else. In that event he would not have been liable to the assignee as regards future debts.[34] On the facts of *Brice* v. *Bannister*, this right of termination would not have made any difference to the result because at the date of notice £500 was already earned, of which the plaintiff held an assignment of £100. Had nothing been earned under the contract at the date of notice of assignment, the result would probably have been different.[35]

---

[32] *Roxburghe* v. *Cox* (1878) 17 Ch.D. 520 at 526. See also *The Evelpidis Era* [1981] 1 Lloyd's Rep. 54 at 56. The discussion in the text assumes that there is no specific provision in the contract permitting post-notice modification or rescission.

[33] (1878) 3 Q.B.D. 569.

[34] *Tooth* v. *Hallett* (1869) L.R. 4 Ch.App. 242. American pre-UCC law distinguished between a post-notice payment of a debt to the assignor and a post-notice advance to the assignor to enable him to perform the contract. The latter, but not the former, was binding on the assignee: *Fricker* v. *Uddo & Taormina Co.* (1957) 312 P. 2d 1085; 2 Gilmore, *Security Interests in Personal Property* (1965), paras. 41.8 *et seq.* In *Peden Iron & Steel Co.* v. *McKnight* (1910) 128 S.W. 156 at 159 the court said:

> "When the existence of the assigned fund is dependent upon performance by the assignor of an executory contract, the anticipatory debtor may do whatever reasonably appears to be necessary to enable the assignor to perform the contract."

UCC, Art. 9–318(2) makes post-notice good faith modifications of an executory contract by the assignor and debtor without the assignee's consent effective against the assignee. This approach is sound and indeed necessary in view of the realities of long-term contracts. The assignee is protected by carrying his rights through to the modified or substituted contract.

[35] (1878) 3 Q.B.D. 569 at 577.

Different considerations arise where a debtor seeks to modify or rescind an executory contract the benefit of which has been assigned, after receiving notice of an assignment. In one sense all contractual rights are vested the moment the contract is made even if the contract is wholly executory. It may therefore be thought that after notice of assignment the debtor and the assignor are no longer free to modify or rescind the contract, at any rate where this involves divestment of the assignee. This analysis has a superficial appeal. If parties to an executory contract cannot modify it to adjust to altered circumstances because the creditor of the debt obligation decides to assign his expectant entitlement before the entitlement is earned, the result is slavery.[36] There is nothing either in principle or in the authorities which compels such a result. Provided the modification or rescission is done in good faith, in response to business needs and before the debt assigned is earned by performance, the debtor should be able to plead such a modification or rescission in complete answer to the assignee's claim.[37] It is unthinkable that where parties enter into a long-term contract an assignment of the debt obligation can prevent them from modifying or rescinding the contract. The point remains undecided in this country, but the American case of *Babson* v. *Village of Ulysses*[38] is in point. There, an electricity company contracted with a village to supply electricity for 20 years in consideration of a fixed periodic premium and a secondary charge based on actual supplies. The periodic premiums were assigned to B who gave notice of the assignment to the village. Ten years later the company was acquired by a third party who, in conjunction with the village, rescinded the original supply contract. B sued the village for moneys due after the mutual rescission. His action failed. The contract being executory as to future obligations, the parties were free to rescind. The assignment did not create any direct contractual relationship between B and the village. Therefore the village had assumed no direct obligation towards him. On the contrary, he took the benefit of the contract subject to all its incidents one of which was the right of the assignor and debtor to rescind. By the rescission his assignor surrendered its right to future payments in return for a release from its future obligations. It is thought that if a similar problem arises in this country this case ought to be considered persuasive. Where the original contracting parties rescind the old agreement and substitute a new one, can the assignee claim the benefit of any debt owed under the new agreement to his assignor? This question is not free from difficulty, but in principle the assignee cannot automatically claim the debt. One reason is that, not being a party to the substituted contract, the privity rule

---

[36] *Ibid.* at 579. Brett L.J. dissented because he considered the building contract executory at the date of notice of the assignment. Had he thought that the money earned at the time of notice exceeded the amount assigned, no doubt he would have concurred in the reasoning of the majority.

[37] This is apparently the position under UCC, Art. 9–318(2). The subsection does not apply where the right to payment has been earned by performance. For a discussion of the interpretational problems arising thereunder, see 2 Gilmore, *Security Interests in Personal Property* (1965), para. 41.10. Under the subsection, the debtor is not always protected: *Honolulu Roofing Co.* v. *Felix* (1967) 429 P. 2d 298.

[38] (1952) 52 N.W. 2d 320.

constitutes a serious procedural obstacle to any action to recover the new debt. Another is that his old assignment does not automatically attach to the substituted contract. This result is harsh but seems inevitable once it is conceded that the debtor's right to modify or rescind the original contract is an equity subject to which an assignee takes. By way of contrast, it is interesting to note that American law recognises the right of the debtor and assignor to vary, modify or rescind the old contract, so long as the right assigned has not become a debt, but protects the assignee by recognising that his assignment automatically becomes attached to the varied, modified or substituted agreement.[39] In England there is no evidence of the magnitude of the problem created by modification and rescission after notice, but if legislative clarification is considered desirable, the American approach should be followed especially as it strikes a desirable balance between the interests of the contracting parties on the one hand and the expectations of the assignee on the other.

Security assignments and the debtor's equities

Technical and analytical problems arise with the enforcement of the **8.5** debtor's equities where the assignee is a secured lender and time for enforcement of his security has not arrived. Since the assignor retains an equity of redemption in the assigned receivables, the assignee is not the complete beneficial owner, neither is the assignor. If the debtor cannot enforce his equities before the security is enforced, he may be seriously prejudiced, for example, if at the time of enforcement the cross-claim has become statute-barred.[40] From the assignee's point of view, things will be disadvantageous if it is true that where his security takes the form of a charge, whether fixed or floating, equities continue to build up in favour of the debtor until the charge is enforced, either by the execution of an assignment or by sale of the charged receivables.[41] Uncertainties also surround the status of receivables collected and deposited in a special or a general account kept by the assignor with the assignee. The treatment of surplus proceeds of the security for set-off purposes is not as clear as would be desirable. These and other questions will be addressed in this section. It is convenient to begin with the position before the security is enforced.

As we have seen,[42] a security over receivables could be by way of a pledge, contractual lien, attornment, mortgage or charge. Where it is a pledge or contractual lien over receivables embodied in a negotiable paper, the debtor who has issued the paper can only plead limited

---

[39] UCC, Art. 9–318(2). It may also be that the widespread use of performance bonds and standby letters of credit would reduce the incidence of the problem of post-notice modification since the obligee can call in the bond if the obligor falls into difficulties.
[40] By s.35 of the Limitation Act 1980, set-off and counter-claim are separate actions deemed to commence on the same date as the original action.
[41] Goode [1984] J.B.L. 172 at 174.
[42] See para. 5.1, *supra*.

equities depending on whether the secured party is a mere holder,[43] a holder for value,[44] or a holder in due course.[45] Even where the secured party becomes a holder for value after the instrument has become overdue, the debtor is not free to set up equities arising from the underlying contract in respect of which the instrument was issued.[46] This is apparently because such equities are collateral to the instrument, and the instrument is regarded as autonomous of the contract of sale or supply in respect of which it was issued. If the secured party is a holder in due course, he holds the instrument free of any defects in the title of prior parties, as well as from mere personal defences available to prior parties among themselves.[47] But a debtor who has a cross-claim against the holder of an instrument, whether the holder be holding for value or in due course, can set it off provided it is a liquidated cross-claim due at or before the maturity of the instrument.[48] Such a cross-claim affords him a procedural defence when sued by the holder. *A fortiori* where either the holder or debtor becomes insolvent.[49]

Similarly, where the security is by attornment, the debtor cannot raise equities arising after he has attorned the receivables to the secured creditor. However, he can raise as equities all proper legal and equitable defences in the nature of monetary cross-claims which he has against his original creditor. If the contract from which the attorned receivables arose was voidable before the date of attornment, by attorning the debts with knowledge of his right to avoid the contract, the debtor affirms the contract and his original right to rescind is no longer an equity subject to which the secured creditor takes. It seems also that after the date of attornment the debtor cannot raise new equities even if they are inseparably connected with, and flow out of, the contract from which the debts arose, and would thus have been eligible for true equitable set-off. One reason for this is that attornment requires the consent of the debtor and where he acknowledges that he holds identified debts to the order of the secured creditor it would be unfair to allow him to deplete the security by fresh credits given to the original creditor, even before the security is enforced.

The position is not so clear in relation to a mortgage or charge of receivables. Such a security may be fixed or floating. Where it is floating,

---

[43] Defined in s.2 of the Bills of Exchange Act 1882 as the payee or indorsee of a bill or note who is in possession of it, or the bearer thereof.

[44] Where value has at any time been given for a bill, the holder is deemed to be a holder for value as regards the acceptor and all parties to the bill who became parties prior to such time: Bills of Exchange Act 1882, s.27(2).

[45] A holder in due course is a holder who takes a bill, complete and regular on its face, in good faith and for value before it is overdue, and without notice of previous dishonour (if any) or of any defect in the title of the person who negotiated it to him: Bills of Exchange Act 1882, s.29(1).

[46] *Burrough* v. *Moss* (1930) 1 B. & C. 558; *Stein* v. *Yglesias* (1834) 1 C. M. & R. 565; *Whitehead* v. *Walker* (1842) 10 M. & W. 696; *Oulds* v. *Harrison* (1854) 10 Exch. 572.

[47] Bills of Exchange Act 1882, s.38(2).

[48] *Agra & Masterman's Bank* v. *Leighton* (1866) L.R. 2 Ex. 56; *Hong Kong & Shanghai Banking Corp.* v. *Kloeckner & Co. AG* [1989] 2 Lloyd's Rep. 323 (letter of credit).

[49] *Re Anglo-Greek Steam Navigation & Trading Co.* (1869) L.R. 4 Ch.App. 174; *Willment Brothers Ltd.* v. *North West Thames RHA* (1984) 26 B.L.R. 51.

the debtor can raise equities arising at any time before the crystallisation of the security,[50] even though he had notice of the floating charge prior to crystallisation.[51] This is because the floating charge, before crystallisation, is considered as an incomplete assignment of debts and other property within its scope.[52] Consequently, notice by the debtor of this incomplete assignment is not disabling for purposes of the rule that a debtor may not set off equities arising after he became aware of the existence of an assignment. This conclusion can be rationalised in at least one of two ways. The first is to say that the incomplete assignment does not break the mutuality between the debtor and the chargor arising from their mutual dealings. The second is that since the incomplete assignment leaves the chargor free to continue trading as regards debts within the charge, the debtor's equities are an incident of the chargor's trading and the chargee is estopped from denying that the chargor has power (not necessarily a right) to create them against the incompletely assigned debts. But even after crystallisation fresh equities remain capable of diminishing the assigned debts if they are eligible for true equitable set-off, that is to say, if they either impeach the title to the debts,[53] or otherwise flow out of, and are inseparably connected with, the assigned debts and arise from obligations existing at crystallisation. So, with regard to floating securities the debtor can assert his equities whether arising before or after the security is enforced.

The position is, however, not quite so clear where the security is a fixed charge or mortgage. A charge transfers no beneficial interest in the assigned debts to the chargee.[54] The security before time for enforcement arrives consists of a right of non-possessory control over the debts corresponding to the restrictions on the chargor's dispositive rights over the debts.[55] He has no right to possession,[56] his remedy being either to take an assignment of the charged debts,[57] or otherwise to apply to the court for an order for sale or appointment of a receiver.[58] Lacking both possession and beneficial ownership, the chargee, it would seem, has no right to call for payment of the charged debts, and even where he does so, the debtor is under an obligation not to honour the call. From this it would, at first sight, appear that the existence of a fixed charge does not break the mutuality between the chargor and the debtor, with the result that the debtor can continue to give fresh credits to the chargor and thus

---

[50] *Edward Nelson & Co. Ltd.* v. *Faber* [1903] 2 K.B. 367.

[51] *Biggerstaff* v. *Rowatt's Wharf Ltd.* [1896] 2 Ch. 93.

[52] *Biggerstaff* v. *Rowatt's Wharf Ltd.*, *supra* at 106; *George Barker (Transport) Ltd.* v. *Eynon* [1974] 1 W.L.R. 462 at 467.

[53] *Forster* v. *Nixon's Navigation Co. Ltd.* (1906) 23 T.L.R. 138; *Parsons* v. *Sovereign Bank of Canada* [1913] A.C. 160; *Rother Iron Works Ltd.* v. *Canterbury Precision Engineers Ltd.* [1974] Q.B. 1.

[54] For a more detailed discussion of the nature of a charge over receivables, see para. 5.6, *supra*.

[55] *Ibid.*

[56] *Vacuum Oil Co. Ltd.* v. *Ellis* [1914] 1 K.B. 693.

[57] *Burlinson* v. *Hall* (1884) 12 Q.B.D. 347 at 350. But the chargee cannot be compelled to take an assignment instead of enforcing a sale: *Matthews* v. *Goodday* (1861) 31 L.J.Ch. 282 at 283.

[58] *Tennant* v. *Trenchard* (1869) L.R. 4 Ch.App. 537.

diminish the value of the charged debts even after notice of the charge.[59] Were this to be taken as the position in law, the effect would be far reaching, not least because it would strike at the very foundation of lending practices based on specific security over receivables. However, there is nothing in principle or in the case law which compels such a result. If anything, the cases are to the contrary.[60] Another reason for rejecting this view is that the conclusion does not follow logically from the premise. That a charge is a mere incumbrance on the debt does not, without more, license the debtor to deplete the obligation by fresh credits given to the chargor after he has become aware of the charge. Indeed were he to have such a licence there would be nothing for the charge to operate upon. It would also mean that he could unilaterally defeat the charge. The view under criticism sees a charge as a purely contractual matter between the chargor and the chargee; it ignores the proprietary aspect of a charge which, properly understood, gives the chargee a right *in rem* over the debts charged, and this right, it is submitted, is enough to prevent equities arising after notice of the charge from being enforceable against the debts, unless, perhaps, such an equity is eligible for true equitable set-off and matures out of an obligation incurred at the date of notice. Of course, after notice the debtor may still enforce collateral equities against any surplus left after the chargee is completely satisfied. In practice it is difficult to separate a charge from a mortgage of receivables, and since most charge instruments will contain a power of attorney and an express power to collect charged receivables, it is idle to continue to accord a charge over receivables a separate treatment from a mortgage.

Also, the degree of management autonomy (over charged or mortgaged receivables) necessary to ensure that the security is recognised as fixed often requires that the proceeds are collected and paid into an account controlled by the chargee or mortgagee even before time for enforcement of the charge arrives. It is difficult to see quite how the debtor can pay the gross amount without deducting his cross-debt against the assignor. Wood[61] suggests that as long as the security subsists and has not been paid off, there should be no mutuality between the assigned debt and the debtor's cross-debt. If there were a set-off, he argues, the security interest of the assignee, though defeasible, would have been used to pay the assignor's debt. Limited to cross-debts arising after notice of the mortgage or charge, the suggestion needs only very little qualification to be accepted as law.[62] But if it is intended to describe the position of cross-debts existing at the date the debtor becomes aware of the security, it is difficult to accept. It is a cardinal rule of assignment that an assignee

[59] Goode [1984] J.B.L. 172 at 174.

[60] *Roxburghe* v. *Cox* (1878) 17 Ch. 570 (fixed charge); *Rendell* v. *Doors & Doors Ltd.* [1975] 2 N.Z.L.R. 191; *Leichhardt Emporium Pty. Ltd.* v. *AGC (Household Finance) Ltd.* [1979] 1 N.S.W.L.R. 701; *W. Pope & Co. Pty Ltd.* v. *Edward Souery & Co. Pty Ltd.* [1983] W.A.R. 117 (floating charge).

[61] Wood, *op. cit.*, para. 16–214.

[62] Notice of assignment does not cut off cross-claims in the nature of true equitable set-off which arise from obligations incurred before the notice but which mature after notice. See n. 98, *supra*.

takes subject to the debtor's equities. If this rule applies to non-security assignments, as it does, there is no reason why it should not apply to subsisting security assignments. That giving effect to such equities would be an indirect way of using the assignee's security to pay off the assignor's debt is hardly to the point. The assignee's security is not the gross amount of the debt assigned, but whatever is left after admitting the debtor's equities valid against the assignee. Seen in this way, at no time does the assignee's security comprise the face value of the debt assigned. Another way of expressing this conclusion is to say that the assignee took as his security no more than what claim the assignor has against the debtor. Cases where set-off was denied to a buyer of goods (subject to an auctioneer's lien) to whom the auctioneer's principal was indebted are relied upon by Wood as "clearly establishing" his suggestion.[63] However, those cases are not in point. The auctioneer has a lien on goods entrusted to him for sale as security for his charges.[64] Where he sells the goods his security carries through to the proceeds, and a buyer seeking to diminish the purchase price by a set-off which he has against the owner of the goods is in effect claiming priority over the goods ahead of the auctioneer. This he cannot do as the auctioneer has a prior lien entitled to priority over the buyer's cross-claim against the auctioneer's principal. This is the converse of the position between the assignee and the debtor before the debt is enforced. The debtor's equities are entitled to priority over the assignee both in equity[65] and under the statute.[66]

When the security is enforced and a surplus is left, the debtor can set off post-notice cross-debts against the surplus which represents the assignor's equity of redemption,[67] since there remains sufficient mutuality between the debtor and the assignor. This much is clear. Can the assignee set off against the surplus any other debts owed to him by the assignor? Ideally this question admits of a relatively straightforward answer. First, in the absence of a contrary agreement, the mortgagee holds surplus proceeds of his security as a constructive trustee for whoever is entitled to the equity of redemption,[68] which is the mortgagee unless there are junior incumbrancers. Where, therefore, surplus proceeds of receivables are in the hands of a mortgagee, they do not create a debt relationship between the mortgagee and the assignor, even where the mortgagee is a bank,[69] unless there is an agreement releasing the surplus from the constructive trust. The agreement may be express or implied, but in either case the question always is whether the assignor intended that the mortgagee should have beneficial use of the surplus. If that is so, the trust is released

---

[63] Wood, *op. cit.*, para. 16–214 and cases there cited.
[64] *Webb* v. *Smith* (1885) 30 Ch.D. 192.
[65] *Roxburghe* v. *Cox, supra*; *Young* v. *Kitchin, supra*.
[66] Law of Property Act 1925, s.136(1).
[67] *Re Asphaltic Wood Pavement Co., Lee & Chapman's Case* (1885) 30 Ch.D. 216.
[68] *Charles* v. *Jones* (1887) 35 Ch.D. 544; *Re Thomson's Mortgage Trusts, Thomson* v. *Bruty* [1920] 1 Ch. 508; *Weld-Blundell* v. *Synott* [1940] 2 K.B. 107; *Adams* v. *Bank of New South Wales* [1984] 1 N.S.W.L.R. 285; *Re G.L. Saunders Ltd.* [1986] 1 W.L.R. 215. See also L.P.A. 1925, s.105; Consumer Credit Act 1974, s.121(3).
[69] *Ex p. Caldicott, re Hart* (1884) 25 Ch.D. 716. *Cf.* Goode, *Legal Problems of Credit and Security* (2nd ed., 1988), p. 129.

and substituted with an ordinary personal liability in debt to repay an equivalent sum. This debt could then be set off against any other debt owed to him by the assignor. But if there is no agreement releasing the surplus from the constructive trust, it remains trust property for the benefit of those entitled to the equity of redemption. If there are no junior incumbrancers and the assignor is solvent, the surplus, although impressed with a constructive trust, is money available for the payment of simple debts. Since there is no objection to preferring one creditor where the assignor is solvent, in order to avoid circuity of action, the mortgagee may retain the balance as set-off. Where, however, there are junior incumbrancers interested in the equity of redemption, the mortgagee may not set off the surplus against another unsecured debt owed to him by the assignor, even if he is solvent. Here, the question is really one of priorities, and the mortgagee may not tack an unsecured debt owed by the assignor to his security, in the name of set-off,[70] unless at the date the unsecured debt was incurred he had no notice of the existence of puisne incumbrancers.[71] Nor, in such cases, is the need to avoid circuity of action sufficiently compelling to justify tacking.

If the assignor is insolvent and there are no junior mortgagees, the position is not at all clear. The authorities are not wholly reconcilable. Some of the cases confuse the nature of surplus proceeds with the rule in *Rose* v. *Hart*.[72] Others proceed on the basis that the surplus is not money given for a special purpose.[73] This is not a very helpful approach because the surplus is not like money given from the beginning for a special purpose which has since been completed,[74] or has failed.[75] A better approach is to proceed in two stages. The first is to characterise the surplus, that is to say, whether it is a debt or money held on trust. Secondly, to consider in the light of the answer to the first inquiry whether the surplus is properly regarded as a credit given to the mortgagee by the assignor. On this approach, the surplus is in the first instance impressed with a constructive trust for the benefit of those entitled to the equity of redemption. Accordingly, it is not available as a

---

[70] *Irby* v. *Irby* (1855) 22 Beav. 217; *Tanner* v. *Heard* (1857) 23 Beav. 553; *Pile* v. *Pile* (1875) 23 W.R. 440; *Talbot* v. *Frere* (1878) 9 Ch.D. 568 at 572–573; *Banner* v. *Berridge* (1881) 18 Ch.D. 254; *Re Gregson* (1887) 36 Ch.D. 223; *Re S. Piscione & Sons Ltd.* [1965] 1 O.R. 515.
[71] *Rolt* v. *Hopkinson* (1861) 9 H.L. 514; *Deeley* v. *Lloyds Bank Ltd.* [1911] A.C. 756, applied in *Siebe Gorman & Co. Ltd.* v. *Barclays Bank Ltd.* [1979] 2 Lloyd's Rep. 142.
[72] (1818) 8 Taunt. 499. The essence of the rule is that where a debtor delivers property to his creditor with directions to convert it into money, so that the credit given by the act of delivery will ordinarily terminate in a debt, then, if the direction is not revoked and the conversion into money is effected after the debtor has become insolvent, there is mutuality between the debtor and his creditor at the date of insolvency, at any rate for purposes of insolvency set-off. The rule assumes that the direction to convert is not, without more, terminated by the debtor's insolvency. But query whether the same assumption can be made in relation to goods delivered by a principal to his agent for sale on terms that the proceeds are to be turned over without deduction. *Cf. Palmer* v. *Day & Sons* [1895] 2 Q.B. 618; *Rolls Razor Ltd.* v. *Cox* [1967] 1 Q.B. 552; *French* v. *Fenn* (1783) 3 Doug.K.B. 257.
[73] *Re H.E. Thorne & Son Ltd.* [1914] 2 Ch. 438.
[74] *Re Mid-Kent Fruit Factory* [1896] 1 Ch. 567; *Re City Equitable Fire Insurance Co. Ltd. (No. 2)* [1930] 2 Ch. 293.
[75] *Re Pollitt* [1893] 1 Q.B. 455; *Barclays Bank Ltd.* v. *Quistclose Investments Ltd.* [1970] A.C. 567.

set-off against an unsecured debt owed to the mortgagee by the assignor.[76] One reason for this is that the surplus, being trust property, cannot be regarded as a credit given to the mortgagee by the assignor for purposes of insolvency set-off.[77] Where the security is realised after the assignor has become insolvent, an additional reason for denying set-off is the absence of mutuality.[78] The unsecured debt is owed by the assignor. The surplus belongs to the liquidator or trustee in bankruptcy, as the case may be. If the security is realised before the insolvency of the assignor, in order to avoid circuity of action, the court may infer an agreement to release the surplus from the constructive trust. In *Re H.E. Thorne & Son Ltd.*,[79] Astbury J. came to the same conclusion, although it is difficult to accept his wide-ranging dicta as correct propositions of law. In particular, it is not easy to accept the proposition[80] that there is always insolvency set-off whenever there are pre-insolvency dealings which result in money claims on either side. For one thing, not all money claims are claims in debt.[81] The money may be impressed with a trust. The preoccupation of Astbury J. with the question whether the surplus was money earmarked for a special purpose was unhelpful since the real question was whether it was a credit given to the mortgagee by the mortgagor. Although a conclusion that it was given for a special purpose would negate the existence of mutual credit, a finding that it was not so given does not necessarily conclude the question whether it was a credit given to the mortgagee. This wrong focus (it is thought) weakens the authority of *Re H.E. Thorne & Son Ltd.* The other cases[82] treating surplus proceeds in insolvency as a credit given to the mortgagee have since been departed from as wrongly decided.[83] *Alsager* v. *Currie*[84] did not raise this question, but was a specific application of the rule in *Rose* v. *Hart.*[85] *Astley* v. *Gurney*[86] is obscure. In that case some coffee and bills of exchange were given to a creditor as security. By a subsequent agreement the security over the coffee was released and power given to the creditor to sell the coffee at any time. At the time the debtor became bankrupt the creditor had some money

---

[76] *Young* v. *Bank of Bengal* (1836) 1 Moo.P.C. 150; *Talbot* v. *Frere, supra*; *Re Gregson, supra*; *Re Gedney* [1908] 1 Ch. 807.

[77] *Pile* v. *Pile* (1875) 23 W.R. 440. See also, *Young* v. *Bank of Bengal, supra.*

[78] See p. 248, n. 70, *supra.*

[79] [1914] 2 Ch. 438.

[80] *Ibid.* at 450, relying on Lord Esher in *Eberle's Hotels & Restaurant Co. Ltd.* v. *Jonas* (1887) 18 Q.B.D. 459 at 465. *Cf.* Fry L.J., *ibid.* at 470.

[81] See p. 248, nts. 74 and 75, *supra.*

[82] *Spalding* v. *Thomson* (1858) 22 Beav. 637; *Re Haselfoot's Estate* (1872) L.R. 13 Eq. 327; *Re General Provident Assurance Co.* (1872) L.R. 14 Eq. 507.

[83] *Talbot* v. *Frere* (1872) 9 Ch.D. 568 (Jessel M.R.). It must be said, however, that Jessell M.R. was counsel for the unsuccessful plaintiffs in *Spalding* v. *Thompson* and *Re Haselfoot's Estate.*

[84] (1844) 12 M. & W. 751. See also, *French* v. *Fenn* (1783) 3 Doug.K.B. 257; *Palmer* v. *Day & Sons* [1895] 2 Q.B. 618; *Rolls Razor Ltd.* v. *Cox* [1967] 1 Q.B. 552 in each of which the creditor was an agent to whom goods had been entrusted for sale. In each the sale was after the insolvency of the principal, but in none was the insolvency regarded as having revoked the authority to sell. It may be that the power of sale was a power coupled with an interest and so irrevocable.

[85] (1818) 8 Taunt. 499.

[86] (1869) L.R. 4 C.P. 714.

belonging to the debtor. This was held available for bankruptcy set-off. It is, however, not clear[87] whether the money came from the coffee, the security over which had since been released, or from the bills. If it was from the coffee, and the heavy reliance on the rule in *Rose* v. *Hart* would suggest so, the case is not authority for the proposition that surplus security is a credit given to the mortgagee by the mortgagor.[88] These pockets of inconclusive and obscure cases are certainly important, but it is submitted that they fall short of what would be required in order to justify treating them as establishing a general rule in favour of set-off against surplus security.

Insolvency proceedings and the debtor's equities

8.6   Under the Insolvency Act 1986, insolvency proceedings may take one of four different forms.[89] In the first instance, a company may enter into a voluntary arrangement with its creditors. Secondly, it may go into administration. Alternatively, it may go into administrative receivership. Finally, it may go into insolvent liquidation. However, our discussion will be limited to the last three procedures. We will begin with administrative receivership.[90]

Where a company goes into administrative receivership, if the floating charge under which the receiver was appointed has not crystallised, the appointment operates as crystallisation and a complete assignment of debts and other property within the charge. Although administrative receivership has now been assimilated into the mainstream of insolvency proceedings, there is no separate body of doctrine applicable to it. The same is true of ordinary receivership.[91] One reason for this is that insolvency set-off[92] applies only when a company goes into liquidation.[93] Another is that despite the assimilation, receivership and administrative receivership remain primarily machineries for the enforcement of real security. Since these matters are not always kept in mind when considering what equities a debenture holder whose debt is secured by a floating charge takes, it is important at the outset to dissipate two sources of error. The first is the concept of mutuality. In considering whether a particular equity is binding on a receiver and hence the mortgagee, the presence or absence of beneficial mutuality is often regarded as critical.[94]

---

[87] The report of the case is not clear as to whether the money came from the coffee or the bills of exchange which were discounted before the bankruptcy of the debtor. At 717, Cleasby B. treats the money as if it came from the bills, but Kelly C.B. at 724–725 treats it as having come from the coffee.

[88] *Cf.* Wood, *English and International Set-Off* (1989), para. 9–287.

[89] Insolvency Act 1986, s.247(1).

[90] The discussion includes receivership and where appropriate receiver and receivership are used in preference to administrative receiver and administrative receivership.

[91] Meagher, Gummow and Lehane, *Equity: Doctrines and Remedies* (2nd ed., 1984), para. 2854.

[92] Insolvency Rules 1986 (S.I. 1986 No. 1925), r. 4.90.

[93] *Farley* v. *Housing & Commercial Developments Ltd.* (1984) 26 B.L.R. 66. A company goes into liquidation when either a resolution for a voluntary winding-up is passed or a winding-up order is made: Insolvency Act 1986, s.247(2).

[94] *Felt & Textiles of New Zealand Ltd.* v. *R. Hubrich Ltd.* [1968] N.Z.L.R. 716.

Thus in *N.W. Robbie and Co. Ltd.* v. *Witney Warehouse Co. Ltd.*,[95] where a debtor of a company took an assignment of a pre-receivership debt owed by the company to a third party with knowledge that the company was already in receivership, the absence of beneficial mutuality between him and the company was one reason why a majority of the Court of Appeal rejected his set-off. The decision is of course correct[96] because the cross-debt sought to be set off arose after the debtor became aware of the completed assignment to the debenture holder and was ineligible for true equitable set-off. It was therefore unnecessary to consider whether there was mutuality. In such a case the absence of mutuality may indeed explain the result reached but it is not the reason for the decision.

Therefore, to generalise this result by saying that a receiver is not bound by post-receivership equities is unsatisfactory for a number of reasons. First, the premise of such a generalisation is incomplete, and the conclusion unsound. Since there is no separate body of doctrine known as receivership set-off, the simple inquiry whether a particular cross-claim is an equity binding on the mortgagee becomes obscured with the quite separate question whether there is mutuality between the receiver and the debtor. Secondly, there is authority for the view that while a receiver acting as an agent of the company is in office, the company remains the beneficial owner of property subject to the receivership, although it has precluded itself by contract from being able to deal with such property.[97] If this is so,[98] it must follow that there is beneficial as well as legal mutuality, and that some other explanation must be found for disallowing post-receivership cross-claims of the debtor. Thirdly, it has been argued[99] powerfully that equity never insisted on mutuality, and that *Robbie's* case is best explained as a case where there was legal mutuality but equity disallowed set-off because the absence of beneficial mutuality made it unconscionable to allow a set-off.[1] It has to be said, however, that the cases[2] relied upon in support of this argument are obscure and inconclusive. Moreover, to decide what equities are binding on a receiver by reference to mutuality is neither entirely consistent with the cases nor just: inconsistent, because post-receivership cross-claims have been held valid against the receiver in the absence of strict mutuality[3]; unjust, because the result of the view being criticised is that after notice of crystallisation, even cross-claims eligible for true equitable set-off and arising from the receiver's trading may be disallowed for lack of mutuality.[4] Finally, if the solution was mutuality then it should be the rule that

---

[95] [1963] 1 W.L.R. 1324.
[96] In *Ferrier* v. *Bottomer* (1971) 126 C.L.R. 597 at 603, Barwick C.J. left open the question whether *Robbie's case* was rightly decided.
[97] *Gosling* v. *Gaskell* [1897] A.C. 575 at 583.
[98] This must be considered doubtful because it over-emphasises the contractual aspects of crystallisation, ignoring its proprietary consequences altogether.
[99] Meagher, Gummow and Lehane, *op. cit.*, para. 2862.
[1] On a principle similar to that affirmed in *Re Whitehouse* (1879) 9 Ch.D. 595 at 597.
[2] *Ex p. Stephens* (1805) II Ves. 24; *Vulliamy* v. *Noble* (1817) 3 Mer. 593.
[3] *Rother Iron Works Ltd.* v. *Canterbury Precision Engineers Ltd.* [1974] Q.B. 1. See also *West Street Properties Pty Ltd.* v. *Jamison* [1974] 2 N.S.W.L.R. 435.
[4] *Rendell* v. *Doors & Doors Ltd.* [1975] 2 N.Z.L.R. 191; *Leichhardt Emporium Pty Ltd.* v. *AGC (Household Finance) Ltd.* [1979] 1 N.S.W.L.R. 701.

the appointment of a receiver or earlier crystallisation of a floating charge cuts off future equities regardless of whether the debtor knew of the appointment or crystallisation, since, from that time, there would be no mutuality. Yet in no case has a post-receivership equity been disallowed by the very fact of receivership in the absence of notice by the debtor that the company was in receivership.

It may, of course, be argued that notice of receivership is relevant because in its absence the receiver is deemed to have waived his right to object to the admission of post-receivership pre-notice equities. A better explanation is that neither the appointment of a receiver nor the earlier crystallization of a floating charge (both break the mutuality between the company and the debtor), without more, prevents cross-claims arising thereafter from being valid against the receiver, just as an uncommunicated assignment does not stop the build-up of equities. Notice of receivership prevents the debtor from giving the company fresh credits which will count as equities subject to which a receiver takes. But even after such notice equities arising afterwards may be valid against the receiver in certain circumstances. One such circumstance is where the cross-claim arises from a pre-receivership contract and is inseparably connected with the contract out of which the debt owed to the company arises so that it is eligible for true equitable set-off.[5] This is so whether the receiver be appointed by the court[6] or by a debenture holder.[7] Another circumstance is where both debt and cross-debt arise out of post-receivership transactions.[8] Here, it matters not whether the cross-debt is eligible only for legal set-off between solvent parties. The justification for this is that the receiver cannot engage in trade without accepting the ordinary incidents of trading unless the debtor renounces his right to plead such equities. We can express this conclusion differently by saying that where both debt and cross-debt arise after receivership the debt does not arise except subject to the burden of the cross-debt. There is no *scintilla temporis* between debt and cross-debt, and the debtor's liability is not the gross amount payable for the goods or services supplied by the receiver, but the net amount remaining after deducting his cross-debt.

The second source of error in relation to equities binding on a receiver is his agency. It is said, and truly so, that a receiver appointed as agent of the company[9] could be a real agent.[10] Based on the reality of his agency, it has been suggested[11] that the position of a receiver in relation to set-off

---

[5] See p. 251, n.3, *supra*.

[6] As in *Forster* v. *Nixon's Navigation Co. Ltd.*, *supra*; *Parsons* v. *Sovereign Bank of Canada*, *supra*.

[7] As in *Rother Iron Works Ltd.* v. *Canterbury Precision Engineers Ltd.*, *supra*.

[8] *Forster* v. *Nixon's Navigation Co. Ltd.*, *supra*; *Parsons* v. *Sovereign Bank of Canada*, *supra*; *Rendell* v. *Doors & Doors Ltd.* [1975] 2 N.Z.L.R. 191 at 202.

[9] Where such a receiver is an administrative receiver his agency is deemed by the statute: Insolvency Act 1986, s.44(1)(a).

[10] *Ratford* v. *Northavon D.C.* [1987] Q.B. 357 at 372. In *Rhodes* v. *Allied Dunbar Pension Services Ltd.* [1989] 1 All E.R. 1161, the reality of the receiver's agency led the Court of Appeal to the conclusion that the company remained beneficially entitled to rents charged to the receiver's appointor. This, however, runs the fiction of agency into the ground.

[11] Lightman & Moss, *The Law of Receivers of Companies* (1986), para. 16–06, cited with approval in *Astor Chemicals Ltd.* v. *Synthetic Technology Ltd.* [1990] B.C.L.C. 1.

can be more clearly understood by asking "which hat is the receiver wearing?" If he is wearing his company hat, that is to say, acting as the agent of the company, the ordinary rules of set-off apply, and he will be bound by any set-off which would bind the company if there were no receiver. But when wearing his mortgagee's hat, he is in the position of an assignee and the general rules of assignment apply. This suggestion has a superficial appeal in so far as it avoids complicated factual and legal analyses of when a cross-debt can be said to have arisen for purposes of the rule that an assignee generally takes free of post-notice cross-claims not eligible for equitable set-off. However, the suggestion needs only to be stated for its difficulties to become obvious. First, it is not easy to say when a receiver appointed as agent of the company is to be taken as wearing his mortgagee's hat.[12] If, as will ordinarily be the case, he continues to wear his company hat, the suggestion, if accepted, would lead to the quite unacceptable result that a debtor can build up equities against an assigned debt after notice of assignment, regardless of whether the equities would be eligible for true equitable set-off. More importantly, the suggestion is at odds with the result of the cases denying set-off to post-receivership cross-claims in cases where the receiver was wearing his company hat.[13] Lastly, the suggestion overlooks the fact that whether the receiver's agency is real or nominal, receivership itself is largely a machinery for the enforcement of real securities.

The position of a receiver in relation to the debtor's equities may be summarised as follows. The relevant principle is that applicable to assignment of debts. A receiver is bound by all equities in existence at the date of notice of receivership or earlier crystallisation.[14] He may also be bound by equities arising after such notice if they flow out of, and are inseparably connected with, the transaction out of which the debt subject to the receivership arose.[15] For this purpose, the debts need not arise out of the same contract but, in general, they must arise from pre-receivership transactions. Exceptionally, a receiver may be bound by post-receivership equities where the debt and the cross-debt arise from post-receivership dealings between the receiver and the debtor.[16] As regards notice, it seems that neither crystallisation nor the registration of the

---

[12] Liquidation terminates the receiver's agency. But outside liquidation, it is not clear how much the mortgagee needs to interfere with the conduct of receivership before the receiver can be treated as his agent: see *American International Banking Corp.* v. *Hurley* [1985] 3 All E.R. 564; *The Maira (No. 1)* [1989] 3 W.L.R. 185 at 194–196, C.A., rvsd. on different grounds [1990] 1 All E.R. 78.

[13] *N.W. Robbie & Co. Ltd.* v. *Witney Warehouse Co. Ltd.* [1963] 1 W.L.R. 1324; *Felt & Textiles of New Zealand Ltd.* v. *R. Hubrich Ltd.* [1968] N.Z.L.R. 716; *Rendell* v. *Doors & Doors Ltd.* [1975] N.Z.L.R. 191; *Leichhardt Emporium Pty Ltd.* v. *AGC (Household Finance) Ltd.* [1979] 1 N.S.W.L.R. 701; *CIBC* v. *Tuckerr Industries Inc.* [1983] 5 W.W.R. 602; *W. Pope & Co. Pty Ltd.* v. *Edward Souery & Co. Pty Ltd.* [1983] W.A.R. 117.

[14] *Biggerstaff* v. *Rowatt's Wharf Ltd.* [1896] 2 Ch. 93; *Edward Nelson & Co. Ltd.* v. *Faber* [1903] 2 K.B. 367.

[15] See cases cited at p. 251, n. 3, *supra*.

[16] *Rendell* v. *Doors & Doors Ltd.* [1975] 2 N.Z.L.R. 191 at 202. *Cf. W. Pope & Co. Ltd.* v. *Edward Souery & Co. Pty Ltd.* [1983] W.A.R. 117.

appointment of a receiver is notice of assignment to the debtor.[17] Of course, if the debtor inspects the Register he is bound by what he finds.

Technically, the question of equities binding on an administrator or a liquidator is outside the scope of this book as neither involves an assignment of a debt owed to the company. However, since we are considering the effect of insolvency proceedings on the debtor's equities, it is desirable for the sake of completeness to say a word or two on the effect of administration and insolvent liquidation on the debtor's set-offs. There is no exact analogy in our law by reference to which set-offs enforceable against an administrator can be ascertained. On one hand, it is clear that the principle of the receivership cases is not readily adaptable to administration.[18] For one thing, receivership crystallizes the charge under which the receiver was appointed. Crystallization effects an assignment of property, including debts, within the scope of the charge. Administration does not necessarily or always have this effect unless there is a provision to that effect. Consequently there remains legal and beneficial mutuality between the company and its debtors for purposes of set-off. On the other hand, insolvency set-off will not apply to a company in administration since that set-off is limited to cases of insolvent liquidation.[19] It follows that administration must be considered as a *tertium quid* between receivership and liquidation and principles relevant to set-off between solvent parties apply unless on grounds of principle or policy set-off is denied.

As to principle, it is not easy to see the grounds upon which set-off against a company in administration is to be denied. The nearest to such a principle is the provision[20] which imposes a moratorium on the enforcement of security and the commencement or continuation of legal proceedings against the company. But for reasons already given,[21] a set-off is not a security for purposes of the moratorium. Also a true set-off (including a counterclaim in the nature of a set-off) is not an independent cross-claim which could for certain purposes be considered as a separate proceeding. Accordingly, no leave is required in order to plead it in an action by the administrator to recover a debt owed to the company.[22] Different considerations may apply to a true counterclaim.[23] The policy considerations seem evenly balanced. On the one hand, to allow the exercise of set-off while attempts are being made to rescue the company may

---

[17] This is so notwithstanding s.711A(2) of the Companies Act 1985, which preserves the wider doctrine of constructive notice. Notice for purposes of the rule that a debtor may not set off post-notice equities means actual as opposed to constructive notice. But even assuming that constructive notice is relevant, it remains true that the debtor is not a person who ought reasonably to make inquiries as to what incumbrances, if any, have been created over his obligation.

[18] *Astor Chemicals Ltd.* v. *Synthetic Technology Ltd.* [1990] B.C.L.C. 1.

[19] Insolvency Rules 1986 (S.I. 1986 No. 1925), r. 4.90(1); *Farley* v. *Housing & Commercial Developments Ltd.* (1984) 26 B.L.R. 66.

[20] Insolvency Act 1986, s.11(3)(c) and (d).

[21] *Supra*, p. 200.

[22] A similar approach is adopted when considering whether a set-off is a "proceeding" or an "execution" in the context of winding-up: *Peat* v. *Jones* (1881) 8 Q.B.D. 147; *Mersey Steel & Iron Co.* v. *Naylor, Benson & Co.* (1882) 9 Q.B.D. 648, affd. (1884) 9 App.Cas. 434.

[23] *Langley Constructions (Brixham) Ltd.* v. *Wells* [1969] 1 W.L.R. 503.

frustrate the very purpose of the administration.[24] On the other, to deny set-off may deprive the debtor of the priority secured by his set-off if the administration eventually fails and the company descends into insolvent liquidation.[25] This dilemma is avoided in the case of cross-claims arising during the administration by the statutory charge[26] imposed for the protection of simple contract creditors of the administrator.

When a company goes into insolvent liquidation, pre-insolvency dealings are capable of set-off.[27] This regime is more generous than set-off between solvent parties in that cross-claims need not impeach the debt; unrelated unliquidated damages may be set off if they arise from mutual dealings[28]; contingent claims which are not accelerated by winding-up[29] are to be valued and set off.[30] So also debts due but payable in future,[31] whether or not ascertained[32] at the date of liquidation. The aim here is not to avoid circuity of action, but to do substantial justice between the parties.[33] By this netting off, insolvency law departs from one of its own central aims, namely, equal treatment of all unsecured creditors who stood in positions of relative equality at the commencement of insolvent liquidation. Although it is not obvious from the language of the insolvency set-off provision, the courts have consistently affirmed that insolvency set-off is mandatory.[34] Unlike solvent parties who can contract not to set off cross-claims arising from mutual dealings[35] or extend set-off beyond the limits allowed by statute or equity, when one of the parties to a mutual dealing becomes insolvent, pre-insolvency agreements designed to exclude, restrict or extend rights of set-off may not be enforced.[36] The vice of this interpretation of insolvency set-off is that it strikes blindly in all directions. Not only agreements which exclude or restrict the insolvent

---

[24] Wood, *op. cit.*, para. 7–19.

[25] *Ibid.*

[26] Insolvency Act 1986, s.19(5).

[27] Insolvency Rules 1986 (S.I. 1986 No. 1925), r. 4.90. For bankruptcy of individuals, see Insolvency Act 1986, s.323.

[28] *Peat* v. *Jones* (1881) 8 Q.B.D. 147; *Mersey Steel & Iron Co.* v. *Naylor, Benson & Co.* (1882) 9 Q.B.D. 648, affd. (1884) 9 App.Cas. 434.

[29] Insolvent liquidation usually, but not always, acts as a repudiation of the insolvent's future and contingent obligations in that when time for performance arrives, it would not be in a position to render the required performance. This anticipatory breach gives rise to a claim for unliquidated damages by the party entitled to receive performance, and is available for set-off: *Re Asphaltic Wood Pavement Co., Lee & Chapman's Case* (1884) 26 Ch.D. 624; *Baker* v. *Lloyds Bank Ltd.* [1920] 2 K.B. 322. See generally, Shea [1986] J.I.B.L. 152 at 156.

[30] Insolvency Rules 1986 (S.I. 1986 No. 1925), r. 13.12. See also, *Day & Dent Constructions Pty Ltd.* v. *North Australian Properties Pty Ltd.* (1982) 150 C.L.R. 85; *Re Charge Card Services Ltd.* [1987] Ch. 150.

[31] *Re National Benefit Assurance Co. Ltd.* [1924] 2 Ch. 338.

[32] *Re Daintrey* [1900] 1 Q.B. 547.

[33] *Forster* v. *Wilson* (1843) 12 M. & W. 191 at 203–204.

[34] *Re Paraquassu Steam Tramroad Co.* (1872) L.R. 8 Ch.App. 254; *Ex p. Barnett* (1874) L.R. 9 Ch.App. 293; *Halesowen Presswork & Assemblies Ltd.* v. *National Westminster Bank Ltd.* [1972] A.C. 785.

[35] *Hong Kong & Shanghai Banking Corp.* v. *Kloeckner & Co. AG* [1989] 2 Lloyd's Rep. 323.

[36] In addition to cases cited in n. 34 above, see also, *Rolls Razor Ltd.* v. *Cox* [1967] 1 Q.B. 552.

party's set-off are denied effect, but also agreements extending that party's right of set-off or restricting or excluding the solvent party's set-off are similarly struck down. The justification for this approach is difficult to discern. Besides, it is neither a necessary nor a logical consequence of the mandatory nature of insolvency set-off. Yet this is apparently the law and, despite recommendations to the contrary,[37] this view of the nature of insolvency set-off remains law.

For insolvency set-off to apply there must be mutual debts, or mutual credits or mutual dealings. It is not necessary that at the moment when insolvent liquidation commences there shall be two enforceable debts, a debt provable in the liquidation and a debt enforceable by the liquidator against the creditor seeking to prove. It is enough that at the time of liquidation mutual dealings exist which create rights and obligations, absolute or contingent, of such a nature that afterwards, in the events that happen, they mature into pecuniary demands capable of set-off.[38] If the end contemplated by the transaction is a claim sounding in debt, so that it is commensurable with the cross-demand,[39] no more is required than that at the date of liquidation liabilities shall have been contracted by the company and the other party respectively from which monetary cross-claims accrue during the course of the winding-up.[40] This rule does not apply where the cross-demand is money given to the other party for a special purpose, whether the purpose has been fulfilled and a surplus is left[41] or has failed.[42] The reason is that money given for a special purpose is not a credit given by one party to the other. There must, however, be mutuality between the parties.[43] Mutuality does not require that both claims should arise at the same time or that they should be connected, one to the other, or that they should have the same pedigree.[44] Thus secured debts and liabilities are just as capable of set-off as unsecured debts, although to the extent that the secured debt or liability is answered by set-off the security is released.[45] All that is implied by mutuality is that the claim and cross-claim be between the same parties in the same right. For this purpose beneficial entitlements and not merely dry legal rights are considered.[46] There is no mutuality between a liquidating company and a person holding a debt or other money claim as a trustee for another.[47] But there is mutuality between the beneficiary and the liquidat-

---

[37] Report of the Review Committee on Insolvency Law and Practice, Cmnd. 8558 (1982), para. 1342.
[38] Hiley v. Peoples Prudential Assurance Co. Ltd. (1938) 60 C.L.R. 468 at 496–497.
[39] Cf. Eberle's Hotels & Restaurant Co. v. Jonas (1887) 18 Q.B.D. 459.
[40] Naoroji v. Chartered Bank of India (1868) L.R. 3 C.P. 444; Astley v. Gurney (1869) L.R. 4 C.P. 714.
[41] Re Mid-Kent Fruit Factory [1896] 1 Ch. 567; Re City Equitable Fire Insurance Co. Ltd. (No. 2) [1930] 2 Ch. 293.
[42] Re Pollitt [1893] 1 Q.B. 455; Barclays Bank Ltd. v. Quistclose Investments Ltd. [1970] A.C. 567.
[43] Derham, Set Off (1987), pp. 136 et seq., on which the accompanying text draws heavily.
[44] Bennett v. White [1910] 2 K.B. 643.
[45] Ex p. Law, re Kennedy (1846) De G. 378; Ex p. Barnett (1874) L.R. 9 Ch.App. 293.
[46] Cochrane v. Green (1860) 9 C.B.(N.S.) 448; Thornton v. Maynard (1875) L.R. 10 C.P. 695.
[47] Bailey v. Finch (1871) L.R. 7 Q.B. 34; Ex p. Morier, re Willis, Percival & Co. (1879) 12 Ch.D. 491; Middleton v. Pollock (1875) L.R. 20 Eq. 515; MPS Constructions Pty Ltd. v. Rural Bank of New South Wales (1980) 4 A.C.L.R. 835.

ing company.[48] Where the fact of trust is disputed and not established, a mere allegation that the legal owner holds in trust for someone else is not enough to establish mutuality between the alleged beneficiary and the person indebted to the alleged trustee,[49] although where one of the parties is insolvent the more elaborate rules of discovery may help to establish the beneficial ownership of money alleged to be held in trust. Also, where a creditor of a company in insolvent liquidation becomes indebted to the liquidator on account of goods or services delivered or supplied after liquidation, there is no mutuality.[50] The debt is due to the liquidator whereas the liquidating company is the debtor of the other party. Where, however, there is mutuality at the date of the liquidation, a subsequent assignment of one of the claims does not destroy mutuality because the rights and liabilities of the parties crystallise at the time of liquidation.[51]

The effect of a pre-liquidation assignment must be noted. If a creditor of an insolvent company has before liquidation assigned his claim to a third party, the assignment destroys the mutuality between the creditor and the company, provided the assignment was other than by way of security.[52] If the assignment was by way of security there is mutuality between the company and the creditor as to any surplus left after the assignee has been satisfied.[53] The rule is the same where the assignment is of a cross-debt owed to the insolvent company by its debtor.[54] If the assignment is voidable and is avoided after the company has gone into insolvent liquidation, there is sufficient mutuality between the company and its debtor based on the company's right to avoid the assignment.[55] The position may be different if the company has no right to avoid so that in avoiding the pre-liquidation assignment, the liquidator is exercising a right given to him by insolvency law. It is for this reason also that a creditor of the company to whom an undue preference has been given cannot, in an action to recover the preference, set up a cross-debt owed by him to the company, even if he is equally insolvent.[56] It may also be added that a company director against whom a successful misfeasance, fraudulent or wrongful trading action is brought cannot diminish the amount ordered to be contributed to the company's assets by setting up a cross-debt owed to him by the company. One reason for this is the absence of mutuality between the director's cross-claim and the right of a liquidator to recover.[57] Another is that the statutory provisions impose a

---

[48] See cases cited at p. 256, n. 46, *supra*.
[49] *Bhogal* v. *Punjab National Bank* [1988] 2 All E.R. 296; *Uttamchandani* v. *Central Bank of India*, *The Times*, February 8, 1989.
[50] *Sankey Brook Coal Co. Ltd.* v. *Marsh* [1871] L.R. 6 Ex. 185; *Ince Hall Rolling Mills Co. Ltd.* v. *Douglas Forge Co.* (1882) 8 Q.B.D. 179.
[51] *Ex p. MacKenzie, re China Steamship Co.* (1869) L.R. 7 Eq. 240; *Farley* v. *Housing & Commercial Developments Ltd.* (1984) 26 B.L.R. 66.
[52] *Re Asphaltic Wood Pavement Co., Lee & Chapman's Case* (1885) 30 Ch.D. 216.
[53] *Ibid.*
[54] *De Mattos* v. *Saunders* (1872) L.R. 7 C.P. 570; *Re City Life Assurance Co. Ltd., Stephenson's Case* [1926] Ch. 191; *Popular Homes Ltd.* v. *Circuit Developments Ltd.* [1979] 2 N.Z.L.R. 642.
[55] *Hiley* v. *Peoples Prudential Assurance Co. Ltd.* (1938) 60 C.L.R. 468.
[56] *N.A. Kratzmann Pty Ltd.* v. *Tucker* (1968) 123 C.L.R. 295.
[57] *Guinness plc* v. *Saunders* [1988] 1 W.L.R. 863, C.A. affd. [1990] 1 All E.R. 652, H.L.

liability to contribute to the company's assets and since they do not give a right of set-off, the statutory liability to contribute extends to the whole amount ordered to be paid.[58] A third reason is that, as a matter of policy, it is wrong that a director guilty of misfeasance or wrongful trading should have his liability to contribute converted into a debt so as to provide him a right of set-off. It may also be said that the statutory liability cannot be considered either as a credit given to him by the company or as resulting from mutual dealings.

A creditor may not set off a cross-demand acquired at a time when he has notice of a meeting of the company at which a resolution for winding-up is to be proposed or when a petition for the winding-up of the company is pending.[59] This makes perfect sense in that it discourages last-minute attempts by some creditors to pull themselves up by their own bootstraps, contrary to the statutory scheme for the distribution of assets to all creditors. Insolvency set-off is a departure from this scheme in favour of creditors with legitimate (as defined by insolvency law) cross-claims. To allow other creditors to opt out of the scheme by acquiring cross-claims merely as insolvency law expedients would significantly undermine the *pari passu* principle and for no good reason. In this sense, the disallowance of last-minute cross-claims for purposes of insolvency set-off is one of several insolvency rules which act to implement the collective nature of insolvency proceedings by preserving the reasons for their existence. As such the disallowance inherently diverges from pre-liquidation rights, for it is part and parcel of the substitution of a collective set of rights for the individualised rights that exist outside liquidation.

One final point. Where a debtor owes two separate debts to his creditor and is owed a cross-debt by the creditor, how may he exercise his right of set-off, assuming his cross-debt is eligible for set-off against both debts? If he sets it off against one of the two debts, that debt alone will bear the burden of the debtor's equity. There may be nothing unfair about this in relations between the debtor and the creditor. But where one or both debts have been assigned to third parties, the result would be harsh on the assignee whose claim suffered the entire burden of the debtor's deduction. In such cases, where no detriment will be suffered by the debtor, it is better to compel him to "marshal" his set-off, so that both assignees bear the burden rateably.[60] The result should be the same, whether or not one or both debts are secured. Where, however, the cross-debt is eligible for set-off against only one of the debts, there cannot, and should not, be set-off against the other debt. But where the debt immune from set-off is unassigned and is still due to the creditor, there should be contribution and indemnity from the assignor to the assignee.

---

[58] *Re Anglo-French Co-operative Society* (1882) 21 Ch.D. 492; *Re Exchange Banking Co.* (1882) 21 Ch.D. 519; *Re Carriage Co-operative Supply Association* (1884) 27 Ch.D. 322.
[59] Insolvency Rules 1986 (S.I. 1986 No. 1925) r. 4.90(3); *Re Eros Films Ltd.* [1963] Ch. 565.
[60] *Smit Tak International* v. *Selco Salvage Ltd.* [1988] 2 Lloyd's Rep. 398. For a similar approach in the context of insolvency set-off, see *Re Unit 2 Windows Ltd.* [1985] 1 W.L.R. 1383. Cf. *Re E.J. Morel (1934) Ltd.* [1962] Ch. 21 at 34.

Unassignable contract rights

By law certain rights are unassignable on grounds of public policy.[61] We **8.7** shall not go into these rights. It is proposed to consider the question whether parties to a contract can lawfully give its subject-matter an unassignable quality. The relevant law is unclear for a number of reasons. First, there is a failure to distinguish between a prohibition of an assignment of the fruits of the creditor's performance on one hand, and a prohibition of delegation of performance by the creditor of the debt obligation on the other. In many cases the aim of a no-assignment clause is to prohibit vicarious performance. This is partiularly true of prohibition clauses in building and construction contracts.[62] By the prohibition the employer excludes the general rule that where the personality of the performer is not crucial to the contract, although the contractor cannot transfer his obligations,[63] he may delegate performance.[64] In such cases the prohibition is the clearest evidence that the contract is personal to the parties. But even so, the expected fruits of a personal contract are assignable, although the contract itself is incapable of assignment.[65] Secondly, the equally important distinction between the effect of a prohibition clause between the assignor and the assignee on the one hand, and between the assignee and the debtor on the other, is not always kept clear. Nor is that between the contractual and proprietary effects of a purported assignment. The effect of the failure to make these distinctions has been profound. For example, it has encouraged the view that a prohibition invalidates any purported assignment, even as between the assignor and assignee.[66] There is no reason to believe that this view is law. However, before we examine the evidence arising from the case law, it is instructive to examine the possible constructions of a prohibition clause.

The nature and extent of a prohibitory clause are matters of interpretation. A prohibition may be absolute or qualified. In the latter case consent of the debtor is required and where it has not been obtained the prohibition is in effect absolute. Whether absolute or qualified, the prohibition may be calculated to do one of many things.[67] In the first place, the prohibition may be a personal promise not to assign the contract or any receivable arising thereunder. What words are sufficient to give a prohibition this limited effect is unclear. An assignment in breach of the promise gives the debtor a right to damages but the promise can no more operate to invalidate the assignment than it could to interfere with the laws of gravitation.[68] Another possible interpretation is

---

[61] For a good general discussion, see Winfield (1919) 35 L.Q.R. 143; *Trendtex Trading Corp.* v. *Credit Suisse* [1980] Q.B. 629 rvsd. [1982] A.C. 679.

[62] *Hudson's Building & Engineering Contracts* (10th ed., 1970), p. 734.

[63] *Tolhurst* v. *Associated Portland Cement Manufacturers* [1902] 2 K.B. 660 at 668.

[64] *British Waggon Co.* v. *Lea* (1880) 5 Q.B.D. 149; *Nokes* v. *Doncaster Amalgamated Collieries Ltd.* [1940] A.C. 1014 at 1019.

[65] *Crouch* v. *Martin* (1707) 2 Vern. 595; *Russell & Co. Ltd.* v. *Austin Fryers* (1909) 25 T.L.R. 414.

[66] *Helstan Securities Ltd.* v. *Hertfordshire CC* [1978] 3 All E.R. 262.

[67] Goode (1979) 42 M.L.R. 553 at 554.

[68] *Tom Shaw & Co.* v. *Moss Empires Ltd.* (1908) 25 T.L.R. 190 at 191; *Hodder & Tooley Ltd.* v. *Cornes* [1923] N.Z.L.R. 876 at 878.

that any purported assignment is to be treated as a breach of a condition giving the debtor a right to terminate the contract and apply any damages suffered in extinction of the debt owed to the assignor. A prohibition clause having this meaning is almost certain to be denied effect in equity as an invalid forfeiture.[69] But where it does not provide for extinction of the debt already earned by the assignor or where nothing has been earned under the contract, the right to terminate is not to be considered a penalty.[70] A third possible meaning of a prohibition clause is that an assignment is to give the assignee no rights against the debtor. If that be so, the debtor may safely disregard any notice of assignment and pay the debt to the assignor.[71] The assignee cannot sue him for the debt.[72] A prohibition having this meaning is for the protection of the debtor and there are many reasons why a debtor may wish to give his contract this strictly personal character. The first is that assignment law may operate harshly on him. His consent is not required. Cross-claims arising after notice of assignment cannot be set off unless they are eligible for true equitable set-off. Where there are many assignees of the same debt, he has to determine the validity and priority of each and if he pays the wrong assignee, the debt is not discharged and he is liable to pay again to the assignee who is entitled. The same is true where he forgets or overlooks an earlier assignment.[73] Secondly, the assignor may be an indulgent creditor; it is obviously prejudicial to the debtor if he finds himself saddled with a vicious assignee. Faced with these problems, it is easy to see why a debtor may wish to protect himself by prohibiting an assignment. There is no reason in principle or policy why such a prohibition should not be enforced. It is therefore an equity subject to which an assignee takes, but an assignment in breach of the prohibition gives the assignee a valid, if unenforceable, right of property in the debt.[74] This property right could be important if there is a competing claim from another assignee or an administrator or liquidator of the assignor, in cases where the debtor has waived the prohibition.

Can a prohibition be so drafted as to render the debt unassignable even as between the assignor and assignee? The case law is inconclusive and academic opinions are divided.[75] In most of the cases usually cited in support of the invalidity of such a prohibition, the point did not arise at all and nothing was said about it,[76] or the debtor had waived the prohibition by interpleading the debt.[77] In some the validity of the

---

[69] *Bysouth* v. *Shire of Blackburn & Mitcham (No. 2)* [1928] V.R. 562.
[70] *Lombard North Central plc* v. *Butterworth* [1987] All E.R. 267 at 271–275.
[71] *Carex* v. *R.* (1983) 21 B.L.R. 200 (Fed.Ct. of Appeal, Canada).
[72] *Helstan Securities Ltd.* v. *Hertfordshire CC* [1978] 3 All E.R. 262.
[73] *Burrows* v. *Lock* (1805) 10 Ves. 470 at 475–476.
[74] *R.* v. *Canada West Interiors Ltd.* (1986) 43 Atla.L.R. (2d) 155.
[75] Compare Goode (1979) 42 M.L.R. 553; Alcock [1983] C.L.J. 328; with Kloss (1979) 41 Conv. 133; *Chitty on Contracts* (26th ed., 1989), Vol. 1, para. 1413.
[76] *Re Griffin* [1899] 1 Ch. 408; *Re Westerton* [1919] 2 Ch. 104.
[77] *Hodder & Tooley Ltd.* v. *Cornes* [1923] N.Z.L.R. 876; *Attwood & Reid* v. *Stephens* [1932] N.Z.L.R. 1332.

prohibition was assumed[78] but its effect evaded.[79] However, in *Helstan Securities Ltd.* v. *Hertfordshire CC*,[80] where the point was unnecessary for the decision, Croom-Johnson J. appeared to have thought that the prohibition invalidated the assignment even as between the assignor and assignee. It is not easy to see how this can possibly be correct.[81] One explanation is to separate the contractual and proprietary aspects of an assignment.[82] On this approach, there is no reason why a prohibition should not render the assignor liable to the assignee for breach of contract and breach of implied warranty of authority to assign. However, it is also claimed that as between assignor and assignee, any purported assignment ought not to operate as an assignment since this would be prejudicial to the debtor.[83] If the assignor is solvent this approach does not harm the assignee because he can recover damages for breach of contract from the assignor or recover the money paid for the ineffectual assignment as on a total failure of consideration. But where, as will often be the case, the assignor is insolvent or the assignment is to secure a debt, a claim for damages or a restitutionary claim for failure of consideration is unlikely to be of much value. In addition, the prejudice to the debtor from a recognition of the assignment as between assignor and assignee is more apparent than real. Since an assignment contrary to the prohibition would give the assignee no enforceable rights against the debtor, the scope for prejudice to the debtor is considerably reduced, if not totally eliminated.

It has also been suggested that the invalidity of a prohibited assignment between assignor and assignee is consistent with analogous case law relating to intervention of an undisclosed principal where the debtor contracted with the agent on terms that he is liable to the agent and to no one else.[84] This suggestion confuses the personal nature of a contract with the slightly different question of assignability of the fruits of such a contract. There is no reason why parties to a contract cannot give it a personal character. But this is different from saying that one of the parties may, by contract, control the disposition of its fruits. Any such purported prohoibition will clearly be repugnant to the creditor's entitlement and on that ground alone denied effect.[85] Besides, the analogy of intervention of an undisclosed principal is strained, if not false. For one thing, a prohibitory condition will prevent the assignee from having any enforceable rights against the debtor; for another, an assignment of the fruits of a contract does not give the assignee a right to interfere in the performance of the contract.

---

[78] *Laurie* v. *West Hartlepool Steamship Thirds Indemnity Association* (1899) 15 T.L.R. 486; *United Dominion Trust (Commercial) Ltd.* v. *Parkway Motors Ltd.* [1955] 1 W.L.R. 719, overruled as to measure of damages in *Wickham Holdings Ltd.* v. *Brooke House Motors Ltd.* [1967] 1 W.L.R. 295. In *Spellman* v. *Spellman* [1961] 1 W.L.R. 921 at 925, 929, Danckwerts and Willmer L.JJ. expressed, *obiter*, conflicting views on the validity of a prohibition against assignment in a hire-purchase agreement.
[79] *Re Turcan* (1888) 40 Ch.D. 5.
[80] [1978] 2 All E.R. 262.
[81] Goode (1979) 42 M.L.R. 553 esp. at 555 *et seq.* *Cf.* Kloss (1979) 41 Conv. 133 at 136.
[82] *Chitty on Contracts* (26th ed., 1989), Vol. 1, para. 1413.
[83] *Ibid.*
[84] Kloss (1970) 41 Conv. 133 at 136.
[85] *Cassidy* v. *Belfast Banking Co.* (1887) 22 L.R.Ir. 68.

The better view is that a prohibition clause cannot invalidate an assignment between assignor and assignee. The assignee gets a valid but unenforceable right of property in the debt.[86] Several consequences flow from this conclusion. The first is that in relations between assignor and assignee the prohibition has no effect whatever. It is for the protection of the debtor. Accordingly, where he waives the prohibition or has no legitimate interest in relying on it, neither the assignor nor those claiming through or under him can challenge the assignment on the ground of the prohibition.[87] Where, therefore, a creditor assigns a debt in breach of a prohibitory condition and subsequently assigns the debt to another assignee with the debtor's consent, priority of the assignees falls to be considered as if there was no prohibition. The prohibition is at best a shield for the protection of the debtor and not a sword by which a junior assignee is to fight his way up to a more favourable position in the pecking order.[88] But since the prohibition prevents the first assignment from being statutory (he cannot sue the debtor and has no remedy against him), priority is determined by the order in which notice of assignment is given to the debtor, unless the second assignee can advance a successful plea of bona fide purchaser for value without notice.[89] In priority disputes between the assignee and the assignor's execution creditors, administrator or liquidator, the prohibition is of no effect: the executioners or liquidators get no better title than the assignor had.[90]

A second consequence of treating a prohibitory condition as of no effect in relations between assignor and assignee is that although the debtor may disregard notice of assignment and pay the debt to the assignor,[91] the assignor, having assigned the debt, holds the payment—proceeds of the debt—as a constructive trustee for the assignee.[92] The assignee has a proprietary tracing claim to recover the payment unless it has been dissipated. If the payment has been converted into goods the assignee may take the goods in satisfaction. Since his primary claim is for the recovery of payment received by the assignor in breach of his assignment, it is not within the Bills of Sale Acts under which an unregistered bill of sale is void even as against the grantor.[93]

---

[86] *R.* v. *Canada West Interiors Ltd.* (1986) 43 Atla.L.R. (2d) 155.

[87] *Fortunato* v. *Patten* (1895) 41 N.E. 572; *Portuguese-American Bank of San Francisco* v. *Welles* (1916) 242 U.S. 7; *Re Bresnan* (1930) 45 F. 2d 193; *Martin* v. *National Surety Co.* (1937) 300 US 588; *R.* v. *Canada West Interiors Ltd.* (1986) 43 Atla.L.R. (2d) 155. See also UCC, Art. 9–318(4).

[88] *Ibid.*

[89] *Cf.* Alcock [1983] C.L.J. 328 at 334–335.

[90] In addition to cases cited in n. 87, *supra*, see also, *Hodder & Tooley Ltd.* v. *Cornes* [1923] N.Z.L.R. 876; *Attwood & Reid Ltd.* v. *Stephens* [1932] N.Z.L.R. 1332.

[91] *Carex* v. *R.* (1983) 21 B.L.R. 200 (Fed.Ct. of Appeal, Canada).

[92] *G.E. Crane Sales Pty Ltd.* v. *Comsr. of Taxation* (1971) 46 A.L.J.R. 15; *International Factors Ltd.* v. *Rodriguez* [1979] Q.B. 351; *Barclays Bank plc* v. *Willowbrook International Ltd.* [1987] 1 F.T.L.R. 386.

[93] Contrast Alcock [1983] C.L.J. 328 at 336.

CHAPTER NINE

CONCLUSIONS

The primary obligation to pay money is probably the most common obligation. In developed economies the bulk of corporate wealth is locked up in debts. The recycling of these valuable assets as well as their utilisation in the provision of working capital has been the focus of this book. The patterns of receivables financing which we have seen show the flexibility of English contract law. As pressures on free corporate assets grow, financiers have been driven to tap the wealth locked up in debts. The indications are that receivables will continue to play an important role in the overall scheme of asset-based financing. Also receivables financing is becoming more sophisticated as witness the development and growth of securitisation of receivables and venture factoring. A few years ago not many people would have considered factoring relevant to corporate acquisitions. Today factoring has been used to gear up management buy-outs. Administrators have also turned to factoring when working capital is needed to carry out the statutory purposes of their appointment. These innovative uses of receivables financing will continue.

Unlike the American receivables financier who, in the pre-UCC days, had to live in the shadow of *Benedict* v. *Ratner*,[1] the English financier benefited from two important factors. The first is the facility of equitable assignment. From the earliest times equity made it possible to buy and sell debts and after *Tailby* v. *Official Receiver*,[2] it was no longer in doubt, if it ever was, that a trader could assign presently all his existing and future receivables. These developments side-stepped the common law procedural obstacle to assignments as well as the common law refusal to recognise, except in limited circumstances, that there could be an effectual present transfer of property which, at the date of transfer, exists only in the contemplation of the parties. The second is the somewhat favourable legislative climate. The doctrine of reputed ownership, which

---

[1] (1925) 268 US 353. The case established that where a creditor assigned all his existing and future receivables and the assignee did not exercise dominion over the receivables, *e.g.* by giving notice to the debtors, the assignment is conclusive evidence of fraud. The decision would have struck at the heart of non-notification financing. But paradoxically it led to its development. For a good account of how this came about, see 1 Gilmore, *Security Interests in Personal Property* (1965), pp. 251 *et seq.* The decision may have prevented the development of the floating charge in America: Goode and Gower, in J. Ziegel and W. Foster (eds), *Aspects of Comparative Commercial Law* (1969), p.318.
[2] (1888) 13 App.Cas. 523.

is the policy consideration underpinning *Benedict* v. *Ratner*, never applied to limited companies. In addition, *Dearle* v. *Hall*[3] provided a simple priority rule. Where there are two or more assignees of a fund insufficient to satisfy all the claimants, the assignee who gives the first notice to the fundholder prevails, provided at the time he took his assignment or gave value, whichever is earlier, he had no notice, actual or constructive, of any other assignee.

Today assignments still provide the primary legal framework for receivables financing. Priorities are largely determined by the rule in *Dearle* v. *Hall*. Some security assignments have to be registered in order to be valid against certain persons and office-holders. Reform has been slow and half-hearted. The general shortcomings of the law governing security interests in personal property and the solutions are too well known and no time need be wasted rehearsing them here.[4] Some improvements and clarifications have been made by the Companies Act 1989[5] but a lot more needs to be done. For example, despite the definition of a charge as any form of consensual security interest over property,[6] no attempt is made to define security interests, an omission which cannot have made the law clearer or simpler. Besides, the new definition of a charge does not add much since there is still a closed list of registrable charges. No one can pretend that these piecemeal responses to particular problems are a satisfactory solution to the problem of making the law relevant to modern business needs.

However, we cannot go into all the areas where the modern law of asset based financing needs improvement. It will take another book to do justice to that subject. What we shall do is to recapitulate some of the problems which we have already highlighted in the course of our previous discussion, which are specific to receivables financing. Several problems arise from the peculiar nature of receivables. The central policy question is how to facilitate receivables financing within the triangular relationship of debtor/creditor/financier. If, for example, receivables are made quasi-negotiable, this will, no doubt, enhance the security of financiers; but it will be at the expense of the debtor whose equities will thereby be destroyed. There are good reasons why the collectible value of receivables should not be higher in the hands of the financier than in those of the original creditor with whom the debtor contracted. The law has vacillated on a number of issues. Where policy considerations are discernible at all, the rules have been an unsatisfactory compromise between the need to protect the debtor on the one hand, and the countervailing need to enhance the quality of the security which "borrowers" can give on the other. In no area is this more pronounced than in relation to the rule that an assignee takes subject to equities. In short, the

---

[3] (1828) 3 Russ. 1.
[4] Most of the issues are usefully examined in *Crowther Committee Report*, Cmnd. 4596; Goode (1984) 100 L.Q.R. 234; *Reform of Personal Property Security Law* (New Zealand Law Reform Commission, Preliminary Paper No. 6, 1988); *A Review of Security Interests in Personal Property* (prepared by A. L. Diamond for the Department of Trade and Industry, 1989).
[5] Pt. IV.
[6] New s.395(2) of the Companies Act 1985.

present law is flawed from the perspective of policy. The law has yet to tackle satisfactorily the treatment of surplus proceeds of security or the question how best to treat matters affecting the performance of a contract in the context of the rule that an assignee takes subject to equities. Also several technical and analytic problems arise from the temporal aspect of equities. Recourse to the necessity for the debtor's equity to impeach title to the debt or to flow out of, and be inseparably connected with, the debt cannot have made the law clear. It is not satisfactory that the title of an assignee should depend on the somewhat muddy waters of equitable set-off. What degree of connection need exist between claim and cross-claim before the debtor can be sure of set off? Why should the validity of an "equity" depend on the accident of timing of accrual of the debtor's cross-claim? In many cases there is no way the debtor can avoid giving effective credit to the original creditor (assignor). Either we make debts negotiable, in which case an assignee takes free of cross-claims arising from the underlying contract between the debtor and the assignor, or we adopt a rule which allows all contract-related claims to be valid against the assignee without the necessity for establishing whether or not they would be eligible for set off.

There has similarly been no response to the problem of contractual prohibition of assignment, post-notice modification of the underlying contract, the source of the receivables, and the obstacle created by *Re Charge Card Services Ltd.*[7] Admittedly the magnitude of these problems is unknown. But this is scarcely an answer to such obvious problems. It is like telling an owner of property not to worry about insurance since it is unknown how much damage an accidental fire might cause. In the area of priorities, the rules are equally confused. *Dearle* v. *Hall* is unsuited to the realities of modern day financing against receivables. The rule was formulated in the context of a competition for priority between three equitable assignees of a trust fund. Given the relatively small number of trustees of a modest fund, it may not have been unreasonable to settle the competing claims in the order in which notice of assignment was given to the trustees. This is especially so where, as in the case itself, an assignee had, before taking his assignment, made enquiries of the trustees and no pre-existing incumbrances were disclosed, and given also the lack of a reliable facility for publicising dealings in debts. In such a situation, preferring an assignee who gave first notice was a reward for diligence even when this was at the expense of making the debtor a kind of public register. For reasons already given,[8] *Dearle* v. *Hall* ought not to govern financing assignments. It imposes an intolerable administrative burden on the debtor who has to keep all the notices and determine their relative priorities. It is inconvenient when applied to expectancies; yet receivables financing is unprofitable without this category of future assets.

---

[7] [1987] Ch. 150. In *Welsh Development Agency* v. *Export Finance Co. Ltd.* (1990) B.C.C. 393 Browne-Wilkinson V.-C. doubted whether he would have reached the same conclusion as did Millett J. in *Charge Card*, but he followed it in the interest of preserving consistency in matters which had an important general commercial impact. This is understandable but sad because *Charge Card* is unsound and commercially undesirable.

[8] See para. 6.6, *supra.*

That rules of equity are sophisticated is beyond doubt. But they can no longer be relied upon to provide a satisfactory solution to the emerging problems of receivables financing for which they were not designed and are ill-suited. A statutory solution to all the problems is impossible. What is most urgently needed is a simple and efficient facility for the creation, disclosure and priority of entitlements. As to creation, assignment is still the best framework and should be retained and clarified particularly in relation to the rule of taking an assignment subject to equities. As for disclosure, a suitable solution is to provide a simple and efficient comprehensive register which will put persons proposing to take an assignment on notice. The register should, as far as possible, be a mirror of all existing claims. Fixing a minimum monetary limit on registrable assignments will keep assignments of trifling amounts out of the register. As for priority, the primary rule should be the date of registration. The law should protect a bona fide assignee for value without notice, whether his assignment be legal or equitable. The case for reform could hardly be stronger or more patent. Given the billions of pounds advanced annually on the strength of receivables, the importance of a simple, inexpensive and efficient facility for the creation, protection, disclosure and priority of dealings in receivables can hardly be overemphasised.

INDEX

Page numbers followed by n refer to footnotes

[267]